Revolutionary Patriots of Maryland, 1775-1783
Second Supplement

Henry C. Peden, Jr.

Willow Bend Books
Westminster, Maryland
2002

Willow Bend Books

65 East Main Street
Westminster, Maryland 21157-5026
1-800-876-6103

WB2128

Source books, early maps, CDs -- Worldwide

For our listing of thousands of titles offered
by hundreds of publishers, see our website
at
www.WillowBendBooks.com

Visit our retail store

©2002 Henry C. Peden, Jr.

International Standard Book Number: 1-58549-771-1

Printed in the United States of America

INTRODUCTION

When I published the supplement to my sixteen volumes on Revolutionary Patriots of Maryland in 2000 I thought at the time that it would be my last book on the subject. However, so much information has since come to light that it has led me to compile this second supplement.

Soldiers, sailors, privateers, and patriots from every county in Maryland are covered in this second supplement, unlike the first one which covered only the five counties in and around Baltimore. Also included are many pension abstracts (both accepted and rejected applications), plus soldiers from Harford County militia companies whose names have never been published before. My thanks goes to Christopher T. Smithson for finding and sharing these records.

Additional information was contributed by family historians who submitted corrections to their respective lines. Information was also gleaned from the *Maryland Historical Magazine* (volumes 6, 7, 13, 69), the *Archives of Maryland* (volumes 11, 12, 16, 18, 21, 43, 45, 47, 48), newspaper obituaries, and county histories.

As with my other books, this compilation is more than just a listing of names. Many patriots have genealogical data included with their respective entries and all information is fully documented. Also, all surnames are cross-referenced within the text and thus precludes the need for a separate index. One should always consult the original records before drawing any conclusions from the data presented herein.

> Henry C. Peden, Jr.
> Bel Air, Maryland
> January 27, 2002

Dedicated to the memory of my fellow compatriots of the
Colonel Aquila Hall Chapter
Maryland Society, Sons of the American Revolution,
who passed away in recent years

Edward Loring Dix Roach Best
(1912-2001)

Augustus Freeborn Brown III
(1915-1998)

Wilford Anderson Hall Councill III
(1950-2001)

Walter Remington Frank, Sr.
(1919-2000)

Walter Remington Frank, Jr.
(1945-2001)

John Garland Green
(1908-1996)

Alvin Seymour Hoffman
(1919-2001)

REVOLUTIONARY PATRIOTS OF MARYLAND
1775-1783: SECOND SUPPLEMENT

ACKRIGHT (AKERIGHT), ISAAC (Baltimore County), private in the militia who enlisted in Baltimore on 20 Jul 1776 and applied for pension in Wayne County, Ohio on 26 May 1824, aged 86; son John Ackright stated his father's house burned down on 15 Mar 1824. {Ref: Archives of Maryland Vol. 18, p. 60; Research by Christopher T. Smithson, citing Federal Pension Application R22}

ACRE, CONOMUS or CRONAMUS (Frederick County), private in the militia who enlisted in Frederick County on 19 Jul 1776 and was in the 7th Maryland Continental Line by 7 Dec 1776; wounded and taken prisoner in the Battle of Staten Island; discharged on 8 Dec 1779; moved to Roane County, Tennessee in 1806 and applied for a pension on 14 May 1818, aged 58; in 1822 his wife Barbara Acre was aged 45 and children were Catharine Acre (aged 31), David Acre (aged 19), Christiana Acre (aged 15), and Louisa Acre (aged 14). {Ref: Archives of Maryland Vol. 18, pp. 51, 183; Research by Virgil D. White, citing Federal Pension Application S39145}

ADAIR, WILLIAM (Maryland Navy), armorer on the State Ship *Defence* in 1777. {Ref: Archives of Maryland Vol. 18, p. 654}

ADAMS, ELIZA, see "Thomas Adams," q.v.

ADAMS, HANS (Baltimore County), private, aged 22, printer, born in Philadelphia, enlisted 23 Feb 1776 in Capt. John Fulford's Company of Matrosses. {Ref: Maryland Historical Magazine, Vol. 69, No. 1, p. 95}

ADAMS, ISAAC (Western Maryland), private in Capt. Michael Cresap's Company in 1775. {Ref: Howard L. Leckey's *The Tenmile Country and Its Pioneer Families*, p. 15}

ADAMS, JAMES (Baltimore County), private, aged 29, farmer, born in Ireland, enlisted 14 Mar 1776 in Capt. John Fulford's Company of Matrosses. {Ref: Maryland Historical Magazine, Vol. 69, No. 1, p. 96}

ADAMS, JOHN (Somerset County), privateer service during the war; born 5 Mar 1763 in Somerset County and married Sophia Smith in 1805; moved to Ross County, Ohio where he applied for a pension on 16 Oct 1833, aged 70; he died on 19 May 1835 and his widow died on 9 Nov 1847 in Fayette County, Ohio; surviving children were Josiah Adams, Celia Moomaw, and Elizabeth Kerr, who filed a claim in 1852. {Ref: Research by Christopher T. Smithson, citing Federal Pension Application R38}

ADAMS, JOHN (Washington County), private who was drafted to serve in the Maryland Continental Line until 10 Dec 1781, but *"being represented unfit for the duty for which he was intended"* was discharged on 30 Oct 1781. {Ref: Archives of Maryland Vol. 45, p. 656}

ADAMS, JOSIAH, see "John Adams," q.v.

ADAMS, LEAH, see "Thomas Adams," q.v.

ADAMS, MARY, see "Thomas Adams," q.v.

ADAMS, MORRIS, see "Thomas Adams," q.v.

ADAMS, RICHARD (Charles County), soldier in the Maryland Continental Line; born 3 Apr 1755 in Charles County and applied for pension in Georgetown, D. C. on 22 Apr 1833, aged 78. {Ref: Research by Virgil D. White, citing Federal Pension Application S11938}

ADAMS, RICHARD (Western Maryland), private in Capt. Michael Cresap's Company in 1775. {Ref: Howard L. Leckey's *The Tenmile Country and Its Pioneer Families*, p. 15}

ADAMS, PETER (Frederick County), colonel in the 1st Maryland Continental Line who received payment for his services in the amount of "1900 Dollars & £3.10s" on 12 Sep 1780. {Ref: Archives of Maryland Vol. 45, p. 97}

ADAMS, SAMUEL, see "Thomas Adams," q.v.

ADAMS, THOMAS (Somerset County), private in the militia in 1780; born 8 Nov 1761 in Somerset County, married Mary ----, and died circa 1832; their children were: Samuel Adams (born 6 Apr 1781, married Mary Ann Wilson); Eliza Adams (married James Smith on 4 Nov 1817); Leah Jane Adams; Emaline Bounds; Mary Pitt; and, Morris Henry Adams. {Ref: Maryland State Society DAR Directory, 1892-1965, p. 113}

ADAMS, WILLIAM (Somerset County), patriot who was appointed by the Council of Maryland on 27 Jan 1776 as one of three persons in Somerset County to collect all gold and silver coin that can be procured in said county. {Ref: Archives of Maryland Vol. 11, p. 132}

ADELON, PEIRE (Maryland Privateer), commander of the brigantine *Le Comptis Denery*, now riding in the Patuxent River, navigated by 25 men and mounting 8 carriage guns and 10 swivel guns, was issued Letters of Marque & Reprisal by the Council of Maryland on 11 Jun 1778. {Ref: Archives of Maryland Vol. 21, p. 131}

ADLUM, JOHN (Frederick County), captain in the Maryland militia who died in April, 1819 *"in his 82nd year, upwards of 50 years an inhabitant of this place; headed a company in the Revolutionary War."* {Ref: *Frederick-Town Herald*, 1 May 1819}

ADY, JONATHAN (Harford County), private in Capt. Robert Harris' Company of the Flying Camp in 1776; born circa 1722, married Rebecca Yorke and died intestate on 17 Jan 1800; their children were: Rachel Ady (born in December, 1743, married Nathan Yearly); William Ady (born 23 Aug 1745, married first Clara Hilton and second Clorinda Standiford); and, Elizabeth Ady (born 13 Aug 1747). {Ref: Maryland State Society DAR Directory, 1892-1965, p. 114}

AHEARN, WILLIAM (Frederick County), private (substitute) in the Maryland Continental Line, Williams' Regiment, enrolled in May, 1778 for 3 years or duration of the war. {Ref: Maryland Historical Magazine, Vol. 6, No. 3, p. 259}

AHRSON, JOHN (Western Maryland), private in Capt. Michael Cresap's Company in 1775. {Ref: Howard L. Leckey's *The Tenmile Country and Its Pioneer Families*, p. 15}

AIKIN, SAMUEL (Harford County), private who was enrolled 10 Mar 1776 in Militia Company No. 18 under Capt. John Jolly. {Ref: George W. Archer Collection and Revolutionary War File, Historical Society of Harford County Archives}

AIRY, THOMAS HILL (Dorchester County), patriot who was commissioned one of the three persons in Dorchester County by the Council of Maryland on 19 Aug 1779 to receive subscriptions for use of the State. {Ref: Archives of Maryland Vol. 21, p. 499}

AISQUITH, WILLIAM (Baltimore County), patriot and sheriff of Baltimore County until 8 May 1777 at which time he resigned. {Ref: Archives of Maryland Vol. 16, p. 244}

ALBRIGHT, JOHN (Baltimore City), soldier who allegedly served in the war and applied for pension under the Act of June 7, 1832, but the claim was suspended because of no proof of service. {Ref: *Rejected or Suspended Applications for Revolutionary War Pensions* (1850 Report), p. 231}

ALCOCK, ROBERT (Anne Arundel County), soldier in the militia who applied for pension in Anne Arundel County on 6 Oct 1832, aged 73. {Ref: Research by Virgil D. White, citing Federal Pension Application S8017}

ALEXANDER, JOHN (Cecil County), private in the militia in 1776 and there were also two men by this name who took the Oath of Allegiance and Fidelity in 1778: (1) one John Alexander married Rebecca Justice and died before 12 Aug 1794 (date of administration bond) and <u>not</u> 6 Jan 1802 as misstated in *Revolutionary Patriots of Cecil County, 1775-1783*; John's daughter Sarah Alexander was under age 16 and son Israel Alexander was under age 21 in 1794; (2) the other John Alexander may have been the one who died on 6 Jan 1802, aged 88 years and 9 months, and was buried in Head of Christiana Creek Presbyterian Church Cemetery (tombstone inscribed *"He was an honest man"*). Additional research will be necessary before drawing any conclusions. {Ref: Information submitted by H. Jack Wells of Cocoa Beach, Florida in 2001}

ALEXANDER, LAWSON (Baltimore Town), patriot and merchant who enrolled in Capt. John Sterrett's Independent Mercantile Company by February, 1777, at which time they were mustered into regular service with the continental army to repress loyalist activities in the Eastern Shore counties of Somerset and Worcester. {Ref: J. Thomas Scharf's *History of Baltimore City and County*, Part I, p. 77}

ALLBAUGH, ZACHARIAH (Frederick County), patriot and soldier who was born 31 Oct 1758 in Frederick County and served in the Maryland and Pennsylvania Lines; after the war he lived in Maryland for 8 years and in Pennsylvania for 36 years; he applied for pension in Licking County, Ohio on 29 Oct 1832, aged 74. {Ref: Research by Christopher T. Smithson, citing Federal Pension Application S2902}

ALLEN, BENJAMIN (Baltimore Privateer), commander of the schooner *Dolphin*, mounting 4 carriage guns, 2 cohorn guns and 7 muskets, was issued Letters of

Marque & Reprisal by the Council of Maryland on 7 Nov 1778. {Ref: Archives of Maryland Vol. 21, p. 232}

ALLEN, JAMES (Maryland Navy), quartermaster on the State Ship *Defence* in 1777. {Ref: Archives of Maryland Vol. 18, p. 654}

ALLEN, JESSEE (Charles County), private in the 1st Maryland Continental Line who had enlisted for 9 months and was discharged on 11 Mar 1779 at which time he received £14.5.6 in clothing. {Ref: Archives of Maryland Vol. 21, p. 320}

ALLEN, RICHARD (Maryland Navy), marine on the State Ship *Defence* in 1777. {Ref: Archives of Maryland Vol. 18, p. 654}

ALLEN, RICHARD, see "John H. Hughes," q.v.

ALLEN, WILLIAM (Washington County), private who was enrolled to serve as a substitute in the Maryland Continental Line until 10 Dec 1781, but *"being represented unfit for the service for which he was intended"* was discharged on 30 Oct 1781. {Ref: Archives of Maryland Vol. 45, p. 656}

ALLENDER, MARY, see "Jesse Foster," q.v.

ALLENDER, PERRY (Queen Anne's County), private who was drafted into the Maryland Continental Line, was discharged on 8 Dec 1781. {Ref: Archives of Maryland Vol. 48, p. 10}

ALLENDER, WILLIAM (Frederick County), private (substitute) in the Maryland Continental Line, Price's Regiment, enrolled in May, 1778 for 3 years or duration of the war. {Ref: Maryland Historical Magazine, Vol. 6, No. 3, p. 261}

ALLENDER, WILLIAM (Harford County), private who was enrolled 25 Mar 1776 in Militia Company No. 19 under Capt. William Morgan; William Allender was administrator of the estate of Ann Allender on 9 Feb 1784 and a William Allender died intestate by 7 May 1793 when Ann Allender was administratrix of his estate. {Ref: George W. Archer Collection and Revolutionary War File, Historical Society of Harford County Archives; Henry C. Peden, Jr.'s *Heirs & Legatees of Harford County, 1774-1802*, pp. 19, 40}

ALLISON, ELIZABETH, see "James Higgins, q.v.

ALLISON, JAMES (Harford County), patriot who was recommended for a commission on 7 Jan 1777 by Col. Aquila Hall who stated, in part, *"that he has a mind to enter into the service of his Country, he is a man of Courage, and is a Friend to the Common Cause, he will accept of an Ensign or second Lieutenant Commission, if they are not all provided for."* {Ref: Archives of Maryland Vol. 16, p. 26}

ALLSOP, JOSEPH (Frederick County), private who enlisted in the 7th Maryland Continental Line on 8 Jun 1778 and was discharged on 30 Mar 1779; married Mary Freeman on 10 Jan 1778 in Frederick and died in 1783; widow Mary Allsop married Peter Casey who died 16 Dec 1794; widow Mary Casey applied for pension in Franklin County, Pennsylvania on 28 Aug 1843, aged 86. {Ref:

Archives of Maryland Vol. 18, p. 184; Research by Virgil D. White, citing Federal Pension Application W3129}

ALSY, WILLIAM (Prince George's County), private (substitute) in the Maryland Continental Line by 1781 and was discharged on 8 Dec 1781. {Ref: Archives of Maryland Vol. 48, p. 10}

AMELUNG, ANN, see "Christopher Taylor," q.v.

AMOS (AMOSS), BENJAMIN (Harford County), captain, elected 30 Nov 1776, commissioned 26 Jan 1777, Militia Company No. 30 in the 8th Battalion. {Ref: Archives of Maryland Vol. 16, p. 77; George W. Archer Collection and Revolutionary War File, Historical Society of Harford County Archives}

AMOS, GEORGE B., see "David Bell," q.v.

AMOS (AMOSS), JOSHUA (Harford County), first lieutenant, elected 30 Nov 1776, commissioned 26 Jan 1777, Militia Company No. 30 under Capt. Benjamin Amoss in the 8th Battalion. {Ref: Archives of Maryland Vol. 16, p. 77; George W. Archer Collection and Revolutionary War File, Historical Society of Harford County Archives}

AMOS, MARTHA, see "William Norris" and "David Bell," q.v.

AMOS (AMOSS), NICHOLAS (Harford County), ensign, commissioned 14 May 1776 in Militia Company No. 25 under Capt. Charles Baker. {Ref: George W. Archer Collection and Revolutionary War File, Historical Society of Harford County Archives}

AMOS (AMOSS), ROBERT (Harford County), second lieutenant on 9 Dec 1775 in Militia Company No. 14 under Capt. William McComas. {Ref: George W. Archer Collection and Revolutionary War File, Historical Society of Harford County Archives}

ANDERSON, ANDREW (Western Maryland), private in Capt. Michael Cresap's Company in 1775. {Ref: Howard L. Leckey's *The Tenmile Country and Its Pioneer Families*, p. 15}

ANDERSON, ANN, see "Charles Gilbert," q.v.

ANDERSON, ANTHONY, see "John Lindsay," q.v.

ANDERSON, BENNETT (St. Mary's County), private who was drafted into the Maryland Continental Line, was discharged on 8 Dec 1781. {Ref: Archives of Maryland Vol. 48, p. 10}

ANDERSON, DANIEL (Harford County, Susquehannah Hundred), private who was enrolled 23 Apr 1776 in Militia Company No. 21 under Capt. George Patterson. {Ref: George W. Archer Collection and Revolutionary War File, Historical Society of Harford County Archives}

ANDERSON, GEORGE (Harford County), private who was enrolled 10 Mar 1776 in Militia Company No. 18 under Capt. John Jolly. {Ref: George W. Archer Collection and Revolutionary War File, Historical Society of Harford County Archives}

ANDERSON, GEORGE (Baltimore County?), major in the 3rd Maryland Continental Line who received payment for his services in the amount of "1900 Dollars & £3.10s" on 12 Sep 1780. {Ref: Archives of Maryland Vol. 45, p. 98}

ANDERSON, JAMES (Queen Anne's County), private (substitute) in the Maryland Continental Line by 1781, was discharged on 10 Dec 1781. {Ref: Archives of Maryland Vol. 48, p. 17}

ANDERSON, JOHN (Baltimore Town), patriot and merchant who enrolled in Capt. John Sterrett's Independent Mercantile Company by February, 1777, at which time they were mustered into regular service with the continental army to repress loyalist activities in the Eastern Shore counties of Somerset and Worcester. {Ref: J. Thomas Scharf's *History of Baltimore City and County*, Part I, p. 77}

ANDERSON, MATTHEW (Harford County), private who was enrolled by 15 Apr 1776 in Militia Company No. 20 under Capt. Robert Glenn. {Ref: George W. Archer Collection and Revolutionary War File, Historical Society of Harford County Archives}

ANDERSON, RICHARD (Frederick and Montgomery Counties), captain in the 7th Maryland Continental Line who received payment for his services in the amount of "1900 Dollars & £3.10s" on 12 Sep 1780. {Ref: Archives of Maryland Vol. 45, p. 98}

ANDERSON, WILLIAM (African American soldier), private in the Maryland troops who applied for pension in Warren County, Ohio on 15 May 1818. {Ref: Research by Christopher T. Smithson, citing Federal Pension Application R203}

ANDREWS, WILLIAM (Harford County), soldier who enlisted in the Maryland Continental Line in Harford County; applied for pension in Amherst County, Virginia on 23 Nov 1820, aged 66, by which time his wife had died; daughters living with him in 1820 were Polly Andrews (aged 26), Ann Andrews (aged 24), and Betsy Andrews (aged 22). {Ref: Research by Virgil D. White, citing Federal Pension Application S37673}

ANDRUS, SALLY, see "Charles Close," q.v.

ANGELE, JAMES (Baltimore Town), patriot and merchant who enrolled in Capt. John Sterrett's Independent Mercantile Company by February, 1777, at which time they were mustered into regular service with the continental army to repress loyalist activities in the Eastern Shore counties of Somerset and Worcester. {Ref: J. Thomas Scharf's *History of Baltimore City and County*, Part I, p. 77}

ANGUS, JOHN (Maryland Privateer), commander of the brigantine *Delaware*, mounting 10 carriage guns, 7 blunderbusses and 7 musquets, was issued Letters of Marque & Reprisal by the Council of Maryland on 28 Mar 1778. {Ref: Archives of Maryland Vol. 16, p. 556}

ANTHONY, JOHN (Queen Anne's County), private who was drafted into the Maryland Continental Line, was discharged on 8 Dec 1781. {Ref: Archives of Maryland Vol. 48, p. 10}

ANTHONY, PHILIP (Washington County), private who was drafted to serve in the Maryland Continental Line until 10 Dec 1781, but *"being represented unfit for the duty for which he was intended"* was discharged on 30 Oct 1781. {Ref: Archives of Maryland Vol. 45, p. 656}

ARBOR, JOHN (Frederick County), private (substitute) in the Maryland Continental Line by 1781, was discharged on 8 Dec 1781. {Ref: Archives of Maryland Vol. 48, p. 11}

ARCHER, JOHN (Harford County), doctor and patriot who was commissioned one of the three persons in Harford County by the Council of Maryland on 19 Aug 1779 to receive subscriptions for use of the State. {Ref: Archives of Maryland Vol. 21, p. 499}

ARCHER, THOMAS (Harford County), private who was reportedly a deserter enrolled (or captured and re-enrolled) by Capt. Praul for the Regiment Extraordinary and sent to Annapolis with Capt. Thompson on board the sloop *Liberty* on 17 Aug 1780. {Ref: Archives of Maryland Vol. 45, p. 50}

ARMITAGE, WILLIAM (Anne Arundel County), private by 18 Oct 1779 at which time the Council of Maryland *"ordered that the western shore Treasurer pay to Richard Welsh $250 the Bounty paid by him to William Armitage enlisted by him to do Garrison Duty &ca within this State and also $16 for enlisting said Armitage."* {Ref: Archives of Maryland Vol. 21, p. 560}

ARMORY, RICHARD, see "Peter Bahan," q.v.

ARMSTRONG, ---- (Maryland Continental Line, Staff and P. Officer), doctor who received payment for his services in the amount of "1900 Dollars & £3.10s" on 12 Sep 1780. {Ref: Archives of Maryland Vol. 45, p. 98}

ARMSTRONG, GEORGE (Baltimore County?), captain in the 3rd Maryland Continental Line who received payment for his services in the amount of "1900 Dollars & £3.10s" on 12 Sep 1780. {Ref: Archives of Maryland Vol. 45, p. 98}

ARMSTRONG, JAMES (Maryland Navy), marine on the State Ship *Defence* in 1777. {Ref: Archives of Maryland Vol. 18, p. 654}

ARMSTRONG, PAUL (Western Maryland), private in Capt. Michael Cresap's Company in 1775. {Ref: Howard L. Leckey's *The Tenmile Country and Its Pioneer Families*, p. 15}

ARN (ARM), JAMES (Maryland Navy), ordinary seaman on the State Ship *Defence* in 1777. {Ref: Archives of Maryland Vol. 18, p. 654}

ARNOLD, HENRY, see "William Arnold," q.v.

ARNOLD, JEREMIAH (Western Maryland), private in Capt. Michael Cresap's Company in 1775. {Ref: Howard L. Leckey's *The Tenmile Country and Its Pioneer Families*, p. 15}

ARNOLD, SUSAN, see "William Arnold," q.v.

ARNOLD, WILLIAM (Harford County), private who was enrolled 10 Mar 1776 in Militia Company No. 18 under Capt. John Jolly; William Arnold died by 8 Mar 1831 (date of final distribution) and his heirs were widow Susan Arnold, sons William Arnold and Henry F. Arnold (administrator), and daughters Harriet Courtney, Sophia Jackson, Mary Mitchell, Elizabeth Coale, and Delia Mitchell. {Ref: George W. Archer Collection and Revolutionary War File, Historical Society

8

of Harford County Archives; Henry C. Peden, Jr.'s *Heirs & Legatees of Harford County, 1802-1846*, p. 37}

ASHFIELD, HENRY (Baltimore County), private, aged 22, labourer, born in England, enlisted 8 Mar 1776 in Capt. John Fulford's Company of Matrosses. {Ref: Maryland Historical Magazine, Vol. 69, No. 1, p. 96}

ASHLEY, JAMES (Frederick County), private (substitute) in the Maryland Continental Line, German Regiment, enrolled in April, 1778 for 3 years or duration of the war. {Ref: Maryland Historical Magazine, Vol. 6, No. 3, p. 257}

ASHMEAD, JOHN (Harford County), captain, commissioned -- Feb 1777, Militia Company No. 31. {Ref: George W. Archer Collection and Revolutionary War File, Historical Society of Harford County Archives}

ASHMY, ---- (Anne Arundel County?), soldier in the Maryland Continental Line *"now remaining in Annapolis"* on 24 Jul 1780 at which time his wife Hannah Ashmy was entitled to rations under the laws of the State. {Ref: Archives of Maryland Vol. 43, p. 227}

ASKEW, JONATHAN (Baltimore Town), patriot and merchant who enrolled in Capt. John Sterrett's Independent Mercantile Company by February, 1777, at which time they were mustered into regular service with the continental army to repress loyalist activities in the Eastern Shore counties of Somerset and Worcester. {Ref: J. Thomas Scharf's *History of Baltimore City and County*, Part I, p. 77}

ASKINS, WILLIAM (Maryland Navy), marine on the State Ship *Defence* in 1777. {Ref: Archives of Maryland Vol. 18, p. 654}

ATCHISON, WILLIAM (Maryland Privateer), commander of the brigantine *St. Patrick*, navigated by 30 men and mounting 6 carriage guns, was issued Letters of Marque & Reprisal by the Council of Maryland on 2 Dec 1782. {Ref: Archives of Maryland Vol. 48, p. 312}

ATKINSON, ANGELO (Worcester County), ensign in the county militia, commissioned 21 Jun 1776. {Ref: Archives of Maryland Vol. 11, p. 506}

AUBBER, JOHN (Annapolis), patriot who was paid 45 shillings by the Maryland Council of Safety for attending the hospital on 1 Oct 1776. {Ref: Archives of Maryland Vol. 12, p. 313}

AUBRE, JOHN (Maryland Navy), seaman or marine on the State Ship *Defence* in 1777. {Ref: Archives of Maryland Vol. 18, p. 654}

AUCHENLECK, HENRY (Maryland Navy), lieutenant on the State Ship *Defence* in 1777. {Ref: Archives of Maryland Vol. 18, p. 654}

AUDETT, JOSEPH (Baltimore Privateer), commander of the schooner *Resource*, navigated by 24 men and mounting 12 carriage guns and 8 swivel guns, was issued Letters of Marque & Reprisal by the Council of Maryland on 9 Sep 1780. {Ref: Archives of Maryland Vol. 43, p. 282}

AVIETS, JOHN (Maryland Navy), sailor or seaman on 7 Jan 1780. {Ref: Calendar of Maryland State Papers, The Brown Books, p. 57}

AYER, DARIUS (Kent County), soldier in the militia; born 22 Oct 1755 in Kent County and applied for pension in Marion District, South Carolina on 17 Mar 1835. {Ref: Research by Virgil D. White, citing Federal Pension Application R332}

AYRES, DANIEL, see "Daniel Eirs," q.v.

AYRES, STEPHEN, see "Stephen Eirs," q.v.

BABB, JOSEPH (Anne Arundel County), corporal in the 1st Maryland Continental Line by 30 Jul 1778 at which time the Council of Maryland noted his *"having a sore Leg has permission to remain at Home three weeks from this Time to endeavour to obtain Relief."* {Ref: Archives of Maryland Vol. 21, p. 170}

BABBS, JOHN (Anne Arundel County), soldier who enlisted in the 1st Maryland Continental Line in Annapolis on 10 Dec 1776 and was discharged on 13 Dec 1779; applied for pension on 30 Apr 1818 in Hamilton County, Ohio; in 1820 he was aged 68 and living with a son (not named) and also mentioned a wife and children (not named). {Ref: Archives of Maryland Vol. 18, p. 81; Research by Christopher T. Smithson, citing Federal Pension Application S45241}

BABLEN, JOHN (Anne Arundel County), patriot who was paid £40 by the Maryland Council of Safety for necessaries for the hospital. {Ref: Archives of Maryland Vol. 12, p. 318}

BACHER, T. H. (Baltimore Town), patriot and merchant who enrolled in Capt. John Sterrett's Independent Mercantile Company by February, 1777, at which time they were mustered into regular service with the continental army to repress loyalist activities in the Eastern Shore counties of Somerset and Worcester. {Ref: J. Thomas Scharf's *History of Baltimore City and County*, Part I, p. 77}

BACKENBAUGH (PECKINPAUGH), LEONARD (Frederick County), soldier in the Maryland Continental Line; born in 1760 in Frederick County, married Catharine Shroyer (aged 16) in 1786 and 19 years after his discharge from the service he moved to Fayette County, Pennsylvania; in 1822 he moved to Union County, Indiana and applied for pension on 9 Sep 1833; moved in April, 1839 to Lebanon, Ohio; his son Michael Peckinbaugh stated his father died at his house on 12 Nov 1842; widow Catharine Backenbaugh applied for pension in Warren County, Ohio on 30 Aug 1848, aged 78, and died about 6 May 1856. {Ref: Research by Christopher T. Smithson, citing Federal Pension Application W4122}

BACQUES (BARGUES), JACQUES (Anne Arundel County), lieutenant in the Maryland Artillery who received payment for his services in the amount of "1900 Dollars & £3.10s" on 12 Sep 1780. {Ref: Archives of Maryland Vol. 45, p. 98}

BAGLEY, LAVINIA, see "Richard Sappington," q.v.

BAHAN (BAYHAN), PETER (Baltimore County?), recruit who had enlisted in the Maryland Continental Line for the duration of the war (no date given) and complained on 29 Aug 1781 to the Council of Maryland *"that he was hired as a substitute by Richard Armory and that Mr. Armory engaged to give him one hundred Bushels of wheat, which he Bayhan has not received"* and the Council directed William Hemsley, Esq., ordering, in part, *"if he has not received a Compensation for becoming a Substitute he will of Course be entitled to the Bounty given to recruits."* {Ref: Archives of Maryland Vol. 45, p. 586}

BAILEY, AQUILA (Harford County, Susquehannah Hundred), private who was enrolled 23 Apr 1776 in Militia Company No. 21 under Capt. George Patterson. {Ref: George W. Archer Collection and Revolutionary War File, Historical Society of Harford County Archives}

BAILEY, CHARLES (Harford County, Susquehannah Hundred), private who was enrolled 23 Apr 1776 in Militia Company No. 21 under Capt. George Patterson. {Ref: George W. Archer Collection and Revolutionary War File, Historical Society of Harford County Archives}

BAILEY, JOSEPHUS (Baltimore County), private who enlisted in the Maryland Continental Line in Baltimore and applied for pension on 24 Jun 1818, aged 63; lived in Harford County. {Ref: Research by Virgil D. White, citing Federal Pension Application S34633}

BAILEY, JOSIAS (Harford County, Susquehannah Hundred), private who was enrolled 23 Apr 1776 in Militia Company No. 21 under Capt. George Patterson. {Ref: George W. Archer Collection and Revolutionary War File, Historical Society of Harford County Archives}

BAILEY, MOUNTJOY (Southern Maryland), captain, commissioned on 27 Jul 1780 to serve in the Regiment Extra by order of the Council of Maryland. {Ref: Archives of Maryland Vol. 43, p. 234}

BAILEY, THOMAS, see "James McCracken," q.v.

BAILEY, THOMAS, JR. (Baltimore Town), patriot and merchant who enrolled in Capt. John Sterrett's Independent Mercantile Company by February, 1777, at which time they were mustered into regular service with the continental army to repress loyalist activities in the Eastern Shore counties of Somerset and Worcester. {Ref: J. Thomas Scharf's *History of Baltimore City and County*, Part I, p. 77}

BAIRD, WILLIAM (Frederick County), patriot who was appointed by the Council of Maryland on 27 Jan 1776 as one of three persons in Frederick County to collect all gold and silver coin that can be procured in said county. {Ref: Archives of Maryland Vol. 11, p. 132}

BAKER, CHARLES (Harford County), captain, commissioned 14 May 1776 in Militia Company No. 25. {Ref: George W. Archer Collection and Revolutionary War File, Historical Society of Harford County Archives}

BAKER, FREDERICK (Baltimore Privateer), commander of the sloop *Hero*, mounting 6 carriage guns, 8 swivel guns, 2 howitz guns and 14 small arms, was issued Letters of Marque & Reprisal by the Council of Maryland on 10 May 1779. {Ref: Archives of Maryland Vol. 21, p. 384}

BAKER, GEORGE (Frederick County), private who was enrolled to serve as a substitute in the Maryland Continental Line until 10 Dec 1781, but *"being*

represented unfit for the service for which he was intended" was discharged on 30 Oct 1781. {Ref: Archives of Maryland Vol. 45, p. 657}

BAKER, GRAFTON (Harford County), private who was enrolled by 15 Apr 1776 in Militia Company No. 20 under Capt. Robert Glenn. {Ref: George W. Archer Collection and Revolutionary War File, Historical Society of Harford County Archives}

BAKER, NATHAN (Baltimore County), private who was drafted into the Maryland Continental Line, was discharged on 8 Dec 1781. {Ref: Archives of Maryland Vol. 48, p. 10}

BAKER, NICHOLAS (Harford County, Susquehannah Hundred), private who was enrolled 23 Apr 1776 in Militia Company No. 21 under Capt. George Patterson. {Ref: George W. Archer Collection and Revolutionary War File, Historical Society of Harford County Archives}

BAKER, VALENTINE (Western Maryland), private in Capt. Michael Cresap's Company in 1775. {Ref: Howard L. Leckey's *The Tenmile Country and Its Pioneer Families*, p. 15}

BAKER, WILLIAM (Harford County), private who was enrolled by 15 Apr 1776 in Militia Company No. 20 under Capt. Robert Glenn. {Ref: George W. Archer Collection and Revolutionary War File, Historical Society of Harford County Archives}

BAKER, WONSLEY (Frederick County), private who enlisted in the Maryland Continental Line in Frederick County and applied for pension in Rockcastle County, Kentucky on 1 Oct 1836, aged 74; lived in Laurel County, Kentucky. {Ref: Research by Virgil D. White, citing Federal Pension Application R439}

BALCH, STEPHEN BLOOMER (Calvert County), private who enlisted in the Maryland Continental Line at Lower Marlborough in Calvert County and applied for pension in Washington, D.C. on 23 Nov 1832, aged 84; his son L. P. W. Balch, who lived in Frederick, Maryland in 1841, stated his parents were married on 10 Jul 1781 and his mother died in 1827 and his father died in 1833. {Ref: Research by Virgil D. White, citing Federal Pension Application S12051}

BALDWIN, FRANCIS, see "Tyler Baldwin," q.v.

BALDWIN, HENRY (Anne Arundel County), lieutenant in the 3rd Maryland Continental Line who received payment for his services in the amount of "1900 Dollars & £3.10s" on 12 Sep 1780. {Ref: Archives of Maryland Vol. 45, p. 97}

BALDWIN, JOHN (Frederick County), private (substitute) in the Maryland Continental Line, Price's Regiment, enrolled in April, 1778 for 3 years or duration of the war. {Ref: Maryland Historical Magazine, Vol. 6, No. 3, p. 256}

BALDWIN, JOHN (Maryland Privateer), commander of the schooner *Lively*, navigated by 12 men and mounting 8 swivel guns and 8 small arms, was issued Letters of Marque & Reprisal by the Council of Maryland on 14 Oct 1778. {Ref: Archives of Maryland Vol. 21, p. 216}

BALDWIN, NICHOLAS, see "Tyler Baldwin," q.v.

BALDWIN, REZIN, see "Tyler Baldwin," q.v.

BALDWIN, SAMUEL (Prince George's County), private who was drafted into the Maryland Continental Line, was discharged on 8 Dec 1781. {Ref: Archives of Maryland Vol. 48, p. 10}

BALDWIN, TYLER (Anne Arundel County), patriot who *"took the Oath of Allegiance agreeable to the Act of the General Assembly administered to the Freemen of the State of the better protection of our Government"* in 1778; born in 1755, married Timsey Davidge on 17 Mar 1785, and died in 1795; their children were: Tyler Baldwin (born 16 Oct 1785, married Sarah Keene); Rezin Baldwin; and, Francis Baldwin; on 21 Dec 1798 Nicholas Baldwin was surviving executor of the estate of Tyler Baldwin, deceased, and halves of the remaining balance were paid to Rezin Baldwin and Tyler Baldwin. {Ref: Maryland State Society DAR Directory, 1892-1965, p. 134; Anne Arundel County Administration Account JG No. 2, p. 51}

BALL, NANCY (ANN), see "George Moore," q.v.

BALTZELL, CHARLES (Frederick County), major in the Maryland Continental Line who *"died at his farm near Woodsborough in Frederick County on 31 Dec 1813 in his 77th year; a native of Germany, he served several campaigns in the 7 years war; upwards of 50 years since he migrated to this country and settled in Maryland; he served in the Revolutionary War until the army was disbanded; became a member of the Society of the Cincinnati."* {Ref: Frederick-Town Herald, 22 Jan 1814}

BANKHEAD, HUGH (Harford County), private who was enrolled by 15 Apr 1776 in Militia Company No. 20 under Capt. Robert Glenn. {Ref: George W. Archer Collection and Revolutionary War File, Historical Society of Harford County Archives}

BANKHEAD, WILLIAM (Harford County), private who was enrolled by 15 Apr 1776 in Militia Company No. 20 under Capt. Robert Glenn. {Ref: George W. Archer Collection and Revolutionary War File, Historical Society of Harford County Archives}

BANTZ, JOHN (Baltimore County), private, aged 18, farmer, born in Talbot County, Maryland, enlisted 12 Mar 1776 in Capt. John Fulford's Company of Matrosses. {Ref: Maryland Historical Magazine, Vol. 69, No. 1, p. 96}

BARBER, FREDERICK (Western Maryland), private in Capt. Michael Cresap's Company in 1775. {Ref: Howard L. Leckey's *The Tenmile Country and Its Pioneer Families*, p. 15}

BARBER, SAMUEL (Anne Arundel County), adjutant to the Severn Battalion of Militia who was paid by the Maryland Council of Safety for four months' service on 28 Nov 1776. {Ref: Archives of Maryland Vol. 12, p. 485}

BARLOW, BENJAMIN (Queen Anne's County), private (substitute) in the Maryland Continental Line by 1781, was discharged on 8 Dec 1781. {Ref: Archives of Maryland Vol. 48, p. 11}

BARNES, BENJAMIN (Harford County), private who was enrolled 25 Mar 1776 in Militia Company No. 19 under Capt. William Morgan. {Ref: George W. Archer Collection and Revolutionary War File, Historical Society of Harford County Archives}

BARNES, CATHERINE, see "John Mitchell," q.v.

BARNES, HENRY (Maryland Navy), seaman or marine on the State Ship *Defence* in 1777. {Ref: Archives of Maryland Vol. 18, p. 654}

BARNES, JAMES (Harford County, Susquehannah Hundred), private who was enrolled 23 Apr 1776 in Militia Company No. 21 under Capt. George Patterson. {Ref: George W. Archer Collection and Revolutionary War File, Historical Society of Harford County Archives}

BARNES, JAMES (Queen Anne's County), second major in the 20th Battalion of Militia, commissioned 8 May 1777. {Ref: Archives of Maryland Vol. 16, p. 244}

BARNES, RICHARD (St. Mary's County), patriot who was appointed by the Council of Maryland on 27 Jan 1776 as one of three persons in St. Mary's County to collect all the gold and silver coin that can be procured in said county; supplied 800 lbs. of beef on the hoof to the State of Maryland on 14 Oct 1780; and, Richard Barnes, Esq., was County Lieutenant in 1780. {Ref: Archives of Maryland Vol. 11, p. 132, Vol. 43, p. 330, and Vol. 45, p. 156}

BARNES, THOMAS (Queen Anne's County), private (substitute) in the Maryland Continental Line by 1781, was discharged on 8 Dec 1781. {Ref: Archives of Maryland Vol. 48, p. 11}

BARNES, THOMAS (Western Maryland), private in Capt. Michael Cresap's Company in 1775. {Ref: Howard L. Leckey's *The Tenmile Country and Its Pioneer Families*, p. 15}

BARNETT, DANIEL (Frederick County), private (substitute) in the Maryland Continental Line, Gunby's Regiment, enrolled in May, 1778 for 3 years or duration of the war. {Ref: Maryland Historical Magazine, Vol. 6, No. 3, p. 259}

BARNETT, ROBERT (Frederick County), private (substitute) in the Maryland Continental Line, German Regiment, enrolled in May, 1778 for 3 years or duration of the war. {Ref: Maryland Historical Magazine, Vol. 6, No. 3, p. 259}

BARNHOUSER, JOHN, see "William B. Rasin," q.v.

BARR, JOHN (Maryland Navy), coxswain on the State Ship *Defence* in 1777. {Ref: Archives of Maryland Vol. 18, p. 654}

BARRANCE, JAMES (Maryland Navy), seaman or marine on the State Ship *Defence* in 1777. {Ref: Archives of Maryland Vol. 18, p. 654}

BARRETT, JAMES (Harford County), soldier whose widow Martha Barrett applied for pension under the Act of July 7, 1838, but the claim was suspended for further proof of marriage and service. {Ref: *Rejected or Suspended Applications for Revolutionary War Pensions* (1850 Report), p. 236}

BARRETT, JOHN (Maryland Navy), seaman or marine on the State Ship *Defence* in 1777. {Ref: Archives of Maryland Vol. 18, p. 654}

BARRETT, JOHN (Harford County), private who was enrolled by 15 Apr 1776 in Militia Company No. 20 under Capt. Robert Glenn; see "Simon Fitzgerald," q.v. {Ref: George W. Archer Collection and Revolutionary War File, Historical Society of Harford County Archives}

BARRETT, JONATHAN (Prince George's County), soldier in the Maryland Continental Line; married Sophia Beck on 14 Feb 1828; applied for pension in Davidson County, North Carolina on 19 Nov 1833, aged 76; died 21 Aug 1840 and widow applied for pension on 19 Nov 1853, aged 71. {Ref: Research by Virgil D. White, citing Federal Pension Application R560}

BARRETT, MARTHA, see "James Barrett," q.v.

BARRICK, JOHN, OF HANDEAL (Frederick County), ensign in Capt. Valentine Creager's Company in Col. James Johnson's Battalion of Militia, commissioned 28 Apr 1779. {Ref: Archives of Maryland Vol. 21, p. 369}

BARRY, STANDISH (Baltimore Town), patriot and merchant who enrolled in Capt. John Sterrett's Independent Mercantile Company by February, 1777, at which time they were mustered into regular service with the continental army to repress loyalist activities in the Eastern Shore counties of Somerset and Worcester. {Ref: J. Thomas Scharf's *History of Baltimore City and County*, Part I, p. 77}

BARRYMAN, JOHN (Maryland Navy), sailor or seaman on 7 Jan 1780. {Ref: Calendar of Maryland State Papers, The Brown Books, p. 57}

BARTOLOMEW, PETER (Frederick County), private (substitute) in the Maryland Continental Line, German Regiment, enrolled in May, 1778 for 3 years or duration of the war. {Ref: Maryland Historical Magazine, Vol. 6, No. 3, p. 260}

BASNET, NATHANIEL (Kent County), private (substitute) in the Maryland Continental Line by 1781, was discharged on 11 Dec 1781. {Ref: Archives of Maryland Vol. 48, p. 18}

BATTERSHELL, FREEMAN (Western Maryland), private in Capt. Michael Cresap's Company in 1775. {Ref: Howard L. Leckey's *The Tenmile Country and Its Pioneer Families*, p. 15}

BATTS, JOSEPH (Anne Arundel County), private in the Maryland Continental Line by 1 Dec 1781 at which time he was on duty guarding the magazine at the Head of Severn River. {Ref: Archives of Maryland Vol. 48, p. 8}

BAUN, JOHN (Frederick County), private (substitute) in the Maryland Continental Line by 1781, was discharged on 8 Dec 1781. {Ref: Archives of Maryland Vol. 48, p. 11}

BAYARD, EPHRAIM (Harford County, Susquehannah Hundred), private who was enrolled 23 Apr 1776 in Militia Company No. 21 under Capt. George Patterson. {Ref: George W. Archer Collection and Revolutionary War File, Historical Society of Harford County Archives}

BAYARD, JAMES (Harford County, Susquehannah Hundred), private who was enrolled 23 Apr 1776 in Militia Company No. 21 under Capt. George Patterson. {Ref: George W. Archer Collection and Revolutionary War File, Historical Society of Harford County Archives}

BAYER, JACOB (Frederick County), patriot buried in Mount Olivet Cemetery. {Ref: Information compiled by Dr. Donald Wolf in Maryland Society SAR Newsletter circa 1996}

BAYLESS, BENJAMIN (Harford County, Susquehannah Hundred), private who was enrolled 23 Apr 1776 in Militia Company No. 21 under Capt. George Patterson; see "Nathaniel Bayless," q.v. {Ref: George W. Archer Collection and Revolutionary War File, Historical Society of Harford County Archives}

BAYLESS, DANIEL (Harford County, Susquehannah Hundred), private who was enrolled 23 Apr 1776 in Militia Company No. 21 under Capt. George Patterson; see "Nathaniel Bayless," q.v. {Ref: George W. Archer Collection and Revolutionary War File, Historical Society of Harford County Archives}

BAYLESS, HARRIOTT, see "Nathaniel Bayless," q.v.

BAYLESS, JAMES, see "Nathaniel Bayless," q.v.

BAYLESS, JONAS (Harford County, Susquehannah Hundred), private who was enrolled 23 Apr 1776 in Militia Company No. 21 under Capt. George Patterson. {Ref: George W. Archer Collection and Revolutionary War File, Historical Society of Harford County Archives}

BAYLESS, MARY, see "Nathaniel Bayless," q.v.

BAYLESS, NATHANIEL (Harford County, Susquehannah Hundred), private who was enrolled 23 Apr 1776 in Militia Company No. 21 under Capt. George Patterson; Nathaniel Bayless died by 27 Mar 1804 (date of final distribution) and his heirs were Ann Whitaker (wife of Platt Whitaker), Samuel Bayless, Daniel Bayless, Elizabeth Kenly (wife of Lemuel Kenly), Benjamin Bayless, Mary Bayless, Harriott Bayless, James Bayless, and Nathaniel Bayless. {Ref: George W. Archer Collection and Revolutionary War File, Historical Society of Harford County Archives; Henry C. Peden, Jr.'s *Heirs & Legatees of Harford County, 1802-1846*, p. 6}

BAYLESS, ROBERT (Harford County, Susquehannah Hundred), private who was enrolled 23 Apr 1776 in Militia Company No. 21 under Capt. George Patterson. {Ref: George W. Archer Collection and Revolutionary War File, Historical Society of Harford County Archives}

BAYLESS, SAMUEL, see "Nathaniel Bayless," q.v.

BAYLEY, JONAS (Harford County), private who was enrolled 25 Mar 1776 in Militia Company No. 19 under Capt. William Morgan. {Ref: George W. Archer Collection and Revolutionary War File, Historical Society of Harford County Archives}

BEACHUM, WILLIAM (Maryland Navy), carpenter's mate on the State Ship *Defence* in 1777. {Ref: Archives of Maryland Vol. 18, p. 654}

BEALL, BARTON (Charles County), private who was drafted to serve in the Maryland Continental Line until 10 Dec 1781, but *"being represented unfit for the duty for which he was intended"* was discharged on 30 Oct 1781. {Ref: Archives of Maryland Vol. 45, p. 656}

BEALL, BROOKES (Montgomery County), patriot who was commissioned one of the three persons in Montgomery County by the Council of Maryland on 19 Aug 1779 to receive subscriptions for use of the State. {Ref: Archives of Maryland Vol. 21, p. 499}

BEALL, HARRIET, see "Thomas Johnson, Jr.," q.v.

BEALL, WILLIAM DENT (Prince George's County), captain in the 6th Maryland Continental Line who received payment for his services in the amount of "1900 Dollars & £3.10s" on 12 Sep 1780. For additional information see Peden's *Revolutionary Patriots of Prince George's County, 1775-1783* (p. 20). {Ref: Archives of Maryland Vol. 45, p. 98}

BEALL, WILLIAM MURDOCK (Frederick County), patriot buried in Mount Olivet Cemetery. For additional information see Peden's *Revolutionary Patriots of Frederick County, 1775-1783* (p. 25). {Ref: Information compiled by Dr. Donald Wolf in Maryland Society SAR Newsletter circa 1996}

BEAN, HENRY H., SR. (Bryantown, Charles County), soldier in the Maryland Continental Line who applied for pension under the Act of June 7, 1832, but the claim was rejected because he did not serve six months and payment was suspended for further proof and specification. {Ref: *Rejected or Suspended Applications for Revolutionary War Pensions* (1850 Report), pp. 229, 231}

BEAN, JOHN (Harford County), private who was enrolled 10 Mar 1776 in Militia Company No. 18 under Capt. John Jolly. {Ref: George W. Archer Collection and Revolutionary War File, Historical Society of Harford County Archives}

BEANS, JOSEPH (Prince George's County), private who was drafted into the Maryland Continental Line, was discharged on 8 Dec 1781. {Ref: Archives of Maryland Vol. 48, p. 10}

BEARD, ---- (Anne Arundel County), soldier in the Maryland Continental Line before 14 Dec 1782 at which time the Council of Maryland granted *"permission to Richard Beard, Jr. of Ann Arundel County to go into New York by Dobbs's Ferry to carry his Son Necessaries who is a Prisoner."* {Ref: Archives of Maryland Vol. 48, p. 322}

BEARD, FREDERICK (Frederick County), private who was enrolled to serve as a substitute in the Maryland Continental Line until 10 Dec 1781, but *"being represented unfit for the service for which he was intended"* was discharged on 30 Oct 1781. {Ref: Archives of Maryland Vol. 45, p. 657}

BEARD, RICHARD, see "---- Beard" and "Thomas Beard," q.v.

BEARD, THOMAS (Somerset County), private who was drafted into the Maryland Continental Line, was discharged on 8 Dec 1781. {Ref: Archives of Maryland Vol. 48, p. 10}

BEARD, THOMAS (Anne Arundel County), private who was enrolled to serve as a substitute in the Maryland Continental Line until 10 Dec 1781, but *"being represented unfit for the service for which he was intended"* was discharged on 30 Oct 1781; Thomas Beard was one of the heirs and executors of Richard Beard, deceased, on 11 Dec 1790. {Ref: Archives of Maryland Vol. 45, p. 657; Anne Arundel County Administration Account JG No. 1, p. 20}

BEARD, WILLIAM (Montgomery County), soldier in the Maryland Continental Line; born 10 Oct 1762 on Bell's Island, one mile below Coonrod's Ferry on the Potomac River, and lived in Montgomery County at the time of his enlistment;

in 1799 he moved to Loudon County, Virginia and in 1827 he moved to Belmont County, Ohio; applied for pension on 15 Jun 1835, aged 72. {Ref: Research by Christopher T. Smithson, citing Federal Pension Application R671}

BEATTY, PHILIP (Baltimore County), private who enlisted in Pulaski's Legion on 11 May 1778 in Baltimore. {Ref: Maryland Historical Magazine, Vol. 13, No. 3, p. 222}

BEATTY, THOMAS (Frederick County), patriot and lieutenant and in the revolution buried in Mount Olivet Cemetery; *"Major Thomas Beatty of Georgetown, a Revolutionary War officer, husband and father, died on 27 Feb 1815 in his 56th year."* {Ref: *Frederick-Town Herald*, 4 Mar 1815; Burial information compiled by Dr. Donald Wolf in Maryland Society SAR Newsletter circa 1996}

BEATTY, THOMAS (Baltimore County), patriot who supplied provisions to the State of Maryland between June and September, 1780. {Ref: Archives of Maryland Vol. 45, p. 84}

BEATTY, WILLIAM (Frederick and Washington Counties), captain in the 7th Maryland Continental Line who received payment for his services in the amount of "1900 Dollars & £3.10s" on 12 Sep 1780; born in 1758 and killed at the battle of Hobkirk's Hill near Camden, South Carolina on 25 Apr 1781. {Ref: Archives of Maryland Vol. 45, p. 98; J. Thomas Scharf's *History of Western Maryland*, Vol. II, p. 1034}

BEATTY, WILLIAM (Harford County), private who was enrolled by 15 Apr 1776 in Militia Company No. 20 under Capt. Robert Glenn. {Ref: George W. Archer Collection and Revolutionary War File, Historical Society of Harford County Archives}

BEAVENS, CHARLES (Prince George's County), lieutenant in the 6th Maryland Continental Line who received payment for his services in the amount of "1900 Dollars & £3.10s" on 12 Sep 1780. {Ref: Archives of Maryland Vol. 45, p. 98}

BEAVER, THOMAS (Harford County), private who was enrolled 25 Mar 1776 in Militia Company No. 19 under Capt. William Morgan; private who was enrolled by Capt. Praul in the Regiment Extraordinary and sent to Annapolis with Capt. Thompson on board the sloop *Liberty* on 17 Aug 1780. {Ref: George W. Archer Collection and Revolutionary War File, Historical Society of Harford County Archives; Archives of Maryland Vol. 45, p. 50}

BECK, SAMUEL (Kent County), second lieutenant in the county militia, commissioned 22 Jun 1776; one Samuel Beck died testate in Kent County by 13 Nov 1790. {Ref: Archives of Maryland Vol. 11, p. 506; Kent County Wills Liber 7, p. 296}

BECK, SIMON (Kent County), private (substitute) in the Maryland Continental Line by 1781, was discharged on 8 Dec 1781. {Ref: Archives of Maryland Vol. 48, p. 11}

BECK, SOPHIA, see "Jonathan Barrett," q.v.

BECKENBACH, SUSANNA, see "John F. Main," q.v.

BECKETT, JOSEPH (Western Maryland), private in Capt. Michael Cresap's Company in 1775. {Ref: Howard L. Leckey's *The Tenmile Country and Its Pioneer Families*, p. 15}

BECRAFT, LURANAH, see "James Higgins," q.v.

BEGERHOFF, LUDWIC (Baltimore or Frederick County), private who enlisted in Pulaski's Legion on 1 Jul 1779. {Ref: Maryland Historical Magazine, Vol. 13, No. 3, p. 224}

BEGGERLY, DAVID (Montgomery County), private in the Maryland Continental Line who was drafted to serve until 10 Dec 1781, was discharged on 8 Dec 1781. {Ref: Archives of Maryland Vol. 48, p. 17}

BELFORD, JAMES (Western Maryland), private in Capt. Michael Cresap's Company in 1775. {Ref: Howard L. Leckey's *The Tenmile Country and Its Pioneer Families*, p. 15}

BELL, CATHARINE, see "Frederick Hook," q.v.

BELL, DAVID (Harford County), private who was enrolled 9 Dec 1775 in Militia Company No. 14 under Capt. William McComas; David Bell died by 16 Oct 1815 (date of final distribution) and his heirs were Elizabeth Bell (widow), Lovice Bell, David Bell, Mary Evans, Elizabeth Bryerly, Ann Hawkins, and Martha and George B. Amos. {Ref: George W. Archer Collection and Revolutionary War File, Historical Society of Harford County Archives; Henry C. Peden, Jr.'s *Heirs & Legatees of Harford County, 1802-1846*, p. 20}

BELL, ELISHA (Frederick County), lieutenant in the revolution who *"died at his residence Sunday evening last in his 93rd year; a native of this county, he entered the Army of the Revolution as a lieutenant and attached himself to the Flying Camp during the war; he was distinguished as a gallant soldier and devoted patriot; after the war he turned his attention to agriculture which he continued to the day of his death."* {Ref: *The Republican Citizen*, 22 Dec 1837}

BELL, ELIZABETH, see "David Bell," q.v.

BELL, JOHN (Harford County), second lieutenant by 15 Apr 1776 in Militia Company No. 20 under Capt. Robert Glenn. {Ref: George W. Archer Collection and Revolutionary War File, Historical Society of Harford County Archives}

BELL, LOVICE, see "David Bell," q.v.

BELL, ROBERT (Harford County), private who was enrolled 9 Dec 1775 in Militia Company No. 14 under Capt. William McComas. {Ref: George W. Archer Collection and Revolutionary War File, Historical Society of Harford County Archives}

BELL, THOMAS (Harford County), captain before 28 Feb 1779 (date of court case). {Ref: Historical Society of Harford County Court Records File 3.09(13)}

BELT, BASIL, see "Robert Orme," q.v.

BELT, HUMPHREY (Prince George's County), lieutenant who served on a General Court-Martial on 6 Jul 1776. {Ref: Archives of Maryland Vol. 11, p. 553}

BELT, JAMES (Maryland Navy and Privateer), captain of the galley *Johnson*, commissioned 8 May 1777; commander of the schooner *Montgomery*, mounting 2 carriage guns, 4 swivel guns and 6 small arms, was issued Letters of Marque & Reprisal by the Council of Maryland on 17 Nov 1778; commander of the brigantine *Lively*, mounting 10 carriage guns, 2 swivel guns and 10 small arms, was issued Letters of Marque & Reprisal by the Council of Maryland on 31 May 1779; commander of the schooner *Montgomery*, mounting 2 carriage guns, 4 swivel guns and 6 small arms, was issued Letters of Marque & Reprisal by the Council of Maryland on 17 Nov 1778; commander of the ship *Matilda*, navigated by 70 men and mounting 22 carriage guns, was issued Letters of Marque & Reprisal by the Council of Maryland on 21 Feb 1782. {Ref: Archives of Maryland Vol. 16, p. 244, Vol. 21, pp. 240, 432, and Vol. 48, p. 83}

BELT, WALTER (Maryland Privateer), commander of the schooner *Whynot*, navigated by himself, his Mate and 7 men, given permission by the Council of Maryland on 15 Mar 1783 *"to pass with the said Vessel under Sanction of a Flag of Truce from the Port of Baltimore in this State to Vienna in Dorchester County there to take in 2,633 Bushels of Indian Corn and to proceed from thence to New York with her said Cargo for the use of the Maryland Prisoners there and to return again."* {Ref: Archives of Maryland Vol. 48, p. 381}

BEN, SAMUEL (Kent County), private (substitute) in the Maryland Continental Line by 1781, was discharged on 8 Dec 1781. {Ref: Archives of Maryland Vol. 48, p. 11}

BENNETT, GEORGE (Maryland Navy), seaman or marine on the State Ship *Defence* in 1777. {Ref: Archives of Maryland Vol. 18, p. 654}

BENNETT, JOHN (Frederick County), private (substitute) in the Maryland Continental Line, German Regiment, enrolled in May, 1778 for 3 years or duration of the war. {Ref: Maryland Historical Magazine, Vol. 6, No. 3, p. 260}

BENNETT, JOEL (Baltimore County), matross soldier by 7 May 1779 at which time he gave a deposition about his enlistment terms. {Ref: Maryland State Archives Record MdHR 6636-14-83}

BENNETT, JOSHUA (Prince George's County), private who was drafted into the Maryland Continental Line, was discharged on 8 Dec 1781. {Ref: Archives of Maryland Vol. 48, p. 10}

BENNETT, LEWIS (Western Maryland), private in Capt. Michael Cresap's Company in 1775. {Ref: Howard L. Leckey's *The Tenmile Country and Its Pioneer Families*, p. 15}

BENNETT, SARAH, see "Parker Gilbert," q.v.

BENNINGTON (BENNITON), HENRY (Harford County), private who was enrolled 10 Mar 1776 in Militia Company No. 18 under Capt. John Jolly. {Ref: George W. Archer Collection and Revolutionary War File, Historical Society of Harford County Archives}

BENSON, JOSEPH (Baltimore City), soldier who applied for pension under the Act of June 7, 1832, but the claim was suspended pending further proof and specification. {Ref: *Rejected or Suspended Applications for Revolutionary War Pensions* (1850 Report), p. 231}

BENSON, PERRY (Washington County), captain in the 5th Maryland Continental Line who received payment for his services in the amount of "1900 Dollars & £3.10s" on 12 Sep 1780; Benson *"displayed conspicuous gallantry at the battles of Cowpens and Guilford Courthouse, at Hobkirk's Hill, and at Ninety-Six, where he led the forlorn hope. At Hobkirk's Hill Capt. Benson commanded the picket guard, consisting of about 220 men, and checked the advance of the whole British Army until the American forces, which were separated and unprepared for an attack, could be concentrated and formed for battle, and did not retire until his command had poured six deadly volleys into the enemy, and he had lost in killed and wounded all but 33 of his men; in the attack on Ninety-Six Capt. Benson commanded the forlorn hope, and was shot down within a few yards of the enemy's works, while encouraging his command; he did not recover from the effects of this wound for many years, and even to the end of his life was occasionally a sufferer from it; during the Whisky Insurrection he joined the army with the rank of colonel and in 1812, in spite of the infirmities of advancing age, he took an active part in the defense of this State as brigadier general of militia, on one occasion handsomely repulsing a British attack on the town of St. Michael's with a small body of raw militia; previous to the War of 1812 he had represented his county in the Lower House of the Assembly, which was the only civil office he ever held; he died on 2 Oct 1827 in his 72nd year, and was interred in the family burial ground."* {Ref: Archives of Maryland Vol. 45, p. 98; J. Thomas Scharf's *History of Western Maryland*, Vol. II, p. 1022}

BENTLEY, WILLIAM (Harford County), private (substitute) in the Maryland Continental Line by 1781, was discharged on 8 Dec 1781. {Ref: Archives of Maryland Vol. 48, p. 11}

BENTON, THOMAS (Maryland Navy), carpenter on the State Ship *Defence* in 1777. {Ref: Archives of Maryland Vol. 18, p. 654}

BENYAU, ALEXANDER (Calvert County), private (substitute) in the Maryland Continental Line by 1781, was discharged on 8 Dec 1781. {Ref: Archives of Maryland Vol. 48, p. 10}

BERMINGHAM, CHRISTOPHER (Maryland Navy), captain of the schooner *Liberty*, commissioned 20 Nov 1780. {Ref: Archives of Maryland Vol. 45, p. 219}

BERRY, JAMES (Maryland Navy), marine on the State Ship *Defence* in 1777. {Ref: Archives of Maryland Vol. 18, p. 654}

BERRY, ROBERT (Maryland Navy), captain of the State Ship *Plater* by 27 Apr 1780 at which time he was paid $1800 and received 1 small keg of powder and 4 dozen musket cartridges. {Ref: Archives of Maryland Vol. 43, p. 154}

BERRYMAN, JOHN (Maryland Navy), gunner on board the State Ship *Defence* in 1777 and lost his right arm in the service of this State, received £250 for his subsistence on 26 Jul 1780. {Ref: Archives of Maryland Vol. 18, p. 654 and Vol. 43, p. 230}

BIDDLE, NOBLE, see "Humphrey Pugh," q.v.

BIER, BETSY, see "John Lanham," q.v.

BIRCKHEAD, FRANCIS (Anne Arundel County), private by 5 Oct 1776 in Capt. Richard Chew's Militia Company, Weems' Battalion. {Ref: Archives of Maryland Vol. 12, p. 323}

BIRCKHEAD, FRANCIS, JR. (Anne Arundel County), private by 5 Oct 1776 in Capt. Richard Chew's Militia Company, Weems' Battalion. {Ref: Archives of Maryland Vol. 12, p. 323}

BIRCKHEAD, JOHN (Anne Arundel County), private by 5 Oct 1776 in Capt. Richard Chew's Militia Company, Weems' Battalion. {Ref: Archives of Maryland Vol. 12, p. 323}

BIRCKHEAD, JOHN, JR. (Anne Arundel County), private by 5 Oct 1776 in Capt. Richard Chew's Militia Company, Weems' Battalion. {Ref: Archives of Maryland Vol. 12, p. 322}

BIRCKHEAD, JOSEPH (Anne Arundel County), private by 5 Oct 1776 in Capt. Richard Chew's Militia Company, Weems' Battalion. {Ref: Archives of Maryland Vol. 12, p. 323}

BIRCKHEAD, MATTHEW (Anne Arundel County), private by 5 Oct 1776 in Capt. Richard Chew's Militia Company, Weems' Battalion. {Ref: Archives of Maryland Vol. 12, p. 323}

BIRCKHEAD, NEHEMIAH (Anne Arundel County), private by 5 Oct 1776 in Capt. Richard Chew's Militia Company, Weems' Battalion; Nehemiah Birkhead was an heir and executor of the estate of Nehemiah Birkhead, Sr., deceased, on 5 Aug 1811. {Ref: Archives of Maryland Vol. 12, p. 322; Anne Arundel County Administration Account JG No. 1, p. 157}

BIRCKHEAD, NEHEMIAH, OF SAMUEL (Anne Arundel County), private by 5 Oct 1776 in Capt. Richard Chew's Militia Company, Weems' Battalion. {Ref: Archives of Maryland Vol. 12, p. 323}

BIRD, RICHARD (Queen Anne's County), captain in the 5th Maryland Continental Line who received payment for his services in the amount of "1900 Dollars & £3.10s" on 12 Sep 1780. {Ref: Archives of Maryland Vol. 45, p. 98}

BIRD, SAMUEL (Maryland Navy), marine on the State Ship *Defence* in 1777. {Ref: Archives of Maryland Vol. 18, p. 654}

BIRD, THOMAS (Prince George's County), private in the 3rd Maryland Continental Line who was a 9 month soldier in the 5th Maryland Regiment in 1778-1779, reenlisted on 22 Apr 1779 and received £11.4.10 in clothing. {Ref: Archives of Maryland Vol. 21, p. 361}

BIRMINGHAM, CHRISTOPHER (Maryland Navy), captain of tender to the State Ship *Defence* in 1777. {Ref: Archives of Maryland Vol. 18, p. 654}

BISCOE, JOSIAH (St. Mary's County), patriot and privateer who applied for pension on 10 Aug 1832, aged 73, under the Act of June 7, 1832; born 30 Mar 1760 (son of Joseph Biscoe, of St. Mary's County), he stated he enlisted in the

Maryland troops, but apparently had no proof of service and the claim was rejected because of only privateer service. {Ref: Research by Virgil D. White, citing Federal Pension Application R859; *Rejected or Suspended Applications for Revolutionary War Pensions* (1850 Report), p. 229}

BISCOE, MACKIE (Maryland Navy), seaman or marine on the State Ship *Defence* in 1777. {Ref: Archives of Maryland Vol. 18, p. 654}

BISHOP, EDWARD (Worcester County), private in the Maryland Continental Line who was drafted to serve until 10 Dec 1781, was discharged on 10 Dec 1781. {Ref: Archives of Maryland Vol. 48, p. 17}

BISHOP, ELIJAH (Queen Anne's County), second major of the 5th Battalion of Militia, commissioned 8 May 1777. {Ref: Archives of Maryland Vol. 16, p. 243}

BISHOP, WILLIAM (Maryland Navy), marine on the State Ship *Defence* in 1777. {Ref: Archives of Maryland Vol. 18, p. 654}

BISSETT, THOMAS (Baltimore County), patriot who was paid £8.10.6 for waggonage by the Committee of Claims on 28 Mar 1778. {Ref: Archives of Maryland Vol. 16, p. 557}

BLACK, HENRY (Baltimore County), private, aged 38, shoemaker, born in Dublin, enlisted 13 Feb 1776 in Capt. John Fulford's Company of Matrosses. {Ref: Maryland Historical Magazine, Vol. 69, No. 1, p. 94}

BLACK, MOSES (Baltimore County), private (substitute) in the Maryland Continental Line by 1781, was discharged on 8 Dec 1781. {Ref: Archives of Maryland Vol. 48, p. 11}

BLACKBURN, JAMES (Western Maryland), private in Capt. Michael Cresap's Company in 1775. {Ref: Howard L. Leckey's *The Tenmile Country and Its Pioneer Families*, p. 15}

BLACKBURN, ROBERT (Western Maryland), private in Capt. Michael Cresap's Company in 1775. {Ref: Howard L. Leckey's *The Tenmile Country and Its Pioneer Families*, p. 15}

BLACKBURN, SAMUEL (Western Maryland), private in Capt. Michael Cresap's Company in 1775. {Ref: Howard L. Leckey's *The Tenmile Country and Its Pioneer Families*, p. 15}

BLACKINSTON, GEORGE N. (Baltimore Town), patriot and merchant who enrolled in Capt. John Sterrett's Independent Mercantile Company by February, 1777, at which time they were mustered into regular service with the continental army to repress loyalist activities in the Eastern Shore counties of Somerset and Worcester. {Ref: J. Thomas Scharf's *History of Baltimore City and County*, Part I, p. 77}

BLACKMAN, STEPHEN (Maryland Navy), seaman on the State Ship *Defence* in 1777. {Ref: Archives of Maryland Vol. 18, p. 654}

BLACKMER, SALISBURY (Baltimore Privateer), commander of the schooner *Widow Wadman*, navigated by 14 men and mounting 4 carriage guns, 2 howitzer guns and 1 swivel gun, was issued Letters of Marque & Reprisal by the Council of Maryland on 10 Aug 1778. {Ref: Archives of Maryland Vol. 21, p. 181}

BLAIK, AARON (Baltimore County), private who was drafted into the Maryland Continental Line, was discharged on 8 Dec 1781. {Ref: Archives of Maryland Vol. 48, p. 10}

BLAIR, JAMES (Western Maryland), private in Capt. Michael Cresap's Company in 1775. {Ref: Howard L. Leckey's *The Tenmile Country and Its Pioneer Families*, p. 15}

BLAKE, JOHN (Maryland Navy), boatswain and quartermaster on the State Ship *Defence* in 1777. {Ref: Archives of Maryland Vol. 18, p. 654}

BLAKENEY, THOMAS (Harford County), private who was enrolled by 15 Apr 1776 in Militia Company No. 20 under Capt. Robert Glenn. {Ref: George W. Archer Collection and Revolutionary War File, Historical Society of Harford County Archives}

BLANFORD (BLANDFORD), IGNATIUS (Calvert County), private in the Maryland Continental Line who enlisted on 23 Aug 1776; commissioned an ensign on 27 Jul 1780 to serve in the Regiment Extra by order of the Council of Maryland. {Ref: Archives of Maryland Vol. 18, p. 33 and Vol. 43, p. 234}

BLANFORD (BLANDFORD), JOSEPH (Calvert and Prince George's Counties), private in the Maryland Continental Line who enlisted on 23 Aug 1776 in Calvert County; he applied for pension under the Act of June 7, 1832 in Prince George's County, but the claim was suspended pending further proof and specification; he never received a pension and died on 28 Apr 1836, aged 85; his only surviving children were Stanislaw Blanford and Elizabeth Dyer (wife of Richard Dyer). {Ref: Archives of Maryland Vol. 18, p. 33; Research by Virgil D. White, citing Federal Pension Application R928; *Rejected or Suspended Applications for Revolutionary War Pensions* (1850 Report), p. 231}

BLANFORD (BLANDFORD), RICHARD (Charles County), private who enlisted in the Maryland Continental Line on 18 Jul 1776; he applied for pension in Bullett County, Kentucky on 2 Oct 1832, aged 76; his brother Walter, aged 66, also lived in Bullett county. {Ref: Research by Virgil D. White, citing Federal Pension Application S10392}

BLANFORD, STANISLAW, see "Joseph Blanford," q.v.

BLANFORD, WALTER, see "Richard Blanford," q.v.

BLITHEN, JOHN (Maryland Navy), corporal of marines on the State Ship *Defence* in 1777. {Ref: Archives of Maryland Vol. 18, p. 654}

BLUNT, CHARLES (Maryland Navy), marine on the State Ship *Defence* in 1777. {Ref: Archives of Maryland Vol. 18, p. 654}

BOARDLY, RICHARD, see "William Simmons," q.v.

BODKIN, ROBERT (Harford County), private who was enrolled 10 Mar 1776 in Militia Company No. 18 under Capt. John Jolly. {Ref: George W. Archer Collection and Revolutionary War File, Historical Society of Harford County Archives}

BODLEY, THOMAS (Baltimore Town), patriot and merchant who enrolled in Capt. John Sterrett's Independent Mercantile Company by February, 1777, at which time they were mustered into regular service with the continental army to repress loyalist activities in the Eastern Shore counties of Somerset and Worcester. {Ref: J. Thomas Scharf's *History of Baltimore City and County*, Part I, p. 77}

BODWIN, HENRY (Baltimore or Frederick County), private in Pulaski's Legion before July, 1782. {Ref: Maryland Historical Magazine, Vol. 13, No. 3, p. 225}

BOLTON, RICHARD (Baltimore County), private, aged 43, shoemaker, 5'5" tall, born in England, enlisted 21 May 1776 in Capt. John Fulford's Company of Matrosses. {Ref: Maryland Historical Magazine, Vol. 69, No. 1, p. 97}

BOMGARDNER, JOHN (Washington County), private who was enrolled to serve as a substitute in the Maryland Continental Line until 10 Dec 1781, but *"being represented unfit for the service for which he was intended"* was discharged on 30 Oct 1781. {Ref: Archives of Maryland Vol. 45, p. 657}

BOND, JOHN (Calvert County), doctor and patriot who was commissioned one of the three persons in Calvert County by the Council of Maryland on 19 Aug 1779 to receive subscriptions for use of the State. {Ref: Archives of Maryland Vol. 21, p. 499}

BOND, NATHANIEL (Maryland Navy), midshipman and purser on the State Ship *Defence* in 1777. {Ref: Archives of Maryland Vol. 18, p. 654}

BOND, THOMAS (Baltimore County), private who enlisted in Pulaski's Legion on 8 May 1778 in Baltimore. {Ref: Maryland Historical Magazine, Vol. 13, No. 3, p. 222}

BOND, ZACCHEUS, see "William Morgan," q.v.

BONER, MATTHEW (Harford County, Susquehannah Hundred), private who was enrolled 23 Apr 1776 in Militia Company No. 21 under Capt. George Patterson. {Ref: George W. Archer Collection and Revolutionary War File, Historical Society of Harford County Archives}

BONER, WILLIAM (Harford County, Susquehannah Hundred), private who was enrolled 23 Apr 1776 in Militia Company No. 21 under Capt. George Patterson. {Ref: George W. Archer Collection and Revolutionary War File, Historical Society of Harford County Archives}

BONNELL, JOHN (Maryland Navy), captain of the State Ship *Defence*, commissioned 5 Apr 1776. {Ref: Archives of Maryland Vol. 11, p. 312}

BOOGHER, GEORGE (Frederick County), private (substitute) in the Maryland Continental Line, German Regiment, enrolled in May, 1778 for 3 years or duration of the war. {Ref: Maryland Historical Magazine, Vol. 6, No. 3, p. 258}

BOONE (BOON), JOHN (Charles County), soldier in the Maryland Continental Line who applied for pension on 26 Nov 1828; he may have also been the John Boone who applied under the Act of June 7, 1832, but the claim was suspended *"for a new declaration according to the printed instructions."* His only surviving child was Mary Jane Boone who stated on 28 Nov 1853 that her father was born in 1758 or 1759 and died on 31 Jan 1837; there was also a John Boone who was an ensign in the 1st Maryland Continental Line and received payment for his services in the amount of "1900 Dollars & £3.10s" on 12 Sep

1780. Additional research will be necessary before drawing conclusions. {Ref: Research by Virgil D. White, citing Federal Pension Application S8076; *Rejected or Suspended Applications for Revolutionary War Pensions* (1850 Report), p. 231; Archives of Maryland Vol. 45, p. 97}

BOONE, IGNATIUS (Southern Maryland), ensign, commissioned on 27 Jul 1780 to serve in the Regiment Extra by order of the Council of Maryland. {Ref: Archives of Maryland Vol. 43, p. 234}

BOONE, MARY JANE, see "John Boone," q.v.

BOOTMAN, JOHN (Baltimore County), private, aged 22, farmer, born in Maryland, enlisted (made his "X" mark) on 14 Mar 1776 in Capt. John Fulford's Company of Matrosses. {Ref: Maryland Historical Magazine, Vol. 69, No. 1, p. 96}

BORAT, PETER (Washington County), private who was enrolled to serve as a substitute in the Maryland Continental Line until 10 Dec 1781, but *"being represented unfit for the service for which he was intended"* was discharged on 30 Oct 1781. {Ref: Archives of Maryland Vol. 45, p. 657}

BORDLEY, WILLIAM (Kent County), colonel of the 13th Battalion of Militia, commissioned 8 May 1777; one of the three persons in Kent County appointed by the Council of Maryland on 19 Aug 1779 to receive subscriptions for use of the State; one William Bordley died testate by 21 Sep 1784. {Ref: Archives of Maryland Vol. 16, p. 243 and Vol. 21, p. 499; Kent County Wills Liber 7, p. 69}

BOTTS, ASAEL, see "John Botts," q.v.

BOTTS, AVARILLA, see "John Botts," q.v.

BOTTS, ELIZABETH, see "John Botts," q.v.

BOTTS, GEORGE (Harford County, Susquehannah Hundred), private who was enrolled 23 Apr 1776 in Militia Company No. 21 under Capt. George Patterson. {Ref: George W. Archer Collection and Revolutionary War File, Historical Society of Harford County Archives}

BOTTS, JAMES, see "John Botts" and "John Hall Hughes," q.v.

BOTTS, JOHN (Harford County, Susquehannah Hundred), private who was enrolled 23 Apr 1776 in Militia Company No. 21 under Capt. George Patterson; John Botts died by 15 Jul 1806 (date of final distribution) and his heirs were Elizabeth Botts (widow), Nancy Hughes, James Botts (administrator), Asael Botts, and Avarilla Botts. {Ref: George W. Archer Collection and Revolutionary War File, Historical Society of Harford County Archives; Henry C. Peden, Jr.'s *Heirs & Legatees of Harford County, 1802-1846*, p. 10}

BOTTS, NANCY, see "John Botts" and "John Hall Hughes," q.v.

BOUCHER, JOHN THOMAS (Maryland Navy), first lieutenant on the State Ship *Defence* until 5 Apr 1776 at which time he resigned. {Ref: Archives of Maryland Vol. 11, p. 312}

BOUNDS, EMALINE, see "Thomas Adams," q.v.

BOUNDS, THOMAS (Montgomery County), recruit who was enlisted by Basil Roberts and discharged from the Maryland Continental Line on 22 Jun 1778 *"on his returning the $60 bounty and paying £10 for the clothes he received."* {Ref: Archives of Maryland Vol. 21, p. 144}

BOWEN, JOSIAS (Baltimore County), private, 31 May 1779, Capt. Benjamin Talbott's Militia Company, Cockey's Battalion. {Ref: Maryland Historical Magazine, Vol. 7, No. 1, p. 90}

BOWIE, FIELDER (Prince George's County), captain who served on a General Court-Martial on 6 Jul 1776. {Ref: Archives of Maryland Vol. 11, p. 553}

BOWIN, WILLIAM (Baltimore Privateer), commander of the schooner *Swallow*, navigated by 12 men and mounting 4 howitz guns, 4 swivel guns and 6 small arms, was issued Letters of Marque & Reprisal by the Council of Maryland on 16 Oct 1778. {Ref: Archives of Maryland Vol. 21, p. 217}

BOWMAN, CHARLES (Western Maryland), private in Capt. Michael Cresap's Company in 1775. {Ref: Howard L. Leckey's *The Tenmile Country and Its Pioneer Families*, p. 15}

BOWMAN, WILLIAM (Baltimore or Frederick County), private in Pulaski's Legion before July, 1782. {Ref: Maryland Historical Magazine, Vol. 13, No. 3, p. 225}

BOYCE, ROGER (Baltimore Privateer), commander of the brigantine *Ranger*, navigated by 30 men and mounting 10 carriage guns, was issued Letters of Marque & Reprisal by the Council of Maryland on 27 Aug 1782. {Ref: Archives of Maryland Vol. 48, p. 246}

BOYD, ROBERT (Maryland Navy), seaman on the State barge *Revenge* on 16 Jun 1781 under Commodore Grason. {Ref: Archives of Maryland Vol. 45, p. 477}

BOYD, THOMAS (Prince George's County), ensign in the 2nd Maryland Continental Line who received payment for his services in the amount of "1900 Dollars & £3.10s" on 12 Sep 1780. {Ref: Archives of Maryland Vol. 45, p. 97}

BOYD, SAMUEL (Chester County, Pennsylvania), private who was enlisted by Ensign Jones into the 3rd Maryland Continental Line, *"sent from camp by General Smallwood as unfit for the service"* and discharged on 22 Jun 1778. {Ref: Archives of Maryland Vol. 21, p. 144}

BOYER, ANDREW (Baltimore County), private, aged 41, carpenter, born in Bucks County, Pennsylvania, enlisted 24 Feb 1776 in Capt. John Fulford's Company of Matrosses. {Ref: Maryland Historical Magazine, Vol. 69, No. 1, p. 95}

BOYLE, JAMES (Maryland Navy), marine on the galley *Baltimore*, took the Oath of Fidelity and Allegiance to the State of Maryland on 31 Mar 1778; commissioned first lieutenant of marines on 18 May 1778. {Ref: Archives of Maryland Vol. 16, p. 559 and Vol. 21, p. 91}

BOYLE, ROBERT (Frederick County), private (substitute) in the Maryland Continental Line, Williams' Regiment, enrolled in May, 1778 for 3 years or duration of the war. {Ref: Maryland Historical Magazine, Vol. 6, No. 3, p. 260}

BRACKEN, WILLIAM (Western Maryland), private in Capt. Michael Cresap's Company in 1775. {Ref: Howard L. Leckey's *The Tenmile Country and Its Pioneer Families*, p. 15}

BRADFORD, JAMES (Maryland Navy), ordinary seaman on the State Ship *Defence* in 1777. {Ref: Archives of Maryland Vol. 18, p. 654}

BRADFORD, WILLIAM (Maryland Navy), sergeant of marines on the State Ship *Defence* in 1777. {Ref: Archives of Maryland Vol. 18, p. 654}

BRADFORD, WILLIAM, see "Benjamin B. Norris," q.v.

BRADING, ROBERT (Harford County), private who was enrolled 10 Mar 1776 in Militia Company No. 18 under Capt. John Jolly. {Ref: George W. Archer Collection and Revolutionary War File, Historical Society of Harford County Archives}

BRADHURST, BENJAMIN (Maryland Privateer), commander of the brigantine *Betsey*, mounting 2 carriage guns, 3 swivel guns, 8 howitz guns and 1 musket, was issued Letters of Marque & Reprisal by the Council of Maryland on 17 Nov 1778; commander of the schooner *Blossom*, navigated by 9 men and mounting 4 carriage guns and 6 small arms, was issued Letters of Marque & Reprisal by the Council of Maryland on 13 Mar 1780. {Ref: Archives of Maryland Vol. 21, p. 240 and Vol. 43, p. 110}

BRADY, MICHAEL (Maryland Navy), seaman or marine on the State Ship *Defence* in 1777. {Ref: Archives of Maryland Vol. 18, p. 654}

BRAITHWAITE, JOHN (Maryland Navy) marine on the State Ship *Defence* in 1777. {Ref: Archives of Maryland Vol. 18, p. 654}

BRAITHWAITE, WILLIAM (Frederick County), private (substitute) in the Maryland Continental Line, Price's Regiment, enrolled in May, 1778 for 3 years or duration of the war. {Ref: Maryland Historical Magazine, Vol. 6, No. 3, p. 258}

BRANAMAN, BENJAMIN (Baltimore City), soldier who applied for pension under the Act of June 7, 1832, but the claim was suspended because he did not serve six months; he applied again in Baltimore on 10 May 1845, aged 85, and stated he had served in the Pennsylvania Line. {Ref: *Rejected or Suspended Applications for Revolutionary War Pensions* (1850 Report), p. 231; Research by Virgil D. White, citing Federal Pension Application R1158}

BRANDY, DAVID (Western Maryland), private in Capt. Michael Cresap's Company in 1775. {Ref: Howard L. Leckey's *The Tenmile Country and Its Pioneer Families*, p. 15}

BRASHEAR, JOSEPH (Western Maryland), private in Capt. Michael Cresap's Company in 1775. {Ref: Howard L. Leckey's *The Tenmile Country and Its Pioneer Families*, p. 15}

BRASHEAR, RICHARD (Western Maryland), private in Capt. Michael Cresap's Company in 1775. {Ref: Howard L. Leckey's *The Tenmile Country and Its Pioneer Families*, p. 15}

BRASHEAR, WILLIAM (Frederick County), captain in the Maryland Continental Line who died on 10 Nov 1813 in his 78th year. {Ref: *Frederick-Town Herald*, 20 Nov 1813}

BRASHEARS, JOHN (Prince George's County), private (substitute) in the Maryland Continental Line by 1781, was discharged on 8 Dec 1781. {Ref: Archives of Maryland Vol. 48, p. 10}

BRAUNER, JOSEPH (Frederick County), private (substitute) in the Maryland Continental Line, German Regiment, enrolled in May, 1778 for 3 years or duration of the war. {Ref: Maryland Historical Magazine, Vol. 6, No. 3, p. 260}

BRAY, HENRY (Washington County), private who was drafted to serve in the Maryland Continental Line until 10 Dec 1781, but *"being represented unfit for the duty for which he was intended"* was discharged on 30 Oct 1781. {Ref: Archives of Maryland Vol. 45, p. 656}

BREIDENHART, ANNA, see "James Sloan," q.v.

BREWER, JACOB (Harford County, Susquehannah Hundred), private who was enrolled 23 Apr 1776 in Militia Company No. 21 under Capt. George Patterson. {Ref: George W. Archer Collection and Revolutionary War File, Historical Society of Harford County Archives}

BREWER, RICHARD (Maryland Privateer), captain of the schooner *Boat* [sic] which was impressed into service by order of the Council of Maryland on 27 Apr 1780 *"to go to the Head of Elk for the Purpose of Transporting a Detachment of the American Army to the State of Virginia."* {Ref: Archives of Maryland Vol. 43, p. 155}

BRIAMANT, PETER (Baltimore Privateer), commander of the brigantine *Nancy*, mounting 6 carriage guns, 7 swivel guns and 6 small arms, was issued Letters of Marque & Reprisal by the Council of Maryland on 6 May 1779. {Ref: Archives of Maryland Vol. 21, p. 380}

BRICE, JACOB (Anne Arundel County), captain in the 3rd Maryland Continental Line who received payment for his services in the amount of "1900 Dollars & £3.10s" on 12 Sep 1780; see "Robert Elliott," q.v. {Ref: Archives of Maryland Vol. 45, p. 98}

BRICE, JAMES (Harford County), private who was enrolled 10 Mar 1776 in Militia Company No. 18 under Capt. John Jolly. {Ref: George W. Archer Collection and Revolutionary War File, Historical Society of Harford County Archives}

BRICE, JUDGE, see "Michael O'Connor," q.v.

BRIDEWELL, THIODORE (Prince George's County), private who was drafted into the Maryland Continental Line, was discharged on 8 Dec 1781. {Ref: Archives of Maryland Vol. 48, p. 10}

BRIGHT, WILLIAM (Baltimore County), private, aged 22, farmer, born in Maryland, enlisted 16 Feb 1776 in Capt. John Fulford's Company of Matrosses. {Ref: Maryland Historical Magazine, Vol. 69, No. 1, p. 95}

BRINA, DANIEL (Washington County), private who was drafted to serve in the Maryland Continental Line until 10 Dec 1781, but *"being represented unfit for the duty for which he was intended"* was discharged on 30 Oct 1781. {Ref: Archives of Maryland Vol. 45, p. 656}

BRISCOE, HANSON (St. Mary's County), officer and patriot who was appointed by the Council of Maryland on 27 Jan 1776 as one of three persons in St. Mary's County to collect all the gold and silver coin that can be procured in said county; supplied 800 lbs. of beef on the hoof to the State of Maryland on 8 Oct 1780; the Council recorded that *"Mr. Hanson Briscoe of Chaptico, St. Mary's County, has Vessels and will engage to transport all the Wheat in that County, and perhaps, in the neighbouring ones"* on 1 Dec 1781; *"Major Hanson Briscoe, Clerk of the County Court, died 12 Sep 1817 in his 68th year, his illness confined him nearly 4 weeks; he was a native of St. Mary's County and held a commission in the militia during the Revolutionary War."* {Ref: Archives of Maryland Vol. 11, p. 132, Vol. 45, p. 156, and Vol. 48, p. 9; *The Republican Gazette & General Advertiser*, 4 Oct 1817}

BRISCOE, HENRY (St. Mary's County), private who was drafted into the Maryland Continental Line, was discharged on 8 Dec 1781. {Ref: Archives of Maryland Vol. 48, p. 10}

BRISCOE, JAMES (Maryland Navy), marine on the State Ship *Defence* in 1777. {Ref: Archives of Maryland Vol. 18, p. 654}

BRISCOE, MARIA, see "William Lamar," q.v.

BRISSENTON, ABRAHAM (Maryland Navy), sailor or seaman on 7 Jan 1780. {Ref: Calendar of Maryland State Papers, The Brown Books, p. 57}

BRISSON, ROBERT (Maryland Privateer), commander of the sloop *Concord*, navigated by 22 men and mounting 6 carriage guns and 10 swivel guns, was issued Letters of Marque & Reprisal by the Council of Maryland on 11 Jun 1778. {Ref: Archives of Maryland Vol. 21, p. 131}

BROGDEN, RICHARD (Maryland Navy), second lieutenant of marines on the galley *Baltimore*, commissioned 18 May 1778. {Ref: Archives of Maryland Vol. 21, p. 91}

BROILS, MRS., see "George Holbrooks," q.v.

BROMFIELD, THOMAS (Maryland Navy), captain of marines on the State Ship *Defence* in 1777. {Ref: Archives of Maryland Vol. 18, p. 654}

BROMWELL, JACOB (Baltimore County), private, aged 23, ship carpenter, born in Virginia, enlisted (made his "X" mark) on 11 Mar 1776 in Capt. John Fulford's Company of Matrosses. {Ref: Maryland Historical Magazine, Vol. 69, No. 1, p. 96}

BRONLOR(?), CORNELIUS (Baltimore County), private, aged 24, farmer, born in Maryland, enlisted 18 Sep 1776 in Capt. John Fulford's Company of Matrosses. {Ref: Maryland Historical Magazine, Vol. 69, No. 1, p. 96}

BROOK, BASIL, see "John Patrick," q.v.

BROOKE, HESTER, see "Henry Hill," q.v.

BROOKE, SARAH, see "Aquila Hall," q.v.

BROOKS (BROOKES), BENJAMIN (Prince George's County), captain in the 3rd Maryland Continental Line who received payment for his services in the amount of "1900 Dollars & £3.10s" on 12 Sep 1780. For additional information see Peden's *Revolutionary Patriots of Prince George's County, 1775-1783* (p. 46). {Ref: Archives of Maryland Vol. 45, p. 97}

BROOKS (BROOKES), HENRY (Prince George's County), lieutenant who served on a General Court-Martial on 6 Jul 1776. {Ref: Archives of Maryland Vol. 11, p. 553}

BROOKS, JAMES (Baltimore County), private, aged 23, weaver, born in England, enlisted (made his "X" mark) on 17 Feb 1776 in Capt. John Fulford's Company of Matrosses. {Ref: Maryland Historical Magazine, Vol. 69, No. 1, p. 95}

BROOKS (BROOKES), JOHN SMITH (Prince George's County), lieutenant who served on a General Court-Martial on 6 Jul 1776; appointed Commissary of Purchases by the Council of Maryland on 8 Jul 1780. {Ref: Archives of Maryland Vol. 11, p. 553 and Vol. 43, p. 215}

BROOKS, THOMAS (Maryland Navy), seaman or marine on the State Ship *Defence* in 1777. {Ref: Archives of Maryland Vol. 18, p. 654}

BROWN, AQUILA (Queen Anne's County), patriot who was commissioned one of the three persons in Queen Anne's County by the Council of Maryland on 19 Aug 1779 to receive subscriptions for use of the State. {Ref: Archives of Maryland Vol. 21, p. 499}

BROWN, COLIN (Maryland Navy), sailor on the State Ship *Defence* in 1777. {Ref: Archives of Maryland Vol. 18, p. 654}

BROWN, GARRETT (Maryland Navy), captain of marines on the State Ship *Defence* in 1777. {Ref: Archives of Maryland Vol. 18, p. 654}

BROWN, GEORGE (Frederick County), private (substitute) in the Maryland Continental Line, Gunby's Regiment, enrolled in April, 1778 for 3 years or duration of the war. {Ref: Maryland Historical Magazine, Vol. 6, No. 3, p. 256}

BROWN, HOLLIDAY, see "Solomon Brown," q.v.

BROWN, JACOB (Baltimore County), second lieutenant in the Baltimore Town Battalion of Militia, commissioned 24 Apr 1781. {Ref: Archives of Maryland Vol. 45, p. 412}

BROWN, JAMES, see "Solomon Brown," q.v.

BROWN, JOHN (Anne Arundel County), sergeant in the Maryland Continental Line by 1 Dec 1781 at which time he was on duty guarding the magazine at the Head of Severn River; Richard and John Brown were two of the heirs and co-executors of the estate of John Brown, deceased, on 14 Oct 1795. {Ref: Archives of Maryland Vol. 48, p. 8; Anne Arundel County Administration Account JG No. 1, p. 59}

BROWN, JOHN (Baltimore or Frederick County), private in Pulaski's Legion before July, 1782. {Ref: Maryland Historical Magazine, Vol. 13, No. 3, p. 225}

BROWN, JOHN, see "Solomon Brown," q.v.

BROWN, JOSEPH (Maryland Navy), seaman or marine on the State Ship *Defence* in 1777. {Ref: Archives of Maryland Vol. 18, p. 654}

BROWN, MARGARET, see "Solomon Brown," q.v.

BROWN, MARTHA, see "Solomon Brown," q.v.

BROWN, RICHARD, see "John Brown," q.v.

BROWN, SAMUEL, see "Solomon Brown," q.v.

BROWN, SOLOMON (Harford County), private who was enrolled by 15 Apr 1776 in Militia Company No. 20 under Capt. Robert Glenn; Solomon Brown died by 30 Sep 1817 (date of final distribution) and his heirs were sons John, James, Thomas, Solomon and Samuel Brown, and daughters Mary Chambers and Holliday, Margaret, and Martha Brown. {Ref: George W. Archer Collection and Revolutionary War File, Historical Society of Harford County Archives; Henry C. Peden, Jr.'s *Heirs & Legatees of Harford County, 1802-1846*, p. 23}

BROWN, THOMAS (Baltimore or Frederick County), private in Pulaski's Legion before July, 1782. {Ref: Maryland Historical Magazine, Vol. 13, No. 3, p. 225}

BROWN, THOMAS (Frederick County), private (substitute) in the Maryland Continental Line, Price's Regiment, enrolled in May, 1778 for 3 years or duration of the war. {Ref: Maryland Historical Magazine, Vol. 6, No. 3, p. 258}

BROWN, THOMAS (Western Maryland), private in Capt. Michael Cresap's Company in 1775. {Ref: Howard L. Leckey's *The Tenmile Country and Its Pioneer Families*, p. 15}

BROWN, WILLIAM (Baltimore County), private, aged 18, labourer, born in Dublin, enlisted (made his "X" mark) 17 Feb 1776 in Capt. John Fulford's Company of Matrosses. {Ref: Maryland Historical Magazine, Vol. 69, No. 1, p. 95}

BROWNE, JOSHUA, see "Acquilla Randall," q.v.

BROWNE, MARGARET, see "Ichabod Davis," q.v.

BRUCE, NORMAND (Frederick County), officer and patriot who was commissioned one of the three persons in Frederick County by the Council of Maryland on 19 Aug 1779 to receive subscriptions for use of the State; also supplied provisions to the State of Maryland between June and September, 1780; *"Col. Normand Bruce, an old and respectable inhabitant of this county, died on Pipe Creek on 25 Apr 1811."* {Ref: Archives of Maryland Vol. 21, p. 499 and Vol. 45, p. 84; *The Hornet; Or Republican Advocate*, 1 May 1811}

BRUCE, WILLIAM (Charles County), captain in the 1st Maryland Continental Line who received payment for his services in the amount of "1900 Dollars & £3.10s" on 12 Sep 1780. {Ref: Archives of Maryland Vol. 45, p. 97}

BRUFF, JOSEPH (Talbot County), patriot who was commissioned one of the three persons in Talbot County by the Council of Maryland on 19 Aug 1779 to receive subscriptions for use of the State. {Ref: Archives of Maryland Vol. 21, p. 499}

BRUMICUM, JOHN (Maryland Navy), seaman on the State Ship *Defence* in 1777. {Ref: Archives of Maryland Vol. 18, p. 655}

BRUMWELL, GEORGE (Maryland Navy), sailor or seaman on 7 Jan 1780. {Ref: Calendar of Maryland State Papers, The Brown Books, p. 57}

BRUNNER, ELIAS (Frederick County), patriot buried in Mount Olivet Cemetery. {Ref: Information compiled by Dr. Donald Wolf in Maryland Society SAR Newsletter circa 1996}

BRUNNER, JOHN (Frederick County), patriot buried in Mount Olivet Cemetery.
{Ref: Information compiled by Dr. Donald Wolf in Maryland Society SAR Newsletter circa 1996}

BRUNNER, JOHN, see "Frederick Kemp," q.v.

BRUNNER, MARY, see "Frederick Kemp," q.v.

BRUNNER, VALENTINE (Frederick County), patriot buried in Mount Olivet
Cemetery. {Ref: Information compiled by Dr. Donald Wolf in Maryland Society SAR
Newsletter circa 1996}

BRYAN, DANIEL (Baltimore County), captain by 5 May 1778 at which time he
received 6 barrels of beef and 6 barrels of pork from the Issuing Commissary
for the Baltimore Matrosses. {Ref: Archives of Maryland Vol. 21, p. 67}

BRYAN, EDWARD (Frederick County), private who was enrolled to serve as a
substitute in the Maryland Continental Line until 10 Dec 1781, but *"being
represented unfit for the service for which he was intended"* was discharged on
30 Oct 1781. {Ref: Archives of Maryland Vol. 45, p. 657}

BRYAN, IGNATIUS (St. Mary's County), private who was drafted into the
Maryland Continental Line, was discharged on 8 Dec 1781. {Ref: Archives of
Maryland Vol. 48, p. 10}

BRYAN, WILLIAM (Maryland Navy), sailor or seaman on 7 Jan 1780. {Ref:
Calendar of Maryland State Papers, The Brown Books, p. 57}

BRYANT, JAMES (Queen Anne's County), private in the 7th Maryland
Continental Line; born 1757 at Piney Neck in Queen Anne's County, was
enlisted by Sgt. John Chambers on 13 Apr 1776 and sent to Annapolis to join
the troops commanded by General Smallwood; transferred to Capt. Morris or
Moore's Company on 13 Apr 1777 in Col. John Gunby's Regiment; discharged
on 13 Apr 1778; his daughter Mary Bryant Clary was 72 years old in 1860; he
also had a son William Bryant, Esq., of Annapolis; James died circa 1841. {Ref:
Research by Virgil D. White, citing Federal Pension Application S14993}

BRYERLY, ELIZABETH, see "David Bell," q.v.

BUCHANAN, ANDREW (Baltimore County), patriot who was commissioned one
of the three persons in Baltimore County by the Council of Maryland on 19
Aug 1779 to receive subscriptions for use of the State. {Ref: Archives of Maryland
Vol. 21, p. 499}

BUCHANAN, ARCHIBALD (Baltimore Town), patriot and merchant who
enrolled in Capt. John Sterrett's Independent Mercantile Company by February,
1777, at which time they were mustered into regular service with the
continental army to repress loyalist activities in the Eastern Shore counties of
Somerset and Worcester. {Ref: J. Thomas Scharf's *History of Baltimore City and County*,
Part I, p. 77}

BUCHANAN, GEORGE (Baltimore Privateer), commander of the brigantine *Fox*,
navigated by 22 men and mounting 14 carriage guns and 14 small arms, was
issued Letters of Marque & Reprisal by the Council of Maryland on 13 Mar
1780; commander of the brigantine *Salisbury*, mounting 6 carriage guns and 3

small arms, was issued Letters of Marque & Reprisal by the Council of Maryland on 19 Dec 1778; commander of the ship *Tom Lee*, navigated by 45 men and mounting 12 carriage guns, was issued Letters of Marque & Reprisal by the Council of Maryland on 22 Feb 1781. {Ref: Archives of Maryland Vol. 21, p. 269, Vol. 43, p. 110, and Vol. 45, p. 322}

BUCHANAN, J. S. (Baltimore Town), patriot and merchant who enrolled in Capt. John Sterrett's Independent Mercantile Company by February, 1777, at which time they were mustered into regular service with the continental army to repress loyalist activities in the Eastern Shore counties of Somerset and Worcester. {Ref: J. Thomas Scharf's *History of Baltimore City and County*, Part I, p. 77}

BUCHANAN, JAMES (Baltimore Privateer), commander of the brigantine *Revenge*, mounting 12 carriage guns, 4 howitz guns and 20 small arms, was issued Letters of Marque & Reprisal by the Council of Maryland on 14 Jun 1779; commander of the brigantine *Fox*, navigated by 22 men and mounting 8 carriage guns, was issued Letters of Marque & Reprisal by the Council of Maryland on 27 Jun 1780; commander of the brigantine *Ranger*, navigated by 42 men and mounting 14 carriage guns and 6 swivel guns, was issued Letters of Marque & Reprisal by the Council of Maryland on 12 Jan 1781. {Ref: Archives of Maryland Vol. 21, p. 453, Vol. 43, p. 206, and Vol. 45, p. 273}

BUCHANAN, JAMES (Western Maryland), sergeant in Capt. Michael Cresap's Company in 1775. {Ref: Howard L. Leckey's *The Tenmile Country and Its Pioneer Families*, p. 15}

BUCHANAN, JAMES A. (Baltimore Town), patriot and merchant who enrolled in Capt. John Sterrett's Independent Mercantile Company by February, 1777, at which time they were mustered into regular service with the continental army to repress loyalist activities in the Eastern Shore counties of Somerset and Worcester. {Ref: J. Thomas Scharf's *History of Baltimore City and County*, Part I, p. 77}

BUCKLER, JOHN, see "James Sloan," q.v.

BUCKLEY, THOMAS (Maryland Navy), marine on the State Ship *Defence* in 1777. {Ref: Archives of Maryland Vol. 18, p. 655}

BUFFINGTON, JONATHAN (Baltimore Privateer), commander of the brigantine *Rambler*, navigated by 25 men and mounting 10 carriage guns, was issued Letters of Marque & Reprisal by the Council of Maryland on 11 Sep 1780. {Ref: Archives of Maryland Vol. 43, p. 285}

BUGLES, WILLIAM (Washington County), private who was drafted to serve in the Maryland Continental Line until 10 Dec 1781, but *"being represented unfit for the duty for which he was intended"* was discharged on 30 Oct 1781. {Ref: Archives of Maryland Vol. 45, p. 656}

BULEY, GEORGE (Dorchester County), private (substitute) in the Maryland Continental Line by 1781, was discharged on 8 Dec 1781. {Ref: Archives of Maryland Vol. 48, p. 10}

BULLEN, JOHN (Anne Arundel County), patriot who was authorized by the Council of Maryland on 15 Jan 1781 to impress wagons to remove the public records in pursuance of a Resolution of the General Assembly on 13 Jan 1781; also, served as Collector of Stores in 1782. {Ref: Archives of Maryland Vol. 45, p. 275 and Vol. 48, p. 78}

BUNYAN, JOHN (Maryland Navy), chief mate on the State Ship *Defence* in 1777. {Ref: Archives of Maryland Vol. 18, p. 655}

BURGE, JOSEPH (Maryland Navy), steward on the State Ship *Defence* in 1777. {Ref: Archives of Maryland Vol. 18, p. 655}

BURGESS, JOSHUA (Anne Arundel County), ensign in the 4th Maryland Continental Line who received payment for his services in the amount of "1900 Dollars & £3.10s" on 12 Sep 1780. {Ref: Archives of Maryland Vol. 45, p. 98}

BURGESS, RICHARD (Anne Arundel County), doctor and surgeon's mate to Colonel Marbury's Battalion of Militia by 28 Jan 1778 at which time he was paid £29 for 58 days service. {Ref: Archives of Maryland Vol. 16, p. 476}

BURGESS, VACHEL (Anne Arundel County), captain, commissioned on 27 Jul 1780 to serve in the Regiment Extra by order of the Council of Maryland; Basil and Thomas D. Burgess were two of the heirs and co-executors of the estate of Vachel Burgess, deceased, on 16 Mar 1830. {Ref: Archives of Maryland Vol. 43, p. 234; Anne Arundel County Administration Account TH No. 1, p. 167}

BURK, JAMES (Frederick County), private (substitute) in the Maryland Continental Line, Williams' Regiment, enrolled in May, 1778 for 3 years or duration of the war. {Ref: Maryland Historical Magazine, Vol. 6, No. 3, p. 259}

BURK, RICHARD (Baltimore County), matross soldier by 7 May 1779 at which time he gave a deposition about his enlistment terms. {Ref: Maryland State Archives Record MdHR 6636-14-83}

BURKE, ELICK (Baltimore County), private, aged 25, labourer, born in Ireland, enlisted 14 Feb 1776 in Capt. John Fulford's Company of Matrosses, discharged 10 May 1776 from any further service, *"having for times been guilty of getting drunk and neglected duty."* {Ref: Maryland Historical Magazine, Vol. 69, No. 1, pp. 95, 97}

BURKHEAD, COLONEL, see "James O'Bryan," q.v.

BURNELL, JOHN (Maryland Navy), master on the State Ship *Defence* in 1777. {Ref: Archives of Maryland Vol. 18, p. 655}

BURNET, ---- (Anne Arundel County?), soldier in the Maryland Continental Line *"now remaining in Annapolis"* on 24 Jul 1780 at which time his wife Mary Burnet was entitled to rations under the laws of the State. {Ref: Archives of Maryland Vol. 43, p. 227}

BURNET, JEMIMA, see "William Jackson," q.v.

BURNET, MARY, see "---- Burnet," q.v.

BURNS, JOHN (Maryland Navy), marine on the sloop *Lincoln* who was taken prisoner and confined in New York before 17 Jan 1781 and was subsequently exchanged. {Ref: Archives of Maryland Vol. 45, p. 277}

BURNS, JOHN (Frederick County), private (substitute) in the Maryland Continental Line, Price's Regiment, enrolled in May, 1778 for 3 years or duration of the war. {Ref: Maryland Historical Magazine, Vol. 6, No. 3, p. 260}

BURNS, TIMOTHY (Baltimore County), private (substitute) in the Maryland Continental Line by 1781, was discharged on 8 Dec 1781. {Ref: Archives of Maryland Vol. 48, p. 11}

BURNSIDE, MATTHEW (Harford County), private who was enrolled by 15 Apr 1776 in Militia Company No. 20 under Capt. Robert Glenn. {Ref: George W. Archer Collection and Revolutionary War File, Historical Society of Harford County Archives}

BURRIS, ELIJAH (St. Mary's County), soldier whose widow Margaret P. Burris applied for pension under the Act of July 7, 1838, but the claim was suspended for further proof. {Ref: *Rejected or Suspended Applications for Revolutionary War Pensions* (1850 Report), p. 236}

BURRIS, ELISHA (St. Mary's County), private (substitute) in the Maryland Continental Line by 1781, was discharged on 8 Dec 1781. {Ref: Archives of Maryland Vol. 48, p. 11}

BURRIS, NORMAN, see "Norman Burroughs," q.v.

BURRIS, ROBERT (Dorchester County), private (substitute) in the Maryland Continental Line by 1781, was discharged on 8 Dec 1781. {Ref: Archives of Maryland Vol. 48, p. 10}

BURROUGHS (BURROUGH), NORMAN or NORMAND (St. Mary's County), soldier in the 2nd Maryland Continental Line whose widow Esther Turner Burroughs (Burrough) applied for pension in Baltimore under the Act of July 7, 1838, but the claim was rejected because he did not serve six months; however, records indicate "Norman Bouroughs" entered the service on 30 May 1778 for 9 months and "Norm. Burris" was discharged on 3 Apr 1779; his widow applied again in Charles County on 30 Mar 1842, aged 78, stating she had married the soldier in 1784 in King & Queen Parish in St. Mary's County (where she was born and where he had enlisted) and he died in 1812. {Ref: *Rejected or Suspended Applications for Revolutionary War Pensions* (1850 Report), p. 235; Research by Virgil D. White, citing Federal Pension Application W3935; Archives of Maryland Vol. 18, pp. 83, 329}

BURROWS, JOHN (Maryland Privateer), commander of the sloop *Washington*, navigated by 20 men and mounting 8 carriage guns, 6 swivel guns and 20 muskets, was issued Letters of Marque & Reprisal by the Council of Maryland on 3 Aug 1778. {Ref: Archives of Maryland Vol. 21, p. 175}

BUSEY, PAUL (Maryland Navy), marine on the sloop *Lincoln* who was taken prisoner and confined in New York before 17 Jan 1781 and was subsequently exchanged. {Ref: Archives of Maryland Vol. 45, p. 277}

BUSSEY, BENNETT, see "Jesse Bussey," q.v.

BUSSEY, EDWARD (Harford County), second lieutenant, commissioned -- Feb 1777, Militia Company No. 31 under Capt. John Ashmead. {Ref: George W. Archer Collection and Revolutionary War File, Historical Society of Harford County Archives}

BUSSEY, JESSE (Harford County), marine aboard the ship *Matilda* who was taken prisoner before 28 Oct 1782 at which time permission was given by the Council of Maryland *"to Captain Bennett Bussey of Harford County to solicit Leave of His Excellency General Washington or the Officers commanding at the Out posts of the American Army for a Flag to go into New York to endeavor to get Jesse Bussey (the son of Jesse Bussey of Baltimore County who lost a limb on board the Matilda and who is now confined on board the prison ship) released from Captivity, and Permission is also given to Edward Parker to go with the said Captain Bennett Bussey to assist in conveying home the said Jesse Bussey in case his release should be obtained."* {Ref: Archives of Maryland Vol. 48, p. 293}

BUSSEY, SAMUEL (Montgomery County), private (substitute) in the Maryland Continental Line by 1781, was discharged on 8 Dec 1781. {Ref: Archives of Maryland Vol. 48, p. 11}

BUTLER, HENRY (Charles County), private who was drafted into the Maryland Continental Line, was discharged on 8 Dec 1781. {Ref: Archives of Maryland Vol. 48, p. 10}

BUTLER, JAMES (Maryland Navy), seaman or marine on the State Ship *Defence* in 1777. {Ref: Archives of Maryland Vol. 18, p. 655}

BUTLER, JOHN (Harford County), private who was enrolled by Capt. Praul in the Regiment Extraordinary and sent to Annapolis with Capt. Thompson on board the sloop *Liberty* on 17 Aug 1780. {Ref: Archives of Maryland Vol. 45, p. 50}

BUTLER, JOSEPH (Baltimore or Frederick County), private in Pulaski's Legion before July, 1782. {Ref: Maryland Historical Magazine, Vol. 13, No. 3, p. 225}

BUTLER, JOSEPH (Charles County), private who was drafted into the Maryland Continental Line, was discharged on 8 Dec 1781. {Ref: Archives of Maryland Vol. 48, p. 10}

BUTLER, MARY, see "Nace Butler," q.v.

BUTLER, NACE (Anne Arundel County), soldier in the Maryland troops whose widow Mary Butler applied for pension on 30 Jul 1840, aged 76, under the Act of July 4, 1836, but the claim was rejected because of no proof that they were ever married (she claimed they were married on 3 or 5 Nov 1782); soldier died on 6 Aug 1809. {Ref: *Rejected or Suspended Applications for Revolutionary War Pensions* (1850 Report), p. 233; Research by Virgil D. White, citing Federal Pension Application R1549}

BUTLER, TIMOTHY (Queen Anne's County), private who was drafted into the Maryland Continental Line, was discharged on 8 Dec 1781. {Ref: Archives of Maryland Vol. 48, p. 10}

BUTLER, WILLIAM (Harford County), private who was drafted into the Maryland Continental Line, was discharged on 8 Dec 1781. {Ref: Archives of Maryland Vol. 48, p. 10}

BUTTON, SAMUEL DYRE (Queen Anne's County), recruiting officer appointed by the Council of Maryland *"to provide for and receive all recruits raised in Queen Ann's County"* on 18 Apr 1781. {Ref: Archives of Maryland Vol. 45, p. 402}

BYERLY, GEORGE (Baltimore Town), patriot and merchant who enrolled in Capt. John Sterrett's Independent Mercantile Company by February, 1777, at which time they were mustered into regular service with the continental army to repress loyalist activities in the Eastern Shore counties of Somerset and Worcester. {Ref: J. Thomas Scharf's *History of Baltimore City and County*, Part I, p. 77}

BYRNES, ALEXANDER (Western Maryland), private in Capt. Michael Cresap's Company in 1775. {Ref: Howard L. Leckey's *The Tenmile Country and Its Pioneer Families*, p. 15}

CAHILL, JAMES (Queen Anne's County), private in the Maryland Continental Line; born 27 Jan 1749 in Queen Anne's County [not Washington County as mistakenly stated in Peden's *Revolutionary Patriots of Washington County, 1776-1783*]; he enlisted in the Maryland Continental Line in Queen Anne's County and after the war moved to Kentucky and then to Ohio circa 1814; applied for pension in Brown County, Ohio on 3 Apr 1834. {Ref: Research by Christopher T. Smithson, citing Federal Pension Application S8186}

CAHILL, THOMAS (Frederick County), private (substitute) in the Maryland Continental Line, German Regiment, enrolled in April, 1778 for 3 years or duration of the war. {Ref: Maryland Historical Magazine, Vol. 6, No. 3, p. 257}

CAIN, ALEXANDER (Baltimore Privateer), commander of the sloop *Fly*, mounting 10 carriage guns, 10 swivel guns and 22 muskets, was issued Letters of Marque & Reprisal by the Council of Maryland on 30 Mar 1779. {Ref: Archives of Maryland Vol. 21, p. 332}

CAIN, ELIZABETH, see "James Cain," q.v.

CAIN, JAMES (Harford County), ensign, commissioned 16 May 1776 in Militia Company No. 26 under Capt. Samuel Smith; James Cain died by 7 Sep 1802 (date of final distribution) and his heirs were Elizabeth Cain (widow) and John, Matthew, Nancy, Mary, and Jane Cain. {Ref: George W. Archer Collection and Revolutionary War File, Historical Society of Harford County Archives; Henry C. Peden, Jr.'s *Heirs & Legatees of Harford County, 1802-1846*, p. 2}

CAIN, JOHN (Baltimore County), private who enlisted in Pulaski's Legion on 4 May 1778 in Baltimore. {Ref: Maryland Historical Magazine, Vol. 13, No. 3, p. 222}

CAINE, JOHN (Western Maryland), private in Capt. Michael Cresap's Company in 1775. {Ref: Howard L. Leckey's *The Tenmile Country and Its Pioneer Families*, p. 15}

CALDWELL, BENJAMIN (Baltimore City), soldier whose widow Mary Caldwell applied for pension under the Act of July 4, 1836, but the claim was rejected because he was "a soldier of the regular army" *[sic]* (and there is no proof of his service listed in the *Archives of Maryland*). {Ref: *Rejected or Suspended Applications for Revolutionary War Pensions* (1850 Report), p. 233}

CALHOUN, JAMES (Baltimore County), patriot who was commissioned one of the three persons in Baltimore County by the Council of Maryland on 19 Aug 1779 to receive subscriptions for use of the State; appointed Commissary of Purchases for Baltimore County on 5 Sep 1780. {Ref: Archives of Maryland Vol. 21, p. 499, and Vol. 43, p. 276}

CALHOUN, JAMES, JR. (Baltimore Town), patriot and merchant who enrolled in Capt. John Sterrett's Independent Mercantile Company by February, 1777, at which time they were mustered into regular service with the continental army to repress loyalist activities in the Eastern Shore counties of Somerset and Worcester. {Ref: J. Thomas Scharf's *History of Baltimore City and County*, Part I, p. 77}

CALLAHAN, DENNIS (Queen Anne's County), private who enlisted in the 5th Maryland Continental Line under Capt. Emory in Queen Anne's County; applied for pension in Adams County, Ohio on 12 Aug 1821, aged 72; had no family. {Ref: Research by Christopher T. Smithson, citing Federal Pension Application S42118}

CALLAHAN, JOHN (Annapolis), patriot who was appointed and commissioned by the Council of Maryland as Register of the Land Office for the Western Shore in the room of St. George Peale, deceased, on 18 Jul 1778. {Ref: Archives of Maryland Vol. 21, p. 161}

CALWELL, CAROLINE, see "Jacob Norris," q.v.

CALWELL, JAMES, see "Samuel Calwell," q.v.

CALWELL, LUCIEN, see "James Sloan," q.v.

CALWELL, SAMUEL (Harford County), signer of the Bush Declaration on 22 Mar 1775; first lieutenant in Militia Company No. 7 on 9 Sep 1775; commissioned captain in the 8th Battalion of Militia, Company No. 24, on 26 Apr 1776; he wrote to the Maryland Council of Safety on 28 Sep 1776 as follows: *"Gentlemen. Inclosed you have my commission. The reason of my laying it down is that on the 10th of the month our Battalion was called together to signalize themselves, but from the cowardice of the greatest part of the Company that I had the command of and I think I cant head them with honour therefore Chuse to Resign my Commission, though not the cause for having the interest of my country at hart as much as ever and am still willing and ready to act in a private capacity with Gentlemen that have distinguished themselves as men of courage. I beg leave to return you thanks and the Gentlemen that recommended me to that honour for the good opinion they had of me. I am Gentlemen Your most Humble Servant, Samuel Calwell."* Subsequently, however, on 17 Feb 1777, he was elected and recommended for commission as second major in the 8th Battalion of Militia in Harford County; on 9 Apr 1778 he was commissioned lieutenant colonel (name listed as "Caldwell"). Samuel married Ann Richardson and had three sons: James

Calwell (moved to Greenbrier, Virginia where he founded the White Sulphur Springs resort); William Calwell (merchant in Bel Air); and, Thomas Calwell (moved to Baltimore where he established large flour mills). Samuel died by 23 Jun 1800 in Harford County. {Ref: George W. Archer Collection and Revolutionary War File, Historical Society of Harford County Archives; Walter W. Preston's *History of Harford County*, pp. 229-230; Archives of Maryland Vol. 11, p. 387, Vol. 12, p. 310, Vol. 16, p. 149, and Vol. 21, p. 24}

CALWELL, THOMAS (Baltimore Town), patriot and merchant who enrolled in Capt. John Sterrett's Independent Mercantile Company by February, 1777, at which time they were mustered into regular service with the continental army to repress loyalist activities in the Eastern Shore counties of Somerset and Worcester. {Ref: J. Thomas Scharf's *History of Baltimore City and County*, Part I, p. 77}

CALWELL, THOMAS, see "Samuel Calwell," q.v.

CALWELL, WILLIAM, see "Samuel Calwell," q.v.

CAMMEL, NICHOLAS (Frederick County), private (substitute) in the Maryland Continental Line, Gunby's Regiment, enrolled in April, 1778 for 3 years or duration of the war. {Ref: Maryland Historical Magazine, Vol. 6, No. 3, p. 256}

CAMPBELL, ALLEN (Prince George's County), private who was drafted into the Maryland Continental Line, was discharged on 8 Dec 1781. {Ref: Archives of Maryland Vol. 48, p. 10}

CAMPBELL, DANIEL (Baltimore Privateer), commander of the schooner *Plunkett*, navigated by 15 men and mounting 4 carriage guns and 8 swivel guns, was issued Letters of Marque & Reprisal by the Council of Maryland on 26 Sep 1782. {Ref: Archives of Maryland Vol. 48, p. 268}

CAMPBELL, J. M. (Baltimore Town), patriot and merchant who enrolled in Capt. John Sterrett's Independent Mercantile Company by February, 1777, at which time they were mustered into regular service with the continental army to repress loyalist activities in the Eastern Shore counties of Somerset and Worcester. {Ref: J. Thomas Scharf's *History of Baltimore City and County*, Part I, p. 77}

CAMPBELL, JAMES (Western Maryland), private in Capt. Michael Cresap's Company in 1775. {Ref: Howard L. Leckey's *The Tenmile Country and Its Pioneer Families*, p. 15}

CAMPBELL, JAMES (Maryland Navy), seaman or marine on the State Ship *Defence* in 1777. {Ref: Archives of Maryland Vol. 18, p. 655}

CAMPBELL, JOHN (Maryland Navy), seaman or marine on the State Ship *Defence* in 1777. {Ref: Archives of Maryland Vol. 18, p. 655}

CAMPBELL, ROBERT (Caroline County), adjutant in Col. Richardson's Regiment in 1776 who was recommended for promotion to captain. {Ref: Archives of Maryland Vol. 18, p. 74}

CAMPBELL, WILLIAM (Baltimore County), private in the 3rd Maryland Continental Line in 1777; the Council of Maryland ordered the Treasurer *"to pay to William Campbell, a soldier of the late Capt. Samuel Griffith's Company of the 3rd Regiment who appears to be an Invalid and an Object deserving Assistance from a wound received in his right Leg at the Battle of German Town in 1777, £100 for his Subsistence"* on 27 Jul 1780; it was also ordered *"that the Issuing Commissary deliver to the said William Campbell six Days Rations."* {Ref: Archives of Maryland Vol. 43, p. 233}

CANNADY, JAMES (Western Maryland), private in Capt. Michael Cresap's Company in 1775. {Ref: Howard L. Leckey's *The Tenmile Country and Its Pioneer Families*, p. 15}

CANNON, JOHN (Baltimore County), patriot who along with Daniel Richardson contracted with the Council of Maryland to make 250 pair of shoes for use of the State on 25 Nov 1776. {Ref: Archives of Maryland Vol. 12, pp. 477-478}

CANNON, NEWTON (Baltimore Privateer), commander of the sloop *General Wayne*, navigated by 10 men and mounting 4 carriage guns, was issued Letters of Marque & Reprisal by the Council of Maryland on 11 Dec 1779. {Ref: Archives of Maryland Vol. 43, p. 35}

CANNON, WILLIAM (Dorchester County), private in the 3rd Maryland Continental Line who was a 9 month soldier in the 3rd Maryland Regiment in 1779, was discharged on 18 Oct 1779 and received £12 in clothing. {Ref: Archives of Maryland Vol. 21, p. 561}

CAPLE, SAMUEL (Anne Arundel and Baltimore Counties), soldier in the Maryland troops who applied for pension under the Act of June 7, 1832, but the claim was suspended *"pending further proof and specification."* He applied again in Carroll County on 3 Apr 1845, aged 92 years and 10 months, stating he was born in Anne Arundel County on 12 May 1752 and lived in Baltimore County at the time of his enlistment. {Ref: *Rejected or Suspended Applications for Revolutionary War Pensions* (1850 Report), p. 231; Research by Virgil D. White, citing Federal Pension Application R1671}

CAREINS, ISAAC, see "Richard Hope," q.v.

CAREINS, NEOME, see "Richard Hope," q.v.

CAREINS, RICHARD, see "Richard Hope," q.v.

CAREY, JOHN (Baltimore Privateer), commander of the brigantine *Hercules*, navigated by 60 men and mounting 16 carriage guns, was issued Letters of Marque & Reprisal by the Council of Maryland on 1 Jul 1780. {Ref: Archives of Maryland Vol. 43, p. 209}

CARLIN, JAMES (Harford County), private who was enrolled by 15 Apr 1776 in Militia Company No. 20 under Capt. Robert Glenn; James Carlin died by 5 Apr 1831 (date of final distribution) and his heirs were son William Carlin and 8 grandchildren (i.e., the children of said son William and wife Elizabeth), namely James Carlin, Ruth Carlin, Rachel Carlin, Josias Carlin, Aaron Carlin, William Carlin, and Thomas Carlin. {Ref: George W. Archer Collection and Revolutionary War File, Historical Society of Harford County Archives; Henry C. Peden, Jr.'s *Heirs & Legatees of Harford County, 1802-1846*, p. 37}

CARMEN, JOHN (Maryland Navy), sergeant of marines on the State Ship *Defence* in 1777. {Ref: Archives of Maryland Vol. 18, p. 655}

CARPENTER, HUMPHREY (Charles County), private in the 1st Maryland Continental Line who was recruited by 28 Feb 1780 at which time he was issued clothing due him. {Ref: Archives of Maryland Vol. 43, p. 98}

CARPENTER, THOMAS (Baltimore County), private, aged 29, weaver, born in England, enlisted 16 Jul 1776 in Capt. John Fulford's Company of Matrosses. {Ref: Maryland Historical Magazine, Vol. 69, No. 1, p. 96}

CARPENTER, WILLIAM (Baltimore County), private, aged 40, labourer, born in England, enlisted (made his "X" mark) on 5 Mar 1776 in Capt. John Fulford's Company of Matrosses. {Ref: Maryland Historical Magazine, Vol. 69, No. 1, p. 96}

CARR, HENRY (Maryland Navy), marine on the State Ship *Defence* in 1777. {Ref: Archives of Maryland Vol. 18, p. 655}

CARR, JOHN (Frederick and Washington Counties), lieutenant in the 3rd Maryland Continental Line who received payment for his services in the amount of "1900 Dollars & £3.10s" on 12 Sep 1780; *"Col. John Carr died on 6 Mar 1819 at his residence in Washington County, a Revolutionary War hero and patriot."* {Ref: Archives of Maryland Vol. 45, pp. 98, 218; *Star of Federalism*, 12 Mar 1819}

CARROLL, CHARLES, OF CARROLLTON (Anne Arundel County), patriot who was appointed by the Council of Maryland on 27 Jan 1776 as one of three persons in Anne Arundel County to collect all gold and silver coin that can be procured in said county; born on 19 Sep 1737 in Annapolis, married Mary Darnall on 5 Jun 1768, served as a delegate to the Continental Congress during the war, supported the ratification of the U. S. Constitution in 1788, held numerous public offices, and died on 14 Nov 1832, aged 95, at "Doughoregan Manor" in Anne Arundel County. For more information about his life and times, see Edward C. Papenfuse's *A Biographical Dictionary of the Maryland Legislature, 1635-1789*, Vol. I, pp. 197-199. {Ref: Archives of Maryland Vol. 11, p. 132}

CARROLL, HENRY (Baltimore County), matross soldier by 7 May 1779 at which time he gave a deposition about his enlistment terms. {Ref: Maryland State Archives Record MdHR 6636-14-83}

CARROLL, JOHN (Frederick County), private (substitute) in the Maryland Continental Line, Williams' Regiment, enrolled in May, 1778 for 3 years or duration of the war. {Ref: Maryland Historical Magazine, Vol. 6, No. 3, p. 260}

CARSON, JAMES (Harford County, Susquehannah Hundred), private who was enrolled 23 Apr 1776 in Militia Company No. 21 under Capt. George Patterson. {Ref: George W. Archer Collection and Revolutionary War File, Historical Society of Harford County Archives}

CARSTON, ISAAC (Baltimore Town), patriot and merchant who enrolled in Capt. John Sterrett's Independent Mercantile Company by February, 1777, at which time they were mustered into regular service with the continental army to repress loyalist activities in the Eastern Shore counties of Somerset and Worcester. {Ref: J. Thomas Scharf's *History of Baltimore City and County*, Part I, p. 77}

CARSWELL, JOHN (Harford County, Susquehannah Hundred), private who was enrolled 23 Apr 1776 in Militia Company No. 21 under Capt. George Patterson. {Ref: George W. Archer Collection and Revolutionary War File, Historical Society of Harford County Archives}

CARTER, EDWARD (Anne Arundel County), private (substitute) in the Maryland Continental Line by 1781, was discharged on 8 Dec 1781. {Ref: Archives of Maryland Vol. 48, p. 11}

CARTER, JAMES (Baltimore County), private who enlisted in Pulaski's Legion on 10 May 1778 in Baltimore. {Ref: Maryland Historical Magazine, Vol. 13, No. 3, p. 222}

CARTER, MARY, see "Nathan Musgrove," q.v.

CARTER, SAMUEL (Baltimore County), private, aged 42, carpenter, born in England, enlisted 6 Apr 1776 in Capt. John Fulford's Company of Matrosses. {Ref: Maryland Historical Magazine, Vol. 69, No. 1, p. 96}

CARTER, THOMAS (Baltimore County), private, aged 35, labourer, born in England, enlisted (made his "X" mark) on 29 Feb 1776 in Capt. John Fulford's Company of Matrosses. {Ref: Maryland Historical Magazine, Vol. 69, No. 1, p. 96}

CARTER, WILLIAM (Maryland Navy), midshipman on the State Ship *Defence* in 1777. {Ref: Archives of Maryland Vol. 18, p. 655}

CARTNEY, WILLIAM (Frederick County), private (substitute) in the Maryland Continental Line, Price's Regiment, enrolled in April, 1778 for 3 years or duration of the war. {Ref: Maryland Historical Magazine, Vol. 6, No. 3, p. 257}

CARY, PATRICK (Frederick County), private (substitute) in the Maryland Continental Line, Price's Regiment, enrolled in May, 1778 for 3 years or duration of the war. {Ref: Maryland Historical Magazine, Vol. 6, No. 3, p. 261}

CASE, JOB (Maryland Navy), sailor or seaman on 7 Jan 1780. {Ref: Calendar of Maryland State Papers, The Brown Books, p. 57}

CASEY, JOHN (Frederick County), private who was enrolled to serve as a substitute in the Maryland Continental Line until 10 Dec 1781, but *"being represented unfit for the service for which he was intended"* was discharged on 30 Oct 1781. {Ref: Archives of Maryland Vol. 45, p. 657}

CASEY, MARY, see "Joseph Allsop," q.v.

CASEY, PETER, see "Joseph Allsop," q.v.

CASNER, CHRISTIAN (Frederick County), private (substitute) in the Maryland Continental Line, German Regiment, enrolled in May, 1778 for 3 years or duration of the war. {Ref: Maryland Historical Magazine, Vol. 6, No. 3, p. 260}

CAULFIELD, ROBERT (Baltimore Privateer), commander of the brigantine *Burling*, navigated by 50 men and mounting 14 carriage guns, 4 swivel guns and 8 small arms, was issued Letters of Marque & Reprisal by the Council of

Maryland on 18 Aug 1778; commander of the schooner *Baltimore*, mounting 6 carriage guns and 6 small arms, was issued Letters of Marque & Reprisal by the Council of Maryland on 26 Jul 1779; commander of the brigantine *Duke of Lemster*, navigated by 45 men and mounting 16 carriage guns and 4 swivel guns, was issued Letters of Marque & Reprisal by the Council of Maryland on 20 Jan 1781. {Ref: Archives of Maryland Vol. 21, pp. 188, 480, and Vol. 45, p. 283}

CAULLIFLOWER, MICHAEL (Frederick and Washington Counties), soldier in the Maryland troops who applied for pension on 3 Mar 1835, aged 76, under the Act of June 7, 1832, stating he was born 27 Sep 1758 in Washington County [although it should be noted that Washington County was not created out of Frederick County until 1776] and he moved to Frederick County in 1804; a brother John was living in 1835 and a brother George had died before that time; the claim was rejected because Michael did not serve six months. {Ref: *Rejected or Suspended Applications for Revolutionary War Pensions* (1850 Report), p. 229; Research by Virgil D. White, citing Federal Pension Application R1817}

CAYTON, ---- (Anne Arundel County?), soldier in the Maryland Continentel Line who died fighting in the defense of his country before 8 Jan 1777 at which time his distressed widow Mary Cayton received £3 from the State Treasurer. {Ref: Archives of Maryland Vol. 16, p. 27}

CHADWICK, GEN'R. (Baltimore Privateer), commander of the schooner *Fountain*, navigated by 20 men and mounting 8 carriage guns and 4 swivel guns, was issued Letters of Marque & Reprisal by the Council of Maryland on 26 Oct 1780. {Ref: Archives of Maryland Vol. 43, p. 341}

CHAILLE, PETER (Worcester County), patriot who was appointed by the Council of Maryland on 27 Jan 1776 as one of three persons in Worcester County to collect all gold and silver coin that can be procured in said county. {Ref: Archives of Maryland Vol. 11, p. 132}

CHAIN, JOHN, see "Michael Payne," q.v.

CHAINE, FRANCIS (Western Maryland), private in Capt. Michael Cresap's Company in 1775. {Ref: Howard L. Leckey's *The Tenmile Country and Its Pioneer Families*, p. 15}

CHALMERS, SARAH, see "Nicholas R. Moore," q.v.

CHAMBERLAIN, CHARLES (Maryland Navy), sailor on the State Ship *Defence* in 1777. {Ref: Archives of Maryland Vol. 18, p. 655}

CHAMBERLAIN, JAMES LLOYD (Talbot County), patriot who was appointed by the Council of Maryland on 27 Jan 1776 as one of three persons in Talbot County to collect all gold and silver coin that can be procured in said county. {Ref: Archives of Maryland Vol. 11, p. 132}

CHAMBERLIN, JONAS (Frederick County), private (substitute) in the Maryland Continental Line, Price's Regiment, enrolled in May, 1778 for 3 years or duration of the war. {Ref: Maryland Historical Magazine, Vol. 6, No. 3, p. 261}

CHAMBERS, JOHN, see "James Bryant," q.v.

CHAMBERS, MARY, see "Solomon Brown," q.v.

CHAMBERS, WILLIAM (Harford County), private who was enrolled 9 Dec 1775 in Militia Company No. 14 under Capt. William McComas. {Ref: George W. Archer Collection and Revolutionary War File, Historical Society of Harford County Archives}

CHAMPINS, JAMES (Frederick County), private (substitute) in the Maryland Continental Line, German Regiment, enrolled in May, 1778 for 3 years or duration of the war. {Ref: Maryland Historical Magazine, Vol. 6, No. 3, p. 259}

CHAMPION, GEORGE (Maryland Navy), boatswain's yeoman on the State Ship *Defence* in 1777. {Ref: Archives of Maryland Vol. 18, p. 655}

CHANNELL, ANN, see "Joseph Hook," q.v.

CHANNING, JOHN (Baltimore Privateer), commander of the schooner *Havana*, navigated by 15 men and mounting 7 carriage guns, was issued Letters of Marque & Reprisal by the Council of Maryland on 14 Mar 1783. {Ref: Archives of Maryland Vol. 48, p. 381}

CHAPLINE, JOSEPH (Washington County), captain and patriot who was commissioned one of the three persons in Washington County by the Council of Maryland on 19 Aug 1779 to receive subscriptions for use of the State; *"Capt. Joseph Chaplin, a soldier of the Revolution, died 31 Aug 1821 in the 75th year of his age."* {Ref: Archives of Maryland Vol. 21, p. 499; J. Thomas Scharf's *History of Western Maryland*, Vol. II, p. 1048}

CHAPMAN, THOMAS (Talbot County), private who was drafted into the Maryland Continental Line, was discharged on 8 Dec 1781. {Ref: Archives of Maryland Vol. 48, p. 10}

CHARLOTON, ANN, see "John Ross Key," q.v.

CHARLTON, JOHN (Harford County), soldier in the Maryland Continental Line who was living in Harford County on 3 Sep 1823 at which time documents were filed in the 6th Judicial District, Harford County Court, stating, in part: *"John Charlton, aged 70 years, resident in Harford County ... does on his oath make the following declaration in order to obtain the provision made by the acts of Congress of the 18th of March of 1818 and the 1st of May 1820 that he the said John Charlton, aged 70 years, enlisted for the term of the war in the year 1780 in the State of Maryland in the marine company under the command of Capt. Jones on the continental establishment, that he continued to serve in the said company for the term of 18 months when he was taken prisoner, that he has never yet been placed on the pension list nor asked for a pension while able to support himself. And in pursuance of the act of the first of May 1820 I do solemnly swear that I was a resident citizen of the United States on the 18th of March 1818 and that I have not since that time by gift, sale or in any manner disposed of my property or any part thereof with intent thereby so as to diminish it as to bring myself within the provision of an Act of Congress entitled an act to provide for certain persons engaged in the land and naval service of* *the United States in the Revolutionary War passed on the 18th day of March 1818 and that I have not, nor has any person in trust for me, any property or securities, contracts or debts due me nor have I any income other than what is contained in the schedule hereto annexed and by me subscribed. The following is a full and correct schedule of my property: one loom and tackle worth about $10 or $15."* Signed: John Charlton (made his mark that resembled a "C" with a curl on the top left side). {Ref: Historical Society of Harford County, Court Records File 25.14}

CHATHAM, JAMES (Queen Anne's County), quartermaster of the 20th Battalion of Militia, commissioned 8 May 1777. {Ref: Archives of Maryland Vol. 16, p. 244}

CHEEK, ANN, see "Humphrey Pugh," q.v.

CHEESELY, JAMES (Talbot County), private (substitute) in the Maryland Continental Line by 1781, was discharged on 8 Dec 1781. {Ref: Archives of Maryland Vol. 48, p. 11}

CHEESLY, ROBERT (Talbot County), private who was drafted into the Maryland Continental Line, was discharged on 8 Dec 1781. {Ref: Archives of Maryland Vol. 48, p. 10}

CHENOWETH, JOSEPH (Baltimore County), private, 31 May 1779, Capt. Benjamin Talbott's Militia Company, Cockey's Battalion. {Ref: Maryland Historical Magazine, Vol. 7, No. 1, p. 90}

CHENOWITH, JOHN (Western Maryland), private in Capt. Michael Cresap's Company in 1775. {Ref: Howard L. Leckey's *The Tenmile Country and Its Pioneer Families*, p. 15}

CHENOWITH, THOMAS (Western Maryland), private in Capt. Michael Cresap's Company in 1775. {Ref: Howard L. Leckey's *The Tenmile Country and Its Pioneer Families*, p. 15}

CHENWOWETH, THOMAS (Baltimore County), lieutenant on 31 May 1779 in Capt. Benjamin Talbott's Militia Company, Cockey's Battalion. {Ref: Maryland Historical Magazine, Vol. 7, No. 1, p. 90}

CHESHIRE, BENJAMIN (Maryland Navy), marine on the State Ship *Defence* in 1777. {Ref: Archives of Maryland Vol. 18, p. 655}

CHEVIER (CHEVEAR), JOHN (Maryland Navy), midshipman on the State Ship *Defence* on 1 Nov 1777; marine on the galley *Baltimore* in 1778 who took the Oath of Fidelity and Allegiance to the State of Maryland on 31 Mar 1778; commissioned lieutenant of marines on the galley *Chester* on 16 Jul 1778, having served on said ship from 10 Apr last; lieutenant in the artillery who received payment for his services in the amount of "1900 Dollars & £3.10s" on 12 Sep 1780. {Ref: Archives of Maryland Vol. 16, p. 559, Vol. 18, p. 655, Vol. 21, p. 160, and Vol. 45, p. 98}

CHEW, ANNE, see "Acquilla Randall," q.v.

CHEW, EMELINE, see "Nathaniel Chew," q.v.

CHEW, HENRIETTA, see "Nathaniel Chew," q.v.

CHEW, JAMES, see "Nathaniel Chew," q.v.

CHEW, JOHN, see "Nathaniel Chew," q.v.

CHEW, MARGARET or MARGARETTA, see "John Eager Howard" and "Nathaniel Chew" and "Acquilla Randall," q.v.

CHEW, NATHANIEL (Cecil and Harford Counties), sailor in the Maryland Navy who lived in Cecil County at the time of his enlistment and died at Chesapeake near Havre de Grace in Harford County in May, 1827, aged 69, by which time he was called captain; his widow Margaret Rodgers Chew (sister of Commodore John Rodgers) applied for pension on 8 May 1844 under the Act of July 7, 1838, but the claim was suspended for further proof as she *"alleges his service as a lieutenant in the navy of the United States of the Revolution."* She died in Cecil County on 21 Apr 1848, leaving four children: John A. Chew (born 17 Sep 1794 and living in Howard County in 1857); Henrietta Mary Chew (married Rev. Cyrus Hamilton, a Presbyterian minister in Howard County in 1857); Emeline R. Chew (living in Howard County in 1857); and, Washington P. Chew (died in 1849, leaving three sons including James W. Chew who was still living in 1857). {Ref: *Rejected or Suspended Applications for Revolutionary War Pensions* (1850 Report), p. 236; Research by Virgil D. White, citing Federal Pension Application W9383}

CHEW, RICHARD (Harford County), private who was enrolled 10 Mar 1776 in Militia Company No. 18 under Capt. John Jolly. {Ref: George W. Archer Collection and Revolutionary War File, Historical Society of Harford County Archives}

CHEW, RICHARD (Harford County), private who was enrolled 25 Mar 1776 in Militia Company No. 19 under Capt. William Morgan; ensign in the 4th Maryland Continental Line who received payment for his services in the amount of "1900 Dollars & £3.10s" on 12 Sep 1780. {Ref: Archives of Maryland Vol. 45, p. 98; George W. Archer Collection and Revolutionary War File, Historical Society of Harford County Archives}

CHEW, THOMAS S., see "William Morgan," q.v.

CHEW, WASHINGTON, see "Nathaniel Chew," q.v.

CHILDS, CUD or CUTHBERT (Maryland Navy), marine on the State Ship *Defence* in 1777. {Ref: Archives of Maryland Vol. 18, p. 655}

CHILDS, MARY, see "James Tootell," q.v.

CHUB (CHOB), JONATHAN (Prince George's County), recruit in the Maryland Continental Line who enlisted for the Extra Regiment and received clothing on 18 Aug 1780, "the Bounty allowed by the General Assembly." {Ref: Archives of Maryland Vol. 18, p. 338, and Vol. 43, p. 257}

CHUNN, LANCELOT (Charles County), private who was drafted into the Maryland Continental Line, was discharged on 8 Dec 1781. {Ref: Archives of Maryland Vol. 48, p. 10}

CHURCHMAN, ENOCH, see "Benjamin B. Norris," q.v.

CISCO, THOMAS (Western Maryland), private in Capt. Michael Cresap's Company in 1775. {Ref: Howard L. Leckey's *The Tenmile Country and Its Pioneer Families*, p. 15}

CLABAUGH, FREDERICK (Frederick County), patriot and farmer in Pipe Creek Hundred whose wagon and horses were impressed into the service of the State of Virginia in 1781 to take loads from Philadelphia to Stemtown in Virginia and, in their behalf, John Ross Key presented to the Governor and Council of Maryland that it could not be legal for Virginia to impress Maryland wagons and horses for their use and requested said property should be returned. {Ref: Archives of Maryland Vol. 47, pp. 502-503}

CLAGETT, HORATIO (Prince George's County), captain in the 3rd Maryland Continental Line who received payment for his services in the amount of "1900 Dollars & £3.10s" on 12 Sep 1780. {Ref: Archives of Maryland Vol. 45, p. 97}

CLAGETT, THOMAS (Prince George's County), patriot who was commissioned one of the three persons in Prince George's County by the Council of Maryland on 19 Aug 1779 to receive subscriptions for use of the State. {Ref: Archives of Maryland Vol. 21, p. 499}

CLARK, JACOB (Baltimore County), private, aged 18, labourer, born in Maryland, enlisted (made his "X" mark) on 13 Feb 1776 in Capt. John Fulford's Company of Matrosses. {Ref: Maryland Historical Magazine, Vol. 69, No. 1, p. 94}

CLARK, JAMES (Maryland Navy), marine on the State Ship *Defence* in 1777. {Ref: Archives of Maryland Vol. 18, p. 655}

CLARK, JONATHAN (Baltimore Privateer), commander of the sloop *Eclipse*, navigated by 12 men and mounting 2 carriage guns and 4 swivel guns, was issued Letters of Marque & Reprisal by the Council of Maryland on 30 Jul 1778. {Ref: Archives of Maryland Vol. 21, p. 170}

CLARK, RICHARD (Talbot County), private (substitute) in the Maryland Continental Line by 1781, was discharged on 8 Dec 1781. {Ref: Archives of Maryland Vol. 48, p. 11}

CLARK, RICHARD (Frederick County), private (substitute) in the Maryland Continental Line, Gunby's Regiment, enrolled in April, 1778 for 3 years or duration of the war. {Ref: Maryland Historical Magazine, Vol. 6, No. 3, p. 257}

CLARY, MARY BRYANT, see "James Bryant," q.v.

CLAY, GEORGE (Western Maryland), private in Capt. Michael Cresap's Company in 1775. {Ref: Howard L. Leckey's *The Tenmile Country and Its Pioneer Families*, p. 15}

CLEGNESS, JOHN FRANCIS (Maryland Navy), surgeon's mate on the State Ship *Defence* in 1777. {Ref: Archives of Maryland Vol. 18, p. 655}

CLEMENS, PATRICK (Harford County), private who was enrolled 9 Dec 1775 in Militia Company No. 14 under Capt. William McComas. {Ref: George W. Archer Collection and Revolutionary War File, Historical Society of Harford County Archives}

CLEMENTS, BENNETT (Charles County), private (substitute) in the Maryland Continental Line by 1781, was discharged on 8 Dec 1781. {Ref: Archives of Maryland Vol. 48, p. 11}

CLEMENTS, HENRY (Charles County), ensign in the 2nd Maryland Continental Line who received payment for his services in the amount of "1900 Dollars & £3.10s" on 12 Sep 1780. {Ref: Archives of Maryland Vol. 45, p. 97}

CLEMENTS, JOHN (Charles County), private (substitute) in the Maryland Continental Line by 1781, was discharged on 8 Dec 1781. {Ref: Archives of Maryland Vol. 48, p. 11}

CLEMENTS, JOSIAS (Baltimore Town), patriot and merchant who enrolled in Capt. John Sterrett's Independent Mercantile Company by February, 1777, at which time they were mustered into regular service with the continental army to repress loyalist activities in the Eastern Shore counties of Somerset and Worcester. {Ref: J. Thomas Scharf's *History of Baltimore City and County*, Part I, p. 77}

CLEMM, WILLIAM (Baltimore City), soldier in the Pennsylvania Line who married Catharine Schultze in 1778 at York, Pennsylvania and died 23 Feb 1807 in Baltimore; his widow Catharine Clemm died 5 Jan 1836 and the only surviving children were Joseph E. Clemm and Elizabeth Tschudy of Baltimore County; they applied for pension on 8 May 1837 in Baltimore City under the Act of July 4, 1836, but their claim was rejected because the soldier and his wife had died before the passage of the act; Christianna Krems, sister of Catharine Clemm, lived in Baltimore in 1837, aged 70, and William Warfield, aged 79, stated he had witnessed the soldier's marriage in 1778. {Ref: *Rejected or Suspended Applications for Revolutionary War Pensions* (1850 Report), p. 233; Research by Virgil D. White, citing Federal Pension Application R2041}

CLEMMONS (CLEMMONDS), JOHN (Caroline County), private in the Maryland Continental Line who applied for pension in Richmond County, North Carolina on 18 Jul 1832, stating he was born in Queen Anne's County on 12 Dec 1751 and lived in Caroline County at the time of his enlistment. {Ref: Research by Virgil D. White, citing Federal Pension Application S8215; Archives of Maryland Vol. 18, p. 66}

CLENDENNIN, JOHN (Western Maryland), sergeant in Capt. Michael Cresap's Company in 1775. {Ref: Howard L. Leckey's *The Tenmile Country and Its Pioneer Families*, p. 15}

CLIFFORD, WILLIAM (Washington County), private who was enrolled to serve as a substitute in the Maryland Continental Line until 10 Dec 1781, but *"being represented unfit for the service for which he was intended"* was discharged on 30 Oct 1781. {Ref: Archives of Maryland Vol. 45, p. 656}

CLIFTON, JAMES (Baltimore Privateer), commander of the brigantine *Hawke*, navigated by 31 men and mounting 10 carriage guns, 6 swivel guns and 14 small arms, was issued Letters of Marque & Reprisal by the Council of Maryland on 14 Aug 1780. {Ref: Archives of Maryland Vol. 43, p. 254}

CLOPPER, ANDREW (Baltimore Town), patriot and merchant who enrolled in Capt. John Sterrett's Independent Mercantile Company by February, 1777, at which time they were mustered into regular service with the continental army to repress loyalist activities in the Eastern Shore counties of Somerset and Worcester. {Ref: J. Thomas Scharf's *History of Baltimore City and County*, Part I, p. 77}

CLOSE (CLOES), CHARLES (Baltimore County), private in the Maryland Continental Line who was born in 1756 in County Antrim, Northern Ireland and enlisted in a Baltimore company of matrosses on 3 Feb 1776 (also see Peden's *Revolutionary Patriots of Baltimore Town and Baltimore County, 1775-1783*, p. 50); married Hannah ---- circa 1784 in Balstown, New York and applied for pension on 4 May 1818 in Ontario County, New York, aged 61, but the claim was rejected (probably due to lack of proof of service); in 1820 he stated he was aged near 70, lived near Penfield, New York, and mentioned children James Cloes (aged 20), Clara Cloes (aged 14), Charles Cloes (aged 11), and Caroline Cloes (aged 9); Charles died on 10 Sep 1838 at Webster, New York [not in Baltimore or Harford County as stated in the aforementioned book] and his widow died on 23 Jun 1842; in 1846 their surviving children were Sally Andrus, Hannah King, Qurella Gregory, Caroline Cloes, Nancy Ray, O'Neil Cloes, and Charles Cloes. {Ref: Research by Virgil D. White, citing Federal Pension Application R2054; Archives of Maryland Vol. 18, pp. 414, 565}

CLYNE, NICHOLAS (Washington County), private who was enrolled to serve as a substitute in the Maryland Continental Line until 10 Dec 1781, but *"being represented unfit for the service for which he was intended"* was discharged on 30 Oct 1781. {Ref: Archives of Maryland Vol. 45, p. 656}

COACHMAN, JOHN (Montgomery County), private who was drafted into the Maryland Continental Line, was discharged on 8 Dec 1781. {Ref: Archives of Maryland Vol. 48, p. 10}

COALE, ELIZABETH, see "William Arnold," q.v.

COALE, RICHARD, see "Joseph Holland," q.v.

COCHRANE, JOSEPH (Western Maryland), private in Capt. Michael Cresap's Company in 1775. {Ref: Howard L. Leckey's *The Tenmile Country and Its Pioneer Families*, p. 15}

COCHRANE, WILLIAM (Baltimore Town), patriot and merchant who enrolled in Capt. John Sterrett's Independent Mercantile Company by February, 1777, at which time they were mustered into regular service with the continental army to repress loyalist activities in the Eastern Shore counties of Somerset and Worcester. {Ref: J. Thomas Scharf's *History of Baltimore City and County*, Part I, p. 77}

COCK, SAMUEL (Southern Maryland), captain lieutenant, commissioned on 27 Jul 1780 to serve in the Regiment Extra by order of the Council of Maryland. {Ref: Archives of Maryland Vol. 43, p. 234}

COCKAYNE, WILLIAM (Maryland Navy), sailor or seaman on 7 Jan 1780. {Ref: Calendar of Maryland State Papers, The Brown Books, p. 57}

COCKERTON, ROBERT (Maryland Navy), cabin steward on the State Ship *Defence* in 1777. {Ref: Archives of Maryland Vol. 18, p. 655}

COCKEY, RICHARD (Maryland Navy), marine on the State Ship *Defence* in 1777. {Ref: Archives of Maryland Vol. 18, p. 655}

COCKRAN, JOHN (Western Maryland), private in Capt. Michael Cresap's Company in 1775. {Ref: Howard L. Leckey's *The Tenmile Country and Its Pioneer Families*, p. 15}

COCKRAN, JOSEPH (Western Maryland), private in Capt. Michael Cresap's Company in 1775. {Ref: Howard L. Leckey's *The Tenmile Country and Its Pioneer Families*, p. 15}

COCKRAN, RICHARD, see "William Evans," q.v.

CODDINGTON, BENJAMIN (Allegany County), soldier who was born 10 Nov 1759 in Middlesex County, New Jersey and served in the New Jersey Line and in privateer service from Essex County during the war; he moved to Allegany County, Maryland in 1785 and received disability payments which began on 25 Apr 1812; he also applied for pension under the Act of June 7, 1832 and, although the claim was suspended pending further proof and specification, he apparently received the pension; died on 14 Mar 1851, leaving sons Joseph and Jent Coddington. {Ref: *Rejected or Suspended Applications for Revolutionary War Pensions* (1850 Report), p. 231; Research by Virgil D. White, citing Federal Pension Application S10468}

CODY, JAMES (Maryland Navy), marine on the State Ship *Defence* in 1777. {Ref: Archives of Maryland Vol. 18, p. 655}

COE, CLARKSON (Kent County), private (substitute) in the Maryland Continental Line by 1781, was discharged on 11 Dec 1781. {Ref: Archives of Maryland Vol. 48, p. 18}

COE, JOB (Maryland Navy), corporal of marines on the State Ship *Defence* in 1777. {Ref: Archives of Maryland Vol. 18, p. 655}

COFFMAN, HENRY (Western Maryland), private in Capt. Michael Cresap's Company in 1775. {Ref: Howard L. Leckey's *The Tenmile Country and Its Pioneer Families*, p. 15}

COLE, BENJAMIN (Frederick County), private (substitute) in the Maryland Continental Line, German Regiment, enrolled in May, 1778 for 3 years or duration of the war. {Ref: Maryland Historical Magazine, Vol. 6, No. 3, p. 261}

COLE, CHARLES (St. Mary's County), private who was drafted into the Maryland Continental Line, was discharged on 8 Dec 1781. {Ref: Archives of Maryland Vol. 48, p. 10}

COLE, PATRICK (Maryland Navy), marine on the State Ship *Defence* in 1777. {Ref: Archives of Maryland Vol. 18, p. 655}

COLE, SARAH, see "Thomas Courtney," q.v.

COLIN, THOMAS (Baltimore County), private, aged 33, founder, born in London, enlisted 14 Mar 1776 in Capt. John Fulford's Company of Matrosses. {Ref: Maryland Historical Magazine, Vol. 69, No. 1, p. 96}

COLINS, JAMES (Maryland Navy), marine on the State Ship *Defence* in 1777. {Ref: Archives of Maryland Vol. 18, p. 655}

COLLIER, ---- (Worcester County), soldier by 13 Sep 1782 at which time the Council of Maryland gave "permission to John Round Morris of Worcester County in the State of Maryland to apply to his Excellency General Washington or the Commanding Officers at the Out Posts of the American Army for leave to go into the City of New York for the purpose of endeavoring to procure the release of ---- Collier, a Prisoner." {Ref: Archives of Maryland Vol. 48, p. 262}

COLLINS, JAMES (Prince George's County?), sergeant in the 2nd Maryland Continental Line by 28 Jan 1780 at which time he was issued clothing *"due him from the United States."* {Ref: Archives of Maryland Vol. 43, p. 72}

COLLINS, JOHN (Baltimore County), private who enlisted in Pulaski's Legion on 28 Apr 1778 in Baltimore. {Ref: Maryland Historical Magazine, Vol. 13, No. 3, p. 222}

COLLINS (COLLENS), JOHN (Harford County), private who was recruited and enrolled by Richard Dallam in the Regiment Extraordinary and sent to Annapolis with Capt. Thompson on board the sloop *Liberty* on 17 Aug 1780. {Ref: Archives of Maryland Vol. 45, pp. 50, 51}

COLLINS, LEVIN (Dorchester County), private (substitute) in the Maryland Continental Line by 1781, was discharged on 10 Dec 1781. {Ref: Archives of Maryland Vol. 48, p. 17}

COLLINS (COLLINGS), ROBERT (Baltimore Privateer), commander of the ship *Friendship*, navigated by 100 men and mounting 24 carriage guns, was issued Letters of Marque & Reprisal by the Council of Maryland on 17 Jul 1782. {Ref: Archives of Maryland Vol. 48, p. 216}

COLLYER, ISAAC (Western Maryland), private in Capt. Michael Cresap's Company in 1775. {Ref: Howard L. Leckey's *The Tenmile Country and Its Pioneer Families*, p. 15}

COLSON (COULSTON), JOHN (Maryland Navy), marine on the State Ship *Defence* in 1777. {Ref: Archives of Maryland Vol. 18, p. 655}

COLT, EDWARD (Baltimore County?), private in Capt. Long's Independent Company in the Maryland Continental Line who was taken prisoner at Fort Washington and released on parole by 11 Dec 1777 at which time he received £31.5.0 due him for wages and subsistence from the State Treasurer. {Ref: Archives of Maryland Vol. 16, p. 433}

COMPTON, EDWARD (Charles County), lieutenant in the 1st Maryland Continental Line who received payment for his services in the amount of "1900 Dollars & £3.10s" on 12 Sep 1780. {Ref: Archives of Maryland Vol. 45, p. 97}

COMPTON, JOHN (Maryland Navy), marine on the State Ship *Defence* in 1777. {Ref: Archives of Maryland Vol. 18, p. 655}

CONDON, WILLIAM (Talbot County), private (substitute) in the Maryland Continental Line by 1781, was discharged on 8 Dec 1781. {Ref: Archives of Maryland Vol. 48, p. 11}

CONDRON, WILLIAM (Harford County), private who was drafted into the Maryland Continental Line, was discharged on 8 Dec 1781. {Ref: Archives of Maryland Vol. 48, p. 10}

CONKLING, MATTHEW (Harford County), private who was enrolled 25 Mar 1776 in Militia Company No. 19 under Capt. William Morgan. {Ref: George W. Archer Collection and Revolutionary War File, Historical Society of Harford County Archives}

CONLEY, CHARITY, see "Thomas Norris," q.v.

CONNALLY, JEREMIAH (Cecil County), private (substitute) in the Maryland Continental Line, who enlisted to serve until 10 Dec 1781, was discharged on 29 Nov 1781. {Ref: Archives of Maryland Vol. 48, p. 7}

CONNALLY, MATTHEW (Cecil County), private (substitute) in the Maryland Continental Line, who enlisted to serve until 10 Dec 1781, was discharged on 29 Nov 1781. {Ref: Archives of Maryland Vol. 48, p. 7}

CONNELLY, JOHN (Baltimore County), private, aged 21, ship carpenter, born in Maryland, enlisted (made his "X" mark) on 11 Mar 1776 in Capt. John Fulford's Company of Matrosses. {Ref: Maryland Historical Magazine, Vol. 69, No. 1, p. 96}

CONNELLY, WILLIAM (Baltimore County), private, aged 22, labourer, born in Ireland, enlisted (made his "X" mark) on 11 Mar 1776 in Capt. John Fulford's Company of Matrosses. {Ref: Maryland Historical Magazine, Vol. 69, No. 1, p. 96}

CONNER, ANN, see "Nathan Musgrove," q.v.

CONNER, DANIEL (Caroline County), private who was drafted into the Maryland Continental Line, was discharged on 8 Dec 1781. {Ref: Archives of Maryland Vol. 48, p. 10}

CONNER, JOHN (Baltimore County), private, aged 20, shoemaker, born in Ireland, enlisted (made his "V" mark) on 15 Feb 1776 in Capt. John Fulford's Company of Matrosses. {Ref: Maryland Historical Magazine, Vol. 69, No. 1, p. 95}

CONNER, MARY, see "Patrick Conner," q.v.

CONNER, PATRICK (Allegany County), soldier who probably served in the Pennsylvania Line and whose widow Mary Conner applied for pension in Maryland under the Act of July 4, 1836, but the claim was rejected because he was "a soldier of the regular army" *[sic]*. {Ref: *Rejected or Suspended Applications for Revolutionary War Pensions* (1850 Report), p. 233}

CONNER, ROBERT (Maryland Navy), marine on the State Ship *Defence* in 1777. {Ref: Archives of Maryland Vol. 18, p. 655}

CONNERLY, ROGER (Caroline County), private who was drafted into the Maryland Continental Line, was discharged on 8 Dec 1781. {Ref: Archives of Maryland Vol. 48, p. 10}

CONNOLLY, ---- (Anne Arundel County?), soldier in the Maryland Continental Line *"now remaining in Annapolis"* on 24 Jul 1780 at which time his wife Mary Connolly was entitled to rations under the laws of the State. {Ref: Archives of Maryland Vol. 43, p. 227}

CONNOLLY, HARMOR (Western Maryland), private in Capt. Michael Cresap's Company in 1775. {Ref: Howard L. Leckey's *The Tenmile Country and Its Pioneer Families,* p. 15}

CONNOLLY, JOHN (Frederick County), private (substitute) in the Maryland Continental Line, who enlisted to serve until 10 Dec 1781, was discharged on 29 Nov 1781. {Ref: Archives of Maryland Vol. 48, p. 7}

CONNOR, CATT (Baltimore County), private, aged 23, carpenter, born in Ireland, enlisted 23 Feb 1776 in Capt. John Fulford's Company of Matrosses. {Ref: Maryland Historical Magazine, Vol. 69, No. 1, p. 95}

CONNOWAY, JAMES (Frederick County), private (substitute) in the Maryland Continental Line, German Regiment, enrolled in May, 1778 for 3 years or duration of the war. {Ref: Maryland Historical Magazine, Vol. 6, No. 3, p. 259}

CONTEE, RICHARD, see "William Sanders," q.v.

CONTEE, THOMAS (Prince George's County), patriot who was appointed by the Council of Maryland on 27 Jan 1776 as one of three persons in Prince George's County to collect all gold and silver coin that can be procured in said county. {Ref: Archives of Maryland Vol. 11, p. 132}

CONWAY, ROBERT (Maryland Privateer), commander of the schooner *Hope,* navigated by 21 men and mounting 6 carriage guns, was issued Letters of Marque & Reprisal by the Council of Maryland on 12 Mar 1781. {Ref: Archives of Maryland Vol. 45, p. 349}

CONWAY, THOMAS (Baltimore Privateer), commander of the sloop *Molly,* commissioned 14 Dec 1776; commander of the brigantine *Alexander,* navigated by 40 men and mounting 12 carriage guns and 20 small arms, was issued Letters of Marque & Reprisal by the Council of Maryland on 18 Nov 1779. {Ref: Archives of Maryland Vol. 12, p. 527 and Vol. 43, pp. 17-18}

COOGLE, JOHN (Washington County), private who was drafted to serve in the Maryland Continental Line until 10 Dec 1781, but *"being represented unfit for the duty for which he was intended"* was discharged on 30 Oct 1781. {Ref: Archives of Maryland Vol. 45, p. 656}

COOK, GEORGE (Maryland Navy), lieutenant on the State Ship *Defence* from 12 Sep 1776 to 15 Nov 1776 and captain from 15 Nov 1776 to 31 Dec 1777. {Ref: Archives of Maryland Vol. 18, p. 655}

COOK, JOHN (Harford County), private who was enrolled by 15 Apr 1776 in Militia Company No. 20 under Capt. Robert Glenn. {Ref: George W. Archer Collection and Revolutionary War File, Historical Society of Harford County Archives}

COOK, MARGARET, see "Daniel Day," q.v.

COOK, SUSAN, see "Christopher Lambert," q.v.

COOK, WILLIAM (Harford County), private who was enrolled by 15 Apr 1776 in Militia Company No. 20 under Capt. Robert Glenn. {Ref: George W. Archer Collection and Revolutionary War File, Historical Society of Harford County Archives}

COOKSON, JOHN (Maryland Navy), sailmaker on the State Ship *Defence* in 1777. {Ref: Archives of Maryland Vol. 18, p. 655}

COOLEY, JOHN (Harford County, Susquehannah Hundred), private who was enrolled 23 Apr 1776 in Militia Company No. 21 under Capt. George Patterson. {Ref: George W. Archer Collection and Revolutionary War File, Historical Society of Harford County Archives}

COOP, BARRACIAH (Harford County), private (substitute) in the Maryland Continental Line by 1781, was discharged on 8 Dec 1781. {Ref: Archives of Maryland Vol. 48, p. 11}

COOP, DEOBERT (Baltimore or Frederick County), private who enlisted in Pulaski's Legion on 1 Sep 1778. {Ref: Maryland Historical Magazine, Vol. 13, No. 3, p. 224}

COOPER, GEORGE (Baltimore County), matross soldier by 7 May 1779 at which time he gave a deposition about his enlistment terms. {Ref: Maryland State Archives Record MdHR 6636-14-83}

COOPER, JOHN (Anne Arundel County), private in the Maryland Continental Line by 1 Dec 1781 at which time he was on duty guarding the magazine at the Head of Severn River. {Ref: Archives of Maryland Vol. 48, p. 8}

COOPER, NATHANIEL (Maryland Navy and Baltimore Privateer), second mate on the State Ship *Defence* from 11 Jan 1777 to 1 Jun 1777; commander of the sloop *Richardson*, navigated by 10 men and mounting 2 carriage guns and 4 swivel guns, was issued Letters of Marque & Reprisal by the Council of Maryland on 25 Jul 1778; commander of the sloop *Lady Washington*, navigated by 12 men and mounting 6 carriage guns, was issued Letters of Marque & Reprisal by the Council of Maryland on 9 Oct 1778. {Ref: Archives of Maryland Vol. 18, p. 655 and Vol. 21, p. 215}

COPPER, ----, see "Michael Payne," q.v.

COPPER, NORRIS (Baltimore Privateer), commander of the sloop *Mars*, navigated by 25 men and mounting 8 carriage guns, was issued Letters of Marque & Reprisal by the Council of Maryland on 10 Dec 1777. {Ref: Archives of Maryland Vol. 16, p. 433}

CORBET, JAMES (Harford County), private who was enrolled 9 Dec 1775 in Militia Company No. 14 under Capt. William McComas. {Ref: George W. Archer Collection and Revolutionary War File, Historical Society of Harford County Archives}

CORBET, LEWIS (Harford County), private who was enrolled by 15 Apr 1776 in Militia Company No. 20 under Capt. Robert Glenn. {Ref: George W. Archer Collection and Revolutionary War File, Historical Society of Harford County Archives}

CORBET, PATRICK (Maryland Navy), yeoman and marine on the State Ship *Defence* in 1777. {Ref: Archives of Maryland Vol. 18, p. 655}

CORBET, SAMUEL (Harford County), private who was enrolled 9 Dec 1775 in Militia Company No. 14 under Capt. William McComas. {Ref: George W. Archer Collection and Revolutionary War File, Historical Society of Harford County Archives}

CORD, JOSHUA (Anne Arundel County), private in a company of matrosses by 24 Dec 1779 at which time he was stationed in the City of Annapolis and was given *"permission to go on Furlough in the Country to see his Friends so that he return back to the same Place on or before the 15 Day of February next."* {Ref: Archives of Maryland Vol. 43, p. 41}

CORD, REBECCA, see "Acquilla Randall," q.v.

CORDRAY, JAMES (Maryland Navy), second mate on the State Ship *Defence* in 1777. {Ref: Archives of Maryland Vol. 18, p. 655}

CORNAFLEAN, WILLIAM (Maryland Navy), midshipman and clerk on the State Ship *Defence* in 1777. {Ref: Archives of Maryland Vol. 18, p. 655}

CORWIN, JAMES (Baltimore County), private, aged 20, labourer, born in Dublin, enlisted (made his "X" mark) on 13 Feb 1776 in Capt. John Fulford's Company of Matrosses. {Ref: Maryland Historical Magazine, Vol. 69, No. 1, p. 94}

COSGROVE, MATTHIAS (Frederick County), private (substitute) in the Maryland Continental Line, German Regiment, enrolled in May, 1778 for 3 years or duration of the war. {Ref: Maryland Historical Magazine, Vol. 6, No. 3, p. 259}

COSTILLO, THOMAS (Maryland Navy), marine on the State Ship *Defence* in 1777. {Ref: Archives of Maryland Vol. 18, p. 655}

COTTER, WILLIAM (Harford County, Susquehannah Hundred), private who was enrolled 23 Apr 1776 in Militia Company No. 21 under Capt. George Patterson. {Ref: George W. Archer Collection and Revolutionary War File, Historical Society of Harford County Archives}

COUGHLAN, MICHAEL (Frederick County), private (substitute) in the Maryland Continental Line, Williams' Regiment, enrolled in May, 1778 for 3 years or duration of the war. {Ref: Maryland Historical Magazine, Vol. 6, No. 3, p. 259}

COULTER, ALEXANDER (Baltimore Town), patriot and merchant who enrolled in Capt. John Sterrett's Independent Mercantile Company by February, 1777, at which time they were mustered into regular service with the continental army to repress loyalist activities in the Eastern Shore counties of Somerset and Worcester. {Ref: J. Thomas Scharf's *History of Baltimore City and County*, Part I, p. 77}

COURTNEY, HARRIET, see "William Arnold," q.v.

COURTNEY, THOMAS (Harford County, Susquehannah Hundred), private who was enrolled 23 Apr 1776 in Militia Company No. 21 under Capt. George Patterson; Thomas Courtney died by 23 Jul 1839 (date of final distribution) and his heirs were widow Sarah Courtney, sons Hollis Courtney, Thomas Courtney, George W. Courtney, and Edward Courtney, daughters Sarah Cole, Milcha Donn, Matilda Hanson's heirs, and grandsons Thomas Courtney, William Courtney, and America Courtney. {Ref: George W. Archer Collection and Revolutionary

War File, Historical Society of Harford County Archives; Henry C. Peden, Jr.'s *Heirs & Legatees of Harford County, 1802-1846*, p. 46}

COVENTRY, PETER (Maryland Navy), sailor or seaman on 7 Jan 1780. {Ref: Calendar of Maryland State Papers, The Brown Books, p. 57}

COWAN, ALEXANDER (Harford County), captain, commissioned 26 Apr 1776 in Militia Company No. 22; patriot who was commissioned one of the three persons in Harford County by the Council of Maryland on 19 Aug 1779 to receive subscriptions for use of the State. {Ref: Archives of Maryland Vol. 21, p. 499; George W. Archer Collection and Revolutionary War File, Historical Society of Harford County Archives}

COWEN, EDWARD (Harford County, Susquehannah Hundred), private who was enrolled 23 Apr 1776 in Militia Company No. 21 under Capt. George Patterson. {Ref: George W. Archer Collection and Revolutionary War File, Historical Society of Harford County Archives}

COWEN, THOMAS (Harford County, Susquehannah Hundred), private who was enrolled 23 Apr 1776 in Militia Company No. 21 under Capt. George Patterson. {Ref: George W. Archer Collection and Revolutionary War File, Historical Society of Harford County Archives}

COWMAN, SAMUEL (Maryland Navy), marine on the sloop *Lincoln* who was taken prisoner and confined in New York before 17 Jan 1781 and was subsequently exchanged. {Ref: Archives of Maryland Vol. 45, p. 277}

COWARD, THOMAS (Dorchester County), captain who was noted by the Council of Maryland on 7 Sep 1778 stating, in part, that he was *"a native of this State and hath been absent therefrom for about 1 year and 8 months, last past a prisoner on board the British ships, and hath lately that is to say within 3 months now last past, returned into this State, appeared before the Council, and before them did take, repeat and Subscribe the Oath of Fidelity and support to this State."* {Ref: Archives of Maryland Vol. 21, p. 194}

COWARD, WILLIAM (Baltimore Privateer), commander of the schooner *Lark*, mounting 4 swivel guns, 1 howitz gun and 4 small arms, was issued Letters of Marque & Reprisal by the Council of Maryland on 18 Aug 1779; commander of the schooner *Holker*, navigated by 17 men and mounting 4 howitz guns and 4 swivel guns, was issued Letters of Marque & Reprisal by the Council of Maryland on 19 Apr 1780; commander of the schooner *Squirrel*, navigated by 22 men and mounting 4 carriage guns, was issued Letters of Marque & Reprisal by the Council of Maryland on 27 Aug 1782. {Ref: Archives of Maryland Vol. 21, p. 498, Vol. 43, p. 145, and Vol. 48, p. 246}

COX, CORNELIUS (Washington County), private who was drafted to serve in the Maryland Continental Line until 10 Dec 1781, but *"being represented unfit for the duty for which he was intended"* was discharged on 30 Oct 1781. {Ref: Archives of Maryland Vol. 45, p. 656}

COX, JOHN (Maryland Navy), marine on the galley *Baltimore*, took the Oath of Fidelity and Allegiance to the State of Maryland on 31 Mar 1778. {Ref: Archives of Maryland Vol. 16, p. 559}

COX, SUSANNA, see "John Manley," q.v.

CRAIG (CRAIGE), ROBERT (Cecil County and Baltimore Privateer), captain from Cecil County by 1776 who was recommended to the Council of Maryland as *"an inhabitant of this County, has now a brigantine well fitted lying in Sassafras River and is very desirous of being employed by the Publick for the purpose of importing Arms and Ammunition. He is a person of property and by his Conduct appears to be well attached to the American Cause, from his long experience at Sea is well acquainted with foreign Ports"* on 29 Jan 1776; commander of the sloop *Bennington*, mounting 6 carriage guns, 4 howitz guns and 10 small arms, was issued Letters of Marque & Reprisal by the Council of Maryland on 18 Aug 1779. {Ref: Archives of Maryland Vol. 11, p. 121 and Vol. 21, p. 498}

CRAMBLETT, MICHAEL, see "Acquilla Randall," q.v.

CRAMER, PETER (Washington County), private who was enrolled to serve as a substitute in the Maryland Continental Line until 10 Dec 1781, but *"being represented unfit for the service for which he was intended"* was discharged on 30 Oct 1781. {Ref: Archives of Maryland Vol. 45, p. 656}

CRANDALL, ANN, see "Acquilla Randall," q.v.

CRAPPER, JOHN (Maryland Navy), sergeant of marines on the State Ship *Defence* in 1777; marine on the galley *Baltimore* in 1778 who took the Oath of Fidelity and Allegiance to the State of Maryland on 31 Mar 1778. {Ref: Archives of Maryland Vol. 16, p. 559 and Vol. 18, p. 655}

CRATCHER, MATTHEW (Maryland Navy), marine on the State Ship *Defence* in 1777. {Ref: Archives of Maryland Vol. 18, p. 655}

CRATING, JAMES (Harford County), private who was enrolled 9 Dec 1775 in Militia Company No. 14 under Capt. William McComas. {Ref: George W. Archer Collection and Revolutionary War File, Historical Society of Harford County Archives}

CRAVEN, ANDREW (Harford County), private in the 6th Maryland Continental Line who was a 9 month soldier in 1779, was discharged on 19 Oct 1779 and received £9.10.0 in clothing. {Ref: Archives of Maryland Vol. 21, p. 562}

CRAWFORD (CRAUFURD), DAVID (Prince George's County), captain who served on a General Court-Martial on 6 Jul 1776; commissioned one of the three persons in Prince George's County by the Council of Maryland on 19 Aug 1779 to receive subscriptions for use of the State. {Ref: Archives of Maryland Vol. 11, p. 553 and Vol. 21, p. 499}

CRAWFORD (CRAUFURD), HUGH (Prince George's County), private who was drafted into the Maryland Continental Line, was discharged on 8 Dec 1781. {Ref: Archives of Maryland Vol. 48, p. 10}

CRAWFORD, JACOB (Prince George's County), ensign and later lieutenant in the 2nd Maryland Continental Line who received payment for his services in the amount of "1900 Dollars & £3.10s" on 12 Sep 1780. {Ref: Archives of Maryland Vol. 45, p. 97}

CRAWFORD, MORDECAI (Harford County), private who was enrolled 25 Mar 1776 in Militia Company No. 19 under Capt. William Morgan. {Ref: George W. Archer Collection and Revolutionary War File, Historical Society of Harford County Archives}

CRAWFORD, STROTHER (Western Maryland), private in Capt. Michael Cresap's Company in 1775. {Ref: Howard L. Leckey's *The Tenmile Country and Its Pioneer Families*, p. 15}

CRAWLEY, JAMES (Maryland Navy), marine on the State Ship *Defence* in 1777. {Ref: Archives of Maryland Vol. 18, p. 655}

CRAWLEY, PATRICK (Frederick County), private in the Maryland Continental Line; born in York County, Pennsylvania, served as a private in the Maryland Continental Line; taken up as a vagrant in Frederick County, *"sent from camp by General Smallwood as unfit for the service"* and was discharged on 22 Jun 1778. {Ref: Archives of Maryland Vol. 21, p. 144}

CREAGER, VALENTINE, see "John Barrick," q.v.

CRESAP, DANIEL, JR. (Western Maryland), sergeant in Capt. Michael Cresap's Company in 1775. {Ref: Howard L. Leckey's *The Tenmile Country and Its Pioneer Families*, p. 15}

CRESAP, JOSEPH (Western Maryland), sergeant, later lieutenant, in Capt. Michael Cresap's Company in 1775. {Ref: Howard L. Leckey's *The Tenmile Country and Its Pioneer Families*, p. 15}

CRESAP, MICHAEL (Western Maryland), captain of a company of Maryland and Pennsylvania troops in 1775; see "George Moore," q.v. {Ref: Howard L. Leckey's *The Tenmile Country and Its Pioneer Families*, p. 15}

CRESAP, MICHAEL, JR. (Western Maryland), lieutenant in Capt. Michael Cresap's Company in 1775. {Ref: Howard L. Leckey's *The Tenmile Country and Its Pioneer Families*, p. 15}

CRESSWELL, MICHAEL (Western Maryland), private in Capt. Michael Cresap's Company in 1775. {Ref: Howard L. Leckey's *The Tenmile Country and Its Pioneer Families*, p. 15}

CRISTY, DANIEL (Western Maryland), private in Capt. Michael Cresap's Company in 1775. {Ref: Howard L. Leckey's *The Tenmile Country and Its Pioneer Families*, p. 15}

CRISWELL, ROBERT (Harford County), private who was enrolled 25 Mar 1776 in Militia Company No. 19 under Capt. William Morgan. {Ref: George W. Archer Collection and Revolutionary War File, Historical Society of Harford County Archives}

CRON, THOMAS (Maryland Navy), marine on the State Ship *Defence* in 1777. {Ref: Archives of Maryland Vol. 18, p. 655}

CRONEY, WILLIAM (Caroline County), private (substitute) in the Maryland Continental Line by 1781, was discharged on 8 Dec 1781. {Ref: Archives of Maryland Vol. 48, p. 10}

CROOKS, HENRY (Harford County), private who was enrolled 10 Mar 1776 in Militia Company No. 18 under Capt. John Jolly. {Ref: George W. Archer Collection and Revolutionary War File, Historical Society of Harford County Archives}

CROSBY, JAMES (Baltimore County), private, aged 36, labourer, born in Ireland, enlisted (made his "X" mark) on 14 Mar 1776 in Capt. John Fulford's Company of Matrosses. {Ref: Maryland Historical Magazine, Vol. 69, No. 1, p. 96}

CROSBY, JOSIAH (Baltimore Town), patriot and merchant who enrolled in Capt. John Sterrett's Independent Mercantile Company by February, 1777, at which time they were mustered into regular service with the continental army to repress loyalist activities in the Eastern Shore counties of Somerset and Worcester. {Ref: J. Thomas Scharf's *History of Baltimore City and County*, Part I, p. 77}

CROSLEY (CROSSLEY), WILLIAM (Maryland Navy), marine on the State Ship *Defence* in 1777. {Ref: Archives of Maryland Vol. 18, p. 655}

CROSS, BRISTOW (Talbot County), private who was drafted into the Maryland Continental Line, was discharged on 8 Dec 1781. {Ref: Archives of Maryland Vol. 48, p. 10}

CROSS, JOSHUA (Maryland Navy), sailor or seaman on 7 Jan 1780. {Ref: Calendar of Maryland State Papers, The Brown Books, p. 57}

CROW, FRANCINA, see "Humphrey Pugh," q.v.

CROXALL, L. (Baltimore Town), patriot and merchant who enrolled in Capt. John Sterrett's Independent Mercantile Company by February, 1777, at which time they were mustered into regular service with the continental army to repress loyalist activities in the Eastern Shore counties of Somerset and Worcester. {Ref: J. Thomas Scharf's *History of Baltimore City and County*, Part I, p. 77}

CROXALL, THOMAS (Baltimore Town), patriot and merchant who enrolled in Capt. John Sterrett's Independent Mercantile Company by February, 1777, at which time they were mustered into regular service with the continental army to repress loyalist activities in the Eastern Shore counties of Somerset and Worcester. {Ref: J. Thomas Scharf's *History of Baltimore City and County*, Part I, p. 77}

CRUCKLY, BENJAMIN (Prince George's County), private (substitute) in the Maryland Continental Line by 1781, was discharged on 8 Dec 1781. {Ref: Archives of Maryland Vol. 48, p. 10}

CUCKLEY, DANIEL (Baltimore County), private, aged 24, shoemaker, born in Ireland, enlisted 28 Feb 1776 in Capt. John Fulford's Company of Matrosses. {Ref: Maryland Historical Magazine, Vol. 69, No. 1, p. 95}

CULBERTSON, WILLIAM (Baltimore County), matross soldier by 7 May 1779 at which time he gave a deposition about his enlistment terms. {Ref: Maryland State Archives Record MdHR 6636-14-83}

CULLEMBER, THOMAS (Annapolis), private in the 2nd Maryland Matross Company who petitioned the Maryland Council on 11 Dec 1776 and requested an exemption from military service; on 1 Sep 1781 he was listed as a maimed soldier in the 2nd Maryland Continental Line at which time he was paid £10. {Ref: Maryland State Archives Record MdHR 4575-6; Archives of Maryland Vol. 45, p. 595}

CULLY, ARMISTEAD (Allegany County), soldier in the Virginia Line who born in 1758 in Kingston Parish in Gloucester or Matthews County, moved to Baltimore in 1818, and died 18 Feb 1839; he applied for pension in Frostburg, Maryland on 9 May 1836 under the Act of June 7, 1832, but the claim was suspended because *"the original papers were mailed to an agent in 1836 and have never been replaced."* {Ref: *Rejected or Suspended Applications for Revolutionary War Pensions* (1850 Report), p. 231; Research by Virgil D. White, citing Federal Pension Application S8270}

CULVER, BENJAMIN (Harford County, Susquehannah Hundred), private who was enrolled 23 Apr 1776 in Militia Company No. 21 under Capt. George Patterson. {Ref: George W. Archer Collection and Revolutionary War File, Historical Society of Harford County Archives}

CULVER, ROBERT (Harford County, Susquehannah Hundred), private who was enrolled 23 Apr 1776 in Militia Company No. 21 under Capt. George Patterson; on 8 Jun 1781 *"Robert Culver, drafted from the Militia of Harford County, appeared before the Board and having produced a Memorial from several of the Inhabitants of the said County and a Certificate from Dr. James Murray of this City of his being incapable of Military Duty, having had a fracture of his Leg near the Ankle which has been improperly reduced, is therefore discharged from the service for which he was Drafted."* {Ref: Archives of Maryland Vol. 45, p. 466; George W. Archer Collection and Revolutionary War File, Historical Society of Harford County Archives}

CUMMING, JAMES (Baltimore Town), patriot and merchant who enrolled in Capt. John Sterrett's Independent Mercantile Company by February, 1777, at which time they were mustered into regular service with the continental army to repress loyalist activities in the Eastern Shore counties of Somerset and Worcester. {Ref: J. Thomas Scharf's *History of Baltimore City and County*, Part I, p. 77}

CUMMINGS, ALEXANDER (Maryland Navy), marine and carpenter's yeoman on the State Ship *Defence* in 1777. {Ref: Archives of Maryland Vol. 18, p. 655}

CUMMINGS, ELIZABETH, see "John Patrick," q.v.

CUMMINGS, JOHN (Harford County), private who was enrolled 9 Dec 1775 in Militia Company No. 14 under Capt. William McComas. {Ref: George W. Archer Collection and Revolutionary War File, Historical Society of Harford County Archives}

CUMMINS, JOHN (Harford County, Susquehannah Hundred), private who was enrolled 23 Apr 1776 in Militia Company No. 21 under Capt. George Patterson. {Ref: George W. Archer Collection and Revolutionary War File, Historical Society of Harford County Archives}

CUMMINS, NATHAN (Talbot County), private (substitute) in the Maryland Continental Line by 1781, was discharged on 8 Dec 1781. {Ref: Archives of Maryland Vol. 48, p. 11}

CUMMINS, PAUL (Harford County, Susquehannah Hundred), private who was enrolled 23 Apr 1776 in Militia Company No. 21 under Capt. George Patterson. {Ref: George W. Archer Collection and Revolutionary War File, Historical Society of Harford County Archives}

CUMMINS, SAMUEL (Harford County, Susquehannah Hundred), private who was enrolled 23 Apr 1776 in Militia Company No. 21 under Capt. George Patterson. {Ref: George W. Archer Collection and Revolutionary War File, Historical Society of Harford County Archives}

CUNNINGHAM, DANIEL, see "Aquila Norris," q.v.

CUNNINGHAM, JOHN (Harford County), private who was enrolled 10 Mar 1776 in Militia Company No. 18 under Capt. John Jolly. {Ref: George W. Archer Collection and Revolutionary War File, Historical Society of Harford County Archives}

CUNNINGHAM, JONATHAN (Frederick County), private (substitute) in the Maryland Continental Line, Gunby's Regiment, enrolled in May, 1778 for 3 years or duration of the war. {Ref: Maryland Historical Magazine, Vol. 6, No. 3, p. 259}

CUNNINGHAM, THOMAS (Harford County), private who was enrolled 9 Dec 1775 in Militia Company No. 14 under Capt. William McComas. {Ref: George W. Archer Collection and Revolutionary War File, Historical Society of Harford County Archives}

CUNNINGHAM, THOMPSON (Maryland Navy), boatswain's mate on the State Ship *Defence* in 1777. {Ref: Archives of Maryland Vol. 18, p. 655}

CURFMAN, REBECCA, see "Frederick Kemp," q.v.

CURRY, JAMES (Harford County), private who was enrolled 9 Dec 1775 in Militia Company No. 14 under Capt. William McComas; James Curry died by 15 Apr 1812 (date of final distribution) and his heirs were Elizabeth Curry (widow) and sons John, James, and Israel Curry. {Ref: George W. Archer Collection and Revolutionary War File, Historical Society of Harford County Archives; Henry C. Peden, Jr.'s *Heirs & Legatees of Harford County, 1802-1846*, p. 21}

CURTIS, ISAAC (Somerset County), lieutenant who "brought up the State Barge from Salisbury" by 27 Sep 1781 at which time he was issued one barrel of flour for the use of the Select Militia of Somerset County. {Ref: Archives of Maryland Vol. 45, p. 627}

CURTIS, SAMUEL (Montgomery County), private who was drafted into the Maryland Continental Line, was discharged on 8 Dec 1781. {Ref: Archives of Maryland Vol. 48, p. 10}

DAEFNEY, JOHN (Maryland Navy), seaman on the State Ship *Defence* in 1777. {Ref: Archives of Maryland Vol. 18, p. 655}

DAEMON, CHARLES (Baltimore County), private who enlisted in Pulaski's Legion on 10 May 1778 in Baltimore. {Ref: Maryland Historical Magazine, Vol. 13, No. 3, p. 222}

DAILEY, JOHN (Harford County), private who was enrolled by 15 Apr 1776 in Militia Company No. 20 under Capt. Robert Glenn. {Ref: George W. Archer Collection and Revolutionary War File, Historical Society of Harford County Archives}

DALE, CAMPBELL (Worcester County), private who served in the militia under Capt. Josiah Dale in Worcester County; applied for pension in Delaware County, Indiana on 15 Jul 1835, aged 79. {Ref: Research by Virgil D. White, citing Federal Pension Application R2630}

DALEY, THOMAS (Frederick County), private (substitute) in the Maryland Continental Line, Price's Regiment, enrolled in May, 1778 for 3 years or duration of the war. {Ref: Maryland Historical Magazine, Vol. 6, No. 3, p. 259}

DALLAM, BRYAN (Baltimore County), private who enlisted in Pulaski's Legion on 28 Apr 1778 in Baltimore. {Ref: Maryland Historical Magazine, Vol. 13, No. 3, p. 222}

DALLAM, RICHARD (Harford County), patriot who was appointed by the Council of Maryland on 27 Jan 1776 as one of three persons in Harford County to collect all the gold and silver coin that can be procured in said county; appointed Commissary of Purchases on 8 Jul 1780; supplied provisions to the State of Maryland between June and September, 1780; also see "John Collins" and "Michael Daugherty" and "James Fitzgerald" and "John Garreguies" and "Edward Hawkins" and "John Jones" and "James O'Brian," q.v. {Ref: Archives of Maryland Vol. 11, p. 132, Vol. 43, p. 215, and Vol. 45, p. 84, which listed his name as "Richd. Dulham"}

DALTON, JOHN (Frederick County), private (substitute) in the Maryland Continental Line, German Regiment, enrolled in April, 1778 for 3 years or duration of the war. {Ref: Maryland Historical Magazine, Vol. 6, No. 3, p. 256}

DANNOR, DAVID (Frederick County), private in the Maryland troops who was born in March, 1759 in Frederick County and enlisted there; at age 32 or 33 he moved to Westmoreland County, Pennsylvania for 8 or 9 years, then to Jefferson County, Kentucky for 3 years, then to Harrison County, Indiana for 28 years, and then to Clay County, Indiana where he applied for a pension on 29 Oct 1833. {Ref: Research by Virgil D. White, citing Federal Pension Application S32208}

DARBY, ROBERT (Harford County), private who was enrolled 25 Mar 1776 in Militia Company No. 19 under Capt. William Morgan. {Ref: George W. Archer Collection and Revolutionary War File, Historical Society of Harford County Archives}

DARE, WILLIAM (Calvert County), first lieutenant in Capt. Frederick Skinner's Company of Militia, commissioned 16 Jun 1778. {Ref: Archives of Maryland Vol. 21, p. 137}

DARNALL, MARY, see "Charles Carroll," q.v.

DASHIELL, GEORGE (Somerset County), patriot who was appointed by the Council of Maryland on 27 Jan 1776 as one of three persons in Somerset County to collect all gold and silver coin that can be procured in said county. {Ref: Archives of Maryland Vol. 11, p. 132}

DASHIELL, JOSEPH (Worcester County), patriot who was appointed Commissary of Purchases by the Council of Maryland on 8 Jul 1780. {Ref: Archives of Maryland Vol. 43, p. 215}

DASHIELL, ROBERT (Maryland Navy and Privateer), captain in the navy on 7 Jan 1780; commander of the schooner *Lady Lee*, navigated by 14 men and mounting 4 carriage guns, was issued Letters of Marque & Reprisal by the Council of Maryland on 19 Oct 1780. {Ref: Archives of Maryland Vol. 43, p. 333; Calendar of Maryland State Papers, The Brown Books, p. 57}

DASHIELL, THERESA, see "Thomas Jones," q.v.

DAUGHERTY, BARNEY (Harford County), private who was enrolled 25 Mar 1776 in Militia Company No. 19 under Capt. William Morgan. {Ref: George W. Archer Collection and Revolutionary War File, Historical Society of Harford County Archives}

DAUGHERTY, MICHAEL (Harford County), private who was recruited and enrolled by Richard Dallam in the Regiment Extraordinary and sent to Annapolis with Capt. Thompson on board the sloop *Liberty* on 17 Aug 1780. {Ref: Archives of Maryland Vol. 45, pp. 50, 51}

DAVENPORT, ARTHUR, see "George Moore," q.v.

DAVID, VALENTINE (Frederick County), private (substitute) in the Maryland Continental Line by 1781, was discharged on 11 Dec 1781. {Ref: Archives of Maryland Vol. 48, p. 18}

DAVIDGE, TIMSEY, see "Tyler Baldwin," q.v.

DAVIDSON, JAMES (Anne Arundel County), private (substitute) in the Maryland Continental Line by 1781, was discharged on 8 Dec 1781; applied for pension in Anne Arundel County on 7 Jul 1818 and applied again in Washington, D.C. on 16 Aug 1832, aged 72; died 28 Nov 1841. {Ref: Research by Virgil D. White, citing Federal Pension Application S8305; Archives of Maryland Vol. 48, p. 11}

DAVIDSON, JOHN (Anne Arundel County), patriot who was paid £6.15.0 by the Maryland Council of Safety for boatage on 30 Sep 1776; captain in the 2nd Maryland Continental Line who received payment for his services in the amount of "1900 Dollars & £3.10s" on 12 Sep 1780. {Ref: Archives of Maryland Vol. 12, p. 310 and Vol. 45, p. 97}

DAVIES (DAVIS), MARMADUKE S. (Anne Arundel County), soldier in the Maryland Continental Line; born 11 Mar 1760 at Warrington Township in York County, Pennsylvania and lived at Elk Ridge Landing in Anne Arundel County at the time of his enlistment; married Eleanor Wilson in Belmont County, Ohio on 30 Jan 1816; applied for pension on 17 Nov 1832 (resident of Richland Township) and died 18 Mar 1855 at St. Clairsville in Belmont County; his widow applied for pension on 2 Feb 1856, aged 75. {Ref: Research by Christopher T. Smithson, citing Federal Pension Application W6967}

DAVIS, CALEB (Prince George's County), private (substitute) in the Maryland Continental Line by 1781, was discharged on 8 Dec 1781. {Ref: Archives of Maryland Vol. 48, p. 10}

64

DAVIS, CORNELIUS (Prince George's County), private in the Maryland Continental Line, who drafted to serve until 10 Dec 1781, was discharged on 29 Nov 1781. {Ref: Archives of Maryland Vol. 48, p. 6}

DAVIS, DAVID (Dorchester County), private (substitute) in the Maryland Continental Line by 1781, was discharged on 8 Dec 1781. {Ref: Archives of Maryland Vol. 48, p. 10}

DAVIS, ELIZABETH, see "James Norris," q.v.

DAVIS, ICHABOD (Anne Arundel County), patriot who took the Oath of Fidelity and Allegiance in 1778 and may have been a private in the militia (although his pension claim was rejected due to lack of proof of service); born 15 Apr 1758 (son of Robert Davis and Ruth Gaither), married Delilah Randall (daughter of Acquilla Randall and Margaret Browne) on 25 Jan 1785; Delilah died 7 Nov 1819 and Ichabod died in Columbiana County, Ohio on 29 Jul 1845; their children were: Nancy Davis; Richard Davis (born 5 Jul 1788, married Elizabeth Slayton); Rachel Davis; Nathan Caleb Davis (born 1790); Robert Davis; John Davis; Rezin Davis; Julia Ann Davis (married Samuel Koffel); Elizabeth Davis (born 5 Nov 1796, married William Diltz Hamilton on 4 Apr 1816 in Ohio, died in 1834); Eleanor Davis; Ruth Davis (married a McCord and died before 1845); Mary Davis (married Josiah Gaskill); Amos Davis (born 25 Aug 1799); and, Isaac R. Davis (born 1800); also see "Acquilla Randall," q.v. {Ref: Research by Christopher T. Smithson, citing Federal Pension Application R2724; *For King or Country*, Vol. I, p. 91; *Rejected or Suspended Applications for Revolutionary War Pensions* (1850 Report), p. 345}

DAVIS, JESSE (Charles County), private who was drafted to serve in the Maryland Continental Line until 10 Dec 1781, but *"being represented unfit for the duty for which he was intended"* was discharged on 30 Oct 1781. {Ref: Archives of Maryland Vol. 45, p. 656}

DAVIS, JOHN (Harford County), private who was enrolled 9 Dec 1775 in Militia Company No. 14 under Capt. William McComas. {Ref: George W. Archer Collection and Revolutionary War File, Historical Society of Harford County Archives}

DAVIS, JOHN (Maryland Navy), corporal of marines on the State Ship *Defence* in 1777. {Ref: Archives of Maryland Vol. 18, p. 655}

DAVIS, JOHN (Anne Arundel County), private in the Maryland Continental Line by 17 Jul 1782 at which time the Council of Maryland requested to Col. James Tootell *"to let John Davis, a sick soldier, have a Shirt and a Pair of Overalls, for which you will be paid at the Time the Payment for the Hats becomes due."* {Ref: Archives of Maryland Vol. 48, p. 216}

DAVIS, PETER (Queen Anne's County), private who was drafted into the Maryland Continental Line, was discharged on 8 Dec 1781. {Ref: Archives of Maryland Vol. 48, p. 10}

DAVIS, REZIN (Frederick and Washington Counties), ensign in the militia in 1776; "*Col. Rezin Davis died 17 Mar 1809, aged 53; served in the*

Revolutionary War and also filled the offices of sheriff and coroner for a number of years." {Ref: J. Thomas Scharf's *History of Western Maryland*, Vol. II, p. 1048}

DAVIS, ROBERT, see "Ichabod Davis," q.v.

DAVIS, RUTH, see "Acquilla Randall," q.v.

DAVIS, SAMUEL (Frederick County), private (substitute) in the Maryland Continental Line, Gunby's Regiment, enrolled in May, 1778 for 3 years or duration of the war. {Ref: Maryland Historical Magazine, Vol. 6, No. 3, p. 260}

DAVIS, SAMUEL (Maryland Privateer), commander of the sloop *Alphin*, navigated by 20 men and mounting 6 carriage guns, was issued Letters of Marque & Reprisal by the Council of Maryland on 18 Jan 1782. {Ref: Archives of Maryland Vol. 48, p. 48}

DAVIS, SARAH, see "Daniel Root," q.v.

DAVIS, THOMAS (Frederick County), private (substitute) in the Maryland Continental Line, who enlisted to serve until 10 Dec 1781, was discharged on 29 Nov 1781. {Ref: Archives of Maryland Vol. 48, p. 7}

DAVIS, THOMAS (Harford County), private who was enrolled 9 Dec 1775 in Militia Company No. 14 under Capt. William McComas. {Ref: George W. Archer Collection and Revolutionary War File, Historical Society of Harford County Archives}

DAVIS, WILLIAM (Baltimore County), private, aged 18, labourer, born in England, enlisted (made his "X" mark) on 16 Feb 1776 in Capt. John Fulford's Company of Matrosses. {Ref: Maryland Historical Magazine, Vol. 69, No. 1, p. 95}

DAVIS, WILLIAM (Maryland Navy), marine on the State Ship *Defence* in 1777. {Ref: Archives of Maryland Vol. 18, p. 655}

DAY, AGNES, see "John B. Howard," q.v.

DAY, DANIEL (Baltimore County), soldier who enlisted in Philadelphia and allegedly served in the Maryland Continental Line; applied for pension in Washington, D. C. on 28 Apr 1818, aged 62, and lived in Baltimore County by 13 Sep 1820 with wife Peggy (aged 55) and a daughter, not named (aged 11); his widow Margaret Day applied for pension under the Act of July 4, 1836 and died before 1839 (daughter Margaret Cook lived in Baltimore in 1839); the claim was suspended *"for proof of marriage and the date of her decease."* {Ref: *Rejected or Suspended Applications for Revolutionary War Pensions* (1850 Report), p. 234; Research by Virgil D. White, citing Federal Pension Application R2789}

DAY, EDWARD, JR. (Harford County), private who was enrolled 16 Sep 1775 in Militia Company No. 6 under Capt. Benjamin Rumsey. {Ref: George W. Archer Collection and Revolutionary War File, Historical Society of Harford County Archives}

DAY, JOHN (Frederick County), private (substitute) in the Maryland Continental Line, Price's Regiment, enrolled in April, 1778 for 3 years or duration of the war. {Ref: Maryland Historical Magazine, Vol. 6, No. 3, p. 256}

DAY, MARGARET, see "Daniel Day," q.v.

DAY, NICHOLAS, see "Jesse Dungan," q.v.

DEAKINS, WILLIAM, JR. (Montgomery County), patriot who was commissioned one of the three persons in Montgomery County by the Council of Maryland on 19 Aug 1779 to receive subscriptions for use of the State; died testate in Georgetown by 12 Mar 1798; wife Jane; no children mentioned in his will. {Ref: Archives of Maryland Vol. 21, p. 499; Montgomery County Wills Liber L#D, p. 1}

DEALE, HENRY (Calvert County), private who was drafted into the Maryland Continental Line, was discharged on 8 Dec 1781. {Ref: Archives of Maryland Vol. 48, p. 10}

DEAMES (DEEMS), FREDERICK (Baltimore Town), captain in the Baltimore Town Battalion of Militia, commissioned 12 Apr 1781. {Ref: Archives of Maryland Vol. 45, p. 393}

DEAN, JOHN (Queen Anne's County), major in the 4th Maryland Continental Line who received payment for his services in the amount of "1900 Dollars & £3.10s" on 12 Sep 1780. {Ref: Archives of Maryland Vol. 45, p. 98}

DEAN, JOHN (Western Maryland), private in Capt. Michael Cresap's Company in 1775. {Ref: Howard L. Leckey's *The Tenmile Country and Its Pioneer Families*, p. 15}

DEARLING, CHRISTIAN (Baltimore County), private who enlisted in Pulaski's Legion on 2 Jan 1779 and still in service in November, 1779. {Ref: Maryland Historical Magazine, Vol. 13, No. 3, p. 224}

DEAVER, AQUILA (Harford County), soldier who was living in Harford County on 1 Sep 1820 at which time documents were filed in the 6th Judicial District, Harford County Court, stating, in part: *"Aquila Deaver, aged 66 years, resident in Harford County ... does on his oath declare that he served in the Revolutionary War as follows: I enlisted under Capt. J. Price attached to the 3rd Regiment Maryland Militia on the 14th day of May in 1777 and served until the year 1783. Number of Certificate 4358. And I do solemnly swear that I was a resident citizen of the United States on the 18th of March 1818 and that I have not since that time by gift, sale or in any manner disposed of my property or any part thereof with intent thereby so as to diminish it as to bring myself within the provision of an Act of Congress entitled an act to provide for certain persons engaged in the land and naval service of the United States in the Revolutionary War passed on the 18th day of March 1818 and that I have not, nor has any person in trust for me, any property or securities, contracts or debts due me nor have I any income other than what is contained in the schedule hereto annexed and by me subscribed. Schedule of real and personal property: one house and lott $150; one mare and colt $30; one cow and calf $12; one sow and pigs $10; one chest drawers $5; 1 cupboard and contents $10; 1 desk $3; 2 tables $2; ½ dozen chairs $1; plow and harness $2; saddle and bridle $2; kitchen furniture $3; 1 stove $5; [total] $235. I have no trade nor family except a wife."* Signed: Aquila Deaver. {Ref: Historical Society of Harford County, Court Records File 25.14}

DEBWORTH, AMOS, see "Acquilla Randall," q.v.

DELAFIELD, SARAH, see "Richard Donovan," q.v.

DELANY, JOHN (Harford County), private who was enrolled 10 Mar 1776 in Militia Company No. 18 under Capt. John Jolly. {Ref: George W. Archer Collection and Revolutionary War File, Historical Society of Harford County Archives}

DELONG, BARTHOLOMEW (Maryland Navy), marine on the State Ship *Defence* in 1777. {Ref: Archives of Maryland Vol. 18, p. 656}

DELOW, MICHAEL (Western Maryland), private in Capt. Michael Cresap's Company in 1775. {Ref: Howard L. Leckey's *The Tenmile Country and Its Pioneer Families*, p. 15}

DENNIS, BENJAMIN (Worcester County), captain in the county militia, commissioned 21 Jun 1776. {Ref: Archives of Maryland Vol. 11, p. 506}

DENNIS, HENRY (Western Maryland), private in Capt. Michael Cresap's Company in 1775. {Ref: Howard L. Leckey's *The Tenmile Country and Its Pioneer Families*, p. 15}

DENNIS, JOHN (Worcester County), patriot who was commissioned one of the three persons in Worcester County by the Council of Maryland on 19 Aug 1779 to receive subscriptions for use of the State. {Ref: Archives of Maryland Vol. 21, p. 499}

DENNIS, JOSEPH (Maryland Navy), seaman or marine on the State Ship *Defence* in 1777. {Ref: Archives of Maryland Vol. 18, p. 656}

DENNY, ROBERT (Annapolis), lieutenant in the 3rd and 7th Maryland Continental Lines; received payment for his services in the amount of "1900 Dollars & £3.10s" on 12 Sep 1780. {Ref: Archives of Maryland Vol. 45, p. 98; Maryland State Archives Records MdHR 19970-5-2/16}

DENT, GEORGE (Charles County), patriot who was commissioned one of the three persons in Charles County by the Council of Maryland on 19 Aug 1779 to receive subscriptions for use of the State. {Ref: Archives of Maryland Vol. 21, p. 499}

DENT, JOHN (Charles County), patriot who was appointed by the Council of Maryland on 27 Jan 1776 as one of three persons in Charles County to collect all gold and silver coin that can be procured in said county. {Ref: Archives of Maryland Vol. 11, p. 132}

DENT, SAMUEL (Charles County), private who was drafted into the Maryland Continental Line, was discharged on 8 Dec 1781. {Ref: Archives of Maryland Vol. 48, p. 10}

DENWOOD, LEVIN (Annapolis), patriot and doctor during the war; surgeon's mate in the 3rd Maryland Continental Line in 1778; surgeon in the 7th Maryland Continental Line by 1780 and received payment for his services in the amount of "1900 Dollars & £3.10s" on 12 Sep 1780; surgeon in the 3rd Maryland Continental Line in 1781. {Ref: Archives of Maryland Vol. 45, p. 98; Maryland State Archives Records MdHR 19970-5-2/16 and 19970-3-5/7}

DERN, SOPHIA, see "Frederick Kemp, Sr.," q.v.

DESHON, DANIEL (Maryland Privateer), commander of the sloop *Molly*, navigated by 30 men and mounting 10 carriage guns, was issued Letters of Marque & Reprisal by the Council of Maryland on 15 May 1778. {Ref: Archives of Maryland Vol. 21, p. 84}

DESKIN, PAUL (Western Maryland), private in Capt. Michael Cresap's Company in 1775. {Ref: Howard L. Leckey's *The Tenmile Country and Its Pioneer Families*, p. 15}

DEVER, SAMUEL (Cecil County), private (substitute) in the Maryland Continental Line by 1781, was discharged on 8 Dec 1781. {Ref: Archives of Maryland Vol. 48, p. 11}

DEWITT, PETER (Western Maryland), private in Capt. Michael Cresap's Company in 1775. {Ref: Howard L. Leckey's *The Tenmile Country and Its Pioneer Families*, p. 15}

DICK, JACOB (Western Maryland), private in Capt. Michael Cresap's Company in 1775. {Ref: Howard L. Leckey's *The Tenmile Country and Its Pioneer Families*, p. 15}

DICK, JOHN (Baltimore County), private, aged 30, tailor, born in England, enlisted 19 Feb 1776 in Capt. John Fulford's Company of Matrosses. {Ref: Maryland Historical Magazine, Vol. 69, No. 1, p. 95}

DICKINSON, BRITTINGHAM (Baltimore County), captain in the Baltimore Town Battalion of Militia in 1781. {Ref: Archives of Maryland Vol. 45, p. 412}

DICKINSON, HENRY (Caroline County), patriot who was appointed by the Council of Maryland on 27 Jan 1776 as one of three persons in Caroline County to collect all gold and silver coin that can be procured in said county. {Ref: Archives of Maryland Vol. 11, p. 132}

DICKMAN, RICHARD (Western Maryland), private in Capt. Michael Cresap's Company in 1775. {Ref: Howard L. Leckey's *The Tenmile Country and Its Pioneer Families*, p. 15}

DICKS, DANIEL (Maryland Navy), seaman or marine on the State Ship *Defence* in 1777. {Ref: Archives of Maryland Vol. 18, p. 656}

DICKS, JOHN (Dorchester County), private (substitute) in the Maryland Continental Line by 1781, was discharged on 8 Dec 1781. {Ref: Archives of Maryland Vol. 48, p. 10}

DICKSON, JOHN (Maryland Navy), seaman on the State Ship *Defence* in 1777. {Ref: Archives of Maryland Vol. 18, p. 656}

DICKSON, THOMAS (Baltimore Privateer), commander of the brigantine *King Tamine*, mounting 10 carriage guns, 4 howitzer guns and 10 small arms, was issued Letters of Marque & Reprisal by the Council of Maryland on 3 May 1779. {Ref: Archives of Maryland Vol. 21, p. 377}

DIDDEROW, JOHN (Frederick County), soldier whose widow Catharine Didderow applied for pension under the Act of July 4, 1836, but the claim was rejected because they were married after his service. {Ref: *Rejected or Suspended Applications for Revolutionary War Pensions* (1850 Report), p. 233}

DIGGES, GEORGE (Prince George's County), patriot who was noted by the Council of Maryland on 12 Aug 1778, in part, that *"he hath been absent therefrom in Great Britain and other Parts beyond the Seas for about 3 months last Past and hath lately that is to say within 3 months now last past, returned into this State, appeared before the Governor and Council, and before them did take, repeat and Subscribe the Oath of Fidelity and Support to this State contained in the Act entitled an Act to Punish certain Crimes and Misdemeanors and to Prevent the Growth of Toryism."* {Ref: Archives of Maryland Vol. 21, p. 182}

DILLOW, THOMAS (Maryland Privateer), captain of the schooner *Liberty* which was impressed into service by order of the Council of Maryland on 27 Apr 1780 *"to go to the Head of Elk for the Purpose of Transporting a Detachment of the American Army to the State of Virginia."* {Ref: Archives of Maryland Vol. 43, p. 155}

DILMAN, CHRISTIAN (Baltimore or Frederick County), private who enlisted in Pulaski's Legion on 8 May 1778. {Ref: Maryland Historical Magazine, Vol. 13, No. 3, p. 224}

DISNEY, EZEKIEL, JR. (Maryland Navy), marine on the State Ship *Defence* in 1777. {Ref: Archives of Maryland Vol. 18, p. 656}

DISNEY, EZEKIEL, SR. (Maryland Navy), marine on the State Ship *Defence* in 1777. {Ref: Archives of Maryland Vol. 18, p. 656}

DIXON, JOHN (Harford County), private who was enrolled 9 Dec 1775 in Militia Company No. 14 under Capt. William McComas; soldier in the 1st Maryland Continental Line by 3 Dec 1781 at which time he received clothing from the Commissary of Stores. {Ref: Archives of Maryland Vol. 48, p. 9; George W. Archer Collection and Revolutionary War File, Historical Society of Harford County Archives}

DIXON, THOMAS (Baltimore County), private, aged 30, farmer, born in England, enlisted (made his "X" mark) on 29 Dec 1776 in Capt. John Fulford's Company of Matrosses. {Ref: Maryland Historical Magazine, Vol. 69, No. 1, p. 97}

DOBSON, HENRY (Cecil County), captain in the 6th Maryland Continental Line who received payment for his services in the amount of "1900 Dollars & £3.10s" on 12 Sep 1780. {Ref: Archives of Maryland Vol. 45, p. 98}

DOBSON, WILLIAM (Frederick County), private who was enrolled to serve as a substitute in the Maryland Continental Line until 10 Dec 1781, but *"being represented unfit for the service for which he was intended"* was discharged on 30 Oct 1781. {Ref: Archives of Maryland Vol. 45, p. 657}

DOBSON, WILLIAM (Calvert County), private who was enrolled to serve as a substitute in the Maryland Continental Line until 10 Dec 1781, but *"being represented unfit for the service for which he was intended"* was discharged on 30 Oct 1781. {Ref: Archives of Maryland Vol. 45, p. 657}

DODSON, JOHN (Anne Arundel County), private in the Maryland Continental Line who was *"sent from camp by General Smallwood as unfit for the service"* (he had the "fits") and was discharged on 22 Jun 1778. {Ref: Archives of Maryland Vol. 21, p. 144}

DOLLING, EDWARD (Western Maryland), private in Capt. Michael Cresap's Company in 1775. {Ref: Howard L. Leckey's *The Tenmile Country and Its Pioneer Families*, p. 15}

DONAHOO, DANIEL (Harford County, Susquehannah Hundred), private who was enrolled 23 Apr 1776 in Militia Company No. 21 under Capt. George Patterson. {Ref: George W. Archer Collection and Revolutionary War File, Historical Society of Harford County Archives}

DONALD, CORNELIUS (Baltimore County), private, aged 34, labourer, birth place not stated, enlisted (made his "X" mark) on 21 Feb 1776 in Capt. John Fulford's Company of Matrosses. {Ref: Maryland Historical Magazine, Vol. 69, No. 1, p. 95}

DONALLY, PATRICK (Frederick County), lieutenant in the 7th Maryland Continental Line who received payment for his services in the amount of "1900 Dollars & £3.10s" on 12 Sep 1780. {Ref: Archives of Maryland Vol. 45, p. 98}

DONAVIN, JOHN (Maryland Navy), marine on the State Ship *Defence* in 1777. {Ref: Archives of Maryland Vol. 18, p. 656}

DONE, JOHN (Worcester County), patriot who was appointed by the Council of Maryland on 27 Jan 1776 as one of three persons in Worcester County to collect all gold and silver coin that can be procured in said county. {Ref: Archives of Maryland Vol. 11, p. 132}

DONHON, DENNIS (Harford County, Susquehannah Hundred), private who was enrolled 23 Apr 1776 in Militia Company No. 21 under Capt. George Patterson. {Ref: George W. Archer Collection and Revolutionary War File, Historical Society of Harford County Archives}

DONN, MILCHA, see "Thomas Courtney," q.v.

DONNALLY, CHARLES (Frederick County), private in the Maryland Continental Line who was drafted to serve until 10 Dec 1781, was discharged on 29 Nov 1781. {Ref: Archives of Maryland Vol. 48, p. 7}

DONNELLAN (DONELLAN), THOMAS (Baltimore County), patriot was served as Commissary of Purchases in 1780. {Ref: Archives of Maryland Vol. 45, pp. 84, 156}

DONNELLY, EDWARD (Baltimore County), private who enlisted in Pulaski's Legion on 10 Apr 1778 in Baltimore, discharged 15 Nov 1783. {Ref: Maryland Historical Magazine, Vol. 13, No. 3, pp. 222, 223}

DONOVAN, PETER (Harford County), private who was enrolled 25 Mar 1776 in Militia Company No. 19 under Capt. William Morgan. {Ref: George W. Archer Collection and Revolutionary War File, Historical Society of Harford County Archives}

DONOVAN, RICHARD (Baltimore County), son of William O'Donovan and Jane Lannin, was born 17 Nov 1731 in County Waterford, Ireland, married Sarah

Ann Delafield of Dublin, Ireland on 19 Mar 1763, migrated to Baltimore in 1764, and died 16 Aug 1780 at the Battle of Camden in South Carolina; their daughter Sarah Donovan (1765-1826) married Robert Gorsuch (1757-1828) in 1782, and they appear to have had a son Valentine Donovan (1769-1835); Richard was a private in 1776, promoted to first sergeant in the Maryland Flying Camp before 7 Dec 1776, promoted to ensign in the Maryland Continental Line on 15 Mar 1777, and promoted to lieutenant on 1 Apr 1778; he served as regimental adjutant from 17 Apr 1777 to 16 Aug 1780 and was listed posthumously as a lieutenant in the 6th Maryland Regiment who was entitled to payment for his services in the amount of "1900 Dollars & £3.10s" on 12 Sep 1780. {Ref: Archives of Maryland Vol. 18, pp. 59, 75, 200, 518, Vol. 21, p. 293, and Vol. 45, p. 98; Francis B. Heitman's *Historical Register officers of the Continental Army*, p. 200; *The Virginia Magazine of History and Biography*, Vol. 27, pp. 187-188; DAR Application No. 377499 (approved in 1948) and SAR Application No. 37340 (approved in 1922); Research by M. Virginia Mills of Orrick, Missouri (a direct descendant) in 1996}

DONOVAN, SARAH, see "Richard Donovan," q.v.

DONOVAN, VALENTINE, see "Richard Donovan," q.v.

DORITY, JOSEPH (Baltimore Privateer), commander of the schooner *Larke*, navigated by 6 men and mounting 4 carriage guns and 2 blunderbusses, was issued Letters of Marque & Reprisal by the Council of Maryland on 8 May 1778; commander of the schooner *General Gates*, mounting 8 carriage guns, 2 swivel guns and 8 small arms, was issued Letters of Marque & Reprisal by the Council of Maryland on 5 Apr 1779; commander of the schooner *Phenix*, navigated by 9 men and mounting 6 swivel guns, was issued Letters of Marque & Reprisal by the Council of Maryland on 18 Mar 1780. {Ref: Archives of Maryland Vol. 21, pp. 71, 336, and Vol. 43, p. 115}

DORSEY, ----, see "John Lindsay," q.v.

DORSEY, ELIZABETH, see "Daniel Smith," q.v.

DORSEY, HENRY (Anne Arundel County), private in the Maryland Continental Line who was drafted to serve until 10 Dec 1781, was discharged on 8 Dec 1781. {Ref: Archives of Maryland Vol. 48, p. 17}

DORSEY, JOHN (Anne Arundel County), patriot who supplied provisions to the State of Maryland between June and September, 1780. {Ref: Archives of Maryland Vol. 45, p. 84}

DORSEY, JOHN W., see "Michael O'Connor," q.v.

DORSEY, JOSEPH (Maryland Navy), marine on the State Ship *Defence* in 1777. {Ref: Archives of Maryland Vol. 18, p. 656}

DORSEY, LEAVEN (Baltimore County), private, aged 21, carpenter, born in Maryland, enlisted 11 Mar 1776 in Capt. John Fulford's Company of Matrosses. {Ref: Maryland Historical Magazine, Vol. 69, No. 1, p. 96, which listed the name as "Leaven Deysey(?)"}

DORSEY, NICHOLAS, OF HENRY (Baltimore County), patriot who was paid £7.5.0 for waggonage by the Committee of Claims on 28 Mar 1778. {Ref: Archives of Maryland Vol. 16, p. 557}

DORSEY, RACHEL, see "John Lindsay," q.v.

DORSEY, RICHARD (Baltimore County), captain of a Company of Artillery in Baltimore Town, commissioned 9 May 1777; captain who received payment for his services in the amount of "1900 Dollars & £3.10s" on 12 Sep 1780; see "Michael O'Connor," q.v. {Ref: Archives of Maryland Vol. 16, p. 245 and Vol. 45, p. 98}

DORSEY, RICHARD (Maryland Navy), midshipman on the State Ship *Defence* in 1777. {Ref: Archives of Maryland Vol. 18, p. 656}

DORSEY, SAMUEL (Anne Arundel County), patriot who was paid £40.1.0 by the Maryland Council of Safety for tents on 2 Oct 1776. {Ref: Archives of Maryland Vol. 12, p. 316}

DORSEY, THOMAS (Anne Arundel County), patriot who was appointed by the Council of Maryland on 27 Jan 1776 as one of three persons in Anne Arundel County to collect all gold and silver coin that can be procured in said county. {Ref: Archives of Maryland Vol. 11, p. 132}

DOUBT, RODGER (Harford County), private who was enrolled 10 Mar 1776 in Militia Company No. 18 under Capt. John Jolly. {Ref: George W. Archer Collection and Revolutionary War File, Historical Society of Harford County Archives}

DOUGHADAY, RICHARD (Baltimore Town), patriot and merchant who enrolled in Capt. John Sterrett's Independent Mercantile Company by February, 1777, at which time they were mustered into regular service with the continental army to repress loyalist activities in the Eastern Shore counties of Somerset and Worcester. {Ref: J. Thomas Scharf's *History of Baltimore City and County*, Part I, p. 77}

DOUGHERTY, GEORGE (Harford County), private who was enrolled 25 Mar 1776 in Militia Company No. 19 under Capt. William Morgan; George Dougherty died by 9 Feb 1802 (date of distribution) and his heirs were Margaret Taylor, formerly Dougherty (widow), John Dougherty, and Mary Ann Dougherty. {Ref: George W. Archer Collection and Revolutionary War File, Historical Society of Harford County Archives; Henry C. Peden, Jr.'s *Heirs & Legatees of Harford County, 1802-1846*, p. 2}

DOUGLAS, ARCHIBALD (Maryland Navy), midshipman in 1776 and on the tender's crew for the State Ship *Defence* in 1777. {Ref: Archives of Maryland Vol. 18, p. 656}

DOUGLASS, JAMES, see "Jesse Greyless," q.v.

DOUGLASS, WILLIAM (Maryland Navy), midshipman on the State Ship *Defence* in 1777. {Ref: Archives of Maryland Vol. 18, p. 656}

DOWALL, RICHARD (Anne Arundel County), private (substitute) in the Maryland Continental Line by 1781, was discharged on 8 Dec 1781. {Ref: Archives of Maryland Vol. 48, p. 11}

DOWNAND, JAMES (Western Maryland), private in Capt. Michael Cresap's Company in 1775. {Ref: Howard L. Leckey's *The Tenmile Country and Its Pioneer Families*, p. 15}

DOWNES, HENRY, JR. (Caroline County), patriot who was commissioned one of the three persons in Caroline County by the Council of Maryland on 19 Aug 1779 to receive subscriptions for use of the State. {Ref: Archives of Maryland Vol. 21, p. 499}

DOWNES, PHILEMON (Queen Anne's County), patriot who was commissioned one of the three persons in Queen Anne's County by the Council of Maryland on 19 Aug 1779 to receive subscriptions for use of the State. {Ref: Archives of Maryland Vol. 21, p. 499}

DOWNING, WILLIAM (Harford County), private who was enrolled 25 Mar 1776 in Militia Company No. 19 under Capt. William Morgan. {Ref: George W. Archer Collection and Revolutionary War File, Historical Society of Harford County Archives}

DRAPIER, JOHN (Frederick County), private (substitute) in the Maryland Continental Line, Price's Regiment, enrolled in May, 1778 for 3 years or duration of the war. {Ref: Maryland Historical Magazine, Vol. 6, No. 3, p. 259}

DRISKILL, JOHN (Maryland Navy), seaman on the State Ship *Defence* in 1777. {Ref: Archives of Maryland Vol. 18, p. 656}

DRUMMOND, HUGH (Anne Arundel County), son of John Drummond who complained to the Council of Maryland and they, in turn, informed Col. Gist on 17 Jun 1778 *"that Capt. Samuel Griffith enlisted his [John's] son Hugh only 14 years old next Valentine's Day. He says his Son is a very weakly Lad and Subject to Fits, and that he was carried away without being passed by a Field Officer. Lads under 16 years old ought not to be inlisted without the consent of their Parents. We wish you to enquire into this Matter and, if the Boy is under 16, we request you to discharge him, on his paying the Money he had received back to you."* {Ref: Archives of Maryland Vol. 21, p. 139}

DRYSDALE, THOMAS (Baltimore Town), patriot and merchant who enrolled in Capt. John Sterrett's Independent Mercantile Company by February, 1777, at which time they were mustered into regular service with the continental army to repress loyalist activities in the Eastern Shore counties of Somerset and Worcester. {Ref: J. Thomas Scharf's *History of Baltimore City and County*, Part I, p. 77}

DUCK, GEORGE (Baltimore Privateer), commander of the brigantine *Sea Bell*, navigated by 21 men and mounting 6 carriage guns, was issued Letters of Marque & Reprisal by the Council of Maryland on 27 Aug 1782. {Ref: Archives of Maryland Vol. 48, p. 246}

DUNBAR, JOSEPH (Maryland Navy), cooper on the State Ship *Defence* in 1777. {Ref: Archives of Maryland Vol. 18, p. 656}

DUNBRACCO, THOMAS (Maryland Navy), sailor or seaman on 7 Jan 1780. {Ref: Calendar of Maryland State Papers, The Brown Books, p. 57}

DUNGAN, JESSE (Harford County), possible patriot who was living in Harford County by 20 Feb 1796 at which time documents were filed stating, in part: *"Know all men by these presents that I, Jesse Dungan of Harford County and State of Maryland, am held and firmly bound unto Nicholas Day (formerly of said county and state aforesaid, now of Westmoreland County and State of Pennsylvania) in the penal sum of $350 specie, for which payment well and truly to be made, I do hereby bind myself, my heirs, executors, administrators and assigns to Nicholas Day, his heirs, executors, administrators and assigns, firmly by these presents. In witness whereof I hath hereunto set my hand and affixed my seal this 20th day of February in the year of Lord 1796. Whereas John Young, a soldier in Col. John Gibson's Detachment of the Virginia Line, did procure from the War Office a certificate (dated on the 22nd day of September in the year of our Lord 1795) signed by William Simmons, Esquire, accountant, under the Seal of the War Office thereunto annexed and affixed or impressed certifying that on the 6th day of December in the year 1784 Josiah Tannehill (agent to Col. John Gibson's Detachment of the Virginia Line) did receive from Andrew Dunscomb, Assistant Commissary of Army Accounts, a number of certificates belonging to the soldiers of said Detachment among which were the following described certificates, the property of the said John Young, to wit: one Certificate No. 78563 on interest from the 1st day of January 1783 for $80; one ditto No. 78709 on interest from the 15th of November 1783 for $123 and 39 parts of a dollar, for which said Tannehill is accountable to said John Young, and the said Young having sold said certificates to the said Jesse Dungan and said Dungan to said Day."* {Ref: Historical Society of Harford County, Court Records File 25.14}

DUNN, ---- (Frederick County?), soldier in the Maryland Continental Line who died fighting in the defense of his country before 8 Jan 1777 at which time his distressed widow Mary Dunn received £3 from the State Treasurer. {Ref: Archives of Maryland Vol. 16, p. 27}

DUNN, WILLIAM (Frederick County), private who was enrolled to serve as a substitute in the Maryland Continental Line until 10 Dec 1781, but *"being represented unfit for the service for which he was intended"* was discharged on 30 Oct 1781. {Ref: Archives of Maryland Vol. 45, p. 657}

DUNNING, JAMES (Charles County), private who was drafted into the Maryland Continental Line, was discharged on 8 Dec 1781. {Ref: Archives of Maryland Vol. 48, p. 10}

DUNNINGTON, GEORGE (Charles County), recommended as an ensign in the 26th Battalion of Militia of Charles County on 20 Mar 1781. {Ref: Archives of Maryland Vol. 47, p. 136}

DUNSCOMB, ANDREW, see "Jesse Dungan," q.v.

DURBIN, CASSANDRA, see "Richard Sappington," q.v.

DURBIN, FRANCIS (Harford County, Susquehannah Hundred), private who was enrolled 23 Apr 1776 in Militia Company No. 21 under Capt. George Patterson. {Ref: George W. Archer Collection and Revolutionary War File, Historical Society of Harford County Archives}

DURDIN, THOMAS (Maryland Navy), seaman or marine on the State Ship *Defence* in 1777. {Ref: Archives of Maryland Vol. 18, p. 656}

DURHAM, DAVIDSON (Maryland Privateer), commander of the schooner *Chance*, navigated by 27 men and mounting 8 carriage guns, 2 swivel guns and 7 small arms, was issued Letters of Marque & Reprisal by the Council of Maryland on 13 Mar 1780. {Ref: Archives of Maryland Vol. 43, p. 109}

DUTTON, SUSANNAH, see "Aquila Norris," q.v.

DUVALL (DUVAL), EDWARD (Prince George's County?), lieutenant in the 2nd Maryland Continental Line who received payment for his services in the amount of "1900 Dollars & £3.10s" on 12 Sep 1780. {Ref: Archives of Maryland Vol. 45, p. 97}

DUVALL, ELIZA, see "Nathan Musgrove," q.v.

DUVALL (DUVAL), ISAAC (Prince George's County), lieutenant in the 3rd Maryland Continental Line who received payment for his services in the amount of "1900 Dollars & £3.10s" on 12 Sep 1780. {Ref: Archives of Maryland Vol. 45, p. 98}

DUZANT, ISAAC (Harford County), private who was enrolled 31 Oct 1775 in Militia Company No. 8 under Capt. Greenberry Dorsey. {Ref: George W. Archer Collection and Revolutionary War File, Historical Society of Harford County Archives}

DUZANT, JACOB (Harford County), private who was enrolled 31 Oct 1775 in Militia Company No. 8 under Capt. Greenberry Dorsey. {Ref: George W. Archer Collection and Revolutionary War File, Historical Society of Harford County Archives}

DYER, EDWARD (Frederick County?), lieutenant in the 2nd Maryland Continental Line who received payment for his services in the amount of "1900 Dollars & £3.10s" on 12 Sep 1780. {Ref: Archives of Maryland Vol. 45, p. 97}

DYER, ELIZABETH, see "Joseph Blanford," q.v.

DYER, JAMES (Frederick County), private (substitute) in the Maryland Continental Line, German Regiment, enrolled in May, 1778 for 3 years or duration of the war. {Ref: Maryland Historical Magazine, Vol. 6, No. 3, p. 258}

DYER, RICHARD, see "Joseph Blanford," q.v.

DYER, WALTER (Charles County), ensign in the 3rd Maryland Continental Line who received payment for his services in the amount of "1900 Dollars & £3.10s" on 12 Sep 1780. {Ref: Archives of Maryland Vol. 45, p. 97}

DYSON, BENNET (Charles County), recommended as captain in the 12th Battalion of Militia of Charles County on 20 Mar 1781. {Ref: Archives of Maryland Vol. 47, p. 136}

EAGLESTON, JOSEPH, see "James McCracken," q.v.

EARLE, JAMES (Baltimore Privateer), commander of the schooner *Baltimore Hero*, mounting 14 carriage guns, 6 swivel guns, 2 cohorn guns and 20 small arms, was issued Letters of Marque & Reprisal by the Council of Maryland on 15 May 1779. {Ref: Archives of Maryland Vol. 21, p. 594}

EARLE, JOHN (Maryland Privateer), commander of the sloop *Rutledge*, navigated by 10 men and mounting 4 swivel guns and 6 small arms, was issued Letters of Marque & Reprisal by the Council of Maryland on 14 Sep 1778. {Ref: Archives of Maryland Vol. 21, p. 202}

EARLE, JOSEPH (Kent County), patriot who was appointed by the Council of Maryland on 27 Jan 1776 as one of three persons in Kent County to collect all gold and silver coin that can be procured in said county. {Ref: Archives of Maryland Vol. 11, p. 132}

EARLE, THOMAS (Baltimore Town), patriot and merchant who enrolled in Capt. John Sterrett's Independent Mercantile Company by February, 1777, at which time they were mustered into regular service with the continental army to repress loyalist activities in the Eastern Shore counties of Somerset and Worcester. {Ref: J. Thomas Scharf's *History of Baltimore City and County*, Part I, p. 77}

EASTBURN, BENJAMIN (Frederick County), captain in the county militia in 1782. {Ref: Archives of Maryland Vol. 48, p. 248}

EDDY, JAMES (Frederick County), private (substitute) in the Maryland Continental Line, Price's Regiment, enrolled in May, 1778 for 3 years or duration of the war. {Ref: Maryland Historical Magazine, Vol. 6, No. 3, p. 258}

EDEN, JOHN (St. Mary's County), patriot who supplied 800 lbs. of beef on the hoof to the State of Maryland on 10 Oct 1780. {Ref: Archives of Maryland Vol. 45, p. 156}

EDGERLY, EDWARD (Annapolis), adjutant in the 2nd Maryland Continental Line in 1777 and later lieutenant who received payment for his services in the amount of "1900 Dollars & £3.10s" on 12 Sep 1780. {Ref: Maryland State Archives Record MdHR 6636-7-171; Archives of Maryland Vol. 45, p. 97}

EDMINSTON, ARCHIBALD (Calvert County), private who was drafted to serve in the Maryland Continental Line until 10 Dec 1781, but *"being represented unfit for the duty for which he was intended"* was discharged on 30 Oct 1781. {Ref: Archives of Maryland Vol. 45, p. 656}

EDMONSON, JAMES (Maryland Navy), sailor or seaman on 7 Jan 1780. {Ref: Calendar of Maryland State Papers, The Brown Books, p. 57}

EDMONSTON, BROOKS, see "Robert Orme," q.v.

EDMONSTON, MR. [SAMUEL?] (Maryland Continental Line, Staff and P. Officer), D.W.G., received payment for his services in the amount of "1900 Dollars & £3.10s" on 12 Sep 1780. {Ref: Archives of Maryland Vol. 45, p. 98}

EDMONSTON, PRISCILLA, see "Robert Orme," q.v.

EDWARDS, SAMUEL (Frederick County), private (substitute) in the Maryland Continental Line, Gunby's Regiment, enrolled in May, 1778 for 3 years or duration of the war. {Ref: Maryland Historical Magazine, Vol. 6, No. 3, p. 260}

EDWARDS, STRUTTON or STRATTON (St. Mary's County), private who was drafted into the Maryland Continental Line and discharged on 8 Dec 1781. {Ref: Archives of Maryland Vol. 48, p. 10}

EIRS, DANIEL (Harford County), private who was enrolled by 15 Apr 1776 in Militia Company No. 20 under Capt. Robert Glenn. {Ref: George W. Archer Collection and Revolutionary War File, Historical Society of Harford County Archives}

EIRS, STEPHEN (Harford County), private who was enrolled by 15 Apr 1776 in Militia Company No. 20 under Capt. Robert Glenn. {Ref: George W. Archer Collection and Revolutionary War File, Historical Society of Harford County Archives}

ELDER, REVEREND, see "John Lindsay," q.v.

ELLIOTT, JOSEPH (Dorchester County Privateer), commander of the schooner *Molly*, navigated by 10 men and mounting 2 carriage guns, 1 swivel gun and 6 small arms, was issued Letters of Marque & Reprisal by the Council of Maryland on 10 Mar 1780; commander of the schooner *Unity*, navigated by 25 men and mounting 8 carriage guns, was issued Letters of Marque & Reprisal by the Council of Maryland on 30 Nov 1780. {Ref: Archives of Maryland Vol. 43, p. 105, and Vol. 45, p. 229}

ELLIOTT (ELLIOT), ROBERT (Harford County), soldier who was living in Harford County on 5 Sep 1820 at which time documents were filed stating, in part: *"Robert Elliott, aged 78 years, resident in Harford County ... on his oath declared that he served in the Revolutionary War as follows: That he was enlisted in the City of Baltimore in April 1777 by Captain Brice for three years or during the war and first mustered in said Brice's Company, joined the 3rd Maryland Regiment commanded by Colonel Ramsey, ordered on to Philadelphia, and then to Kingston and Princeton and from thence to Brunswick and from thence to Brandewine [Brandywine] at which place I fought during the whole engagement and from thence we fell back to Chester and from thence to the Peole [Paoli] at which place I fought and got shot through the mouth which prevented me from doing military duty, but I was ordered on to New Ark, Deleware [Newark, Delaware] to make shoes for the army at which place I remained two years. Then ordered to West Point to join my regiment at which place I remained about one month, but not being well enough to do military duty, ordered on to Albany to make shoes for the army at which place I remained one year. And from thence ordered on to Elkton, Maryland to join my regiment and from thence to Annapolis and from thence to Petersburg, Virginia at which we had a general review, and by the flash of a gun I lost the sight of one of my eyes, and from thence sent to the hospital at Chesterfield Court House at which place I was honourably discharged by Col.*

Davis not being fit for military service in the year 1781 or 2, and lost my discharge. That he hath been placed on the Revolutionary pension list of the Maryland Agency as will more fully appear by his pension certificate bearing date the 9th March 1819 and numbered on the back 7501. And I do solemnly swear that I was a resident citizen of the United States on the 18th March 1818 and that I have not since that time, by gift, sale or any manner, disposed of my property or any part thereof with intent thereby so to diminish it as to bring myself within the provisions of an Act of Congress entitled an act to provide for certain persons engaged in the land and naval service of the United States in the Revolutionary War passed on the 18th March 1818 and that I have not, nor has any person in trust for me, any property or securities, contracts or debts due me nor have I any income other than what is contained in the schedule hereto annexed and by me subscribed. Schedule referred to, viz., one bed and bedding $10; one pot and tea kettle $1.50; 3 chairs and 1 table $2.50; one pail, one tub and sundry crockery ware worth $2.00; 3 knives and forks and spoons 75 cents; and, one pig $1.25; [total] $18. That he is a shoemaker by trade but nearly lost the sight of the remaining eye. That he lives on a gentleman's place which by his assistance and my pension I am enabled to live, until I received the pension I was in Harford County's alms house, and I have no family except a woman that keeps house for me and if it was not for my pension I should have to return to the alms house again." Signed: Robert Elliot (made his "X" mark). {Ref: Historical Society of Harford County, Court Records File 25.14}

ELLIOTT, THOMAS (Baltimore County), patriot who was appointed and commissioned as one of the coroners for Baltimore County on 7 May 1777; commissioned first lieutenant in Capt. George Hunter's Company of Matrosses formed in the defense of the harbor of Baltimore on 30 Mar 1781. {Ref: Archives of Maryland Vol. 45, p. 368}

ELLIS, ELLIS (Harford County), private who was enrolled 25 Mar 1776 in Militia Company No. 19 under Capt. William Morgan. {Ref: George W. Archer Collection and Revolutionary War File, Historical Society of Harford County Archives}

ELLIS, THOMAS (Harford County), soldier who was living in Harford County on 20 Nov 1820 at which time documents were filed in Harford County Court, stating, in part: *"Thomas Ellis, aged 71 years, resident in Harford County ... does on his oath declare that he served in the Revolutionary War as follows: That he enlisted in the 6th Maryland Regiment and served under Capt. Joshua Miles' Company and that he has received a pension and that the number of his pension certificate 16058. And I do solemnly swear that I was a resident citizen of the United States on the 18th of March 1818 and that I have not since that time by gift, sale or in any manner disposed of my property or any part thereof with intent thereby so as to diminish it as to bring myself within the provision of an Act of Congress entitled An Act to provide for certain persons engaged*

in the land and naval service of the United States in the Revolutionary War
passed on the 18th day of March 1818 and that I have not, nor has any person
in trust for me, any property or securities, contracts or debts due me nor have
I any income other than what is contained in the schedule hereto annexed and
by me subscribed. Property, none of any kind or description, that he was a
labourer and unable to labour, that he has no family." {Ref: Historical Society of
Harford County, Court Records File 25.14}

ELLOTT, BENJAMIN (Frederick County), private (substitute) in the Maryland
Continental Line, German Regiment, enrolled in May, 1778 for 3 years or
duration of the war. {Ref: Maryland Historical Magazine, Vol. 6, No. 3, p. 261}

ELTON, ---- (Anne Arundel County?), soldier in the Maryland Continental Line
"now remaining in Annapolis" on 24 Jul 1780 at which time his wife Jane Elton
was entitled to rations under the laws of the State. {Ref: Archives of Maryland Vol.
43, p. 227}

EMERIE, SAMUEL (Baltimore or Frederick County), sergeant in Pulaski's Legion
before July, 1782. {Ref: Maryland Historical Magazine, Vol. 13, No. 3, p. 225}

EMERTEN, HENRY (Caroline County), private in the Maryland Continental Line
who was drafted to serve until 10 Dec 1781, was discharged on 29 Nov 1781.
{Ref: Archives of Maryland Vol. 48, p. 7}

EMMART, SARAH, see "George Zimmerman," q.v.

EMORY, CAPTAIN, see "Dennis Callahan," q.v.

EMORY, ARTHUR (Queen Anne's County), lieutenant colonel of the 20th
Battalion of Militia, commissioned 8 May 1777. {Ref: Archives of Maryland Vol. 16,
p. 244}

ENGLE, SARAH, see "Robert Orme," q.v.

ENNALLS, JOSEPH, see "Thomas Pitt," q.v.

ENNALLS, WILLIAM (Dorchester County), patriot who was appointed by the
Council of Maryland on 27 Jan 1776 as one of three persons in Dorchester
County to collect all the gold and silver coin that can be procured in said
county; commissioned on 19 Aug 1779 as one of the three persons in
Dorchester County to receive subscriptions for use of the State. {Ref: Archives of
Maryland Vol. 11, p. 132 and Vol. 21, p. 499}

ENNIS, ---- (Anne Arundel County?), soldier in the Maryland Continental Line
"now remaining in Annapolis" on 24 Jul 1780 at which time his wife Christian
Ennis was entitled to rations under the laws of the State. {Ref: Archives of Maryland
Vol. 43, p. 227}

ENNIS, GEORGE (Prince George's County), private who was recruited for a term
of 3 years in the Continental Army as procured by Robert Orme (who was
himself a draft for 9 months) and was paid $60 on 25 Jun 1778. {Ref: Archives of
Maryland Vol. 21, p. 150}

ERP, ERASMUS (Frederick and Montgomery Counties), soldier who was born in
1757 in Frederick County and enlisted in the Maryland militia; applied for

pension on 21 Dec 1840, aged 83, in Montgomery County under the Act of June 7, 1832, but the claim was rejected because he did not serve six months. {Ref: *Rejected or Suspended Applications for Revolutionary War Pensions* (1850 Report), p. 229; Research by Virgil D. White, citing Federal Pension Application R3364}

ETTING, REUBEN (Baltimore Town), patriot and merchant who enrolled in Capt. John Sterrett's Independent Mercantile Company by February, 1777, at which time they were mustered into regular service with the continental army to repress loyalist activities in the Eastern Shore counties of Somerset and Worcester. {Ref: J. Thomas Scharf's *History of Baltimore City and County*, Part I, p. 77}

ETTLEMAN, LEONARD (Washington County), private (substitute) in the Maryland Continental Line by 1781, was discharged on 10 Dec 1781. {Ref: Archives of Maryland Vol. 48, p. 17}

EVANS, DAVID (Harford County), private who was enrolled 9 Dec 1775 in Militia Company No. 14 under Capt. William McComas. {Ref: George W. Archer Collection and Revolutionary War File, Historical Society of Harford County Archives}

EVANS, GRIFFITH (Harford County), private who was enrolled 9 Dec 1775 in Militia Company No. 14 under Capt. William McComas. {Ref: George W. Archer Collection and Revolutionary War File, Historical Society of Harford County Archives}

EVANS, GRIFFITH (Harford County), private who was enrolled by 15 Apr 1776 in Militia Company No. 20 under Capt. Robert Glenn. {Ref: George W. Archer Collection and Revolutionary War File, Historical Society of Harford County Archives}

EVANS, JANE, see "Abraham Mitchell," q.v.

EVANS, JOHN (Baltimore County), private, aged 36, sawyer, born in Wales, enlisted (made his "X" mark) on 4 Mar 1776 in Capt. John Fulford's Company of Matrosses. {Ref: Maryland Historical Magazine, Vol. 69, No. 1, p. 96, which listed the name as "John Evanie(?)"}

EVANS, JOHN (Harford County, Susquehannah Hundred), private who was enrolled 23 Apr 1776 in Militia Company No. 21 under Capt. George Patterson. {Ref: George W. Archer Collection and Revolutionary War File, Historical Society of Harford County Archives}

EVANS, MARY, see "David Bell," q.v.

EVANS, NATHAN (Harford County), private who was enrolled by 15 Apr 1776 in Militia Company No. 20 under Capt. Robert Glenn. {Ref: George W. Archer Collection and Revolutionary War File, Historical Society of Harford County Archives}

EVANS, ROBERT (Maryland Navy), seaman or marine on the State Ship *Defence* in 1777. {Ref: Archives of Maryland Vol. 18, p. 656}

EVANS, WILLIAM (Queen Anne's County), enlisted by Richard Cockran in Baltimore Town, was private in the Maryland Continental Line who was *"sent from camp by General Smallwood as unfit for the service"* and was discharged on 22 Jun 1778. {Ref: Archives of Maryland Vol. 21, p. 144}

EVERETT, ANN, see "John H. Hughes," q.v.

EVERRET, L. (Baltimore Town), patriot and merchant who enrolled in Capt. John Sterrett's Independent Mercantile Company by February, 1777, at which time they were mustered into regular service with the continental army to repress loyalist activities in the Eastern Shore counties of Somerset and Worcester. {Ref: J. Thomas Scharf's *History of Baltimore City and County*, Part I, p. 77}

EWING, JAMES (Caroline County), patriot who was appointed ensign in the 14th Militia Battalion by the Council of Maryland on 28 Jun 1780. {Ref: Archives of Maryland Vol. 43, p. 207}

EWING, JAMES (Harford and Allegany Counties), lieutenant in the 2nd Maryland Continental Line who received payment for his services in the amount of "1900 Dollars & £3.10s" on 12 Sep 1780. {Ref: Archives of Maryland Vol. 45, p. 97}

EYLER, CONRAD, see "Frederick Kemp, Sr.," q.v.

FAIRLEY, ANDREW (Western Maryland), private in Capt. Michael Cresap's Company in 1775. {Ref: Howard L. Leckey's *The Tenmile Country and Its Pioneer Families*, p. 15}

FALCON, BICKET (Maryland Privateer), commander of the schooner *Resource*, navigated by 12 men and mounting 3 carriage guns and 8 howitz guns, was issued Letters of Marque & Reprisal by the Council of Maryland on 9 Sep 1780. {Ref: Archives of Maryland Vol. 43, p. 282}

FALL, PATRICK (Maryland Navy), seaman or marine on the State Ship *Defence* in 1777. {Ref: Archives of Maryland Vol. 18, p. 656}

FANNELL, JOHN (Frederick County), private (substitute) in the Maryland Continental Line, German Regiment, enrolled in May, 1778 for 3 years or duration of the war. {Ref: Maryland Historical Magazine, Vol. 6, No. 3, p. 261}

FANNING, JOHN (Baltimore Privateer), commander of the schooner *Baltimore*, navigated by 6 men and mounting 4 swivel guns, was issued Letters of Marque & Reprisal by the Council of Maryland on 8 Jun 1778. {Ref: Archives of Maryland Vol. 21, p. 125}

FARDING, AARON (Frederick County), private (substitute) in the Maryland Continental Line by 1781, was discharged on 8 Dec 1781. {Ref: Archives of Maryland Vol. 48, p. 11}

FARIBAULT (FARRIBAULT), JOSEPH (Baltimore Privateer), commander of the brigantine *The Lady De Miralles*, navigated by 34 men and mounting 10 carriage guns, 8 swivel guns and 19 small arms, was issued Letters of Marque & Reprisal by the Council of Maryland on 4 Nov 1779; commander of the brigantine *Porgie*, navigated by 20 men and mounting 4 carriage guns, was issued Letters of Marque & Reprisal by the Council of Maryland on 19 Jun 1780. {Ref: Archives of Maryland Vol. 43, pp. 8, 199}

FARMER, SAMUEL (Baltimore County), lieutenant and later captain in the 3rd Maryland Continental Line who received payment for his services in the amount of "1900 Dollars & £3.10s" on 12 Sep 1780. {Ref: Archives of Maryland Vol. 45, p. 97}

FARMER, JOHN (Harford County), first lieutenant on 25 Mar 1776 in Militia Company No. 19 under Capt. William Morgan. {Ref: George W. Archer Collection and Revolutionary War File, Historical Society of Harford County Archives}

FARMER, ROBERT (Western Maryland), private in Capt. Michael Cresap's Company in 1775. {Ref: Howard L. Leckey's *The Tenmile Country and Its Pioneer Families*, p. 15}

FARRAJARA, JOHN (Maryland Navy), midshipman on the State Ship *Defence* in 1777. {Ref: Archives of Maryland Vol. 18, p. 656}

FAUX, PATRICK (Cecil County), soldier who served in a Pennsylvania company of artificers, married Rebecca Good in Philadelphia on 24 Dec 1780, and died in October, 1796, leaving a widow and seven children (not named); his widow Rebecca Faux applied for pension in Cecil County on 18 Jul 1842, aged nearly 90, under the Act of July 7, 1838, but the claim was suspended because *"service admitted -- marriage in suspense."* Elizabeth Faux of Cecil County, an heir of the deceased widow, signed a power of attorney on 25 Dec 1852. {Ref: *Rejected or Suspended Applications for Revolutionary War Pensions* (1850 Report), p. 236; Research by Virgil D. White, citing Federal Pension Application W27525}

FEAR, IGNATIUS (Maryland Navy), gunner's mate on the State Ship *Defence* in 1777. {Ref: Archives of Maryland Vol. 18, p. 656}

FEARLEY, WILLIAM (Frederick County), private (substitute) in the Maryland Continental Line, Price's Regiment, enrolled in May, 1778 for 3 years or duration of the war. {Ref: Maryland Historical Magazine, Vol. 6, No. 3, p. 260}

FEBUS, GEORGE (Somerset County), private (substitute) in the Maryland Continental Line by 1781, was discharged on 8 Dec 1781. {Ref: Archives of Maryland Vol. 48, p. 11}

FELL, ELIZABETH, see "Thomas Jones," q.v.

FENNELL, ---- (Anne Arundel County?), soldier in the Maryland Continental Line *"now remaining in Annapolis"* on 24 Jul 1780 at which time his wife Mary Fennell was entitled to rations under the laws of the State. {Ref: Archives of Maryland Vol. 43, p. 227}

FENTON, CORNELIUS (Maryland Navy), marine on the State Ship *Defence* in 1777. {Ref: Archives of Maryland Vol. 18, p. 656}

FENWICK, IGNATIUS (Baltimore Privateer), commander of the brigantine *Sally*, mounting 10 carriage guns, 4 swivel guns and 15 small arms, was issued Letters of Marque & Reprisal by the Council of Maryland on 27 Aug 1782. {Ref: Archives of Maryland Vol. 21, p. 277}

FENWICK, RICHARD (Maryland Navy), marine on the State Ship *Defence* in 1777. {Ref: Archives of Maryland Vol. 18, p. 656}

FERELL, JOHN (Baltimore or Frederick County), private who enlisted in Pulaski's Legion on 15 Jun 1779. {Ref: Maryland Historical Magazine, Vol. 13, No. 3, p. 224}

FERGUSON, ANDREW (Harford County, Susquehannah Hundred), private who was enrolled 23 Apr 1776 in Militia Company No. 21 under Capt. George

Patterson. {Ref: George W. Archer Collection and Revolutionary War File, Historical Society of Harford County Archives}

FERGUSON, DAVID (Maryland Navy), marine on the galley *Conqueror*, took the Oath of Fidelity and Allegiance to the State of Maryland on 2 Apr 1778. {Ref: Archives of Maryland Vol. 21, p. 1}

FERGUSON, THOMAS (Frederick County), private (substitute) in the Maryland Continental Line, who enlisted to serve until 10 Dec 1781, was discharged on 29 Nov 1781. {Ref: Archives of Maryland Vol. 48, p. 7}

FERGUSON, WILLIAM (Baltimore Town), patriot and merchant who enrolled in Capt. John Sterrett's Independent Mercantile Company by February, 1777, at which time they were mustered into regular service with the continental army to repress loyalist activities in the Eastern Shore counties of Somerset and Worcester. {Ref: J. Thomas Scharf's *History of Baltimore City and County*, Part I, p. 77}

FERNANDES, JAMES (Southern Maryland), captain, commissioned on 27 Jul 1780 to serve in the Regiment Extra by order of the Council of Maryland. {Ref: Archives of Maryland Vol. 43, p. 234}

FERRELL, THOMAS (Frederick County), private (substitute) in the Maryland Continental Line, Price's Regiment, enrolled in May, 1778 for 3 years or duration of the war. {Ref: Maryland Historical Magazine, Vol. 6, No. 3, p. 258}

FERRENCE, HENRY (Frederick County), private (substitute) in the Maryland Continental Line, German Regiment, enrolled in May, 1778 for 3 years or duration of the war. {Ref: Maryland Historical Magazine, Vol. 6, No. 3, p. 261}

FERROL, JOSEPH, see "Joseph Pherill," q.v.

FICKLE, BENJAMIN (Frederick County), sergeant and later ensign in the 7th Maryland Continental Line who received payment for his services in the amount of "1900 Dollars & £3.10s" on 12 Sep 1780. {Ref: Archives of Maryland Vol. 45, p. 98}

FIDDEMAN, PHILIP (Queen Anne's County), colonel and contractor for horses in Queen Anne's County by 11 Sep 1780 at which time he was paid £6400 to be expended and accounted for. {Ref: Archives of Maryland Vol. 43, p. 285}

FIELD, MARY, see "Cooper Oram," q.v.

FIELDS, CHARLES (Baltimore County), private (substitute) in the Maryland Continental Line by 1781, was discharged on 8 Dec 1781. {Ref: Archives of Maryland Vol. 48, p. 11}

FIELDS, MICHAEL (St. Mary's County), private who enlisted in the Maryland Continental Line by 17 Jun 1778 at which time he received £3 due him as bounty pay. {Ref: Archives of Maryland Vol. 21, p. 138}

FINCH, GEORGE (Somerset County), private (substitute) in the Maryland Continental Line by 1781, was discharged on 8 Dec 1781. {Ref: Archives of Maryland Vol. 48, p. 11}

FINLEY (FINLAY), EBENEZER (Baltimore County), captain in the Maryland Artillery who received payment for his services in the amount of "1900 Dollars

& £3.10s" on 12 Sep 1780. For additional information see Peden's *Revolutionary Patriots of Baltimore Town and Baltimore County, 1775-1783*, p. 87. {Ref: Archives of Maryland Vol. 45, p. 98}

FINLEY, JAMES (Harford County), private who was enrolled 9 Dec 1775 in Militia Company No. 14 under Capt. William McComas. {Ref: George W. Archer Collection and Revolutionary War File, Historical Society of Harford County Archives}

FINLEY, JOHN (Harford County), private who was enrolled 9 Dec 1775 in Militia Company No. 14 under Capt. William McComas. {Ref: George W. Archer Collection and Revolutionary War File, Historical Society of Harford County Archives}

FINNEY, WILLIAM (Dorchester County), recruit *"from Dorset, blind"* who was a private in the Maryland Continental Line, *"sent from camp by General Smallwood as unfit for the service"* and was discharged on 22 Jun 1778. {Ref: Archives of Maryland Vol. 21, p. 144}

FINNIGAN, TORRENCE (Western Maryland), private in Capt. Michael Cresap's Company in 1775. {Ref: Howard L. Leckey's *The Tenmile Country and Its Pioneer Families*, p. 15}

FISCHER, PHILIP (Frederick County), soldier in the Revolution who *"had enlisted under Captain Fistar in the Dutch Battalion and was wounded in fighting the battles for his country, died in Middletown on 9 Jan 1839 in about his 82nd year; he received the Honors of War from the surviving worthies of the Revolution in this section of the county."* {Ref: *Frederick Visiter and Temperance Advocate*, 17 Jan 1839}

FISH, GENERAL, see "William Fitzhugh," q.v.

FISHER, HENRY (Frederick County), private (substitute) in the Maryland Continental Line, German Regiment, enrolled in April, 1778 for 3 years or duration of the war. {Ref: Maryland Historical Magazine, Vol. 6, No. 3, p. 256}

FISHER, JOHN (Washington County), private who was enrolled to serve as a substitute in the Maryland Continental Line until 10 Dec 1781, but *"being represented unfit for the service for which he was intended"* was discharged on 30 Oct 1781. {Ref: Archives of Maryland Vol. 45, p. 657}

FISHER, WILLIAM (Anne Arundel County), private by 5 Oct 1776 in Capt. Richard Chew's Militia Company, Weems' Battalion; John Sellman was administrator of the estate of William Fisher, deceased, on 9 Dec 1826. {Ref: Archives of Maryland Vol. 12, p. 323; Anne Arundel County Administration Account TH No. 1, p. 94}

FISHPAW, JOHN, see "Frederick Hook," q.v.

FISTAR, CAPTAIN, see "Philip Fischer," q.v.

FITCH, GEORGE, see "George Moore," q.v.

FITCHER, BENJAMIN (Dorchester County), private (substitute) in the Maryland Continental Line by 1781, was discharged on 8 Dec 1781. {Ref: Archives of Maryland Vol. 48, p. 10}

FITZGERALD (FITZGERAL), JAMES (Harford County), private who was recruited and twice deserted from Richard Dallam; possibly enrolled in the Regiment Extraordinary and sent to Annapolis with Capt. Thompson on board the sloop *Liberty* on 17 Aug 1780. {Ref: Archives of Maryland Vol. 45, pp. 50, 51}

FITZGERALD, JOHN (Dorchester County), private in the Maryland Continental Line who was drafted to serve until 10 Dec 1781, was discharged on 29 Nov 1781. {Ref: Archives of Maryland Vol. 48, p. 7}

FITZGERALD, SIMON (Harford County), soldier who was living in Harford County on 28 Aug 1822 at which time documents were filed in Harford County Court, stating, in part: *"Simon Fitzgerald, resident of Harford County, aged 69 years ... does on his oath make the following declaration in order to obtain the provision made by the acts of Congress of the 18th March 1818 and the 1st May 1820, that he enlisted for the term of 18 months on the ---- day of ---- in the year 1775 in the State of Delaware in the company commanded by Captain Williams in the regiment commanded by Colonel Dehorse in the line of the State of Pennsylvania on the W. S. continental establishment; that he continued to serve in the said corps until May 1777 when he was discharged from the said service in Philadelphia in the State of Pennsylvania. That he the said Simon Fitzgerald is a taylor but totally unable to pursue that or any other mode(?) of obtaining a competent or decent subsistence. That he has no family except a decrepid and infirm wife age 69 years. That he was in the battle of Ticonderoga and that he has no other evidence, now in his power, of his said services, except the affidavit of John Barrett herewith produced. And in pursuance of the act of the 1st May 1820 I do solemnly swear that I was a resident citizen of the United States on the 18th of March 1818 and that I have not since that time by gift, sale or in any manner disposed of my property or any part thereof with intent thereby so as to diminish it as to bring myself within the provision of an Act of Congress entitled An Act to provide for certain persons engaged in the land and naval service of the United States in the Revolutionary War passed on the 18th day of March 1818 and that I have not, nor has any person in trust for me, any property or securities, contracts or debts due me nor have I any income other than what is contained in the schedule hereto annexed and by me subscribed. To wit, one lot of ground situate in Dublin, Harford County, one cow, one bureau, one bed and bedding, six chairs, one pot and kettle, and I owe debts which amount to the value of the said property."* Signed: Simon Fitzgerald (made his "X" mark). {Ref: Historical Society of Harford County, Court Records File 25.14}

FITZHUGH, WILLIAM (Washington County), lieutenant and later a colonel who was a *"patriot of the Washington School in the War of Independence, a lieutenant of dragoons at the seize of Yorktown, aide-de-camp of General Fish of Maryland, and formerly of Washington County, Maryland, died at his residence in Livingston County, New York on 27 Dec 1839 in the 79th year of his age."* {Ref: *The Visiter*, Frederick County, 16 Jan 1840}

FITZHUGH, WILLIAM (Calvert County), patriot who was appointed recruiting officer in Calvert County for the Maryland Continental Line by the Council of Maryland on 23 Jun 1780. {Ref: Archives of Maryland Vol. 43, p. 202}

FITZJEFFRYS, AARON (Maryland Navy), seaman or marine on the State Ship *Defence* in 1777. {Ref: Archives of Maryland Vol. 18, p. 656}

FITZPATRICK, HUGH (Baltimore County), private who enlisted in Pulaski's Legion on 10 Apr 1778 and still in service in November, 1779. {Ref: Maryland Historical Magazine, Vol. 13, No. 3, p. 223}

FITZPATRICK, JOHN (Western Maryland), private in Capt. Michael Cresap's Company in 1775. {Ref: Howard L. Leckey's *The Tenmile Country and Its Pioneer Families*, p. 15}

FITZPATRICK, JOSEPH (Baltimore County), private who enlisted in Pulaski's Legion on 28 Aug 1779 and still in service in November, 1779. {Ref: Maryland Historical Magazine, Vol. 13, No. 3, p. 224}

FITZPATRICK, WILLIAM (Maryland Navy), sailor or seaman on 7 Jan 1780. {Ref: Calendar of Maryland State Papers, The Brown Books, p. 57}

FITZSIMMONS, Thomas (Cecil County), private who was enrolled to serve as a substitute in the Maryland Continental Line until 10 Dec 1781, but *"being represented unfit for the service for which he was intended"* was discharged on 30 Oct 1781. {Ref: Archives of Maryland Vol. 45, p. 657}

FLANNAGAN, HENRY (Dorchester County), private in the 2nd and 3rd Maryland Continental Lines by 1780 who *"lately returned from captivity in Charles Town, South Carolina"* and was issued clothing due him on 3 Dec 1781. {Ref: Archives of Maryland Vol. 18, p. 339, and Vol. 48, p. 9}

FLANNAGAN, JOHN (Maryland Navy), seaman or marine on the State Ship *Defence* in 1777. {Ref: Archives of Maryland Vol. 18, p. 656}

FLARITY, STEPHEN (Western Maryland), private in Capt. Michael Cresap's Company in 1775. {Ref: Howard L. Leckey's *The Tenmile Country and Its Pioneer Families*, p. 15}

FLAT, JOHN (Washington County), private who was drafted to serve in the Maryland Continental Line until 10 Dec 1781, but *"being represented unfit for the duty for which he was intended"* was discharged on 30 Oct 1781. {Ref: Archives of Maryland Vol. 45, p. 656}

FLEMMING, JOHN (Maryland Navy), sergeant of marines on the State Ship *Defence* in 1777. {Ref: Archives of Maryland Vol. 18, p. 656}

FLEMMING, THOMAS (Frederick County), captain in the Maryland troops who *"fought for American Independence and glory at the head of his company in the Battles of Brandywine, Germantown, etc., died on Wednesday morning last at his residence at Big Small Mill in Butler County, Ohio, at the age of 88; formerly a native of Frederick, he survived nearly all his contemporaries and was survived by his wife and several small children."* {Ref: *The Times and Democratic Advocate,* 28 Dec 1837}

FLEMMING, WILLIAM (Maryland Navy), sergeant of marines on the State Ship *Defence* in 1777. {Ref: Archives of Maryland Vol. 18, p. 656}

FLETCHER, SAMUEL (Frederick County), private (substitute) in the Maryland Continental Line, German Regiment, enrolled in May, 1778 for 3 years or duration of the war. {Ref: Maryland Historical Magazine, Vol. 6, No. 3, p. 261}

FOGGET, RICHARD (Anne Arundel County), private who was enrolled to serve as a substitute in the Maryland Continental Line until 10 Dec 1781, but *"being represented unfit for the service for which he was intended"* was discharged on 30 Oct 1781. {Ref: Archives of Maryland Vol. 45, p. 657}

FOLGER, FREDERICK (Baltimore Privateer), commander of the schooner *Felicity*, navigated by 25 men and mounting 10 carriage guns, was issued Letters of Marque & Reprisal by the Council of Maryland on 17 Aug 1780. {Ref: Archives of Maryland Vol. 43, p. 257}

FOLLETT, JOSEPH (Baltimore or Frederick County), private in Pulaski's Legion before July, 1782. {Ref: Maryland Historical Magazine, Vol. 13, No. 3, p. 225}

FORBES, JAMES (Baltimore Privateer), commander of the sloop *Annapolis*, mounting 2 howitz guns, 2 swivel guns and 4 small arms, was issued Letters of Marque & Reprisal by the Council of Maryland on 8 Jan 1779; commander of the brigantine *Hercules*, mounting 12 carriage guns and 12 small arms, was issued Letters of Marque & Reprisal by the Council of Maryland on 3 Jan 1780; commander of the brigantine *Nisbett*, navigated by 30 men and mounting 14 carriage guns and 20 small arms, was issued Letters of Marque & Reprisal by the Council of Maryland on 23 Jun 1780; commander of the brigantine *Nesbitt*, navigated by 80 men and mounting 16 carriage guns, was issued Letters of Marque & Reprisal by the Council of Maryland on 11 May 1781. {Ref: Archives of Maryland Vol. 21, p. 276, Vol. 43, pp. 47, 201-202, and Vol. 45, p. 432}

FORD (FOARD), BENJAMIN (Cecil County), colonel in the 2nd Maryland Continental Line who received payment for his services in the amount of "1900 Dollars & £3.10s" on 12 Sep 1780. {Ref: Archives of Maryland Vol. 45, p. 97}

FORD, BENJAMIN (Baltimore County), ensign, 31 May 1779, Capt. Benjamin Talbott's Militia Company, Cockey's Battalion. {Ref: Maryland Historical Magazine, Vol. 7, No. 1, p. 90}

FORD (FOARD), HEZEKIAH (Cecil County), lieutenant in the 2nd Maryland Continental Line who received payment for his services in the amount of "1900 Dollars & £3.10s" on 12 Sep 1780. {Ref: Archives of Maryland Vol. 45, p. 97}

FORD, JOHN (Maryland Navy), sailor or seaman on 7 Jan 1780. {Ref: Calendar of Maryland State Papers, The Brown Books, p. 57}

FORD, JOSEPH (St. Mary's County), patriot who was appointed Commissary of Purchases on 8 Jul 1780 by the Council of Maryland; contractor for horses in

St. Mary's County by 8 Sep 1780 at which time he was paid £6500 to be expended and accounted for. {Ref: Archives of Maryland Vol. 43, pp. 215, 281}

FORD, JOSEPH (Western Maryland), sergeant in Capt. Michael Cresap's Company in 1775. {Ref: Howard L. Leckey's *The Tenmile Country and Its Pioneer Families*, p. 15}

FORD, LOYD (Baltimore County), private, 31 May 1779, Capt. Benjamin Talbott's Militia Company, Cockey's Battalion. {Ref: Maryland Historical Magazine, Vol. 7, No. 1, p. 90}

FORD, THOMAS (Baltimore County), private, 31 May 1779, Capt. Benjamin Talbott's Militia Company, Cockey's Battalion. {Ref: Maryland Historical Magazine, Vol. 7, No. 1, p. 90}

FORD, THOMAS COCKEY DEYE (Baltimore County), private, 31 May 1779, Capt. Benjamin Talbott's Militia Company, Cockey's Battalion. {Ref: Maryland Historical Magazine, Vol. 7, No. 1, p. 90}

FORD, WILLIAM (Cecil County), private who was enrolled to serve as a substitute in the Maryland Continental Line until 10 Dec 1781, but *"being represented unfit for the service for which he was intended"* was discharged on 30 Oct 1781. {Ref: Archives of Maryland Vol. 45, p. 657}

FORHEE, THOMAS (Western Maryland), private in Capt. Michael Cresap's Company in 1775. {Ref: Howard L. Leckey's *The Tenmile Country and Its Pioneer Families*, p. 15}

FORREST, URIAH (Annapolis), colonel in the 7th Maryland Continental Line who received payment for his services in the amount of "1900 Dollars & £3.10s" on 12 Sep 1780. {Ref: Archives of Maryland Vol. 45, p. 98}

FORRESTER, ALEXANDER (Baltimore County), matross soldier by 7 May 1779 at which time he gave a deposition about his enlistment terms. {Ref: Maryland State Archives Record MdHR 6636-14-83}

FORRESTER, JOHN (Baltimore County), matross soldier by 7 May 1779 at which time he gave a deposition about his enlistment terms. {Ref: Maryland State Archives Record MdHR 6636-14-83}

FORSHAY, OBADIAH, see "George Moore," q.v.

FOSTER, FIDELIS (Harford County), private who was enrolled 10 Mar 1776 in Militia Company No. 18 under Capt. John Jolly. {Ref: George W. Archer Collection and Revolutionary War File, Historical Society of Harford County Archives}

FOSTER, JEREMIAH, see "Jesse Foster," q.v.

FOSTER, JESSE (Harford County), private who was enrolled 25 Mar 1776 in Militia Company No. 19 under Capt. William Morgan; Jesse Foster died by 26 Mar 1817 (date of final distribution) and his heirs were sons Jeremiah, Thomas, and John Foster, and daughters Mary Allender, Ann Hammitt, Faithfull McFaddon, Sarah Foster, and Rachel Foster. {Ref: George W. Archer Collection and Revolutionary War File, Historical Society of Harford County Archives; Henry C. Peden, Jr.'s *Heirs & Legatees of Harford County, 1802-1846*, p. 22}

FOSTER, JOHN, see "Jesse Foster," q.v.

FOSTER, MOSES (Frederick County), private (substitute) in the Maryland Continental Line, Gunby's Regiment, enrolled in April, 1778 for 3 years or duration of the war. {Ref: Maryland Historical Magazine, Vol. 6, No. 3, p. 256}

FOSTER, NATHAN (Talbot County), private who was drafted into the Maryland Continental Line, was discharged on 8 Dec 1781. {Ref: Archives of Maryland Vol. 48, p. 10}

FOSTER, RACHEL, see "Jesse Foster," q.v.

FOSTER, SARAH, see "Jesse Foster," q.v.

FOSTER, THOMAS, see "Jesse Foster," q.v.

FOSTER, WILLIAM (Maryland Navy), seaman or marine on the State Ship *Defence* in 1777. {Ref: Archives of Maryland Vol. 18, p. 656}

FOUT, PETER (Frederick County), patriot buried in Mount Olivet Cemetery. {Ref: Information compiled by Dr. Donald Wolf in Maryland Society SAR Newsletter circa 1996}

FOWKE, GERARD (Charles County), captain in the Maryland troops who *"died on 19 Mar 1783 in his 59th year; he was taken ill from home and his death was surprisingly sudden; he was a gentleman of great humanity, honesty, and hospitable beyond what is common."* {Ref: *Maryland Gazette*, 3 Apr 1783}

FOWLER, HANNAH, see "Jubb Fowler," q.v.

FOWLER, JOSEPH (Maryland Navy), cabin boy on the State Ship *Defence* in 1777. {Ref: Archives of Maryland Vol. 18, p. 656}

FOWLER, JUBB (Annapolis), patriot who was appointed as messenger to the Governor and Council of Maryland on 6 Feb 1781, replacing Robert Reith who had died; John Fowler died before 1 Jan 1807 at which time halves of the remaining balance of his estate were paid to his widow Hannah Fowler and his father Jub Fowler. {Ref: Archives of Maryland Vol. 45, p. 302; Anne Arundel County Administration Account JG No. 2, p. 98}

FOWLER, PATRICK (Harford County, Susquehannah Hundred), private who was enrolled 23 Apr 1776 in Militia Company No. 21 under Capt. George Patterson. {Ref: George W. Archer Collection and Revolutionary War File, Historical Society of Harford County Archives}

FOWLER, SADOC (Frederick County), soldier in the Maryland troops who was born in 1762 in Prince George's County and lived in Frederick County at the time of his enlistment; applied for pension on 12 May 1834, aged 71, under the Act of June 7, 1832, but the claim was rejected because he did not serve six months. {Ref: *Rejected or Suspended Applications for Revolutionary War Pensions* (1850 Report), p. 229; Research by Virgil D. White, citing Federal Pension Application R3714}

FOWLER, THOMAS (Frederick County), private in the 1st Maryland Continental Line who was recruited by 28 Feb 1780 at which time he was issued clothing due him. {Ref: Archives of Maryland Vol. 43, p. 98}

FOX, GEORGE, see "Daniel Root," q.v.

FOX, PATRICK, see "Patrick Faux," q.v.

FOXWELL, ADAM (Dorchester County), private (substitute) in the Maryland Continental Line by 1781, was discharged on 8 Dec 1781. {Ref: Archives of Maryland Vol. 48, p. 10}

FOY, JANE, see "Henry Jamar," q.v.

FOY, JOHN (Frederick County), patriot and private soldier buried in Mount Olivet Cemetery. {Ref: Information compiled by Dr. Donald Wolf in Maryland Society SAR Newsletter circa 1996}

FOY, PATRICK, see "Henry Jamar," q.v.

FRAINEMAKER, FRANCIS (Baltimore or Frederick County), sergeant, enlisted in Pulaski's Legion on 12 Mar 1778. {Ref: Maryland Historical Magazine, Vol. 13, No. 3, p. 224}

FRANCEWAY, JOHN (Maryland Navy), marine on the State Ship *Defence* in 1777. {Ref: Archives of Maryland Vol. 18, p. 656}

FRANKLIN, JOHN (Frederick County), private who was drafted to serve in the Maryland Continental Line until 10 Dec 1781, but *"being represented unfit for the duty for which he was intended"* was discharged on 30 Oct 1781. {Ref: Archives of Maryland Vol. 45, p. 656}

FRAZER, LEVIN (Maryland Navy), marine on the galley *Independence*, took the Oath of Fidelity and Allegiance to the State of Maryland on 2 Apr 1778. {Ref: Archives of Maryland Vol. 21, p. 1}

FRAZIER, DANIEL (Baltimore County), private, aged 25, farmer, born in Maryland, enlisted 3 Feb 1776 in Capt. John Fulford's Company of Matrosses. {Ref: Maryland Historical Magazine, Vol. 69, No. 1, p. 97}

FRAZIER, JAMES (Dorchester County Privateer), commander of the schooner *Dorchester*, navigated by 10 men and mounting 4 carriage guns and 2 swivel guns, was issued Letters of Marque & Reprisal by the Council of Maryland on 24 Jun 1780. {Ref: Archives of Maryland Vol. 43, p. 203}

FRAZIER, JOHN (Annapolis Privateer), commander of the sloop *Dispatch*, mounting 110 guns, was issued Letters of Marque & Reprisal by the Council of Maryland on 30 Mar 1779. {Ref: Archives of Maryland Vol. 21, p. 332}

FRAZIER, SOLOMON (Dorchester County Privateer), commander of the schooner *Dorchester*, navigated by 10 men and mounting 1 carriage gun, 2 howitz guns and 4 small arms, was issued Letters of Marque & Reprisal by the Council of Maryland on 26 Oct 1778; commander of the brigantine *Talbot*, navigated by 25 men and mounting 10 carriage guns, 10 swivel guns and 24 small arms, was issued Letters of Marque & Reprisal by the Council of Maryland on 3 Dec 1779. {Ref: Archives of Maryland Vol. 21, p. 224 and Vol. 43, p. 28}

FREAM, WILLIAM (Frederick County), private (substitute) in the Maryland Continental Line by 1781, was discharged on 11 Dec 1781. {Ref: Archives of Maryland Vol. 48, p. 18}

FREDERICK, PHILIP (Baltimore County), private who enlisted in Pulaski's Legion on 1 Sep 1778 and still in service in November, 1779. {Ref: Maryland Historical Magazine, Vol. 13, No. 3, p. 223}

FREEMAN, EDWARD (Harford County), private who was enrolled by Capt. Praul in the Regiment Extraordinary and sent to Annapolis with Capt. Thompson on board the sloop *Liberty* on 17 Aug 1780; reported as a recruit sent before by Capt. Praul and deserted from Annapolis with Capt. Thompson. {Ref: Archives of Maryland Vol. 45, p. 50}

FREEMAN, HANNAH, see "William B. Rasin," q.v.

FREEMAN, MARY, see "Joseph Allsop," q.v.

FREEMAN, SARAH, see "William B. Rasin," q.v.

FRENCH, MARTIN (Baltimore or Frederick County?), private in the 1st Maryland Continental Line by 31 Jan 1780 at which time he was issued clothing *"due him from the Continent."* {Ref: Archives of Maryland Vol. 43, p. 73}

FRENDO, BENJAMIN (Anne Arundel County), private by 5 Oct 1776 (made his "X" mark) in Capt. Richard Chew's Militia Company, Weems' Battalion. {Ref: Archives of Maryland Vol. 12, p. 323}

FRICK, HARRIET (HENRIETTA), see "William Norris" and "James Sloan," q.v.

FRICK, PETER, see "James Sloan," q.v.

FRICK, WILLIAM, see "James Sloan," q.v.

FRICKER, JOHN (Frederick County), private (substitute) in the Maryland Continental Line, Price's Regiment, enrolled in May, 1778 for 3 years or duration of the war. {Ref: Maryland Historical Magazine, Vol. 6, No. 3, p. 259}

FRY, BARNA (Washington County), private who was drafted to serve in the Maryland Continental Line until 10 Dec 1781, but *"being represented unfit for the duty for which he was intended"* was discharged on 30 Oct 1781. {Ref: Archives of Maryland Vol. 45, p. 656}

FRY, JACOB (Western Maryland), private in Capt. Michael Cresap's Company in 1775. {Ref: Howard L. Leckey's *The Tenmile Country and Its Pioneer Families*, p. 15}

FULHAM, CHARLES (Frederick County), private (substitute) in the Maryland Continental Line, German Regiment, enrolled in April, 1778 for 3 years or duration of the war. {Ref: Maryland Historical Magazine, Vol. 6, No. 3, p. 257}

FULTON, JAMES P. (Montgomery County), private who was drafted into the Maryland Continental Line, was discharged on 8 Dec 1781. {Ref: Archives of Maryland Vol. 48, p. 10}

FURNISS, MARY, see "Levi Stevens," q.v.

FURNIVAL, ALEXANDER, see "Michael O'Connor," q.v.

GADDIS, WILLIAM (Harford County), private who was enrolled by 15 Apr 1776 in Militia Company No. 20 under Capt. Robert Glenn. {Ref: George W. Archer Collection and Revolutionary War File, Historical Society of Harford County Archives}

GADSBY, JOHN, see "Benjamin B. Norris," q.v.

GAGGEN (GAGAN), JAMES (Maryland Navy), cook on the State Ship *Defence* in 1777. {Ref: Archives of Maryland Vol. 18, p. 656}

GAGGEN, WILLIAM (Maryland Navy), ordinary sailor on the State Ship *Defence* in 1777. {Ref: Archives of Maryland Vol. 18, p. 656}

GAITHER, BASIL (Southern Maryland), ensign, commissioned on 27 Jul 1780 to serve in the Regiment Extra by order of the Council of Maryland. {Ref: Archives of Maryland Vol. 43, p. 234}

GAITHER, EDWARD (Anne Arundel County), colonel, appointed Commissary of Purchases by the Council of Maryland on 8 Jul 1780; also supplied provisions to the State of Maryland between June and September, 1780. {Ref: Archives of Maryland Vol. 43, p. 215, and Vol. 45, p. 84, which listed his name as "Edwd. Gather"}

GAITHER, JOSEPH (Maryland Navy), clerk on the State Ship *Defence* in 1777. {Ref: Archives of Maryland Vol. 18, p. 656}

GAITHER, RUTH, see "Ichabod Davis," q.v.

GALE, EDWARD, see "Silvanus Smith," q.v.

GALE, JOHN (Somerset County), captain in the 2nd Maryland Continental Line who received payment for his services in the amount of "1900 Dollars & £3.10s" on 12 Sep 1780. For additional information see Peden's *Revolutionary Patriots of Worcester and Somerset Counties, 1775-1783* (p. 105); also see "Michael Payne," q.v. {Ref: Archives of Maryland Vol. 45, p. 97}

GALLION, AVARILLA, see "Jacob Norris," q.v.

GALLION, GREGORY (Harford County), private who was enrolled 25 Mar 1776 in Militia Company No. 19 under Capt. William Morgan. {Ref: George W. Archer Collection and Revolutionary War File, Historical Society of Harford County Archives}

GALLION, JOHN (Harford County, Susquehannah Hundred), private who was enrolled 23 Apr 1776 in Militia Company No. 21 under Capt. George Patterson. {Ref: George W. Archer Collection and Revolutionary War File, Historical Society of Harford County Archives}

GALLOWAY, JOSEPH (Baltimore County?), private in the 2nd Maryland Continental Line by 31 Jan 1780 at which time he was issued clothing *"due him from the Continent."* {Ref: Archives of Maryland Vol. 43, p. 74}

GALLOWAY, MARY, see "David Lynn," q.v.

GANTT, ERASMUS (Prince George's County), patriot who was appointed cornet in Capt. Lingan's "Company of Cavalry directed to be raised by the Act for the Defence of the Bay" on 25 Apr 1781. {Ref: Archives of Maryland Vol. 45, p. 414}

GARDINER, RICHARD (Charles County), private in the 2nd Maryland Continental Line by 31 Jan 1780 at which time he was issued clothing "due him from the Continent." {Ref: Archives of Maryland Vol. 43, p. 74}

GARDNER (GARNER), CLEMENT (Charles County), marine on the State Ship *Defence* in 1777. {Ref: Archives of Maryland Vol. 18, p. 656}

GARDNER, GEORGE (Frederick County), private (substitute) in the Maryland Continental Line, Gunby's Regiment, enrolled in May, 1778 for 3 years or duration of the war. {Ref: Maryland Historical Magazine, Vol. 6, No. 3, p. 260}

GARDNER, SAMUEL (Maryland Navy), sailor or seaman on 7 Jan 1780. {Ref: Calendar of Maryland State Papers, The Brown Books, p. 57}

GARDNER, THOMAS (Maryland Navy), seaman or marine on the State Ship *Defence* in 1777. {Ref: Archives of Maryland Vol. 18, p. 656}

GAREY, JOHN (Maryland Navy), marine on the State Ship *Defence* in 1777. {Ref: Archives of Maryland Vol. 18, p. 656}

GARNER, ABEL (Dorchester County), private (substitute) in the Maryland Continental Line by 1781, was discharged on 8 Dec 1781. {Ref: Archives of Maryland Vol. 48, p. 10}

GARNER, GEORGE (Harford County), private who was enrolled 9 Dec 1775 in Militia Company No. 14 under Capt. William McComas. {Ref: George W. Archer Collection and Revolutionary War File, Historical Society of Harford County Archives}

GARNETT, BENJAMIN (Queen Anne's County?), lieutenant in the 5th Maryland Continental Line who received payment for his services in the amount of "1900 Dollars & £3.10s" on 12 Sep 1780. {Ref: Archives of Maryland Vol. 45, p. 98}

GARREGUIES, JOHN (Harford County), recruit who enlisted for the 8th Regiment and entitled *"to receive £14.1.3 as part of the bounty engaged to be given him by Richard Dallam, Lieutenant of Harford County"* on 16 Oct 1780. {Ref: Archives of Maryland Vol. 43, p. 330}

GARRETT, ELINOR, see "James Higgins," q.v.

GARRETTSON, FRANCES, see "Samuel Griffith," q.v.

GARROTT, MR., see "Abner Meek," q.v.

GARSTON, GEORGE (Baltimore Privateer), commander of the sloop *Hope*, navigated by 7 men and mounting 2 wall pieces and 2 muskets, was issued Letters of Marque & Reprisal by the Council of Maryland on 19 Oct 1779; commander of the schooner *Antelope*, navigated by 32 men and mounting 6 carriage guns, was issued Letters of Marque & Reprisal by the Council of Maryland on 30 Aug 1782. {Ref: Archives of Maryland Vol. 21, p. 563 and Vol. 48, p. 250}

GARTRELL, CALEB, see "Nathan Musgrove," q.v.

GARY, RICHARD (Baltimore County), private in the Maryland Continental Line who lived in Baltimore at the time of his enlistment; applied for pension in Armstrong County, Pennsylvania on 18 Sep 1832, aged 81 (resident of Buffalo Township); in 1824 he stated all his children had left except the oldest (aged 23) and the youngest (no names were given). {Ref: Research by Virgil D. White, citing Federal Pension Application R3933}

GASH, WILLIAM (Harford County), private in the 3rd Maryland Continental Line who was a 9 month soldier in the 3rd Maryland Regiment in 1779, was

94

discharged on 18 Oct 1779 and received £12 in clothing. {Ref: Archives of Maryland Vol. 21, p. 561}

GASKILL, JOSIAH, see "Ichabod Davis," q.v.

GASSAWAY, ELIZABETH, see "William Sanders," q.v.

GASSAWAY, HENRY (Anne Arundel County), ensign in the 2nd Maryland Continental Line who received payment for his services in the amount of "1900 Dollars & £3.10s" on 12 Sep 1780. For additional information see Peden's *Revolutionary Patriots of Anne Arundel County, 1775-1783* (p. 75). {Ref: Archives of Maryland Vol. 45, p. 97}

GASSAWAY, JOHN (Anne Arundel County), captain in the 2nd Maryland Continental Line who received payment for his services in the amount of "1900 Dollars & £3.10s" on 12 Sep 1780. For additional information see Peden's *Revolutionary Patriots of Anne Arundel County, 1775-1783* (p. 76). {Ref: Archives of Maryland Vol. 45, p. 97}

GASSAWAY, NICHOLAS (Anne Arundel County), lieutenant in the 3rd Maryland Continental Line who received payment for his services in the amount of "1900 Dollars & £3.10s" on 12 Sep 1780. {Ref: Archives of Maryland Vol. 45, p. 97}

GATTON, AZARIAH (Montgomery County), private (substitute) in the Maryland Continental Line by 1781, was discharged on 11 Dec 1781. {Ref: Archives of Maryland Vol. 48, p. 18}

GAUL, RICHARD (Frederick County), private (substitute) in the Maryland Continental Line, German Regiment, enrolled in May, 1778 for 3 years or duration of the war. {Ref: Maryland Historical Magazine, Vol. 6, No. 3, p. 259}

GAUNT, LEVI (Prince George's County), patriot who was noted by the Council of Maryland on 10 Aug 1779 as stating, in part, that he was *"a person who took the Oath of Fidelity and Support to the State according to Act of Assembly, having requested Leave to have an Interview on the Lines with his Uncle Lieut. Rignal Hilliary of the Maryland Continental Troops now a Prisoner in New York in Order to supply him with what is necessary to render his Situation less disagreeable and for a Recommendation to the commanding Officer on the Lines to promote such Interview. This Board gives the Leave requested."* {Ref: Archives of Maryland Vol. 21, p. 490}

GEARY, SAMUEL (Prince George's County), private (substitute) in the Maryland Continental Line by 1781, was discharged on 8 Dec 1781. {Ref: Archives of Maryland Vol. 48, p. 10}

GEDDIS (GEDDES), HENRY (Baltimore Privateer), commander of the sloop *Rising Sun*, navigated by 8 men and mounting 2 carriage guns and 4 carbines, was issued Letters of Marque & Reprisal by the Council of Maryland on 3 Apr 1778; commander of the sloop *Savage*, navigated by 12 men and mounting 4 carriage guns and 4 swivel guns, was issued Letters of Marque & Reprisal by the Council of Maryland on 25 Jun 1778; commander of the sloop *Richmond*, navigated by 12 men and mounting 2 carriage guns, 6 cohorn guns and 6 small arms, was issued Letters of Marque & Reprisal by the Council of Maryland on 25 Jun 1778; commander of the schooner *Greyhound*, mounting 6 carriage guns, 6 swivel guns and 11 small arms, was issued Letters of Marque & Reprisal by the Council of Maryland on 17 Jul 1779. {Ref: Archives of Maryland Vol. 21, pp. 6, 150, 210, 475}

GEORGE, ANDREW (Baltimore County), private who enlisted in Pulaski's Legion on 22 Mar 1778 and still in service in November, 1779. {Ref: Maryland Historical Magazine, Vol. 13, No. 3, p. 223}

GERNSLY, HENRY (Maryland Navy), sailor or seaman on 7 Jan 1780. {Ref: Calendar of Maryland State Papers, The Brown Books, p. 57}

GHISELIN, MARY (Annapolis), patriot who was paid £42 by the State Treasurer *"for the hire of her negro man to work at the Tanyard per account passed by the Auditor General"* on 5 Jun 1778. {Ref: Archives of Maryland Vol. 21, p. 123}

GHISELIN, REVERDY, see "Elijah Robosson," q.v.

GIBBONS, EDWARD (Maryland Navy), marine on the State Ship *Defence* in 1777. {Ref: Archives of Maryland Vol. 18, p. 656}

GIBBONS, JOHN (Baltimore Town), recommendation made on 5 Nov 1776 to the Council of Maryland by Jesse Hollingsworth stating, in part, that he *"has been in Baltimore this 2 years, and has behaved himself sober and well as far as I have heard, and is a Industrious yongue man, is willing to take charge of the Skooner Frendship and I believe him fit for the Task, he waits on you to No it if is agreeable."* {Ref: Archives of Maryland Vol. 12, p. 424}

GIBSON, JOHN (Harford County), private who was enrolled by 15 Apr 1776 in Militia Company No. 20 under Capt. Robert Glenn; see "Jesse Dungan," q.v. {Ref: George W. Archer Collection and Revolutionary War File, Historical Society of Harford County Archives}

GIBSON, JOHN LEE (Harford County), patriot who was commissioned one of the three persons in Harford County by the Council of Maryland on 19 Aug 1779 to receive subscriptions for use of the State. {Ref: Archives of Maryland Vol. 21, p. 499}

GIBSON, JONATHAN (Queen Anne's County), captain in the 5th Maryland Continental Line who received payment for his services in the amount of "1900 Dollars & £3.10s" on 12 Sep 1780. {Ref: Archives of Maryland Vol. 45, p. 98}

GIBSON, JOSHUA (Maryland Navy), marine on the State Ship *Defence* in 1777. {Ref: Archives of Maryland Vol. 18, p. 656}

GIBSON, RACHEL, see "Jonathan Hopkins," q.v.

GIBSON, WOOLMAN, see "Jonathan Hopkins," q.v.

GIFFORD, JOHN (Baltimore Privateer), commander of the brigantine *Randolph*, navigated by 28 men and mounting 8 carriage guns, was issued Letters of Marque & Reprisal by the Council of Maryland on 7 Sep 1780. {Ref: Archives of Maryland Vol. 43, p. 280}

GILBERT, ABNER, see "Parker Gilbert," q.v.

GILBERT, AQUILA (Harford County, Susquehannah Hundred), private who was enrolled 23 Apr 1776 in Militia Company No. 21 under Capt. George Patterson. {Ref: George W. Archer Collection and Revolutionary War File, Historical Society of Harford County Archives}

GILBERT, CHARLES (Harford County, Susquehannah Hundred), private who was enrolled 23 Apr 1776 in Militia Company No. 21 under Capt. George Patterson; one Charles Gilbert died by 8 Mar 1825 (date of final distribution) and his heirs were sons Jarvis, James, Charles, Michael, Ephraim, John, and Taylor Gilbert, and daughters Ann Anderson, Mary Weeks, and Elizabeth and Comfort Gilbert. {Ref: George W. Archer Collection and Revolutionary War File, Historical Society of Harford County Archives; Henry C. Peden, Jr.'s *Heirs & Legatees of Harford County, 1802-1846*, p. 32}

GILBERT, COMFORT, see "Charles Gilbert," q.v.

GILBERT, ELIZABETH, see "Parker Gilbert" and "Charles Gilbert," q.v.

GILBERT, EPHRAIM, see "Charles Gilbert," q.v.

GILBERT, HANNAH, see "John H. Hughes," q.v.

GILBERT, JAMES (Harford County, Susquehannah Hundred), private who was enrolled 23 Apr 1776 in Militia Company No. 21 under Capt. George Patterson. {Ref: George W. Archer Collection and Revolutionary War File, Historical Society of Harford County Archives}

GILBERT, JAMES, see "Charles Gilbert," q.v.

GILBERT, JARVIS, see "Charles Gilbert," q.v.

GILBERT, JOHN, see "Charles Gilbert," q.v.

GILBERT, MARTHA, see "Aaron McComas," q.v.

GILBERT, MARY, see "John H. Hughes," q.v.

GILBERT, MICHAEL (Harford County, Susquehannah Hundred), ensign on 23 Apr 1776 in Militia Company No. 21 under Capt. George Patterson. {Ref: George W. Archer Collection and Revolutionary War File, Historical Society of Harford County Archives}

GILBERT, MICHAEL, see "Charles Gilbert," q.v.

GILBERT, PARKER (Harford County, Susquehannah Hundred), private who was enrolled 23 Apr 1776 in Militia Company No. 21 under Capt. George Patterson; Parker Gilbert died by 13 Oct 1812 (date of final distribution) and his heirs were: Elizabeth Gilbert (widow); son Abner Gilbert; daughters Sarah Bennett, Priscilla Mitchell, and Hannah Hughes; heirs of Parker Gilbert; and, heirs of Mary McComas. {Ref: George W. Archer Collection and Revolutionary War File, Historical Society of Harford County Archives; Henry C. Peden, Jr.'s *Heirs & Legatees of Harford County, 1802-1846*, p. 18}

GILBERT, PARKER, JR., see "John H. Hughes," q.v.

GILBERT, SAMUEL (Harford County, Susquehannah Hundred), private who was enrolled 23 Apr 1776 in Militia Company No. 21 under Capt. George Patterson.

{Ref: George W. Archer Collection and Revolutionary War File, Historical Society of Harford County Archives}

TAYLOR, TAYLOR, see "Charles Gilbert," q.v.

GILBY, HENRY (Maryland Navy), ordinary sailor on the State Ship *Defence* in 1777. {Ref: Archives of Maryland Vol. 18, p. 656}

GILBY, THOMAS (Maryland Navy), ordinary sailor on the State Ship *Defence* in 1777. {Ref: Archives of Maryland Vol. 18, p. 656}

GILES, EDWARD (Southern Maryland), major, commissioned on 27 Jul 1780 to serve in the Regiment Extra by order of the Council of Maryland. {Ref: Archives of Maryland Vol. 43, p. 234}

GILFORD, JAMES (Maryland Navy), ordinary sailor on the State Ship *Defence* in 1777. {Ref: Archives of Maryland Vol. 18, p. 656}

GILLILAND, THOMAS (Western Maryland), private in Capt. Michael Cresap's Company in 1775. {Ref: Howard L. Leckey's *The Tenmile Country and Its Pioneer Families*, p. 15}

GILLIS, THOMAS (Maryland Navy), third mate on the State Ship *Defence* in 1777. {Ref: Archives of Maryland Vol. 18, p. 656}

GILLISPIE, JAMES (Southern Maryland), captain, commissioned on 27 Jul 1780 to serve in the Regiment Extra by order of the Council of Maryland. {Ref: Archives of Maryland Vol. 43, p. 234}

GILLUM, THOMAS (Charles County), private (substitute) in the Maryland Continental Line by 1781, was discharged on 11 Dec 1781. {Ref: Archives of Maryland Vol. 48, p. 18}

GILMORE, JANE, see "John E. Howard," q.v.

GILPIN, BENJAMIN (Montgomery County), private (substitute) in the Maryland Continental Line by 1781, was discharged on 10 Dec 1781. {Ref: Archives of Maryland Vol. 48, p. 17}

GILPIN, JOSEPH (Cecil County), patriot who was appointed by the Council of Maryland on 27 Jan 1776 as one of three persons in Cecil County to collect all the gold and silver coin that can be procured in said county; commissioned on 19 Aug 1779 as one of the three persons in Cecil County to receive subscriptions for use of the State. {Ref: Archives of Maryland Vol. 11, p. 132 and Vol. 21, p. 499}

GILMOR, ROBERT, JR. (Baltimore Town), patriot and merchant who enrolled in Capt. John Sterrett's Independent Mercantile Company by February, 1777, at which time they were mustered into regular service with the continental army to repress loyalist activities in the Eastern Shore counties of Somerset and Worcester. {Ref: J. Thomas Scharf's *History of Baltimore City and County*, Part I, p. 77}

GILMOR, WILLIAM (Baltimore Town), patriot and merchant who enrolled in Capt. John Sterrett's Independent Mercantile Company by February, 1777, at which time they were mustered into regular service with the continental army

98

to repress loyalist activities in the Eastern Shore counties of Somerset and Worcester. {Ref: J. Thomas Scharf's *History of Baltimore City and County*, Part I, p. 77}

GIST, JOHN (Maryland Continental Line, Staff Officer, Gist's Regiment), captain who received payment for his services in the amount of "1900 Dollars & £3.10s" on 12 Sep 1780. {Ref: Archives of Maryland Vol. 45, p. 98}

GIST, MORDECAI (Baltimore County), colonel of the 3rd Maryland Continental Line in 1776 and brigadier general of the 2nd Maryland Continental Line in 1779; received payment for his services in the amount of "1900 Dollars & £3.10s" on 12 Sep 1780. For additional information see Peden's *Revolutionary Patriots of Baltimore Town and Baltimore County, 1775-1783* (pp. 101-102). {Ref: Archives of Maryland Vol. 45, p. 97}

GITTING (GEETING), GEORGE (Washington County), private in the German Regiment, 1776-1779, as noted in Peden's *Revolutionary Patriots of Washington County, 1776-1783* (p. 136); subsequent research indicates that *"Rev. George Gitting was born in 1741, not 1711, came to America at the age of 18, lived near Antietam, and was pastor of Evangelical United Brethren Church in Washington County; he attended a session at Otterbein Church in Baltimore in 1812 and died on his way home."* {Ref: Research by Jane Newhart of Edgewood, Maryland (a direct descendant) in 1999, citing C. David Wright's *Encyclopedia of World Methodism*}

GIVENS, GEORGE (Baltimore County), private, aged 20, labourer, born in Ireland, enlisted 26 Feb 1776 in Capt. John Fulford's Company of Matrosses. {Ref: Maryland Historical Magazine, Vol. 69, No. 1, p. 95}

GLASCOW, WILLIAM (Charles County), private (substitute) in the Maryland Continental Line by 1781, was discharged on 8 Dec 1781. {Ref: Archives of Maryland Vol. 48, p. 11}

GLAZE, JOHN (Western Maryland), private in Capt. Michael Cresap's Company in 1775. {Ref: Howard L. Leckey's *The Tenmile Country and Its Pioneer Families*, p. 15}

GLENN, JAMES (Maryland Navy), midshipman on 7 Jan 1780. {Ref: Calendar of Maryland State Papers, The Brown Books, p. 57}

GLENN, JOSEPH (Harford County), private who was enrolled 10 Mar 1776 in Militia Company No. 18 under Capt. John Jolly. {Ref: George W. Archer Collection and Revolutionary War File, Historical Society of Harford County Archives}

GLENN, MICHAEL (Maryland Navy), sailor or seaman on 7 Jan 1780. {Ref: Calendar of Maryland State Papers, The Brown Books, p. 57}

GLENN, ROBERT (Harford County), private who was enrolled 10 Mar 1776 in Militia Company No. 18 under Capt. John Jolly. {Ref: George W. Archer Collection and Revolutionary War File, Historical Society of Harford County Archives}

GLENN, ROBERT (Harford County), captain by 15 Apr 1776 in Militia Company No. 20. {Ref: George W. Archer Collection and Revolutionary War File, Historical Society of Harford County Archives}

GLOURY, WILLIAM (Harford County), private who was enrolled by Capt. Praul in the Regiment Extraordinary and sent to Annapolis with Capt. Thompson on board the sloop *Liberty* on 17 Aug 1780. {Ref: Archives of Maryland Vol. 45, p. 50}

GODWIN, WILLIAM, JR. (Baltimore Town), patriot and merchant who enrolled in Capt. John Sterrett's Independent Mercantile Company by February, 1777, at which time they were mustered into regular service with the continental army to repress loyalist activities in the Eastern Shore counties of Somerset and Worcester. {Ref: J. Thomas Scharf's *History of Baltimore City and County*, Part I, p. 77}

GOLDER, ARCHIBALD (Annapolis), lieutenant, commissioned on 27 Jul 1780 to serve in the Regiment Extra by order of the Council of Maryland; he was appointed *"to provide Quarters for the French Army, on their March through, and during their Stay in this State, and to procure Waggons, Carts, Teams and Drivers, Vessels and hands for the Carriages and Transportation of their Baggage through the State"* on 18 Jul 1782; John Golder was administrator of the estate of Archibald Golder, deceased, on 2 Apr 1812 and the heirs were widow Sarah and children John Golder, Henrietta Golder, Archibald Golder, Robert Golder, and George Golder. {Ref: Archives of Maryland Vol. 43, p. 234 and Vol. 48, p. 217; Anne Arundel County Administration Account JG No. 3, p. 4}

GOLDSBOROUGH, ANN, see "Jacob Jeffers," q.v.

GOLDSBOROUGH, GREENBURY (Talbot County), patriot who was appointed by the Council of Maryland on 27 Jan 1776 as one of three persons in Talbot County to collect all gold and silver coin that can be procured in said county. {Ref: Archives of Maryland Vol. 11, p. 132}

GOLDSBURY, JOHN (Maryland Navy), marine on the State Ship *Defence* in 1777. {Ref: Archives of Maryland Vol. 18, p. 656}

GOLDSBURY, STEPHEN (Maryland Navy), marine on the State Ship *Defence* from 23 Oct 1777 to 15 Nov 1777 when *"discharged, being unfit for duty."* {Ref: Archives of Maryland Vol. 18, p. 656}

GOMAS, JOHN (Maryland Navy), sailor or seaman on 7 Jan 1780. {Ref: Calendar of Maryland State Papers, The Brown Books, p. 57}

GOOD, REBECCA, see "Patrick Faux," q.v.

GOODWIN, LYDE (Baltimore Town), doctor who was appointed Surgeon of the Troops of Horse raised in this State and ordered into actual service on 9 Jun 1781. {Ref: Archives of Maryland Vol. 45, p. 467}

GOODWIN, RICHARD (Anne Arundel County), patriot who took the Oath of Fidelity and Allegiance to the State of Maryland on 31 Mar 1778; Thomas Robinson was executor of the estate of Richard Goodwin, deceased, on 19 Jan 1797. {Ref: Archives of Maryland Vol. 16, p. 559; Anne Arundel County Administration Account JG No. 1, p. 71}

GORDON, DANIEL (Frederick County), soldier in the Revolution who died in Harbaugh's Valley on 5 Jul 1838, aged 81. {Ref: *Frederick Times and Democratic Advocate*, 2 Aug 1838}

GORDON, FRANCIS (Harford County), private who was enrolled by 15 Apr 1776 in Militia Company No. 20 under Capt. Robert Glenn. {Ref: George W. Archer Collection and Revolutionary War File, Historical Society of Harford County Archives}

GORDON, GEORGE (Harford County), patriot who contracted with the Council of Safety on 24 Sep 1776 to make 2,000 cartouch boxes, bayonet belts, and gun slings. {Ref: Archives of Maryland Vol. 12, p. 297}

GORDON, HENRY, see "Daniel Smith," q.v.

GORDON, ISAAC MOUNT (Maryland Navy), sergeant of marines on the State Ship *Defence* in 1777. {Ref: Archives of Maryland Vol. 18, p. 656}

GORDON, JAMES (Harford County), private who was enrolled 10 Mar 1776 in Militia Company No. 18 under Capt. John Jolly. {Ref: George W. Archer Collection and Revolutionary War File, Historical Society of Harford County Archives}

GORDON, JOHN (Baltimore Town), patriot and merchant who enrolled in Capt. John Sterrett's Independent Mercantile Company by February, 1777, at which time they were mustered into regular service with the continental army to repress loyalist activities in the Eastern Shore counties of Somerset and Worcester. {Ref: J. Thomas Scharf's *History of Baltimore City and County*, Part I, p. 77}

GORDON, JOHN (Maryland Navy), first lieutenant of the row galley *Johnson*, commissioned 8 May 1777; captain by 7 Jan 1780. {Ref: Archives of Maryland Vol. 16, p. 244; Calendar of Maryland State Papers, The Brown Books, p. 57}

GORDON, ROBERT (Harford County), private who was enrolled 25 Mar 1776 in Militia Company No. 19 under Capt. William Morgan. {Ref: George W. Archer Collection and Revolutionary War File, Historical Society of Harford County Archives}

GORDON, ROBERT (Harford County), private who was enrolled by 15 Apr 1776 in Militia Company No. 20 under Capt. Robert Glenn. {Ref: George W. Archer Collection and Revolutionary War File, Historical Society of Harford County Archives}

GORDON, SERGEANT, see "James Marr," q.v.

GORDON, WILLIAM (Frederick County), patriot buried in Mount Olivet Cemetery. {Ref: Information compiled by Dr. Donald Wolf in Maryland Society SAR Newsletter circa 1996}

GORMAN, JOHN (Baltimore County), private, aged 27, labourer, born in Ireland, enlisted (made his "X" mark) on 1 Mar 1776 in Capt. John Fulford's Company of Matrosses. {Ref: Maryland Historical Magazine, Vol. 69, No. 1, p. 96}

GORRELL, JOHN (Harford County, Susquehannah Hundred), private who was enrolled 23 Apr 1776 in Militia Company No. 21 under Capt. George Patterson. {Ref: George W. Archer Collection and Revolutionary War File, Historical Society of Harford County Archives}

GORRELL, THOMAS (Harford County, Susquehannah Hundred), private who was enrolled 23 Apr 1776 in Militia Company No. 21 under Capt. George Patterson. {Ref: George W. Archer Collection and Revolutionary War File, Historical Society of Harford County Archives}

GORSUCH, ELIZABETH, see "Luke Merryman," q.v.

GORSUCH, JOHN (Baltimore County), private, 31 May 1779, Capt. Benjamin Talbott's Militia Company, Cockey's Battalion. {Ref: Maryland Historical Magazine, Vol. 7, No. 1, p. 90}

GORSUCH, ROBERT, see "Richard Donovan," q.v.

GOTT, RICHARD (Baltimore County), private, 31 May 1779, Capt. Benjamin Talbott's Militia Company, Cockey's Battalion. {Ref: Maryland Historical Magazine, Vol. 7, No. 1, p. 90}

GOUGH, BAPTIST (St. Mary's County), private (substitute) in the Maryland Continental Line by 1781, was discharged on 8 Dec 1781. {Ref: Archives of Maryland Vol. 48, p. 11}

GOUGH, CHARLES (St. Mary's County), private (substitute) in the Maryland Continental Line by 1781, was discharged on 8 Dec 1781. {Ref: Archives of Maryland Vol. 48, p. 11}

GOULD, JAMES (Queen Anne's County), lieutenant in the 5th Maryland Continental Line who received payment for his services in the amount of "1900 Dollars & £3.10s" on 12 Sep 1780. {Ref: Archives of Maryland Vol. 45, p. 98}

GOULD, JAMES (Maryland Privateer), commander of the schooner *Hope*, navigated by 12 men and mounting 6 carriage guns and 5 small arms, was issued Letters of Marque & Reprisal by the Council of Maryland on 12 Jan 1781. {Ref: Archives of Maryland Vol. 45, pp. 272-273}

GOVANE, JAMES (Baltimore County), contractor for horses in Baltimore County in 1781. {Ref: Archives of Maryland Vol. 45, p. 391}

GOVER, MARTHA, see "William Prigg," q.v.

GRAHAME, JOHN, see "Thomas Johnson, Jr.," q.v.

GRANT, JOHN (Maryland Navy), carpenter's mate on the State Ship *Defence* in 1777. {Ref: Archives of Maryland Vol. 18, p. 656}

GRANT, THOMAS (Baltimore County), private (substitute) in the Maryland Continental Line by 1781, was discharged on 8 Dec 1781. {Ref: Archives of Maryland Vol. 48, p. 11}

GRANTHAM, HENRY (Frederick County), private (substitute) in the Maryland Continental Line, Williams' Regiment, enrolled in May, 1778 for 3 years or duration of the war. {Ref: Maryland Historical Magazine, Vol. 6, No. 3, p. 258}

GRANTHAM, WILLIAM (Maryland Navy), marine on the State Ship *Defence* in 1777. {Ref: Archives of Maryland Vol. 18, p. 656}

GRASON, GEORGE (Maryland Navy), sailor or seaman on 7 Jan 1780. {Ref: Calendar of Maryland State Papers, The Brown Books, p. 57}

GRASON, RICHARD (Maryland Navy), midshipman on 7 Jan 1780. {Ref: Calendar of Maryland State Papers, The Brown Books, p. 57}

GRASON, THOMAS (Maryland Navy), commodore by 7 Jan 1780; commodore of the State barge *Revenge* on 16 Jun 1781 at which time he received provisions from the Issuing Commissary. {Ref: Archives of Maryland Vol. 45, pp. 476-477; Calendar of Maryland State Papers, The Brown Books, p. 57}

GRASON, THOMAS, JR. (Maryland Navy), lieutenant on 7 Jan 1780. {Ref: Calendar of Maryland State Papers, The Brown Books, p. 57}

GRAVES, RICHARD (Kent County), first major of the 13th Battalion of Militia, commissioned 8 May 1777; one Richard Graves died testate in Kent County by 15 Oct 1792. {Ref: Archives of Maryland Vol. 16, p. 243; Kent County Wills Liber 7, p. 368}

GRAY, WOOLFORD, see "William Simmons," q.v.

GRAYBELL, ISAAC (Baltimore Town), patriot and merchant who enrolled in Capt. John Sterrett's Independent Mercantile Company by February, 1777, at which time they were mustered into regular service with the continental army to repress loyalist activities in the Eastern Shore counties of Somerset and Worcester. {Ref: J. Thomas Scharf's *History of Baltimore City and County*, Part I, p. 77}

GRAYHAM, RICHARD (Maryland Navy), sailor or seaman on 7 Jan 1780. {Ref: Calendar of Maryland State Papers, The Brown Books, p. 57}

GREATHOUSE, DANIEL (Western Maryland), sergeant in Capt. Michael Cresap's Company in 1775. {Ref: Howard L. Leckey's *The Tenmile Country and Its Pioneer Families*, p. 15}

GREEN, DAVID (Frederick and Montgomery Counties), private and later ensign in the 1st and 7th Maryland Continental Lines who received payment for his services in the amount of "1900 Dollars & £3.10s" on 12 Sep 1780. {Ref: Archives of Maryland Vol. 45, p. 98}

GREEN, ELISHA (Somerset County), private who was drafted into the Maryland Continental Line, was discharged on 8 Dec 1781. {Ref: Archives of Maryland Vol. 48, p. 10}

GREEN, JAMES (Maryland Navy), midshipman on the State Ship *Defence* in 1777. {Ref: Archives of Maryland Vol. 18, p. 656}

GREEN, JOHN (Maryland Navy), captain on 7 Jan 1780. {Ref: Calendar of Maryland State Papers, The Brown Books, p. 57}

GREEN, ROBERT (Frederick and Montgomery Counties), sergeant and later ensign in the 1st and 7th Maryland Continental Lines who received payment for his services in the amount of "1900 Dollars & £3.10s" on 12 Sep 1780. For additional information see Peden's *Revolutionary Patriots of Montgomery County, 1776-1783* (p. 134). {Ref: Archives of Maryland Vol. 45, p. 98}

GREEN, RICHARD (Harford County), private who was enrolled by 15 Apr 1776 in Militia Company No. 20 under Capt. Robert Glenn. {Ref: George W. Archer Collection and Revolutionary War File, Historical Society of Harford County Archives}

GREENLAND, RICHARD (Harford County, Susquehannah Hundred), private who was enrolled 23 Apr 1776 in Militia Company No. 21 under Capt. George Patterson. {Ref: George W. Archer Collection and Revolutionary War File, Historical Society of Harford County Archives}

GREENWAY, JOSEPH (Maryland Privateer), commander of the brigantine *Virginia*, navigated by 24 men and mounting 8 carriage guns, 4 swivel guns and

8 muskets, was issued Letters of Marque & Reprisal by the Council of Maryland on 11 Apr 1780. {Ref: Archives of Maryland Vol. 43, p. 137}

GREENWOOD, JOHN (Dorchester County), private (substitute) in the Maryland Continental Line by 1781, was discharged on 8 Dec 1781. {Ref: Archives of Maryland Vol. 48, p. 10}

GREER, JAMES (Maryland Navy), marine on the State Ship *Defence* in 1777. {Ref: Archives of Maryland Vol. 18, p. 656}

GREER, MOSES (Maryland Navy), marine on the State Ship *Defence* in 1777. {Ref: Archives of Maryland Vol. 18, p. 656}

GREGORY, QURELLA, see "Charles Close," q.v.

GREYER, MOSES (Worcester County), private (substitute) in the Maryland Continental Line by 1781, was discharged on 8 Dec 1781. {Ref: Archives of Maryland Vol. 48, p. 11}

GREYLESS, JESSE (Caroline County), patriot who was appointed captain in the 14th Militia Battalion by the Council of Maryland on 28 Jun 1780 in the room of James Douglass. {Ref: Archives of Maryland Vol. 43, p. 207}

GRIDER, MICHAEL (Frederick County), soldier who allegedly served in the Pennsylvania Line and applied for pension in Frederick County on 17 Sep 1835, aged 75, under the Act of June 7, 1832, but the claim was suspended *"pending proof from the archives at Harrisburg."* {Ref: *Rejected or Suspended Applications for Revolutionary War Pensions* (1850 Report), p. 231; Research by Virgil D. White, citing Federal Pension Application R4303}

GRIFFIN, IGNATIUS (St. Mary's County), private who was drafted to serve in the Maryland Continental Line until 10 Dec 1781, but *"being represented unfit for the duty for which he was intended"* was discharged on 30 Oct 1781. {Ref: Archives of Maryland Vol. 45, p. 656}

GRIFFIN, WILLIAM (Prince George's County), private who was drafted into the Maryland Continental Line, was discharged on 8 Dec 1781. {Ref: Archives of Maryland Vol. 48, p. 10}

GRIFFITH, ALEXANDER, see "Samuel Griffith," q.v.

GRIFFITH, BENJAMIN (Baltimore County), patriot who was *"appointed Agent for Purchasing Provisions in Baltimore County in the room of John Sterrett who declined by reason of his having lately removed into Anne Arundel County"* on 9 Apr 1778; served as Commissary of Stores in 1782. {Ref: Archives of Maryland Vol. 21, p. 22 and Vol. 48, p. 78}

GRIFFITH, CHRISTOPHER GREENBURY (Montgomery County), patriot who was commissioned one of the three persons in Montgomery County by the Council of Maryland on 19 Aug 1779 to receive subscriptions for use of the State. {Ref: Archives of Maryland Vol. 21, p. 499}

GRIFFITH, EDWARD, see "Samuel Griffith," q.v.

GRIFFITH, ESTHER, see "Thomas Longfellow," q.v.

GRIFFITH, EVAN (Harford County), private who was enrolled 10 Mar 1776 in Militia Company No. 18 under Capt. John Jolly. {Ref: George W. Archer Collection and Revolutionary War File, Historical Society of Harford County Archives}

GRIFFITH, FRANCES, see "Samuel Griffith," q.v.

GRIFFITH, HENRY (Frederick County), patriot who was appointed by the Council of Maryland on 27 Jan 1776 as one of three persons in Frederick County to collect all gold and silver coin that can be procured in said county. {Ref: Archives of Maryland Vol. 11, p. 132}

GRIFFITH, JOHN (Anne Arundel County), private by 5 Oct 1776 (made his "X" mark) in Capt. Richard Chew's Militia Company, Weems' Battalion. {Ref: Archives of Maryland Vol. 12, p. 323}

GRIFFITH, JOHN H., see "Samuel Griffith," q.v.

GRIFFITH, LUKE, see "Samuel Griffith," q.v.

GRIFFITH, MARTHA, see "Samuel Griffith," q.v.

GRIFFITH, PHILIMON (Frederick County), colonel and *"veteran of the Revolutionary War who died at his home near New Market on Sunday evening last in his 82nd year; throughout a long life he maintained an unblemished character."* {Ref: *The Times and Democratic Advocate*, 3 May 1838}

GRIFFITH, SALLY, see "Samuel Griffith," q.v.

GRIFFITH, SAMUEL (Harford County), captain, commissioned 16 May 1776 in Militia Company No. 27; Samuel Griffith died by 1 Mar 1803 (date of final distribution) and his heirs were Martha Griffith (widow), Miss Frances Griffith, Miss Sally Griffith, Samuel G. Griffith, John Hall Griffith, Edward Griffith, Luke Griffith, Alexander Griffith, Martha Smith, and Miss Frances Garrettson. {Ref: George W. Archer Collection and Revolutionary War File, Historical Society of Harford County Archives; Henry C. Peden, Jr.'s *Heirs & Legatees of Harford County, 1802-1846*, p. 5}

GRIFFITH, THOMAS (Western Maryland), private in Capt. Michael Cresap's Company in 1775. {Ref: Howard L. Leckey's *The Tenmile Country and Its Pioneer Families*, p. 15}

GRINAGE, BENJAMIN (Queen Anne's County), private (substitute) in the Maryland Continental Line by 1781, was discharged on 8 Dec 1781. {Ref: Archives of Maryland Vol. 48, p. 11}

GRINNAL, JOHN (St. Mary's County), private (substitute) in the Maryland Continental Line by 1781, was discharged on 8 Dec 1781. {Ref: Archives of Maryland Vol. 48, p. 11}

GROOME, CHARLES (Baltimore County), private, aged 34, barber, born in England, enlisted 16 Feb 1776 in Capt. John Fulford's Company of Matrosses. {Ref: Maryland Historical Magazine, Vol. 69, No. 1, p. 95}

GROSH, ANDREW (Frederick County), private soldier who had neglected to march with the militia, petitioned the Council of Maryland on 14 Sep 1782 stating, in part, that *"he was fined by a Militia Court Martial for a neglect of Militia Duty to the amount of £20, and that he is not an able bodied man or fit for Militia Duty having had a rupture for ten years past and other Sickness, which has rendered him hardly able to assist his Family and having a Wife and six small Children who depend on his labour for Subsistence."* Both he and the fine were subsequently discharged. {Ref: Archives of Maryland Vol. 48, p. 263}

GUESS, BASIL (Anne Arundel County), private by 5 Oct 1776 (made his "+" mark) in Capt. Richard Chew's Militia Company, Weems' Battalion. {Ref: Archives of Maryland Vol. 12, p. 323}

GULLEHAN, JOHN (Maryland Navy), seaman or marine on the State Ship *Defence* in 1777. {Ref: Archives of Maryland Vol. 18, p. 656}

GUNBY, JOHN (Somerset County), colonel in the 7th Maryland Continental Line who received payment for his services in the amount of "1900 Dollars & £3.10s" on 12 Sep 1780; see "James Bryant," q.v. {Ref: Archives of Maryland Vol. 45, p. 98}

GUYTON, ABRAM (Harford County), private who was enrolled by 15 Apr 1776 in Militia Company No. 20 under Capt. Robert Glenn. {Ref: George W. Archer Collection and Revolutionary War File, Historical Society of Harford County Archives}

GUYTON, JOSHUA (Harford County), private who was enrolled by 15 Apr 1776 in Militia Company No. 20 under Capt. Robert Glenn. {Ref: George W. Archer Collection and Revolutionary War File, Historical Society of Harford County Archives}

HACK, DANIEL (Frederick County), private (substitute) in the Maryland Continental Line, who enlisted to serve until 10 Dec 1781, was discharged on 29 Nov 1781. {Ref: Archives of Maryland Vol. 48, p. 7}

HACKET, JAMES (Caroline County), private in Col. Richardson's Regiment in 1776 who was *"a prisoner and good soldier"* recommended for promotion. {Ref: Archives of Maryland Vol. 18, p. 74}

HADDAWAY, OAKLEY (Caroline County), private in Col. Richardson's Regiment in 1776 who was recommended for promotion. {Ref: Archives of Maryland Vol. 18, p. 74}

HADLEY, SAMUEL (Queen Anne's County), private (substitute) in the Maryland Continental Line by 1781, was discharged on 8 Dec 1781. {Ref: Archives of Maryland Vol. 48, p. 10}

HAFLEY, STEPHEN (Frederick County), private (substitute) in the Maryland Continental Line by 1781, was discharged on 8 Dec 1781. {Ref: Archives of Maryland Vol. 48, p. 11}

HAGAN (HAGANS), CHARLES (Maryland Navy), cooper's mate on the State Ship *Defence* in 1777. {Ref: Archives of Maryland Vol. 18, p. 657}

HAGERTY, GEORGE (Frederick County), private (substitute) in the Maryland Continental Line, Price's Regiment, enrolled in May, 1778 for 3 years or duration of the war. {Ref: Maryland Historical Magazine, Vol. 6, No. 3, p. 259}

HAGIN, CHARLES (Prince George's County), private (substitute) in the Maryland Continental Line by 1781, was discharged on 8 Dec 1781. {Ref: Archives of Maryland Vol. 48, p. 10}

HAIR, ROBERT (Harford County), private who was enrolled by 15 Apr 1776 in Militia Company No. 20 under Capt. Robert Glenn. {Ref: George W. Archer Collection and Revolutionary War File, Historical Society of Harford County Archives}

HALDUP, THOMAS (Frederick County), private (substitute) in the Maryland Continental Line, German Regiment, enrolled in April, 1778 for 3 years or duration of the war. {Ref: Maryland Historical Magazine, Vol. 6, No. 3, p. 257}

HALE, HENRY (Baltimore County), private, 31 May 1779, Capt. Benjamin Talbott's Militia Company, Cockey's Battalion. {Ref: Maryland Historical Magazine, Vol. 7, No. 1, p. 90}

HALE, JOHN, see "John Hall," q.v.

HALE, NATHAN (Baltimore County), sergeant, 31 May 1779, Capt. Benjamin Talbott's Militia Company, Cockey's Battalion. {Ref: Maryland Historical Magazine, Vol. 7, No. 1, p. 90}

HALE, NICHOLAS, OF G. (Baltimore County), private, 31 May 1779, Capt. Benjamin Talbott's Militia Company, Cockey's Battalion. {Ref: Maryland Historical Magazine, Vol. 7, No. 1, p. 90}

HALE, NICHOLAS, JR. (Baltimore County), private, 31 May 1779, Capt. Benjamin Talbott's Militia Company, Cockey's Battalion. {Ref: Maryland Historical Magazine, Vol. 7, No. 1, p. 90}

HALES, HUGH, see "Lawrence Keenan," q.v.

HALES, MARY, see "Lawrence Keenan," q.v.

HALEY, THOMAS (Baltimore County), private, aged 20, farmer, born in Maryland, enlisted 12 Mar 1776 in Capt. John Fulford's Company of Matrosses. {Ref: Maryland Historical Magazine, Vol. 69, No. 1, p. 96}

HALFPENNY, THOMAS (Frederick County), private (substitute) in the Maryland Continental Line, enrolled in April, 1778 for 3 years or duration of the war. {Ref: Maryland Historical Magazine, Vol. 6, No. 3, p. 256}

HALKERSTON (HALKERSTONE), ROBERT (Charles County), sergeant in the 3rd Maryland Continental Line, 1777-1780; commissioned ensign on 9 Jan 1780 and later lieutenant in the 4th Maryland Line; received payment for his services in the amount of "1900 Dollars & £3.10s" on 12 Sep 1780. For additional information see Peden's *Revolutionary Patriots of Charles County, 1775-1783* (pp. 126-127). {Ref: Archives of Maryland Vol. 45, p. 97}

HALL, ANN, see "Thomas Hall," q.v.

HALL, AQUILA (Harford County), signer of the Bush Declaration on 22 Mar 1775, captain of militia on 9 Sep 1775, and colonel of the Upper Battalion on 1 Jan 1776; one of three persons appointed by the Council of Maryland to collect all gold and silver coin that can be procured in said county on 28 Jan 1776; appointed County Lieutenant on 29 Jun 1777 and also served as a Justice of the Orphans Court; born 10 Jan 1727 in Baltimore County, Aquila Hall married Sophia White on 14 Feb 1750 and died testate at *Sophia's Dairy* in Harford County by 10 Apr 1779 (date of probate); his heirs were widow Sophia

Hall (who died testate on 2 Jan 1785, aged 54) and children: Thomas Hall (born 27 Dec 1750, married Isabella Presbury); Aquila Hall (born 2 Sep 1753); James White Hall (born 8 Dec 1765, married Sarah Stokes Brooke); William Hall (born 31 Jul 1756, married Sophia Presbury); Charlotte Hall (born 11 Feb 1758, married Nathaniel Ramsay); Mary Hall (born 25 Jan 1760, married Richard Key Heath); John Hall (born 8 Mar 1762); Edward Hall (born 30 Dec 1763); Sophia Hall (born 6 Dec 1765, married Philip Key); Martha Hall (born 8 Mar 1768, married John Henry or McHenry); Elizabeth Hall (born 7 Feb 1770); and, Benedict Hall (born 11 Dec 1771); also see "James Allison," q.v. {Ref: Archives of Maryland Vol. 11, p. 132; Harford County Wills Liber AJ No. 2, pp. 274-275, 280-281; *Harford Historical Bulletin* (No. 34, Fall, 1987, pp. 71-75); Maryland State Society DAR Directory, 1892-1965, p. 356}

HALL, BENEDICT, see "Aquila Hall," q.v.

HALL, BLANCHE, see "John B. Howard," q.v.

HALL, CHARLOTTE, see "Aquila Hall," q.v.

HALL, EDWARD, see "Aquila Hall," q.v.

HALL, GEORGE (Baltimore County), private, aged 25, weaver, born in England, enlisted (made his "X" mark) on 6 Jun 1776 in Capt. John Fulford's Company of Matrosses. {Ref: Maryland Historical Magazine, Vol. 69, No. 1, p. 96}

HALL, JAMES W., see "Aquila Hall," q.v.

HALL (HALE?), JOHN (Maryland Navy), third mate on the State Ship *Defence* in 1777. {Ref: Archives of Maryland Vol. 18, p. 657}

HALL, JOHN, see "Aquila Hall," q.v.

HALL, JOSIAS CARVEL (Harford County), colonel in the 4th Maryland Continental Line who received payment for his services in the amount of "1900 Dollars & £3.10s" on 12 Sep 1780. For additional information see Peden's *Revolutionary Patriots of Harford County, 1775-1783.* {Ref: Archives of Maryland Vol. 45, p. 98}

HALL, MARTHA, see "Aquila Hall," q.v.

HALL, MARY, see "Aquila Hall," q.v.

HALL, SOPHIA, see "Aquila Hall," q.v.

HALL, STEPHEN (Maryland Navy), mate on the State Ship *Defence* in 1777. {Ref: Archives of Maryland Vol. 18, p. 657}

HALL, THOMAS (Baltimore City), soldier who allegedly served in the Virginia Line and died in 1826 in Gloucester County; his widow Ann Hall applied for pension in Baltimore on 24 Nov 1838, aged 67, under the Act of July 7, 1838, but the claim was suspended "for further proof -- claims as sergeant." {Ref: *Rejected or Suspended Applications for Revolutionary War Pensions* (1850 Report), p. 236; Research by Virgil D. White, citing Federal Pension Application R4453}

HALL, THOMAS, see "Aquila Hall," q.v.

HALL, WILLIAM (Harford County), private who was enrolled by 15 Apr 1776 in Militia Company No. 20 under Capt. Robert Glenn. {Ref: George W. Archer Collection and Revolutionary War File, Historical Society of Harford County Archives}

HALL, WILLIAM (Kent County), private (substitute) in the Maryland Continental Line by 1781, was discharged on 8 Dec 1781. {Ref: Archives of Maryland Vol. 48, p. 11}

HALL, WILLIAM (Maryland Navy), seaman or marine on the State Ship *Defence* in 1777. {Ref: Archives of Maryland Vol. 18, p. 657}

HALL, WILLIAM (Western Maryland), private in Capt. Michael Cresap's Company in 1775. {Ref: Howard L. Leckey's *The Tenmile Country and Its Pioneer Families*, p. 15}

HALL, WILLIAM, see "Aquila Hall," q.v.

HALY, OLIVER (Maryland Navy), marine on the State Ship *Defence* in 1777. {Ref: Archives of Maryland Vol. 18, p. 657}

HAMBEL, ARCHIBALD (Harford County), private who was enrolled 9 Dec 1775 in Militia Company No. 14 under Capt. William McComas. {Ref: George W. Archer Collection and Revolutionary War File, Historical Society of Harford County Archives}

HAMBLETON, CHARLES (Maryland Navy), sergeant of marines on the State Ship *Defence* in 1777. {Ref: Archives of Maryland Vol. 18, p. 657}

HAMBLETON, JONATHAN (Harford County), private who was enrolled 10 Mar 1776 in Militia Company No. 18 under Capt. John Jolly. {Ref: George W. Archer Collection and Revolutionary War File, Historical Society of Harford County Archives}

HAMER (HARMER?), JOHN (Maryland Navy), tailor on the State Ship *Defence* in 1777. {Ref: Archives of Maryland Vol. 18, p. 657}

HAMILTON, ----, see "William Lamar," q.v.

HAMILTON, CYRUS, see "Nathaniel Chew," q.v

HAMILTON, GEORGE (Queen Anne's County), captain in the 5th Maryland Continental Line who received payment for his services in the amount of "1900 Dollars & £3.10s" on 12 Sep 1780. {Ref: Archives of Maryland Vol. 45, p. 98}

HAMILTON, JOHN (Baltimore County), lieutenant and paymaster in the 4th Maryland Continental Line who received payment for his services in the amount of "1900 Dollars & £3.10s" on 12 Sep 1780. {Ref: Archives of Maryland Vol. 45, p. 98}

HAMILTON, JOHN (Dorchester County), private (substitute) in the Maryland Continental Line by 1781, was discharged on 8 Dec 1781. {Ref: Archives of Maryland Vol. 48, p. 10}

HAMILTON, JOHN (Baltimore or Frederick County), waggoner in Pulaski's Legion in 1779. {Ref: Maryland Historical Magazine, Vol. 13, No. 3, p. 224}

HAMILTON, JOHN (Frederick County), private (substitute) in the Maryland Continental Line, German Regiment, enrolled in April, 1778 for 3 years or duration of the war. {Ref: Maryland Historical Magazine, Vol. 6, No. 3, p. 257}

HAMILTON, MARGARET, see "Richard Sappington," q.v.

HAMILTON, SAMUEL (Charles County?), lieutenant commissioned on 27 Jul 1780 to serve in the Regiment Extra by order of the Council of Maryland; possibly the lieutenant in the 6th Maryland Continental Line who received payment for his services in the amount of "1900 Dollars & £3.10s" on 12 Sep 1780. Additional research may be necessary before drawing conclusions. {Ref: Archives of Maryland Vol. 43, p. 234, and Vol. 45, p. 98}

HAMILTON, WILLIAM, see "Ichabod Davis," q.v.

HAMMERSLY, JOHN (Frederick County), private (substitute) in the Maryland Continental Line, German Regiment, enrolled in April, 1778 for 3 years or duration of the war. {Ref: Maryland Historical Magazine, Vol. 6, No. 3, p. 257}

HAMMETT, DAVID, see "Daniel Smith," q.v.

HAMMITT, ANN, see "Jesse Foster," q.v.

HAMMOND, VACHEL, see "William Stevens," q.v.

HAMON, WILLIAM (Frederick County), private (substitute) in the Maryland Continental Line, Gunby's Regiment, enrolled in May, 1778 for 3 years or duration of the war. {Ref: Maryland Historical Magazine, Vol. 6, No. 3, p. 259}

HAMRICKHOUSE, PETER, see "Peter Humrichouse," q.v.

HAMTON, DAVID (Harford County, Susquehannah Hundred), private who was enrolled 23 Apr 1776 in Militia Company No. 21 under Capt. George Patterson. {Ref: George W. Archer Collection and Revolutionary War File, Historical Society of Harford County Archives}

HANAN, THOMAS (Harford County), private who was recruited and enrolled by Capt. Praul in the Regiment Extraordinary and sent to Annapolis with Capt. Thompson on board the sloop *Liberty* on 17 Aug 1780, *"from thence deserted and again taken up and reenlisted on pretence of being discharged by the Council."* {Ref: Archives of Maryland Vol. 45, pp. 50, 51}

HANARY, JAMES (Frederick County), taken up as a vagrant in Frederick, was private in the Maryland Continental Line who was *"sent from camp by General Smallwood as unfit for the service"* and was discharged on 22 Jun 1778. {Ref: Archives of Maryland Vol. 21, p. 144}

HANDWOOD, ROBERT (Baltimore or Frederick County), private in Pulaski's Legion before July, 1782. {Ref: Maryland Historical Magazine, Vol. 13, No. 3, p. 225}

HANDY, GEORGE (Caroline County), private in Col. Richardson's Regiment in 1776 who was recommended for promotion. {Ref: Archives of Maryland Vol. 18, p. 74}

HANDY, JAMES (Baltimore Privateer), commander of the sloop *Abingdon*, navigated by 14 men and mounting 8 carriage guns, 4 swivel guns and 16 small arms, was issued Letters of Marque & Reprisal by the Council of Maryland on 14 Sep 1778. {Ref: Archives of Maryland Vol. 21, p. 203}

HANDY, JOSEPH (Maryland Navy), first lieutenant on the barge *Protector*, in the service of this state, commissioned 16 Jun 1781 under Capt. Zedekiah Walley. {Ref: Archives of Maryland Vol. 45, p. 476}

HANDY, LEVIN (Maryland Continental Line, Staff Officer, Lee's Regiment), captain who received payment for his services in the amount of "1900 Dollars & £3.10s" on 12 Sep 1780. {Ref: Archives of Maryland Vol. 45, p. 98}

HANDY, SAMUEL (Worcester County), patriot who was appointed by the Council of Maryland on 27 Jan 1776 as one of three persons in Worcester County to collect all gold and silver coin that can be procured in said county. {Ref: Archives of Maryland Vol. 11, p. 132}

HANE, JACOB (Frederick County), soldier in the Maryland troops *"who served in the Dutch Battalion and was taken sick in Philadelphia which prevented him from participating in the Battle of Germantown, died in Frederick on 2 Jan 1839 in his 86th year, one of the oldest citizens of the city."* {Ref: *Frederick Visiter and Temperance Advocate*, 17 Jan 1839}

HANEY, EZEKIEL (Charles County?), patriot and doctor in the 2nd Maryland Continental Line who received payment for his services in the amount of "1900 Dollars & £3.10s" on 12 Sep 1780. {Ref: Archives of Maryland Vol. 18, p. 445, and Vol. 45, p. 97}

HANNA, JAMES (Harford County, Susquehannah Hundred), private who was enrolled 23 Apr 1776 in Militia Company No. 21 under Capt. George Patterson. {Ref: George W. Archer Collection and Revolutionary War File, Historical Society of Harford County Archives}

HANNA, ROBERT (Harford County), private who was enrolled 9 Dec 1775 in Militia Company No. 14 under Capt. William McComas. {Ref: George W. Archer Collection and Revolutionary War File, Historical Society of Harford County Archives}

HANNESEY, JAMES (Frederick County), soldier in the Maryland troops *"who was sent to camp as a Vagrant from Frederick County, returned to General Smallwood and sent on board the Gallies, Appearing to be unfit for Duty, was discharged from the Service"* on 30 Sep 1778. {Ref: Archives of Maryland Vol. 21, p. 213}

HANSON, GEORGE (Charles County), patriot who was paid 15 shillings by the Maryland Council of Safety for cleaning guns on 9 Oct 1776. {Ref: Archives of Maryland Vol. 12, p. 327}

HANSON, ISAAC (Anne Arundel County), lieutenant in the 4th Maryland Continental Line who received payment for his services in the amount of "1900 Dollars & £3.10s" on 12 Sep 1780. {Ref: Archives of Maryland Vol. 45, p. 98}

HANSON, JANE, see "Peter C. Hanson," q.v.

HANSON, JOHN, see "Peter C. Hanson," q.v.

HANSON, JOHN (Maryland Navy and Baltimore Privateer), midshipman on the State Ship *Defence* in 1777; marine on the galley *Independence* in 1778 who took the Oath of Fidelity and Allegiance to the State of Maryland on 31 Mar 1778; commander of the brigantine *Viper*, navigated by 50 men and mounting 14 carriage guns, was issued Letters of Marque & Reprisal by the Council of

Maryland on 17 Aug 1780. {Ref: Archives of Maryland Vol. 16, p. 559, Vol. 18, p. 657, and Vol. 43, p. 257}

HANSON, JOHN, JR. (Charles, Frederick and Prince George's Counties), patriot who was appointed by the Council of Maryland on 27 Jan 1776 as one of three persons in Frederick County to collect all gold and silver coin that can be procured in said county; born on 3 Apr 1721 in Charles County and died on 15 Nov 1783 at "Oxen Hill," the seat of his nephew Thomas Hanson in Prince George's County, *"this gentleman had long been a servant to this country, in a wide variety of employments, the last of which was President of Congress; he had been ill since he returned home, sick then for several months, then had a relapse while on a visit to Oxen Hill."* For more information about his life and times, see Edward C. Papenfuse's *A Biographical Dictionary of the Maryland Legislature, 1635-1789,* Vol. I, pp. 405-406. {Ref: Archives of Maryland Vol. 11, p. 132; *Maryland Gazette,* 27 Nov 1783}

HANSON, MATILDA, see "Thomas Courtney," q.v.

HANSON, PETER CONTEE (Frederick County), lieutenant in the Maryland troops who fell in the battle at Fort Washington in 1776; son of John Hanson (President of the United States in Congress Assembled, 1781-1782) and his wife Jane (died 21 Feb 1812, aged 85). {Ref: *Frederick-Town Herald,* 22 Feb 1812; Archives of Maryland Vol. 18, p. 48}

HANSON, SAMUEL (Charles County), lieutenant in the 1st Maryland Continental Line who received payment for his services in the amount of "1900 Dollars & £3.10s" on 12 Sep 1780. {Ref: Archives of Maryland Vol. 45, p. 97}

HANSON, SAMUEL (Charles County), patriot who was commissioned one of the three persons in Charles County by the Council of Maryland on 19 Aug 1779 to receive subscriptions for use of the State. {Ref: Archives of Maryland Vol. 21, p. 499}

HANSON, SAMUEL, OF WALTER (Southern Maryland), lieutenant, commissioned on 27 Jul 1780 to serve in the Regiment Extra by order of the Council of Maryland. {Ref: Archives of Maryland Vol. 43, p. 234}

HANSON, SAMUEL, JR. (Charles County), second major in the 26th Battalion of Militia by 17 Jun 1778 at which time he resigned his commission. {Ref: Archives of Maryland Vol. 21, p. 138}

HANSON, THOMAS, see "John Hanson, Jr.," q.v.

HANSON, WALTER (Charles County), patriot who was commissioned one of the three persons in Charles County by the Council of Maryland on 19 Aug 1779 to receive subscriptions for use of the State. {Ref: Archives of Maryland Vol. 21, p. 499}

HANWICK, ELIE (Worcester County), private (substitute) in the Maryland Continental Line by 1781, was discharged on 8 Dec 1781. {Ref: Archives of Maryland Vol. 48, p. 11}

HARBERT, FRANCIS, see "Francis Hurbert," q.v.

HARBERT, RICHARD (Harford County, Susquehannah Hundred), private who was enrolled 23 Apr 1776 in Militia Company No. 21 under Capt. George Patterson. {Ref: George W. Archer Collection and Revolutionary War File, Historical Society of Harford County Archives}

HARBERT (HARBEST?), THOMAS (Maryland Navy), marine on the State Ship *Defence* in 1777. {Ref: Archives of Maryland Vol. 18, p. 657}

HARBERT, WILLIAM (Maryland Navy), sailor on the State Ship *Defence* in 1777. {Ref: Archives of Maryland Vol. 18, p. 657}

HARDCASTLE, PETER (Talbot County), lieutenant in the 7th Maryland Continental Line who received payment for his services in the amount of "1900 Dollars & £3.10s" on 12 Sep 1780. {Ref: Archives of Maryland Vol. 45, p. 98}

HARDESTY, JAMES (Baltimore County), private, aged 23, labourer, born in Maryland, enlisted (made his "X" mark) on 3 Jul 1776 in Capt. John Fulford's Company of Matrosses, deserted 3 Sep 1776 and took his regimentals, hunting shirt and trousers with him. {Ref: Maryland Historical Magazine, Vol. 69, No. 1, pp. 96, 97}

HARDGRO, WILLIAM (Harford County, Susquehannah Hundred), private who was enrolled 23 Apr 1776 in Militia Company No. 21 under Capt. George Patterson. {Ref: George W. Archer Collection and Revolutionary War File, Historical Society of Harford County Archives}

HARDING, RICHARD (Maryland Navy), seaman or marine on the State Ship *Defence* in 1777. {Ref: Archives of Maryland Vol. 18, p. 657}

HARDMAN, JOHN (Frederick County?), captain in the 2nd Maryland Continental Line who received payment for his services in the amount of "1900 Dollars & £3.10s" on 12 Sep 1780. {Ref: Archives of Maryland Vol. 45, p. 97}

HARDMAN, HENRY (Frederick and Washington Counties), major in the 6th Maryland Continental Line who received payment for his services in the amount of "1900 Dollars & £3.10s" on 12 Sep 1780. {Ref: Archives of Maryland Vol. 45, p. 98}

HARDMAN, MICHAEL (Frederick County), private (substitute) in the Maryland Continental Line, German Regiment, enrolled in April, 1778 for 3 years or duration of the war. {Ref: Maryland Historical Magazine, Vol. 6, No. 3, p. 256}

HARDY, KINSEY (Montgomery County), private (substitute) in the Maryland Continental Line by 1781, was discharged on 8 Dec 1781. {Ref: Archives of Maryland Vol. 48, p. 11}

HARGETT, ABRAHAM (Frederick County), patriot buried in Mount Olivet Cemetery. {Ref: Information compiled by Dr. Donald Wolf in Maryland Society SAR Newsletter circa 1996}

HARGUS, JOHN (Western Maryland), private in Capt. Michael Cresap's Company in 1775. {Ref: Howard L. Leckey's *The Tenmile Country and Its Pioneer Families*, p. 15}

HARKINS, GEORGE (Baltimore Town), patriot and merchant who enrolled in Capt. John Sterrett's Independent Mercantile Company by February, 1777, at which time they were mustered into regular service with the continental army to repress loyalist activities in the Eastern Shore counties of Somerset and Worcester. {Ref: J. Thomas Scharf's *History of Baltimore City and County*, Part I, p. 77}

HARMER, JOHN, see "John Hamer," q.v.

HARPER, BETHULA, see "William Harper," q.v.

HARPER, DANIEL (Maryland Navy), boatswain on the State Ship *Defence* in 1777. {Ref: Archives of Maryland Vol. 18, p. 657}

HARPER, FRANCIS, JR. (Harford County), private who was enrolled 25 Mar 1776 in Militia Company No. 19 under Capt. William Morgan. {Ref: George W. Archer Collection and Revolutionary War File, Historical Society of Harford County Archives}

HARPER, HENRY (Dorchester County), private (substitute) in the Maryland Continental Line by 1781, was discharged on 8 Dec 1781. {Ref: Archives of Maryland Vol. 48, p. 10}

HARPER, WILLIAM (Dorchester County), soldier in the Maryland troops who married Bethula Wallace circa 1793 and died 17 Feb 1814; widow Bethula Harper applied for pension on 10 Jan 1846, aged 86, under the Act of July 7, 1838, but the claim was suspended for proof of the date of the marriage; she died 5 Oct 1855; they had children and a son was living in 1858, but no names were given. {Ref: *Rejected or Suspended Applications for Revolutionary War Pensions* (1850 Report), p. 236; Research by Virgil D. White, citing Federal Pension Application W3679}

HARR, JOHN (Maryland Privateer), commander of the brigantine *Donia Antoney*, navigated by 32 men and mounting 10 carriage guns and 12 small arms, was issued Letters of Marque & Reprisal by the Council of Maryland on 29 Nov 1779. {Ref: Archives of Maryland Vol. 43, p. 25}

HARRINGTON, PETER (Dorchester County), soldier in the Maryland militia who was born 20 Nov 1754 and applied for pension on 21 Oct 1833, aged 78, under the Act of June 7, 1832; however, the claim was suspended because of *"no proof or specification, Minute-man's service overrated."* {Ref: *Rejected or Suspended Applications for Revolutionary War Pensions* (1850 Report), p. 231; Research by Virgil D. White, citing Federal Pension Application R4626}

HARRIS, ARTHUR (Queen Anne's County?), lieutenant in the 5th Maryland Continental Line who received payment for his services in the amount of "1900 Dollars & £3.10s" on 12 Sep 1780. {Ref: Archives of Maryland Vol. 45, p. 98}

HARRIS, JAMES (Charles County), private who was enrolled to serve as a substitute in the Maryland Continental Line until 10 Dec 1781, but *"being represented unfit for the service for which he was intended"* was discharged on 30 Oct 1781. {Ref: Archives of Maryland Vol. 45, p. 657}

HARRIS, JOSEPH (Harford County, Susquehannah Hundred), private who was enrolled 23 Apr 1776 in Militia Company No. 21 under Capt. George Patterson. {Ref: George W. Archer Collection and Revolutionary War File, Historical Society of Harford County Archives}

HARRIS, WILLIAM (Maryland Navy), armorer on the State Ship *Defence* in 1777. {Ref: Archives of Maryland Vol. 18, p. 657}

HARRISON, CHARLES (Maryland Privateer), commander of the schooner *Morrice*, navigated by 14 men and mounting 4 carriage guns, 4 swivel guns and 6 muskets, was issued Letters of Marque & Reprisal by the Council of Maryland on 19 Apr 1780; see "Michael O'Connor," q.v. {Ref: Archives of Maryland Vol. 43, p. 145}

HARRISON, CLEMENT (Maryland Privateer), commander of the sloop *Dispatch*, mounting 4 swivel guns and 8 small arms, was issued Letters of Marque & Reprisal by the Council of Maryland on 18 Dec 1778. {Ref: Archives of Maryland Vol. 21, p. 268}

HARRISON, JAMES (Queen Anne's County), private (substitute) in the Maryland Continental Line by 1781, was discharged on 8 Dec 1781. {Ref: Archives of Maryland Vol. 48, p. 10}

HARRISON, JOHN (Maryland Privateer), commander of the sloop *General Lincoln*, mounting 10 carriage guns, 10 swivel guns and 16 small arms, was issued Letters of Marque & Reprisal by the Council of Maryland on 18 Oct 1779; captain of the sloop *Lincoln* "riding in the Patuxent River" on 1 Sep 1780; possibly the Capt. John Harrison who was taken prisoner and confined in New York before 17 Jan 1781. {Ref: Archives of Maryland Vol. 21, p. 561 and Vol. 37, pp. 71, 277}

HARRISON, JOHN C. (Dorchester County), patriot who was appointed Commissary of Purchases by the Council of Maryland on 8 Jul 1780. {Ref: Archives of Maryland Vol. 43, p. 215}

HARRISON, JOSEPH HANSON (Baltimore or Anne Arundel County), patriot who rendered service by contracting to erect a salt-works for use of the State on 22 Jun 1776. {Ref: Archives of Maryland Vol. 11, p. 506}

HARRISON, RICHARD (Maryland Privateer), captain of the schooner *Decoy*, "fitted out to Cruise in this Bay," commissioned 11 May 1781; see "John Mitchell," q.v. {Ref: Archives of Maryland Vol. 45, p. 432}

HARRISON, ROBERT (Dorchester County), patriot who was commissioned one of the three persons in Dorchester County by the Council of Maryland on 19 Aug 1779 to receive subscriptions for use of the State. {Ref: Archives of Maryland Vol. 21, p. 499}

HARRYMAN, TEMPERANCE, see "Joshua Marsh," q.v.

HART, MICHAEL (Baltimore County), private, aged 25, butcher, born in Ireland, enlisted (made his "X" mark) on 4 Mar 1776 in Capt. John Fulford's Company of Matrosses; on 7 Jul 1776 Gen. William Smallwood wrote to the Council of Safety stating: *"The bearers Michael Hart and Laurence Keenan, of the Artillery Company, having been released from jail, prosecution against them being withdrawn, have applied for a discharge, the date of which will properly commence the 7th day of May, when they were imprisoned, as I ordered them to be given up at that time to the Civil Power and having no authority to discharge them, must refer them to the Honorable Council of Safety for their discharges"* and on 8 Jul 1776 the Council of Safety *"ordered that Michael Hart and Lawrence Keenan of Capt. John Fulford's [Company] of Artillery be discharged from the Service of this Colony."* On 18 Jul 1776 Michael Hart and Larrons Keenan (among others who were enlisted by Capt. Thomas Yates) were reviewed and passed by Major Thomas Jones of the Baltimore Town Battalion of Militia. {Ref: Archives of Maryland Vol. 12, pp. 7, 9, and Vol. 18, p. 58; Maryland Historical Magazine, Vol. 69, No. 1, p. 96}

HART, WILLIAM (Harford County), private who was enrolled 25 Mar 1776 in Militia Company No. 19 under Capt. William Morgan. {Ref: George W. Archer Collection and Revolutionary War File, Historical Society of Harford County Archives}

HARTIE (HASTIE?), JAMES (Maryland Navy), quartermaster on the State Ship *Defence* in 1777. {Ref: Archives of Maryland Vol. 18, p. 657}

HARTSHORN, JOHN (Queen Anne's County), lieutenant in the 4th Maryland Continental Line who received payment for his services in the amount of "1900 Dollars & £3.10s" on 12 Sep 1780. {Ref: Archives of Maryland Vol. 45, p. 98}

HARTSHORN, JONATHAN (Cecil County), private who was drafted to serve in the Maryland Continental Line until 10 Dec 1781, but *"being represented unfit for the duty for which he was intended"* was discharged on 30 Oct 1781; he died in 1807. {Ref: Archives of Maryland Vol. 45, p. 656; West Nottingham Presbyterian Cemetery}

HARVEY, ARCHIBALD (Harford County), soldier who served in the Pennsylvania Line and married Elizabeth McFadden on 12 Aug 1777 in York County, Pennsylvania and died 28 Nov 1807; his widow Elizabeth Harvey applied for pension on 12 Feb 1842, aged 87, in Harford County, under the Act of July 7, 1838, but the claim was rejected because he did not serve six months. {Ref: *Rejected or Suspended Applications for Revolutionary War Pensions* (1850 Report), p. 235; Research by Virgil D. White, citing Federal Pension Application R4708}

HARVEY, ELIZABETH, see "Archibald Harvey," q.v.

HARVEY (HARVY), NATHANIEL (Montgomery County), private (substitute) in the 6th Maryland Continental Line by 1781, was discharged on 8 Dec 1781. {Ref: Archives of Maryland Vol. 48, p. 11}

HARVEY (HARVY), RICHARD (Montgomery County), private (substitute) in the Maryland Continental Line by 1781, was discharged on 8 Dec 1781. {Ref: Archives of Maryland Vol. 48, p. 11}

HARVEY (HARVY), WILLIAM (Montgomery County), private who was a 9 month soldier in the 6th Maryland Continental Line in 1778-1779, was discharged on 12 Aug 1779 and received £20 in clothing. {Ref: Archives of Maryland Vol. 21, p. 491}

HARVEY, WILLIAM (Harford County), private who was enrolled 9 Dec 1775 in Militia Company No. 14 under Capt. William McComas. {Ref: George W. Archer Collection and Revolutionary War File, Historical Society of Harford County Archives}

HARWOOD, RICHARD, JR. (Anne Arundel County), patriot who was commissioned one of the three persons in Anne Arundel County by the Council of Maryland on 19 Aug 1779 to receive subscriptions for use of the State. {Ref: Archives of Maryland Vol. 21, p. 499}

HASEN, JACOB (Washington County), private who was enrolled to serve as a substitute in the Maryland Continental Line until 10 Dec 1781, but *"being represented unfit for the service for which he was intended"* was discharged on 30 Oct 1781. {Ref: Archives of Maryland Vol. 45, p. 657}

HASTIE, JAMES, see "James Hartie," q.v.

HATCH, DAVIS (Maryland Privateer), captain and master of the sloop *Susannah* who was granted permission by the Council of Maryland *"to load with Flour and Grain within this State for the consumption of the Eastern States"* on 16 Sep 1778. {Ref: Archives of Maryland Vol. 21, p. 204}

HATHAWAY, PHILLIP (Western Maryland), private in Capt. Michael Cresap's Company in 1775. {Ref: Howard L. Leckey's *The Tenmile Country and Its Pioneer Families*, p. 15}

HATKINSON, MARTIN (Baltimore or Frederick County), private who enlisted in Pulaski's Legion on 13 Apr 1778 or 1779. {Ref: Maryland Historical Magazine, Vol. 13, No. 3, p. 224}

HATTENSTEIN, SAMUEL (Frederick County), private (substitute) in the Maryland Continental Line, German Regiment, enrolled in April, 1778 for 3 years or duration of the war. {Ref: Maryland Historical Magazine, Vol. 6, No. 3, p. 258}

HAUSER, JOHN (Maryland Navy), sailor or seaman on 7 Jan 1780. {Ref: Calendar of Maryland State Papers, The Brown Books, p. 57}

HAVARD, WILLIAM (Maryland Navy), seaman on the State Ship *Defence* in 1777. {Ref: Archives of Maryland Vol. 18, p. 657}

HAVERS, JOHN (Maryland Navy), cooper's crew on the State Ship *Defence* in 1777. {Ref: Archives of Maryland Vol. 18, p. 657}

HAWKINS, ANN, see "David Bell," q.v.

HAWKINS, EDWARD (Anne Arundel County), private who was a deserter from Annapolis and possibly enrolled by Richard Dallam in the Regiment Extraordinary and sent to Annapolis with Capt. Thompson on board the sloop *Liberty* on 17 Aug 1780. {Ref: Archives of Maryland Vol. 45, pp. 50, 51}

HAWKINS, JAMES (Maryland Navy), midshipman on the State Ship *Defence* from 1 Mar to 15 Aug 1777, served with ship's tender from 15 Aug to 15 Nov 1777 and skipper from 15 Nov to 24 Nov 1777. {Ref: Archives of Maryland Vol. 18, p. 657}

HAWKINS, JOHN see "William Simmons," q.v.

HAWKINS, RICHARD (Harford County), private who was enrolled 25 Mar 1776 in Militia Company No. 19 under Capt. William Morgan. {Ref: George W. Archer Collection and Revolutionary War File, Historical Society of Harford County Archives}

HAWKINS, WILLIAM (Western Maryland), private in Capt. Michael Cresap's Company in 1775. {Ref: Howard L. Leckey's *The Tenmile Country and Its Pioneer Families*, p. 15}

HAYCOCK, SOLOMON (Queen Anne's County), private who was drafted into the Maryland Continental Line, was discharged on 8 Dec 1781. {Ref: Archives of Maryland Vol. 48, p. 10}

HAYLIP, RICHARD (Frederick County), private (substitute) in the Maryland Continental Line, German Regiment, enrolled in April, 1778 for 3 years or duration of the war. {Ref: Maryland Historical Magazine, Vol. 6, No. 3, p. 257}

HAYS, RICHARD (Dorchester County), private (substitute) in the Maryland Continental Line by 1781, was discharged on 8 Dec 1781. {Ref: Archives of Maryland Vol. 48, p. 10}

HAYS, THOMAS (Queen Anne's County), private (substitute) in the Maryland Continental Line by 1781, was discharged on 8 Dec 1781. {Ref: Archives of Maryland Vol. 48, p. 10}

HAZELWOOD, THOMAS (Frederick County), private (substitute) in the Maryland Continental Line, German Regiment enrolled in May, 1778 for 3 years or duration of the war. {Ref: Maryland Historical Magazine, Vol. 6, No. 3, p. 258}

HAZLE, EDWARD (St. Mary's County), private (substitute) in the Maryland Continental Line by 1781, was discharged on 8 Dec 1781. {Ref: Archives of Maryland Vol. 48, p. 11}

HAZLE, JEREMIAH (St. Mary's County), private who was drafted into the Maryland Continental Line, was discharged on 8 Dec 1781. {Ref: Archives of Maryland Vol. 48, p. 10}

HEALY, CALEB (Prince George's County), patriot who took the Oath of Fidelity and Support to the State of Maryland on 2 Apr 1778. {Ref: Archives of Maryland Vol. 21, p. 1}

HEALY, DANIEL (Harford County), private who was enrolled 25 Mar 1776 in Militia Company No. 19 under Capt. William Morgan. {Ref: George W. Archer Collection and Revolutionary War File, Historical Society of Harford County Archives}

HEALY, JOHN (Harford County), private who was enrolled 25 Mar 1776 in Militia Company No. 19 under Capt. William Morgan. {Ref: George W. Archer Collection and Revolutionary War File, Historical Society of Harford County Archives}

HEAPES, ROBERT (Harford County), private who was enrolled 9 Dec 1775 in Militia Company No. 14 under Capt. William McComas. {Ref: George W. Archer Collection and Revolutionary War File, Historical Society of Harford County Archives}

HEATH, RICHARD, see "Aquila Hall," q.v.

HEBB, VERNON (St. Mary's County), patriot who was commissioned one of the three persons in St. Mary's County by the Council of Maryland on 19 Aug 1779 to receive subscriptions for use of the State. {Ref: Archives of Maryland Vol. 21, p. 499}

HECKETON, MARTIN (Frederick County), private who was enrolled to serve as a substitute in the Maryland Continental Line until 10 Dec 1781, but *"being*

represented unfit for the service for which he was intended" was discharged on 30 Oct 1781. {Ref: Archives of Maryland Vol. 45, p. 657}

HEMSLEY, WILLIAM (Queen Anne's County), patriot who was appointed by the Council of Maryland on 27 Jan 1776 as one of three persons in Queen Anne's County to collect all the gold and silver coin that can be procured in said county; commissioned lieutenant colonel of the 20th Battalion of Militia on 8 May 1777; commissioned as one of the three persons in Queen Anne's County to receive subscriptions for use of the State on 19 Aug 1779. {Ref: Archives of Maryland Vol. 11, p. 132, Vol. 16, p. 244, and Vol. 21, p. 499}

HENCHMAN, WILLIAM (Dorchester County), confined in Annapolis jail on 4 Sep 1780 on charges of trading with the enemy, petitioned the Governor and Council of Maryland stating, in part, that *"he took the Oath of Allegiance to this State in the Manner and time prescribed by Law; that he constantly performed his Duty as a private in the Militia; and ever behaved himself as a good and faithfull Subject while in the service of the State on board the schooner Molly and the General Smallwood, and ever since Your Petitioner solemnly denies that he ever dealt with or ever had any Connection or Communication with the Enemy, or any of their Privateers or Cruisers in the Bay and declares that any Declarations by him of his Trading with them were made without any foundation in Truth, and in the Hour of Indiscretion and Folly when the Behavior, Conduct and Conversation of the company, induced him, greatly intoxicated with Liquor to utter sentiments foreign to the Truth, and to accuse himself with Crimes of which he is intirely innocent. Your Petitioner further begs leave to represent that he had a Wife and three small Children, with two orphan Girls, who depend altogether on his Labour for their Support."* Signed: William Henchman (made his "X" mark). {Ref: Archives of Maryland Vol. 45, pp. 74-75}

HENDERSON, JAMES (Baltimore County), matross soldier by 7 May 1779 at which time he gave a deposition about his enlistment terms. {Ref: Maryland State Archives Record MdHR 6636-14-83}

HENNISY, JAMES (Frederick County), private (substitute) in the Maryland Continental Line, Price's Regiment, enrolled in May, 1778 for 3 years or duration of the war. {Ref: Maryland Historical Magazine, Vol. 6, No. 3, p. 259}

HENRY, JAMES (Maryland Navy), marine on the State Ship *Defence* in 1777. {Ref: Archives of Maryland Vol. 18, p. 657}

HENRY, JOHN, see "Aquila Hall," q.v.

HENRY, WILLIAM (Kent County), lieutenant colonel of the 27th Battalion of Militia, commissioned 8 May 1777; also commissioned one of the three persons in Kent County by the Council of Maryland on 19 Aug 1779 to receive subscriptions for use of the State; William Henry, of Georgetown in Kent

County, died testate by 28 Mar 1785. {Ref: Archives of Maryland Vol. 16, p. 243 and Vol. 21, p. 499; Kent County Wills Liber 7, p. 89}

HERBERT, JEREMIAH (St. Mary's County), private who was drafted into the Maryland Continental Line, was discharged on 8 Dec 1781. {Ref: Archives of Maryland Vol. 48, p. 10}

HERLITY, WILLIAM (Baltimore County), private who enlisted in Pulaski's Legion on 6 May 1778 in Baltimore. {Ref: Maryland Historical Magazine, Vol. 13, No. 3, p. 222}

HERRING, DANIEL (Kent County), private (substitute) in the Maryland Continental Line, who enlisted to serve until 10 Dec 1781, was discharged on 30 Nov 1781. {Ref: Archives of Maryland Vol. 48, p. 8}

HERSHBERGER, DOROTHY, see "Frederick Kemp," q.v.

HESSE, GODFRIED (Baltimore or Frederick County), private who enlisted in Pulaski's Legion on 10 Sep 1778 and still in service in November, 1779. {Ref: Maryland Historical Magazine, Vol. 13, No. 3, p. 224}

HESSELINS, MISS, see "Thomas Johnson, Jr.," q.v.

HEULINGS, ASHAEL (Baltimore County), private, aged 25, tailor, born in Philadelphia, enlisted 28 Feb 1776 in Capt. John Fulford's Company of Matrosses. {Ref: Maryland Historical Magazine, Vol. 69, No. 1, p. 95}

HEYSER, WILLIAM (Washington County), captain in the Maryland Continental Line and an early settler in the Hagerstown Valley; on 12 Oct 1776 his nine-year-old son William Heyser wrote to his father who was stationed at the American Camp in Philadelphia stating, in part: *"My Dear father, my greatest grief is, that I am incapable of the military Service, that I might enjoy the company of so loving a father, and serve my country in so glorious a cause."* {Ref: J. Thomas Scharf's *History of Western Maryland*, Vol. II, pp. 1035-1036}

HICHINBOTEM (HIGGINBOTHAM), JAMES (Kent County), private (substitute) in the Maryland Continental Line by 1781, was discharged on 8 Dec 1781. {Ref: Archives of Maryland Vol. 48, p. 11}

HICKMAN, JOSHUA (Montgomery County), private (substitute) in the Maryland Continental Line by 1781, was discharged on 8 Dec 1781; died testate by 17 Mar 1818, leaving widow Mary Hickman, son Joshua Hickman, daughters Margaret White Strider and Mary Waters Hickman, and grandson John Strider. {Ref: Archives of Maryland Vol. 48, p. 11; Montgomery County Wills Liber L#L, p. 80}

HIDE, JOHN (Baltimore County), private, aged 18, sailmaker, born in Dublin, enlisted 16 Feb 1776 in Capt. John Fulford's Company of Matrosses, deserted 24 Jun 1776 and took his hunting shirt, trousers and breeches with him. {Ref: Maryland Historical Magazine, Vol. 69, No. 1, pp. 95, 97}

HIGDON, JOSEPH (Baltimore or Frederick County), private in Pulaski's Legion before July, 1782. {Ref: Maryland Historical Magazine, Vol. 13, No. 3, p. 225}

HIGGINBOTTOM, JOEL (Baltimore County), private, aged 19, joiner, born in Maryland, enlisted 19 Feb 1776 in Capt. John Fulford's Company of Matrosses;

marine on the galley *Independence*, took the Oath of Fidelity and Allegiance to the State of Maryland on 2 Apr 1778. {Ref: Maryland Historical Magazine, Vol. 69, No. 1, p. 95; Archives of Maryland Vol. 21, p. 1}

HIGGINS, JAMES (Montgomery County), private who served in the militia, 1777-1780, died in 1816, and buried in Higgins Cemetery located off Twinbrook Parkway in Rockville, Maryland (situated on what is left of the old Higgins farm where James once lived); died testate by 18 Jan 1816, leaving wife ---- Higgins, sons Benjamin Higgins, James Becraft Higgins and John Higgins, and daughters Sarah Prather, Ann Prather, Rebeckah Soper, Susannah Swearingen, Luranah Becraft, Elizabeth Allison and Elinor Garrett. {Ref: Article in Gen. William Smallwood Chapter SAR Newsletter, 1999; Montgomery County Wills Liber L#I, p. 437}

HIGH, GEORGE (Maryland Navy), ordinary sailor on the State Ship *Defence* in 1777. {Ref: Archives of Maryland Vol. 18, p. 657}

HILL, ANNE, see "Henry Hill," q.v.

HILL, CLEMENT, see "Henry Hill," q.v.

HILL, HARMON (Harford County, Susquehannah Hundred), private who was enrolled 23 Apr 1776 in Militia Company No. 21 under Capt. George Patterson. {Ref: George W. Archer Collection and Revolutionary War File, Historical Society of Harford County Archives}

HILL, HENRY (Prince George's County), captain in the Maryland troops who married Hetta or Hesther Brooke (born 9 Oct 1760) on 23 or 24 Apr 1781 and died on 27 Apr 1822; his widow Hester Hill applied for pension in Washington, D. C. on 17 Oct 1838, aged 78, under the Act of July 7, 1838, but the claim was suspended *"for want of proof of service, and papers withdrawn by Silas Wright, Jr., December 26, 1838."* She died on 15 Aug 1842, leaving children Anne T. Hill, Joseph B. Hill, Clement B. Hill, and Henrietta J. Kennedy. {Ref: *Rejected or Suspended Applications for Revolutionary War Pensions* (1850 Report), p. 236; Research by Virgil D. White, citing Federal Pension Application W14907}

HILL, HENRY, OF HENRY (Prince George's County), lieutenant who served on a General Court-Martial on 6 Jul 1776; commissioned captain on 27 Jul 1780 to serve in the Regiment Extra by order of the Council of Maryland. {Ref: Archives of Maryland Vol. 11, p. 553 and Vol. 43, p. 234}

HILL, HESTER, see "Henry Hill," q.v.

HILL, JOHN (Anne Arundel County), private in the 7th Maryland Continental Line before 10 Dec 1779, "a 9 months soldier discharged" and at which time he was issued cloathing due him. {Ref: Archives of Maryland Vol. 43, p. 34}

HILL, JOSEPH, see "Henry Hill," q.v.

HILL, JOSES (Baltimore Privateer), commander of the schooner *Grampus*, navigated by 10 men and mounting 4 carriage guns, 4 swivel guns and 4 small arms, was issued Letters of Marque & Reprisal by the Council of Maryland on 17 Aug 1780. {Ref: Archives of Maryland Vol. 43, p. 257}

HILL, JOSIAH (Maryland Privateer), commander of the sloop *Mercury*, navigated by 45 men and mounting 11 carriage guns, 4 swivel guns and 16 small arms, was issued Letters of Marque & Reprisal by the Council of Maryland on 14 Sep 1778. {Ref: Archives of Maryland Vol. 21, p. 202}

HILL, PHILIP (Prince George's County), patriot who was appointed lieutenant in Capt. Lingan's *"Company of Cavalry directed to be raised by the Act for the Defence of the Bay"* on 25 Apr 1781. {Ref: Archives of Maryland Vol. 45, p. 414}

HILL, REBECCA, see "Henry Hoffman," q.v.

HILL, ROBERT (Baltimore County), private, aged 19, labourer, born in England, enlisted (made his "C" mark) on 28 Feb 1776 in Capt. John Fulford's Company of Matrosses, deserted 24 Jun 1776 and took his hunting shirt and trousers with him. {Ref: Maryland Historical Magazine, Vol. 69, No. 1, pp. 95, 97}

HILL, THOMAS (Charles County), private (substitute) in the Maryland Continental Line by 1781, was discharged on 8 Dec 1781. {Ref: Archives of Maryland Vol. 48, p. 11}

HILLEN, JOHN (Baltimore Town), patriot and merchant who enrolled in Capt. John Sterrett's Independent Mercantile Company by February, 1777, at which time they were mustered into regular service with the continental army to repress loyalist activities in the Eastern Shore counties of Somerset and Worcester. {Ref: J. Thomas Scharf's *History of Baltimore City and County*, Part I, p. 77}

HILLIARY, RIGNAL, see "Levi Gaunt," q.v.

HILLS, CHARLES (Frederick County), private (substitute) in the Maryland Continental Line, Williams' Regiment, enrolled in April, 1778 for 3 years or duration of the war. {Ref: Maryland Historical Magazine, Vol. 6, No. 3, p. 257}

HILTON, CLARA, see "Jonathan Ady," q.v.

HINCH, GEORGE (Western Maryland), private in Capt. Michael Cresap's Company in 1775. {Ref: Howard L. Leckey's *The Tenmile Country and Its Pioneer Families*, p. 15}

HINDMAN, EDWARD (Talbot County), patriot who was commissioned one of the three persons in Talbot County by the Council of Maryland on 19 Aug 1779 to receive subscriptions for use of the State. {Ref: Archives of Maryland Vol. 21, p. 499}

HINDMAN, JAMES (Talbot County), colonel and contractor for horses in 1780; appointed Commissary of Purchases by the Council of Maryland on 8 Jul 1780. {Ref: Archives of Maryland Vol. 43, p. 215, and Vol. 45, p. 219}

HINGSON, THOMAS (Maryland Privateer), captain of the schooner *Speedwell* which was impressed into service by order of the Council of Maryland on 27 Apr 1780 *"to go to the Head of Elk for the Purpose of Transporting a Detachment of the American Army to the State of Virginia."* {Ref: Archives of Maryland Vol. 43, p. 155}

HISSEY, MARY, see "George Zimmerman," q.v.

HITCHCOCK, JOSIAH (Harford County), ensign, elected 30 Nov 1776, commissioned -- Jan 1777, Militia Company No. 30 under Capt. Benjamin Amoss. {Ref: George W. Archer Collection and Revolutionary War File, Historical Society of Harford County Archives}

HIVER, RICHARD (Baltimore County), private, 31 May 1779, Capt. Benjamin Talbott's Militia Company, Cockey's Battalion. {Ref: Maryland Historical Magazine, Vol. 7, No. 1, p. 90}

HOBBS, THOMAS, see "Nathan Musgrove," q.v.

HOCK, WILLIAM (Baltimore County), private, aged 20, farmer, born in Talbot County, Maryland, enlisted (made his "X" mark) on 12 Mar 1776 in Capt. John Fulford's Company of Matrosses. {Ref: Maryland Historical Magazine, Vol. 69, No. 1, p. 96}

HODSKINS, SAMUEL (Harford County), private who was enrolled 9 Dec 1775 in Militia Company No. 14 under Capt. William McComas. {Ref: George W. Archer Collection and Revolutionary War File, Historical Society of Harford County Archives}

HODSON, GEORGE (Charles County), private who was drafted into the Maryland Continental Line, was discharged on 8 Dec 1781. {Ref: Archives of Maryland Vol. 48, p. 10}

HODSON, HOOPER (Caroline County), private (substitute) in the Maryland Continental Line by 1781, was discharged on 8 Dec 1781. {Ref: Archives of Maryland Vol. 48, p. 10}

HOFFMAN, ADAM, see "Henry Hoffman," q.v.

HOFFMAN, CASPAR, see "Henry Hoffman," q.v.

HOFFMAN, CHARLOTTE, see "Henry Hoffman," q.v.

HOFFMAN, ELIZABETH, see "Henry Hoffman," q.v.

HOFFMAN, GEORGE, see "Henry Hoffman," q.v.

HOFFMAN, HENRY (Frederick County), soldier who served in the Pennsylvania Line and married Elizabeth Wickard of Lancaster, Pennsylvania in August, 1783; he applied for pension on 29 Oct 1834, aged 77, in Frederick County where he lived at the time of his enlistment; Henry died in November, 1838 and Elizabeth died on 19 Feb 1842, leaving these heirs: George Hoffman; Caspar Hoffman; John Hoffman; Henry Hoffman (living in 1846); Catharine Travise, Rebecca Hill and Charlotte Hoffman (heirs of Adam Hoffman); and, Jacob Hoffman; widow Elizabeth Hoffman had applied for pension under the Act of July 4, 1836, but the claim was suspended, stating *"no claim -- married after service -- died before August 16, 1842"* (i.e., the widow had died). {Ref: *Rejected or Suspended Applications for Revolutionary War Pensions* (1850 Report), p. 234; Research by Virgil D. White, citing Federal Pension Application R5096}

HOFFMAN, JACOB, see "Henry Hoffman," q.v.

HOFFMAN, JOHN (Frederick County), patriot buried in Mount Olivet Cemetery. {Ref: Information compiled by Dr. Donald Wolf in Maryland Society SAR Newsletter circa 1996}

HOFFMAN, JOHN, see "Henry Hoffman," q.v.

HOFFMAN, MARY, see "Henry Young," q.v.

HOFFMAN, MOSES (Western Maryland), private in Capt. Michael Cresap's Company in 1775. {Ref: Howard L. Leckey's *The Tenmile Country and Its Pioneer Families*, p. 15}

HOFFMAN (HUFFMAN), PHILIP (Montgomery County), soldier in the Virginia troops who applied for pension on 12 Jun 1838 in Montgomery County, Maryland under the Act of June 7, 1832, but the claim was rejected because he did not serve six months. {Ref: *Rejected or Suspended Applications for Revolutionary War Pensions* (1850 Report), p. 229; Research by Virgil D. White, citing Federal Pension Application R5099}

HOGAN, JAMES (Maryland Navy), ordinary sailor on the State Ship *Defence* in 1777. {Ref: Archives of Maryland Vol. 18, p. 657}

HOHN (HOHNE), CHRISTOPHER (Annapolis, Anne Arundel County), soldier in the Maryland troops in the Revolutionary War and in the War of 1812; born in Frederick Town where he lived at the time of his enlistment, he moved to Anne Arundel County in 1786 and married Mary Holland on 7 Jan 1792; he died in Annapolis on 29 Mar 1833 and his widow Mary Hohn (Hohne) applied for pension on 27 Nov 1838, aged 70, under the Act of July 7, 1838, but the claim was rejected for further proof of military service; payment was also suspended because *"the Annapolis records show his service, but not its length -- marriage admitted."* Mary was still living in 1855. {Ref: *Rejected or Suspended Applications for Revolutionary War Pensions* (1850 Report), pp. 235, 236; Research by Virgil D. White, citing Federal Pension Application R5110}

HOLBROOKS, GEORGE (Frederick County), soldier in the Revolution who married on 4 May 1836, in the 93rd year of his age, to Mrs. Broils who was aged about 50. {Ref: *Political Examiner*, 18 May 1836}

HOLDEN, JEREMIAH (Maryland Privateer), captain of a schooner [not named] in April, 1776. {Ref: Archives of Maryland Vol. 11, p. 396}

HOLLAND, GABRIEL (Frederick County), private (substitute) in the Maryland Continental Line, Williams' Regiment, enrolled in April, 1778 for 3 years or duration of the war. {Ref: Maryland Historical Magazine, Vol. 6, No. 3, p. 257}

HOLLAND, JOSEPH (Frederick County), private in the Maryland Continental Line and *"volunteer in the service of his country, died at his residence in New Market on 8 Feb 1839 in the 80th year of his age; his illness was protracted and often severe; his remains were interred in the burying ground of the Methodist Protestant Church, of which he was an active member, with the Honors of War by troops under the command of Capt. Richard Coale of Liberty Town."* {Ref: *Frederick Visiter and Temperance Advocate*, 13 Feb 1839}

HOLLAND, MARY, see "Christopher Hohn," q.v.

HOLLAND, NEHEMIAH (Worcester County), patriot who was commissioned one of the three persons in Worcester County by the Council of Maryland on 19

124

Aug 1779 to receive subscriptions for use of the State. {Ref: Archives of Maryland Vol. 21, p. 499}

HOLLINGSWORTH, FRANCIS (Baltimore Town), patriot and merchant who enrolled in Capt. John Sterrett's Independent Mercantile Company by February, 1777, at which time they were mustered into regular service with the continental army to repress loyalist activities in the Eastern Shore counties of Somerset and Worcester. {Ref: J. Thomas Scharf's *History of Baltimore City and County*, Part I, p. 77}

HOLLINGSWORTH, GEORGE, see "Micajah Mitchell," q.v.

HOLLINGSWORTH, JESSE, see "John Gibbons," q.v.

HOLLIS, MARY, see "Jacob Norris," q.v.

HOLLIS, RICHARD F., see "Jacob Norris," q.v.

HOLLSMAN, HENRY (Frederick County), private (substitute) in the Maryland Continental Line, who enlisted to serve until 10 Dec 1781, was discharged on 29 Nov 1781. {Ref: Archives of Maryland Vol. 48, p. 7}

HOLT, JOHN (Talbot County), private who was drafted into the Maryland Continental Line, was discharged on 8 Dec 1781. {Ref: Archives of Maryland Vol. 48, p. 10}

HOLTZMAN, HENRY (Frederick County), private (substitute) in the Maryland Continental Line, Gunby's Regiment, enrolled in May, 1778 for 3 years or duration of the war. {Ref: Maryland Historical Magazine, Vol. 6, No. 3, p. 259}

HOOD, ANDREW (Harford County), private who was enrolled 10 Mar 1776 in Militia Company No. 18 under Capt. John Jolly. {Ref: George W. Archer Collection and Revolutionary War File, Historical Society of Harford County Archives}

HOOE, ROBERT TOWNSEND (Charles County), patriot who was appointed by the Council of Maryland on 27 Jan 1776 as one of three persons in Charles County to collect all gold and silver coin that can be procured in said county. {Ref: Archives of Maryland Vol. 11, p. 132}

HOOK, ANN, see "Joseph Hook," q.v.

HOOK, FREDERICK (Baltimore County), soldier in the Maryland Troops who married Sarah ---- shortly after the war and died in Baltimore County (date not given); widow Sarah Hook applied for pension under the Act of July 7, 1838, but the claim was suspended *"to lie until called for -- see letter on file from John Munroe, October 17, 1848."* Sarah was still living in February, 1848 at which time affidavits were submitted in her behalf from William Kissey, John Fishpaw, and Catharine Bell (aged 85), all of Baltimore County. {Ref: *Rejected or Suspended Applications for Revolutionary War Pensions* (1850 Report), p. 236; Research by Virgil D. White, citing Federal Pension Application R5196}

HOOK, JOSEPH (Baltimore City), soldier in the Maryland troops who married Ann Channell on 16 Apr 1821 in Baltimore, applied for pension on 2 Jul 1832, and died on 18 Sep 1837; widow Ann Hook applied for pension on 10 May 1853, aged 74. {Ref: Research by Virgil D. White, citing Federal Pension Application W669}

HOOK, SARAH, see "Frederick Hook," q.v.

HOOK, STEPHEN (Frederick County), soldier in the Maryland troops who was born in 1756 in Frederick County and applied for pension in Alleghany County, Virginia on 8 Jul 1833. {Ref: Research by Virgil D. White, citing Federal Pension Application S8733}

HOOPER, ABRAHAM (Baltimore County), private (substitute) in the Maryland Continental Line by 1781, was discharged on 8 Dec 1781. {Ref: Archives of Maryland Vol. 48, p. 11}

HOOPER, ABRAHAM (Harford County), soldier in the Maryland Continental Line who was living in Harford County on 1 Sep 1820 at which time documents were filed in the 6th Judicial District, Harford County Court stating, in part: *"Abraham Hooper, aged 64 years, resident in Harford County ... does on his oath declare that he served in the Revolutionary War as follows: I enlisted under Capt. Robert Harris attached to the 6th Maryland Regiment and served until October 1781. Number of Certificate 7502. And I do also swear that I was a resident citizen of the United States on the 18th of March 1818 and that I have not since that time by gift, sale or in any manner disposed of my property or any part thereof with intent thereby so as to diminish it as to bring myself within the provision of an Act of Congress entitled an act to provide for certain persons engaged in the land and naval service of the United States in the Revolutionary War passed on the 18th day of March 1818 and that I have not, nor has any person in trust for me, any property or securities, contracts or debts due me nor have I any income other than what is contained in the schedule hereto annexed and by me subscribed. Schedule: 1 old horse worth $18; 2 cows at $14 each, $28; 1 bed and furniture $15; 4 shoats [young hogs] $12; 1 walnut and pine table $2; 1 house and 2 acres of land but not paid for, $57; 4 old rush bottom chairs $1.50; [total] $131.50. My occupation was a blacksmith when able to pursue it but old age has left me unable. Family: wife age 53 years, Sarah age 28 years, William age 21 years, John age 17 years, Eliza age 12 years."* Signed: Abraham Hooper (made his "X" mark). {Ref: Historical Society of Harford County, Court Records File 25.14}

HOOPER, JOHN (Baltimore County), private who enlisted in Pulaski's Legion in 1778 in Baltimore. {Ref: Maryland Historical Magazine, Vol. 13, No. 3, p. 223}

HOOPER, JOHN (Caroline County), patriot who was appointed captain in the 14th Militia Battalion by the Council of Maryland on 28 Jun 1780 in the room of Shadrack Lyden who had resigned. {Ref: Archives of Maryland Vol. 43, p. 207}

HOOPER, MARY, see "Abraham Mitchell," q.v.

HOOPER, THOMAS (Baltimore County), private, 31 May 1779, Capt. Benjamin Talbott's Militia Company, Cockey's Battalion. {Ref: Maryland Historical Magazine, Vol. 7, No. 1, p. 90}

126

HOOPS, ADAM (Southern Maryland?), lieutenant in Hazen's Regiment, 1777-1779, prisoner of war, captain in the 2nd and 4th Maryland Continental Lines, 1780-1781, and received payment for his services in the amount of "1900 Dollars & £3.10s" on 12 Sep 1780. {Ref: Archives of Maryland Vol. 18, pp. 123, 363, 520, and Vol. 45, p. 98}

HOPE, ANDREW, see "Richard Hope" and "James Kidd," q.v.

HOPE, ANNIE, see "Thomas Hope," q.v.

HOPE, EZRA, see "Thomas Hope," q.v.

HOPE, HANNAH, see "Thomas Hope," q.v.

HOPE, ISAAC, see "Richard Hope," q.v.

HOPE, JAMES, see "Richard Hope," q.v.

HOPE, JANNET, see "Richard Hope," q.v.

HOPE, JOHN, see "Thomas Hope," q.v.

HOPE, LOUISA, see "Thomas Hope," q.v.

HOPE, RICHARD (Harford County), private who was enrolled 9 Dec 1775 in Militia Company No. 14 under Capt. William McComas; born 29 Sep 1744, Richard Hope married Jannet or Jennett Wilson on 6 Jun 1769, died by 8 Apr 1823 (date of final distribution) and was buried in Bethel Presbyterian Church Cemetery near Jarrettsville; his heirs were: Jannet Hope (widow); James, Isaac, and Andrew Hope; Richard, Nancy, and Jane Kirkwood; Isaac, Rebecca, Neome, and Richard Hope Careins; and, Hannah Thompson. {Ref: George W. Archer Collection and Revolutionary War File, Historical Society of Harford County Archives; Henry C. Peden, Jr.'s *Heirs & Legatees of Harford County, 1802-1846*, p. 29; Bethel Church Cemetery Records}

HOPE, ROBERT (Maryland Navy), ordinary sailor on the State Ship *Defence* in 1777. {Ref: Archives of Maryland Vol. 18, p. 657}

HOPE, THOMAS (Harford County), first lieutenant by 15 Apr 1776 in Militia Company No. 20 under Capt. Robert Glenn; born 10 Jun 1742, married Hannah Nelson, died 20 Mar 1815 (aged 72 years, 9 months and 10 days) and buried in Bethel Presbyterian Church Cemetery near Jarrettsville; their children were Thomas Hope, Ezra Hope, John Hope, William Hope, Annie Hope, Louisa Hope, and Hannah Hope. {Ref: George W. Archer Collection and Revolutionary War File, Historical Society of Harford County Archives; Bethel Church Cemetery Records}

HOPE, WILLIAM, see "Thomas Hope," q.v.

HOPEWELL, THOMAS (Maryland Navy), midshipman on the State Ship *Defence* in 1777. {Ref: Archives of Maryland Vol. 18, p. 657}

HOPKINS, ---- (Charles County), soldier in the Maryland Continental Line by 16 Sep 1780 at which time his wife Elizabeth Hopkins received "4 days Rations to enable her to proceed to Charles County." {Ref: Archives of Maryland Vol. 43, p. 293}

HOPKINS, EPHRAIM, see "William Morgan," q.v.

HOPKINS, GERRARD (Anne Arundel County), patriot who took the Oath of Fidelity and Support to the State of Maryland (affirmed) on 8 Apr 1778. {Ref: Archives of Maryland Vol. 21, p. 16}

HOPKINS, JOHN, see "William Morgan," q.v.

HOPKINS, JONATHAN (Talbot County), sailor in 1780; on 15 Nov 1780 Rachel Gibson, wife of Woolman Gibson, petitioned the Governor and Council of Maryland *"asking discharge of Jonathan Hopkins, her son by a former marriage, who is deficient in his intellect and having straggled away last winter was induced to enlist on the Chester Galley. He is unfit for service and is exposed to the Mockery & Insult of the Sailors and to the Hazard of being corrupted by their example and of learning the bad words."* {Ref: Archives of Maryland Vol. 43, p. 367}

HOPKINS, JOSEPH, see "William Morgan," q.v.

HOPKINS, ROGER (Maryland Navy), seaman or marine on the State Ship *Defence* in 1777. {Ref: Archives of Maryland Vol. 18, p. 657}

HOPKINS, WILLIAM (Anne Arundel County), patriot who took the Oath of Fidelity and Support to the State of Maryland (affirmed) on 8 Apr 1778. {Ref: Archives of Maryland Vol. 21, p. 16}

HOPPE, JEREMIE (Baltimore County), private who enlisted in Pulaski's Legion on 22 Mar 1778 and still in service in November, 1779. {Ref: Maryland Historical Magazine, Vol. 13, No. 3, p. 223}

HORN, GEORGE (Frederick County), private who was drafted into the Maryland Continental Line, was discharged on 8 Dec 1781. {Ref: Archives of Maryland Vol. 48, p. 10}

HORNER, GUSTAVUS (Annapolis), doctor and State Surgeon's Mate in the Hospital Department of the Maryland Continental Line by 19 Jun 1780 at which time he was paid $150 gratuity under a resolution passed by the General Assembly on 11 Dec 1778; also paid $2000 under the resolution passed on 17 Jun 1780 as it related to officers and soldiers in the American Army. {Ref: Archives of Maryland Vol. 43, p. 199}

HORNEY, JOHN (Kent County), private in the 5th Maryland Continental Line who was a 9 month soldier in the 5th Maryland Regiment in 1778-1779, was discharged on 22 Apr 1779 and received £27 in clothing. {Ref: Archives of Maryland Vol. 21, p. 360}

HORNEY, THOMAS (Kent County), private in the 5th Maryland Continental Line who was a 9 month soldier in the 5th Maryland Regiment in 1778-1779, was discharged on 22 Apr 1779 and received £27.10.0 in clothing. {Ref: Archives of Maryland Vol. 21, p. 360}

HORSEFIELD, JOSEPH (Frederick County), private (substitute) in the Maryland Continental Line, Price's Regiment, enrolled in May, 1778 for 3 years or duration of the war. {Ref: Maryland Historical Magazine, Vol. 6, No. 3, p. 261}

HORSEFIELD, LUKE (Frederick County), private (substitute) in the Maryland Continental Line, Price's Regiment, enrolled in May, 1778 for 3 years or duration of the war. {Ref: Maryland Historical Magazine, Vol. 6, No. 3, p. 261}

HORTON, JOSEPH (Baltimore County), private who enlisted in Pulaski's Legion on 28 Aug 1779 and still in service in November, 1779. {Ref: Maryland Historical Magazine, Vol. 13, No. 3, p. 224}

HOSIER, JOSHUA (Maryland Navy), seaman on the State Ship *Defence* in 1777. {Ref: Archives of Maryland Vol. 18, p. 657}

HOSKINS, JOSEPH (Washington County), private who was enrolled to serve as a substitute in the Maryland Continental Line until 10 Dec 1781, but *"being represented unfit for the service for which he was intended"* was discharged on 30 Oct 1781. {Ref: Archives of Maryland Vol. 45, p. 656}

HOSKINS, THOMAS (Harford County), private who was enrolled 9 Dec 1775 in Militia Company No. 14 under Capt. William McComas. {Ref: George W. Archer Collection and Revolutionary War File, Historical Society of Harford County Archives}

HOULDEN, JOHN (Frederick County), private (substitute) in the Maryland Continental Line, Price's Regiment, enrolled in April, 1778 for 3 years or duration of the war. {Ref: Maryland Historical Magazine, Vol. 6, No. 3, p. 256}

HOULT, THOMAS (Baltimore County), private who enlisted in Pulaski's Legion on 9 May 1778 in Baltimore. {Ref: Maryland Historical Magazine, Vol. 13, No. 3, p. 222}

HOUSE, BENJAMIN (Frederick County), patriot buried in Mount Olivet Cemetery. {Ref: Information compiled by Dr. Donald Wolf in Maryland Society SAR Newsletter circa 1996}

HOUSER, MARTIN AND PHILIP (Montgomery County), served as privates in the militia in 1777 and rendered material aid (supplied wheat) to the continental army in 1781; see Peden's *Revolutionary Patriots of Montgomery County, 1776-1783* and subsequent research that has revealed the following clarification: *"Martin and Philip were probably brothers as Philip died in 1782 and Martin was listed as 'kindred.' Martin later married the widow Mary Offutt and had four children, the youngest named Philip. The Ref: V-72 applies only to Martin and his son Philip who was born after the Revolutionary War. The patriot was not the son of Martin and, most likely, his brother."* [Note: Ref: V-72 above refers to *Abstracts of Montgomery County Wills, 1776-1825*, page 72]. The original will of Martin Howser *[sic]* in 1812 is recorded in Wills Liber L#H, p. 20. {Ref: Research by Sue Houser of Montgomery Village, Maryland (a direct descendant) in 1999}

HOVER, DANIEL (Washington County), private who was enrolled to serve as a substitute in the Maryland Continental Line until 10 Dec 1781, but *"being represented unfit for the service for which he was intended"* was discharged on 30 Oct 1781. {Ref: Archives of Maryland Vol. 45, p. 656}

HOVEY, DANIEL (Baltimore County), private, aged 26, gunsmith, born in Dublin, enlisted (made his "X" mark) on 15 Feb 1776 in Capt. John Fulford's Company of Matrosses. {Ref: Maryland Historical Magazine, Vol. 69, No. 1, p. 95}

HOWARD, ---- (Anne Arundel County?), soldier in the Maryland Continental Line *"now remaining in Annapolis"* on 24 Jul 1780 at which time his wife Biddy Howard was entitled to rations under the laws of the State. {Ref: Archives of Maryland Vol. 43, p. 227}

HOWARD, BENJAMIN, JR. (Harford County), soldier in the Maryland militia by 25 Jul 1781 at which time he petitioned the Governor and Council of Maryland regarding the estate of his late father Benjamin Howard, deceased (his father had also been fined for preaching the Gospel) and stated he (the petitioner) had associated himself and enrolled in the militia and had no other subsistence for himself and a large helpless family of orphans except his father's property. {Ref: Archives of Maryland Vol. 47, pp. 367-368}

HOWARD, BIDDY, see "---- Howard," q.v.

HOWARD, JOHN BEALE (Harford County), first lieutenant, commissioned 26 Apr 1776 in Militia Company No. 22 under Capt. Alexander Cowan; born 1735 in England, married Blanche Carvel Hall (1743-1800) on 18 Apr 1765, and died 15 Jul 1799; their children were: Parker Howard (born 13 Mar 1766, died 2 Sep 1766); Matthias Howard (born 9 Dec 1777, died in November, 1781); John Beale Howard (born 3 Apr 1774, married Margaret West); Edward Aquilla Howard (born 15 Nov 1775, married first Charlotte Rumsey and second Agnes Young Day); and, Elizabeth Howard (born 7 Sep 1767, married Rev. Benjamin Richardson). {Ref: George W. Archer Collection and Revolutionary War File, Historical Society of Harford County Archives; Maryland State Society DAR Directory, 1892-1965, p. 405}

HOWARD, JOHN BEALE (Baltimore County), patriot who was commissioned one of the three persons in Baltimore County by the Council of Maryland on 19 Aug 1779 to receive subscriptions for use of the State. {Ref: Archives of Maryland Vol. 21, p. 499}

HOWARD, JOHN EAGER (Baltimore County), colonel in the 6th Maryland Continental Line who received payment for his services in the amount of "1900 Dollars & £3.10s" on 12 Sep 1780; known as the hero of the Battle of Cowpens, John was born on 11 Jun 1752 in Baltimore County, married Margaretta Chew (1761-1824) on 18 Jun 1787, and died 12 Oct 1827; their children were: John Eager Howard (born 1788, married Cornelia Read); George Howard (born 1789, married Prudence Ridgely); Benjamin Howard (born 1791, married Jane Gilmore); William Howard (born 1793, married Rebecca Key); Juliana Howard (born 1796, married John McHenry); James Howard (born 1797, married first Sophia Ridgely and second Catherine Ross); Sophia Chew Howard (born 1800, married William George Read); and, Charles Howard (born 1802, married Elizabeth Key). {Ref: Archives of Maryland Vol. 45, p. 98; Maryland State Society DAR Directory, 1892-1965, p. 405}

HOWARD, JOSEPH (Frederick County), patriot buried in Mount Olivet Cemetery. {Ref: Information compiled by Dr. Donald Wolf in Maryland Society SAR Newsletter circa 1996}

HOWARD, NATHAN (Kent County), private in the Maryland Continental Line who was *"sent from camp by General Smallwood as unfit for the service"* and was discharged on 22 Jun 1778. {Ref: Archives of Maryland Vol. 21, p. 144}

HOWARD, SAMUEL HARVEY (Anne Arundel County), patriot who was Purchaser of Clothing for Anne Arundel County until 16 Jun 1781 when he resigned. {Ref: Archives of Maryland Vol. 45, p. 476}

HOWARD, THOMAS (Maryland Navy), midshipman on the State Ship *Defence* from 15 Aug to 31 Dec 1777; marine on the galley *Baltimore* in 1778 who took the Oath of Fidelity and Allegiance to the State of Maryland on 31 Mar 1778. {Ref: Archives of Maryland Vol. 16, p. 559 and Vol. 18, p. 657}

HOWARD, WILLIAM (Maryland Navy), carpenter's mate on the State Ship *Defence* in 1777. {Ref: Archives of Maryland Vol. 18, p. 657}

HOWARD, WILLIAM (Maryland Navy), marine on the State Ship *Defence* in 1777. {Ref: Archives of Maryland Vol. 18, p. 657}

HOWE, GENERAL, see "Baruch Williams," q.v.

HOWLET, ANDREW (Harford County), private who was enrolled 10 Mar 1776 in Militia Company No. 18 under Capt. John Jolly. {Ref: George W. Archer Collection and Revolutionary War File, Historical Society of Harford County Archives}

HOWLET, JAMES (Harford County), private who was enrolled 10 Mar 1776 in Militia Company No. 18 under Capt. John Jolly. {Ref: George W. Archer Collection and Revolutionary War File, Historical Society of Harford County Archives}

HUBBERD, JOB (Dorchester County), private who was drafted into the Maryland Continental Line, was discharged on 8 Dec 1781. {Ref: Archives of Maryland Vol. 48, p. 10}

HUDSON, JONATHAN (Baltimore County), patriot who supplied provisions to the State of Maryland between June and September, 1780. {Ref: Archives of Maryland Vol. 45, p. 84}

HUDSON, WILLIAM (Maryland Navy), seaman on the State Ship *Defence* in 1777. {Ref: Archives of Maryland Vol. 18, p. 657}

HUESTON, THOMAS (Frederick County), private who was enrolled to serve as a substitute in the Maryland Continental Line until 10 Dec 1781, but *"being represented unfit for the service for which he was intended"* was discharged on 30 Oct 1781. {Ref: Archives of Maryland Vol. 45, p. 657}

HUFFMAN, PHILIP, see "Philip Hoffman," q.v.

HUGGARD, WILLIAM (Maryland Navy), marine on the State Ship *Defence* in 1777. {Ref: Archives of Maryland Vol. 18, p. 657}

HUGGINS, WILLIAM (Maryland Navy), marine on the State Ship *Defence* in 1777. {Ref: Archives of Maryland Vol. 18, p. 657}

HUGHES, ANDREW (Harford County), private who was enrolled 9 Sep 1775 in Militia Company No. 7 under Capt. John Taylor. {Ref: George W. Archer Collection and Revolutionary War File, Historical Society of Harford County Archives}

HUGHES, DANIEL (Washington County), officer and patriot who was commissioned one of the three persons in Washington County by the Council of Maryland on 19 Aug 1779 to receive subscriptions for use of the State. *"Col. Daniel Hughes, of Washington County, died 5 Dec 1818 in his 74th year."* For more information on the Hughes family, see J. Thomas Scharf's *History of Western Maryland*, Vol. II, pp. 1011-1012. {Ref: Archives of Maryland Vol. 21, p. 499; *Frederick-Town Herald*, 12 Dec 1818}

HUGHES, HANNAH, see "Parker Gilbert," q.v.

HUGHES, JOHN (Harford County, Susquehannah Hundred), private who was enrolled 23 Apr 1776 in Militia Company No. 21 under Capt. George Patterson. {Ref: George W. Archer Collection and Revolutionary War File, Historical Society of Harford County Archives}

HUGHES, JOHN (Prince George's County), private in the Maryland troops circa 1780 who petitioned the Governor and Council of Maryland [no date given], as follows: *"Your Humble Petitioner most Honourable Gentlemen Begs leave to offer to Your Consideration, a series of Continued Hardships Undergone in the many Campaignes he has served in 15 in the service of Britain & 4 in the American Service; which together with the Increase of Age (now 51 years) Has occasioned many Corporal Disorders in Particular Rheumatic Pains, allmost without Intermission By which means the Duties of Camp & Fatigues of march are Become too arduous for me to Endure. My Wife and Family in the next Place Honour'd Gentlemen thro' Poverty and Informity are Suffering for the Common Necessaries of Life, During my absence. All which taken Gentlemen into Your Consideration, I hope will Induce you to Commiserate my hard Fortune & to Discharge from the Service Your most Humble Petitioner and Obedient servant."* {Ref: Archives of Maryland Vol. 43, p. 532}

HUGHES, JOHN (Western Maryland), private in Capt. Michael Cresap's Company in 1775. {Ref: Howard L. Leckey's *The Tenmile Country and Its Pioneer Families*, p. 15}

HUGHES, JOHN HALL (Harford County), first lieutenant, commissioned 16 May 1776 in Militia Company No. 27 under Capt. Samuel Griffith; born 10 Jul 1742 in Baltimore County, married Ann Everett (1754-1821) on 26 Jan 1769, and died 7 Feb 1802; their children were: Everett Hughes (born 11 Mar 1770, married Nancy Botts); John Hall Hughes (born 21 Aug 1772, married Charlotte Mitchell); Scott Hughes (born 24 Aug 1774, married Mary Gilbert); James Hughes (born 1776, married Hannah Elizabeth Gilbert); Martha Hughes (married Parker Gilbert, Jr.); Sarah Mitchell Hughes (born 1780, married Richard Allen); and, Ann Hughes (born 7 Apr 1784, married James Botts); also see "John Botts," q.v. {Ref: George W. Archer Collection and Revolutionary War File,

Historical Society of Harford County Archives; Maryland State Society DAR Directory, 1892-1965, p. 409}

HUGHES, JOSEPH (Western Maryland), private in Capt. Michael Cresap's Company in 1775. {Ref: Howard L. Leckey's *The Tenmile Country and Its Pioneer Families*, p. 15}

HUGHES, NAT. (Harford County, Susquehannah Hundred), private who was enrolled 23 Apr 1776 in Militia Company No. 21 under Capt. George Patterson. {Ref: George W. Archer Collection and Revolutionary War File, Historical Society of Harford County Archives}

HUGHES, WILLIAM (Kent County), private (substitute) in the Maryland Continental Line by 1781, was discharged on 8 Dec 1781. {Ref: Archives of Maryland Vol. 48, p. 11}

HUGOU, THOMAS B. (Baltimore County), lieutenant in the 5th Maryland Continental Line who received payment for his services in the amount of "1900 Dollars & £3.10s" on 12 Sep 1780. {Ref: Archives of Maryland Vol. 45, p. 98}

HUMPHREYS, LEWIS (Maryland Navy), seaman or marine on the State Ship *Defence* in 1777. {Ref: Archives of Maryland Vol. 18, p. 657}

HUMRICHOUSE, PETER (Washington County), soldier in the Pennsylvania Line whose widow Mary Hamrickhouse *[sic]* applied for pension under the Act of July 7, 1838, but the claim was suspended *"for proof of the day of her decease and the names of her children must be certified by the court."* Peter was the soldier described in one account as follows: *"The father of Frederick Humrichouse enlisted as a private in the Revolutionary army two months before the Declaration of Independence was signed, and on the 1st of July, 1776, was commissioned as an ensign; he participated in the great battles of the war, was at Valley Forge, and did not lay down his sword until the struggle was ended; he then lived in Philadelphia until the yellow fever epidemic, when he removed to Hagerstown."* For additional information see Federal Pension Application W27514. {Ref: *Rejected or Suspended Applications for Revolutionary War Pensions* (1850 Report), p. 236; J. Thomas Scharf's *History of Western Maryland*, Vol. II, p. 1035}

HUNTER, ELIZA (Anne Arundel County?), patriot who was paid 4 shilings and 3 pence by the Maryland Council of Safety for ferriage of General Lee on 4 Oct 1776. {Ref: Archives of Maryland Vol. 12, p. 321}

HUNTER, GEORGE (Baltimore County), captain of a company of matrosses formed in the defense of the harbor of Baltimore, commissioned 30 Mar 1781. {Ref: Archives of Maryland Vol. 45, p. 368}

HUNTER, JAMES (Talbot County), private (substitute) in the Maryland Continental Line by 1781, was discharged on 8 Dec 1781. {Ref: Archives of Maryland Vol. 48, p. 11}

HURBERT, FRANCIS (Maryland Navy), boatswain's mate on the State Ship *Defence* in 1777. {Ref: Archives of Maryland Vol. 18, p. 657}

HURD, BENNETT (Baltimore County), private (substitute) in the Maryland Continental Line, who enlisted to serve until 10 Dec 1781, was discharged on 29 Nov 1781. {Ref: Archives of Maryland Vol. 48, p. 7}

HURST, CUTHBERT or CATWOOD (Maryland Navy), seaman or marine on the State Ship *Defence* in 1777. {Ref: Archives of Maryland Vol. 18, p. 657}

HUSE, SAMUEL (Anne Arundel County), private by 5 Oct 1776 (made his "X" mark) in Capt. Richard Chew's Militia Company, Weems' Battalion. {Ref: Archives of Maryland Vol. 12, p. 323}

HUSSEY, PAUL (Maryland Privateer), captain and master of the sloop *Hannah* who was granted permission by the Council of Maryland *"to load with Flour and Grain within this State for the consumption of the Eastern States"* on 21 Sep 1778; commander of the schooner *Lizard*, navigated by 10 men and mounting 4 carriage guns and 6 small arms, was issued Letters of Marque & Reprisal by the Council of Maryland on 13 Mar 1780. {Ref: Archives of Maryland Vol. 21, p. 209 and Vol. 43, p. 110}

HUSTEAD, ROBERT (Western Maryland), private in Capt. Michael Cresap's Company in 1775. {Ref: Howard L. Leckey's *The Tenmile Country and Its Pioneer Families*, p. 15}

HUTCHCRAFT, THOMAS (Frederick County), private (substitute) in the Maryland Continental Line, German Regiment, enrolled in May, 1778 for 3 years or duration of the war. {Ref: Maryland Historical Magazine, Vol. 6, No. 3, p. 260}

HUTCHENS, WILLIAM (Maryland Navy), sailor or seaman on 7 Jan 1780. {Ref: Calendar of Maryland State Papers, The Brown Books, p. 57}

HUTCHINS, RICHARD (Harford County), second lieutenant, commissioned 14 May 1776 in Militia Company No. 25 under Capt. Charles Baker. {Ref: George W. Archer Collection and Revolutionary War File, Historical Society of Harford County Archives}

HUTCHINS, THOMAS (Harford County), first lieutenant, commissioned 26 Apr 1776 in Militia Company No. 24 under Capt. Samuel Calwell. {Ref: George W. Archer Collection and Revolutionary War File, Historical Society of Harford County Archives}

HUTCHINSON, WILLIAM (Baltimore City), soldier who applied for pension under the Act of June 7, 1832, but the claim was suspended because *"service in the Maryland militia was not proved by evidence; applicable only to a soldier of the line"* (and noted also that he was deceased, but no date was given). {Ref: *Rejected or Suspended Applications for Revolutionary War Pensions* (1850 Report), p. 231}

HUTSON, SOLOMON (Somerset County), private, Maryland Continental Line, Continental Army, 1780. {Ref: Archives of Maryland Vol. 45, p. 67}

HUTTON, PAUL (Montgomery County), private in the Maryland Continental Line by 1778, was retained in the service on 22 Jun 1778 and sent on board the galleys. {Ref: Archives of Maryland Vol. 21, p. 144}

HYNDSON, ANTHONY (Maryland Navy), boatswain on the State Ship *Defence* in 1777. {Ref: Archives of Maryland Vol. 18, p. 657}

HYNES, ANDREW (Western Maryland), private in Capt. Michael Cresap's Company in 1775. {Ref: Howard L. Leckey's *The Tenmile Country and Its Pioneer Families*, p. 16}

IJAMS (IIAMES), THOMAS (Anne Arundel County), private who enlisted in the 2nd Maryland Continental Line on 10 Jan 1777 and was a sergeant at the time of his discharge on 1 Jan 1780; received clothing *"to be charged to the Continent"* on 1 Feb 1780. {Ref: Archives of Maryland Vol. 45, p. 126, and Vol. 43, p. 74}

IRELAND, WILLIAM (Calvert County), patriot who was commissioned one of the three persons in Calvert County by the Council of Maryland on 19 Aug 1779 to receive subscriptions for use of the State. {Ref: Archives of Maryland Vol. 21, p. 499}

ISABEL (ISSABELL), ROBERT (Anne Arundel County?), drummer in 10 Feb 1776 and sergeant by 10 Jan 1780 in the 2nd Maryland Continental Line; soldier *"now remaining in Annapolis"* on 24 Jul 1780 at which time his wife Betsy Isabel was entitled to rations under the laws of the State; the Council of Maryland ordered *"That the Armourer deliver to Serjeant Issabell two Axes for the use of the Hospital"* on 29 Nov 1781. {Ref: Archives of Maryland Vol. 43, p. 227, Vol. 45, p. 126, and Vol. 48, p. 6}

ITNIRE (ITNEUR), DANIEL (Washington County), private in the Maryland militia; born in 1756 in Frederick County and lived in Washington County at the time of his enlistment; applied for pension there on 9 Apr 1833. {Ref: Research by Virgil D. White, citing Federal Pension Application S9744}

JACKELEN, FRANCIS (Maryland Navy), marine on the State Ship *Defence* in 1777. {Ref: Archives of Maryland Vol. 18, p. 657}

JACKSON, GEORGE (Kent County), ensign in the county militia, commissioned 22 Jun 1776; one George Jackson died testate in Kent County by 9 Nov 1798. {Ref: Archives of Maryland Vol. 11, p. 506; Kent County Wills Liber 7, p. 619}

JACKSON, HENRY (Somerset County), patriot who was commissioned one of the three persons in Somerset County by the Council of Maryland on 19 Aug 1779 to receive subscriptions for use of the State; appointed Commissary of Purchases on 8 Jul 1780. {Ref: Archives of Maryland Vol. 21, p. 499, and Vol. 43, p. 215}

JACKSON, JOHN (Dorchester County), patriot who took the Oath of Fidelity and Support to the State of Maryland on 2 Apr 1778. {Ref: Archives of Maryland Vol. 21, p. 1}

JACKSON, JOHN (Queen Anne's County), private (substitute) in the Maryland Continental Line by 1781, was discharged on 8 Dec 1781. {Ref: Archives of Maryland Vol. 48, p. 11}

JACKSON, SOPHIA, see "William Arnold," q.v.

JACKSON, WILLIAM (Eastern Shore), private in the 3rd Maryland Continental Line who was born on the Eastern Shore of Maryland (county not specified, possibly Caroline County) and enlisted there on 25 Apr 1778; married Jemima Burnet on 8 Aug 1814; applied for pension as William Sullivan Jackson in Grayson County, Virginia on 12 Nov 1834, aged 76; died 22 Aug 1849 and his widow applied for pension in Carroll County, Virginia on 3 Oct 1853, aged 66. {Ref: Archives of Maryland Vol. 18, p. 127; Research by Virgil D. White, citing Federal Pension Application W7883}

JACOB, GABRIEL (Frederick and Prince George's Counties), ensign in the 6th Maryland Continental Line by 1 May 1781 at which time he received payment due in the amount of £22.8.10. {Ref: Archives of Maryland Vol. 45, p. 421}

JACOB, GEORGE (Prince George's County), lieutenant in the 6th Maryland Continental Line who received payment for his services in the amount of "1900 Dollars & £3.10s" on 12 Sep 1780. {Ref: Archives of Maryland Vol. 45, p. 98}

JACOB, JOSEPH (Anne Arundel County), patriot who took the Oath of Fidelity and Support to the State of Maryland on 9 Apr 1778. {Ref: Archives of Maryland Vol. 21, p. 22}

JACOBS, HENRY (Anne Arundel County), private in the Maryland Continental Line who died by 12 Sep 1835 in Anne Arundel County at which time he left a son John Jacobs as his only heir. {Ref: Bounty Land Warrant 2124-100}

JACOBS, J. (Frederick or Prince George's County), lieutenant in the 6th Maryland Continental Line who received payment for his services in the amount of "1900 Dollars & £3.10s" on 12 Sep 1780. {Ref: Archives of Maryland Vol. 45, p. 98}

JACOBS, JOHN (Western Maryland), private in Capt. Michael Cresap's Company in 1775. {Ref: Howard L. Leckey's *The Tenmile Country and Its Pioneer Families*, p. 16}

JACOBS, JOHN, see "Henry Jacobs," q.v.

JAFFRAY, JAMES (Baltimore County), patriot who was noted by the Council of Maryland on 29 Sep 1778 stating, in part, *"that he hath been absent in parts beyond the Seas for about 14 months last past and hath lately that is to say within 3 months last past, returned into this State, appeared before the Governor & Council, and before them did take, repeat and Subscribe the Oath of Fidelity and Support to this State contained in the Act entitled An Act to punish certain Crimes and Misdemeanors and to prevent the Growth of Toryism."* {Ref: Archives of Maryland Vol. 21, p. 212}

JAMAR, HENRY (Baltimore City), soldier who allegedly served in the Pennsylvania Line, married Jane --- in 1786 or 1787, and died in December, 1793; his widow Jane Jamar married second to Patrick Foy and he died 5 years later; Jane Foy applied for pension in Baltimore on 2 Mar 1843, aged 82, under the Act of July 7, 1838, but the claim was suspended for further proof of service and marriage. {Ref: *Rejected or Suspended Applications for Revolutionary War Pensions* (1850 Report), p. 236; Research by Virgil D. White, citing Federal Pension Application R3535}

JAMES, ROBERT (Baltimore County), private who enlisted in Pulaski's Legion on 28 Mar 1778 and still in service in November, 1779. {Ref: Maryland Historical Magazine, Vol. 13, No. 3, p. 223}

JAMES, THOMAS, JR. (Harford County), private who was enrolled 9 Dec 1775 in Militia Company No. 14 under Capt. William McComas. {Ref: George W. Archer Collection and Revolutionary War File, Historical Society of Harford County Archives}

JAMES, WALTER (Baltimore County), private, 31 May 1779, Capt. Benjamin Talbott's Militia Company, Cockey's Battalion. {Ref: Maryland Historical Magazine, Vol. 7, No. 1, p. 90}

JAMESON, MR. [ADAM?] (Maryland Continental Line, Staff and P. Officer), A.C.I., received payment for his services in the amount of "1900 Dollars & £3.10s" on 12 Sep 1780. {Ref: Archives of Maryland Vol. 45, p. 98}

JAMISON, LEONARD (Frederick County), captain and patriot buried in Mount Olivet Cemetery. {Ref: Information compiled by Dr. Donald Wolf in Maryland Society SAR Newsletter circa 1996}

JANQUARY, ABRAHAM (Anne Arundel County), private by 5 Oct 1776 (made his "X" mark) in Capt. Richard Chew's Militia Company, Weems' Battalion. {Ref: Archives of Maryland Vol. 12, p. 323}

JARBOE, PETER (St. Mary's County), private (substitute) in the Maryland Continental Line by 1781, was discharged on 8 Dec 1781. {Ref: Archives of Maryland Vol. 48, p. 11, which listed the name as "Peter Jarber"}

JARVIS, ELISHA (Montgomery County), private in the Maryland Continental Line; born 14 Dec 1757 in Montgomery County and lived there at the time of his enlistment; moved to Rowan County, North Carolina in 1781 and married Drucilla Smith on 27 May 1785; moved to Wilkes County, Georgia in 1790, and then to Clark County, Georgia, and to Pickens District, South Carolina in 1827; applied for pension on 9 Oct 1833 and died on 4 Sep 1837; his widow applied for pension on 31 Dec 1844, aged about 78. {Ref: Research by Virgil D. White, citing Federal Pension Application W11929}

JARVIS, HANNAH, see "Solomon Jarvis," q.v.

JARVIS, LEWIS, see "Solomon Jarvis," q.v.

JARVIS (JERVIS), SOLOMON (Kent and Harford Counties), private in the militia who lived near Bellaire, Maryland at the time of his enlistment in 1776; sergeant in the Maryland Line by 7 Oct 1776 at which time he was serving in Philadelphia and petitioned the Council of Safety stating, in part, that he [Solomon Jervis of Kent County] *"has served in Capt. Watkins' Company for these Eight Months past in the Quality of a Serjint, he therefore prays your Honours to apoint him a Commission in one of the Battalions now to be raised in this Province."* After the war he moved to Kentucky and applied for pension in Fleming County on 10 Mar 1829, aged 76; his mother Hannah Jarvis, aged 99, was a witness; he moved to Scott County by 1839 (residence of his son

Lewis Jarvis) and was still there in 1842. {Ref: Archives of Maryland Vol. 12, p. 325; Research by Virgil D. White, citing Federal Pension Application R5560}

JARVIS, WILLIAM, see "William Jervis," q.v.

JEFFERS, JACOB (Kent and Queen Anne's Counties), soldier in the Maryland troops who married Ann Goldsborough in December, 1793 and applied for pension in Queen Anne's County on 27 Jun 1818; in 1820 he was aged 59 with wife Ann Jeffers (aged about 40) and children Rachel Jeffers (aged 15) and Rebecca Jeffers (aged 11); Jacob died 3 Nov 1841 and his widow Ann applied for pension in Kent County in March, 1847, aged about 70, under the Act of July 7, 1838, but the claim was suspended, stating *"service admitted -- marriage requires proof."* She died 25 Jun 1853 leaving children Joseph Jeffers, William Jeffers, Washington Jeffers, Rainey Jeffers, and Julia Jeffers (according to affidavits in 1857). {Ref: *Rejected or Suspended Applications for Revolutionary War Pensions* (1850 Report), p. 236; Research by Virgil D. White, citing Federal Pension Application W5561}

JEMMISON, WILLIAM (Baltimore County), private, aged 18, labourer, born in Pennsylvania, enlisted (made his "X" mark) on 28 Feb 1776 in Capt. John Fulford's Company of Matrosses, deserted 6 Apr 1776 and took his breeches with him. {Ref: Maryland Historical Magazine, Vol. 69, No. 1, pp. 95, 97}

JENIFER, DANIEL (Charles County), patriot who was appointed Commissary of Purchases by the Council of Maryland on 8 Jul 1780. {Ref: Archives of Maryland Vol. 43, p. 215}

JENKINS, EDWARD (Montgomery County), private (substitute) in the Maryland Continental Line by 1781, was discharged on 8 Dec 1781. {Ref: Archives of Maryland Vol. 48, p. 11}

JENKINS, JOSEPH (Talbot County), private (substitute) in the Maryland Continental Line by 1781, was discharged on 8 Dec 1781. {Ref: Archives of Maryland Vol. 48, p. 11}

JENKINS, PHILIP (Montgomery County), private (substitute) in the Maryland Continental Line, who enlisted to serve until 10 Dec 1781, was discharged on 29 Nov 1781. {Ref: Archives of Maryland Vol. 48, p. 7}

JENKINS, SAMUEL (Harford County), private who was enrolled 25 Mar 1776 in Militia Company No. 19 under Capt. William Morgan. {Ref: George W. Archer Collection and Revolutionary War File, Historical Society of Harford County Archives}

JENNETT, GREEN (Maryland Navy), marine on the State Ship *Defence* in 1777. {Ref: Archives of Maryland Vol. 18, p. 657}

JENNINGS, ANN, see "Thomas Johnson, Jr.," q.v.

JERRIAL, JOHN (Maryland Navy), marine on the State Ship *Defence* in 1777. {Ref: Archives of Maryland Vol. 18, p. 657}

JERVIS, SOLOMON, see "Solomon Jarvis," q.v.

JERVIS, WILLIAM (Harford County, Susquehannah Hundred), private who was enrolled 23 Apr 1776 in Militia Company No. 21 under Capt. George Patterson.

{Ref: George W. Archer Collection and Revolutionary War File, Historical Society of Harford County Archives}

JOHNS, AQUILA (Maryland Navy and Baltimore Privateer), second lieutenant on the State Ship *Defence*, commissioned 5 Apr 1776; lieutenant on said ship in 1777; commander of the ship *Buckskin*, mounting 28 carriage guns and 24 small arms, was issued Letters of Marque & Reprisal by the Council of Maryland on 9 Jan 1779; commander of the brigantine *Buckskin Merchantman* and a prisoner of war in New York by 16 Dec 1780 at which time an exchange was offered with the British. {Ref: Archives of Maryland Vol. 11, p. 312, Vol. 18, p. 657, Vol. 21, p. 277, Vol. 45, p. 244, and Vol. 47, p. 40}

JOHNS, AQUILA, see "Thomas Johns," q.v.

JOHNS, CASSANDRA, see "Thomas Jones," q.v.

JOHNS, JANE, see "David Lynn," q.v.

JOHNS, LEONARD, see "Thomas Johns," q.v.

JOHNS, MARGARETT, see "Thomas Johns," q.v.

JOHNS, RICHARD, see "Thomas Johns," q.v.

JOHNS, SARAH, see "Thomas Johns," q.v.

JOHNS, THOMAS (Montgomery County), patriot who was commissioned Register of Wills on 6 May 1779 and served as Commissioner of Loans for Montgomery County in 1780; died testate by 25 Jul 1794, leaving sons Richard Johns and Leonard Hollyday Johns, daughters Margarett Crabb Johns, Sarah Johns, and brothers Aquila Johns and Richard Johns. {Ref: Archives of Maryland Vol. 21, p. 380 and Vol. 43, p. 291}

JOHNSON, BAKER (Frederick County), colonel who died in June, 1811 and *"during 15 months of severe indisposition preceding his death, suffered every poignant extreme of excruciating pain; he was a native of Calvert County, but immigrated early in life to Frederick where he entered into the profession of the law; he marched at the head of his regiment during the Revolutionary War, then resumed his vocation at the Bar"* [very long obituary; buried in Mount Olivet Cemetery]. Mrs. Catharine Johnson, widow of the late Col. Baker Johnson, died in Frederick on 9 Jun 1814, and their son Baker Johnson, also a colonel, died near Tallahassee, Florida on 13 Jul 1838 in his 50th year [his obituary gives some information about his father's service in the Revolutionary War]. {Ref: Burial information compiled by Dr. Donald Wolf in Maryland Society SAR Newsletter circa 1996; *Frederick-Town Herald*, 22 Jun 1811; *Bartgis's Republican Gazette*, 25 Jun 1814; *The Republican Citizen*, 10 Aug 1838}

JOHNSON, BENJAMIN (Charles County), private (substitute) in the Maryland Continental Line by 1781, was discharged on 8 Dec 1781. {Ref: Archives of Maryland Vol. 48, p. 11}

JOHNSON, CATHARINE, see "Baker Johnson," q.v.

JOHNSON, EDWARD (Baltimore Town), patriot and merchant who enrolled in Capt. John Sterrett's Independent Mercantile Company by February, 1777, at which time they were mustered into regular service with the continental army to repress loyalist activities in the Eastern Shore counties of Somerset and Worcester. {Ref: J. Thomas Scharf's *History of Baltimore City and County*, Part I, p. 77}

JOHNSON, EPHRAIM, see "Richard Johnson," q.v.

JOHNSON, FREDERICK (Dorchester County), private (substitute) in the Maryland Continental Line by 1781, was discharged on 8 Dec 1781. {Ref: Archives of Maryland Vol. 48, p. 10}

JOHNSON, HORSFORD (Maryland Navy), marine on the State Ship *Defence* in 1777. {Ref: Archives of Maryland Vol. 18, p. 657}

JOHNSON, JAMES (Frederick County), colonel and patriot buried in Mount Olivet Cemetery; *"Mrs. Margaret Johnson, relict of the late Col. James Johnson, died at Springfields in Frederick County in September, 1813, in her 64th year."* {Ref: *Frederick-Town Herald*, 11 Sep 1813; Burial information compiled by Dr. Donald Wolf in Maryland Society SAR Newsletter circa 1996}

JOHNSON, JAMES (Frederick County), private (substitute) in the Maryland Continental Line, German Regiment, enrolled in May, 1778 for 3 years or duration of the war. {Ref: Maryland Historical Magazine, Vol. 6, No. 3, p. 261}

JOHNSON, JAMES (Western Maryland), private in Capt. Michael Cresap's Company in 1775. {Ref: Howard L. Leckey's *The Tenmile Country and Its Pioneer Families*, p. 16}

JOHNSON, JAMES, see "John Barrick," q.v.

JOHNSON, JEMIMA, see "Richard Johnson," q.v.

JOHNSON, JOHN (Frederick County), patriot buried in Mount Olivet Cemetery; one John Johnson, aged 56, *"died of the prevailing epidemic after a short and painful illness of 4 days"* in March, 1815. {Ref: *Frederick-Town Herald*, 18 Mar 1815; Burial information compiled by Dr. Donald Wolf in Maryland Society SAR Newsletter circa 1996}

JOHNSON, JOHN (Maryland Navy), seaman on the State Ship *Defence* in 1777. {Ref: Archives of Maryland Vol. 18, p. 657}

JOHNSON, JOHN, see "Jacob Norris," q.v.

JOHNSON, MARGARET, see "James Johnson," q.v.

JOHNSON, MICHAEL (Western Maryland), private in Capt. Michael Cresap's Company in 1775. {Ref: Howard L. Leckey's *The Tenmile Country and Its Pioneer Families*, p. 16}

JOHNSON, MOSES (Harford County), first lieutenant, commissioned 14 May 1776 in Militia Company No. 25 under Capt. Charles Baker. {Ref: George W. Archer Collection and Revolutionary War File, Historical Society of Harford County Archives}

JOHNSON, NELSON (Charles County), private (substitute) in the Maryland Continental Line by 1781, was discharged on 8 Dec 1781. {Ref: Archives of Maryland Vol. 48, p. 11}

JOHNSON, NICHOLAS (Baltimore County), private, aged 21, labourer, born in Belfast, enlisted (made his "X" mark) on 13 Feb 1776 in Capt. John Fulford's Company of Matrosses. {Ref: Maryland Historical Magazine, Vol. 69, No. 1, p. 95}

JOHNSON, RICHARD (Montgomery County), soldier in the Maryland Continental Line who applied for pension under the Act of June 7, 1832, but the claim was suspended for *"proof of identity with soldier of the same name of the 3rd Regiment, Maryland Continental Line, mentioned in the certificate of the register of the land office."* He died on 26 Mar 1841, aged 86 years, 6 months and 10 days, and his wife Jemima died several years before him (affidavit of Ephraim Johnson in 1847, aged 56, only surviving child). {Ref: *Rejected or Suspended Applications for Revolutionary War Pensions* (1850 Report), p. 231; Research by Virgil D. White, citing Federal Pension Application R5657}

JOHNSON, ROGER (Frederick County), patriot buried in Mount Olivet Cemetery. {Ref: Information compiled by Dr. Donald Wolf in Maryland Society SAR Newsletter circa 1996}

JOHNSON, SIMON (Frederick County), private (substitute) in the Maryland Continental Line, Gunby's Regiment, enrolled in April, 1778 for 3 years or duration of the war. {Ref: Maryland Historical Magazine, Vol. 6, No. 3, p. 258}

JOHNSON, THOMAS (Baltimore Town), patriot and merchant who enrolled in Capt. John Sterrett's Independent Mercantile Company by February, 1777, at which time they were mustered into regular service with the continental army to repress loyalist activities in the Eastern Shore counties of Somerset and Worcester. {Ref: J. Thomas Scharf's *History of Baltimore City and County*, Part I, p. 77}

JOHNSON, THOMAS (Baltimore Privateer), commander of the schooner *Dragon*, mounting 2 carriage guns, 2 swivel guns and 7 small arms, was issued Letters of Marque & Reprisal by the Council of Maryland on 25 Dec 1778; captain of the schooner *Sea Flower* which was impressed into service by order of the Council of Maryland on 27 Apr 1780 *"to go to the Head of Elk for the Purpose of Transporting a Detachment of the American Army to the State of Virginia."* {Ref: Archives of Maryland Vol. 21, p. 273 and Vol. 43, p. 155}

JOHNSON, THOMAS (Harford County), private who was enrolled 10 Mar 1776 in Militia Company No. 18 under Capt. John Jolly. {Ref: George W. Archer Collection and Revolutionary War File, Historical Society of Harford County Archives}

JOHNSON, THOMAS, JR. (Frederick County), brigadier general and patriot buried in Mount Olivet Cemetery; served on the Council of Safety and nominated George Washington to be Commander-in-Chief of the Continental Army; elected first Governor of Maryland; born 24 Nov 1732 in Calvert County, married Ann Jennings on 16 Feb 1766, and their children were: Thomas Jennings Johnson ("married Elizabeth Russell, first Miss Hesselins"); Ann Jennings Johnson (married Major John Colin Grahame); Rebecca Johnson (died in infancy); Elizabeth Johnson (married Thomas Johnson); Rebecca Johnson; James Johnson; Joshua Johnson (married Harriet Beall); and, Dorcas

Johnson. *"Thomas Johnson, Esq., died at Rose Hill, seat of John Grahame, near the close of his 87th year; revolutionary patriot and native of Calvert County in this state; for the last 40 years a resident of this county; first governor of the state after the Declaration of Independence"* on 26 Sep 1819; also see "Richard Potts," q.v. {Ref: Burial information compiled by Dr. Donald Wolf in Maryland Society SAR Newsletter circa 1996; Maryland State Society DAR Directory, 1892-1965, p. 426-427; *Frederick-Town Herald*, 30 Oct 1819}

JOHNSON, WILLIAM (Frederick County), private (substitute) in the Maryland Continental Line, German Regiment, enrolled in May, 1778 for 3 years or duration of the war. {Ref: Maryland Historical Magazine, Vol. 6, No. 3, p. 259}

JOHNSON, WORTHINGTON, see "Richard Potts," q.v.

JOHNSTON, ---- (Harford County), fourth sergeant, enrolled by 15 Apr 1776 in Militia Company No. 20 under Capt. Robert Glenn. {Ref: George W. Archer Collection and Revolutionary War File, Historical Society of Harford County Archives}

JOHNSTON, ISAAC (Harford County), private who was enrolled 25 Mar 1776 in Militia Company No. 19 under Capt. William Morgan. {Ref: George W. Archer Collection and Revolutionary War File, Historical Society of Harford County Archives}

JOHNSTON, JOHN (Harford County), private who was enrolled by 15 Apr 1776 in Militia Company No. 20 under Capt. Robert Glenn. {Ref: George W. Archer Collection and Revolutionary War File, Historical Society of Harford County Archives}

JOICE (JOYCE), RICHARD (Anne Arundel County), private by 5 Oct 1776 in Capt. Richard Chew's Militia Company, Weems' Battalion; one Richard Joyce died by 28 Apr 1788 (date of distribution), leaving a widow (not named) and children Richard Joyce, William Joyce, and Elijah Joyce. {Ref: Archives of Maryland Vol. 12, p. 323; Anne Arundel County Administration Account JG No. 1, p. 2}

JOLLY, EDWARD (Harford County), private who was enrolled 10 Mar 1776 in Militia Company No. 18 under Capt. John Jolly. {Ref: George W. Archer Collection and Revolutionary War File, Historical Society of Harford County Archives}

JOLLY, JOHN (Harford County), captain, 10 Mar 1776 in Militia Company No. 18. {Ref: George W. Archer Collection and Revolutionary War File, Historical Society of Harford County Archives}

JONES, AQUILA, JR. (Harford County), private who was enrolled 10 Mar 1776 in Militia Company No. 18 under Capt. John Jolly. {Ref: George W. Archer Collection and Revolutionary War File, Historical Society of Harford County Archives}

JONES, AQUILA, SR. (Harford County), private who was enrolled 10 Mar 1776 in Militia Company No. 18 under Capt. John Jolly. {Ref: George W. Archer Collection and Revolutionary War File, Historical Society of Harford County Archives}

JONES, BENJAMIN (Baltimore County), matross soldier by 7 May 1779 at which time he gave a deposition about his enlistment terms. {Ref: Maryland State Archives Record MdHR 6636-14-83}

JONES, BENJAMIN (Harford County), soldier in the Pennsylvania Line who was born in Baltimore County on 10 Oct 1757 and lived in Harford County at the time of his enlistment in York County, Pennsylvania; applied for pension in

York County on 28 Nov 1845. {Ref: Research by Virgil D. White, citing Federal Pension Application S5626}

JONES, BENJAMIN (Somerset County), soldier in the Maryland Continental Line who applied for pension under the Act of June 7, 1832, but the claim was rejected because he did not serve six months. {Ref: *Rejected or Suspended Applications for Revolutionary War Pensions* (1850 Report), p. 229}

JONES, BLACKWELL (Queen Anne's County), private (substitute) in the Maryland Continental Line by 1781, was discharged on 8 Dec 1781. {Ref: Archives of Maryland Vol. 48, p. 11}

JONES, CHARLES, see "Thomas Jones," q.v.

JONES, CHARLES (Frederick County), private (substitute) in the Maryland Continental Line, German Regiment, enrolled in May, 1778 for 3 years or duration of the war. {Ref: Maryland Historical Magazine, Vol. 6, No. 3, p. 261}

JONES, CUD or CUTHBERT (St. Mary's County), private in the 3rd Maryland Continental Line who was drafted to serve until 10 Dec 1781, was discharged on 29 Nov 1781 and issued clothing due him on 3 Dec 1781. {Ref: Archives of Maryland Vol. 48, pp. 6, 10}

JONES, DAVID (Anne Arundel County), patriot who took the Oath of Fidelity and Support to the State of Maryland on 9 Apr 1778. {Ref: Archives of Maryland Vol. 21, p. 22}

JONES, EBY, see "Thomas Jones," q.v.

JONES, ELIZABETH, see "William Jones" and "Jason Jones," q.v.

JONES, EZEBELLA, see "Thomas Jones," q.v.

JONES, HORATIO, see "Thomas Jones," q.v.

JONES, IGNATIUS (Western Maryland), private in Capt. Michael Cresap's Company in 1775. {Ref: Howard L. Leckey's *The Tenmile Country and Its Pioneer Families*, p. 16}

JONES, JAMES (Calvert County?), private in the 7th Maryland Continental Line by 31 Jan 1780 at which time he was "late a 9 month soldier in the 7th Regiment Discharged the amount of £25.10 in Cloathing due him by Act of Assembly to procure Troops for the American Army." {Ref: Archives of Maryland Vol. 43, p. 74}

JONES, JAMES, see "Thomas Jones," q.v.

JONES, JASON (Anne Arundel County), private in the Maryland militia whose widow Elizabeth Jones applied for pension in Annapolis under the Act of July 7, 1838, but the claim was rejected because *"two husbands, but last marriage after January 1, 1794."* Also see Peden's *Revolutionary Patriots of Maryland, 1775-1783: A Supplement* (p. 119). {Ref: *Rejected or Suspended Applications for Revolutionary War Pensions* (1850 Report), p. 235}

JONES, JOHN, see "Thomas Jones," q.v.

JONES, JOHN (Dorchester County), soldier who applied for pension under the Act of June 7, 1832, but the claim was suspended "pending further proof and specification of other service in the militia; his service in the flying camp was only five months." {Ref: *Rejected or Suspended Applications for Revolutionary War Pensions* (1850 Report), p. 231}

JONES, JOHN (Frederick County), private (substitute) in the Maryland Continental Line, Gunby's Regiment, enrolled in May, 1778 for 3 years or duration of the war. {Ref: Maryland Historical Magazine, Vol. 6, No. 3, p. 259}

JONES, JOHN (Montgomery County), private in the Maryland Continental Line who was *"sent from camp by General Smallwood as unfit for the service"* and was discharged on 22 Jun 1778. {Ref: Archives of Maryland Vol. 21, p. 144}

JONES, JOHN (Baltimore County), private who was a deserter from Baltimore Town, twice deserted; possibly enrolled by Richard Dallam in the Regiment Extraordinary and sent to Annapolis with Capt. Thompson on board the sloop *Liberty* on 17 Aug 1780. {Ref: Archives of Maryland Vol. 45, pp. 50, 51}

JONES, JOHN COURTS (Frederick and Washington Counties), lieutenant and later captain in the 7th Maryland Continental Line who received payment for his services in the amount of "1900 Dollars & £3.10s" on 12 Sep 1780. {Ref: Archives of Maryland Vol. 45, p. 98}

JONES, JOSEPH (Harford County), private in the Maryland Continental Line who was *"sent from camp by General Smallwood as unfit for the service"* (deemed to be an "idiot") and was discharged on 22 Jun 1778. {Ref: Archives of Maryland Vol. 21, p. 144}

JONES, JOSEPH (Harford County), private who was enrolled 9 Dec 1775 in Militia Company No. 14 under Capt. William McComas. {Ref: George W. Archer Collection and Revolutionary War File, Historical Society of Harford County Archives}

JONES, JOSEPH (Maryland Navy), marine on the State Ship *Defence* in 1777. {Ref: Archives of Maryland Vol. 18, p. 657}

JONES, LEVIN, see "Thomas Jones," q.v.

JONES, MICHAEL (Montgomery County), private who was drafted into the Maryland Continental Line, was discharged on 8 Dec 1781. {Ref: Archives of Maryland Vol. 48, p. 10}

JONES, MORGAN (Anne Arundel County), private by 5 Oct 1776 in Capt. Richard Chew's Militia Company, Weems' Battalion. {Ref: Archives of Maryland Vol. 12, p. 323}

JONES, NATHAN (Maryland Navy), seaman or marine on the State Ship *Defence* in 1777. {Ref: Archives of Maryland Vol. 18, p. 657}

JONES, OSGOOD (Western Maryland), private in Capt. Michael Cresap's Company in 1775. {Ref: Howard L. Leckey's *The Tenmile Country and Its Pioneer Families*, p. 16}

JONES, SAMUEL (Baltimore County), private (substitute) in the Maryland Continental Line by 1781, was discharged on 8 Dec 1781. {Ref: Archives of Maryland Vol. 48, p. 11}

JONES, SAMUEL (Southern Maryland), lieutenant colonel, commissioned on 27 Jul 1780 to serve in the Regiment Extra by order of the Council of Maryland. {Ref: Archives of Maryland Vol. 43, p. 234}

JONES, SOLOMON (Baltimore County), private, aged 17, farmer, born in Maryland, enlisted (made his "X" mark) on 10 Sep 1776 in Capt. John Fulford's Company of Matrosses. {Ref: Maryland Historical Magazine, Vol. 69, No. 1, p. 96}

JONES, THOMAS (Calvert County), contractor for horses in Calvert County by 8 Sep 1780 at which time he was paid £6500 to be expended and accounted for. {Ref: Archives of Maryland Vol. 43, p. 281}

JONES, THOMAS (Dorchester County), colonel of the Lower Battalion of Militia, commissioned 20 May 1778 and again on 15 Jan 1783; born 1723 in Dorchester County, married Elizabeth Fell (1733-1819) in 1756, and died 24 Mar 1808; their children were: John Jones (born 4 Sep 1755, commissioned second lieutenant on 20 May 1778, married Cassandra Johns); Thomas Jones (married Nancy ----); Charles Jones (born 1 Feb 1760); William (born 8 Mar 1762); Levin Jones (married Mary ----); Eby Jones (born 10 Aug 1766); Sarah Jones (born 21 Feb 1769); James Jones (born 19 Jul 1771); Horatio Jones (born 25 Oct 1772, married Mary Woolford); Ezebella Jones (married William Woolford); and, Washington Jones (born 1777, married Theresa Dashiell). {Ref: Archives of Maryland Vol. 48, p. 344; Maryland State Society DAR Directory, 1892-1965, p. 432}

JONES, THOMAS (Montgomery County), private (substitute) in the Maryland Continental Line, who enlisted to serve until 10 Dec 1781, was discharged on 30 Nov 1781. {Ref: Archives of Maryland Vol. 48, p. 8}

JONES, WASHINGTON, see "Thomas Jones," q.v.

JONES, WILLIAM, see "Thomas Jones," q.v.

JONES, WILLIAM (Caroline County), soldier in the Maryland Continental Line who applied for pension under the Act of June 7, 1832, but the claim was rejected because he did not serve six months. {Ref: Rejected or Suspended Applications for Revolutionary War Pensions (1850 Report), p. 229}

JONES, WILLIAM (Maryland Privateer), commander of the schooner Two Sisters, navigated by 11 men and mounting 4 swivel guns and 6 small arms, was issued Letters of Marque & Reprisal by the Council of Maryland on 6 May 1780. {Ref: Archives of Maryland Vol. 43, p. 164}

JONES, WILLIAM (Baltimore City), soldier who was referred to as William Jones 1st and whose widow Elizabeth Jones applied for pension under the Act of July 7, 1838, but the claim was suspended "for proof of identity that he was the William Jones named in the certificate of the land office at Annapolis" (and noted also that she was deceased, but no date was given). {Ref: Rejected or Suspended Applications for Revolutionary War Pensions (1850 Report), p. 236}

JORDAN, SAMUEL (Maryland Navy), corporal of marines on the State Ship Defence in 1777. {Ref: Archives of Maryland Vol. 18, p. 657}

JORDAN, THOMAS (Charles County), private in the 1st Maryland Continental Line who was recruited by 28 Feb 1780 at which time he was issued clothing due him. {Ref: Archives of Maryland Vol. 43, p. 98}

JORDON, JOHN (Baltimore County?), captain in the 1st Maryland Continental Line who received payment for his services in the amount of "1900 Dollars & £3.10s" on 12 Sep 1780. {Ref: Archives of Maryland Vol. 45, p. 97}

JORDON, JEREMIAH (St. Mary's County), patriot who was commissioned one of the three persons in St. Mary's County by the Council of Maryland on 19 Aug 1779 to receive subscriptions for use of the State. {Ref: Archives of Maryland Vol. 21, p. 499}

JOURDAN (JORDEN), JEREMIAH (Maryland Navy), seaman or marine on the State Ship *Defence* in 1777. {Ref: Archives of Maryland Vol. 18, p. 657}

JOURDAN (JORDEN), JOHN (Maryland Navy), sergeant of marines on the State Ship *Defence* in 1777. {Ref: Archives of Maryland Vol. 18, p. 657}

JOYCE, RICHARD, see "Richard Joice," q.v.

JUDGES, WILLIAM (Maryland Navy), ordinary seaman on the State Ship *Defence* in 1777. {Ref: Archives of Maryland Vol. 18, p. 657}

JUSTICE, ELIJAH (Somerset County), private, Maryland Continental Line, Continental Army, 1780. {Ref: Archives of Maryland Vol. 45, p. 67}

KAHILL, NATHANIEL (St. Mary's County), private who was drafted into the Maryland Continental Line, was discharged on 8 Dec 1781. {Ref: Archives of Maryland Vol. 48, p. 10}

KAUFMAN, JACOB (Frederick County), private (substitute) in the Maryland Continental Line, German Regiment, enrolled in May, 1778 for 3 years or duration of the war. {Ref: Maryland Historical Magazine, Vol. 6, No. 3, p. 259}

KEATES (KEATS), THOMAS (Anne Arundel County), private in the 4th Maryland Continental Line on 28 Jan 1778, corporal on 1 Feb 1780, and sergeant on 1 Mar 1780; applied for pension in Tuscaloosa County, Alabama on 18 Oct 1826, aged 70; his wife Martha was aged 68 and they had two daughters at home, Nancy Keates (age 18) and Martha Keates (age 16); Thomas was still living in 1839. {Ref: Archives of Maryland Vol. 18, p. 131; Research by Virgil D. White, citing Federal Pension Application S38109}

KEEN, RICHARD (Frederick County), private (substitute) in the Maryland Continental Line, Gunby's Regiment, enrolled in April, 1778 for 3 years or duration of the war. {Ref: Maryland Historical Magazine, Vol. 6, No. 3, p. 257}

KEENAN, LAWRENCE (Baltimore County), private, aged 24, tailor, born in Ireland, enlisted 26 Feb 1776 in Capt. John Fulford's Company of Matrosses. On 7 Jul 1776 Gen. William Smallwood wrote to the Council of Safety stating: *"The bearers Michael Hart and Laurence Keenan, of the Artillery Company, having been released from jail, prosecution against them being withdrawn, have applied for a discharge, the date of which will properly commence the 7th day of May, when they were imprisoned, as I ordered them to be given up at that time to the Civil Power and having no authority to discharge them, must refer them to the Honorable Council of Safety for their discharges."* On 8 Jul 1776 the Council of Safety *"ordered that Michael Hart and Lawrence Keenan of Capt. John Fulford's [Company] of Artillery be discharged from the Service of this Colony."* On 18 Jul 1776 Michael Hart and Larrons Keenan (among others who were enlisted by Capt. Thomas Yates) were reviewed and passed by Major Thomas Jones of the Baltimore Town Battalion of Militia. On 31 Oct 1799 a Laurence Keinan married Mary (Polly) Hales at St. Peter's Roman Catholic Church in Baltimore City. Mary or Polly, daughter of Hugh Hales, Sr., was born in Baltimore on 11 Dec 1778. Lawrence was a "pedlar" in Fells Point from 1800 to 1802 and then moved to Pughton in (now) West Virginia until circa 1835 (date of death not known). Mary Keenan died before 1867 at Fostoria in Seneca County, Ohio. Whether this Lawrence Keenan was related or not to the Revolutionary War soldier is undetermined since there is a paucity in Maryland records in this regard. {Ref: Archives of Maryland Vol. 12, pp. 7, 9, and Vol. 18, p. 58; Maryland Historical Magazine, Vol. 69, No. 1, p. 95 (which mistakenly listed the name as "Lawrence Kenney"); Mary A. and Stanley G. Piet's *Early Catholic Church Records in Baltimore, Maryland, 1782-1800,* p. 127; Baltimore City Directories, 1800-1802; Research by Dr. Francis W. Keenan of Brockport, New York in 2001, citing some information from website *Ancestry.com*}

KEENE, SARAH, see "Tyler Baldwin," q.v.

KEENER, PETER (Baltimore County), contractor for State Arms in Baltimore County in 1781. {Ref: Archives of Maryland Vol. 47, p. 14}

KELLER, JOHN (Frederick County), patriot buried in Mount Olivet Cemetery. {Ref: Information compiled by Dr. Donald Wolf in Maryland Society SAR Newsletter circa 1996}

KELLEY, JAMES (Washington County), private in the Maryland Continental Line who was *"sent from camp by General Smallwood as unfit for the service"* and was discharged on 22 Jun 1778. {Ref: Archives of Maryland Vol. 21, p. 144}

KELLEY, JOSHUA (Baltimore County), private in the Maryland militia; born 1751 in Maryland and lived in Baltimore County at the time of his enlistment; moved to Huntington County, Pennsylvania in 1793 and moved in 1797 to Ross County, Ohio for 2 years and 5 months, after which he moved to Kentucky for 7 or 8 years and then to Owen County, Indiana; applied for pension on 18 Oct 1833 and mentioned his brother William Kelley was a captain in the war; Moses Kelley stated he and Joshua were born in Baltimore County and they had enlisted together; also see "Moses Kelley" and "William Kelley," q.v. {Ref: Research by Christopher T. Smithson, citing Federal Pension Application R21796}

KELLEY, MOSES (Baltimore County), private in the militia who enlisted with Joshua Kelley; applied for pension in Owen County, Indiana on 17 Oct 1833, aged 81, stating he had moved to Washington County, Tennessee about 1792 for 3 years, to Washington County, Virginia for 9 years, to Grant County,

Kentucky and then to Indiana (short periods of time in Dearborn, Ripley, Green and Marion Counties), and to Owen County, Indiana in 1833; by 1835 he was in Hamilton County, Ohio and he was in Carroll County, Maryland by 1839, aged 89; see "Joshua Kelley," q.v. {Ref: Research by Christopher T. Smithson, citing Federal Pension Application S8786}

KELLEY, WILLIAM (Baltimore County), ensign and later captain in the militia in Soldier's Delight Battalion; married Martha Lovell on 1 Jan 1778 and their children were: Sarah Kelley (born 26 Oct 1778, died 12 Apr 1791); John Kelley (born 17 May 1781); Mary Kelley (born 30 Jul 1784); Nicholas Kelley (born 18 Jul 1785, died 20 Nov 1788); Urath Kelley (born 22 Jun 1789, died 19 Feb 1793); Nicholas Kelley (born 11 Feb 1793 and still living in 1839); Sarah Kelley (born 21 May 1796); Joshua Kelley (born 21 Nov 1799); Rachel Kelley (born 19 Apr 1803); Elizabeth Kelley (born 22 Mar 1807); and, William Kelley (no birth date given; he was Carroll County sheriff in 1839); also mentioned Moses Kelley of Carroll County, Maryland, aged 89, in 1839 and William Lovell of Huntington County, Pennsylvania in 1838; see "Joshua Kelley," q.v. {Ref: Research by Virgil D. White, citing Federal Pension Application R5831}

KELLY, BENJAMIN (Western Maryland), private in Capt. Michael Cresap's Company in 1775. {Ref: Howard L. Leckey's *The Tenmile Country and Its Pioneer Families*, p. 16}

KELLY, DARBY (Baltimore County), private, aged 26, labourer, born in Ireland, enlisted 4 Mar 1776 in Capt. John Fulford's Company of Matrosses. {Ref: Maryland Historical Magazine, Vol. 69, No. 1, p. 96}

KELLY, EDMUND (Annapolis), patriot who was *"formerly a Subject of Great Britain who hath lately arrived in this State, appeared before this Board and did voluntarily make, repeat and Subscribe a Declaration of his Belief in the Christian Religion and took, repeated and Subscribed to the Oath of Fidelity and Support to this State directed by the Act to punish certain Crimes and Misdemeanors and to prevent the growth of Toryism and also the Oath prescribed by the Act for Naturalization wherefore he is now become a Subject of this State."* {Ref: Archives of Maryland Vol. 48, p. 345}

KELLY, JOSEPH (St. Mary's County), private (substitute) in the Maryland Continental Line by 1781, was discharged on 8 Dec 1781. {Ref: Archives of Maryland Vol. 48, p. 11}

KELLY, ROBERT (Harford County), private who was enrolled 10 Mar 1776 in Militia Company No. 18 under Capt. John Jolly. {Ref: George W. Archer Collection and Revolutionary War File, Historical Society of Harford County Archives}

KELLY, WILLIAM (Carroll County), soldier whose widow Martha Kelly applied for pension under the Act of July 4, 1836, but the claim was rejected because he did not serve six months. {Ref: *Rejected or Suspended Applications for Revolutionary War Pensions* (1850 Report), p. 233}

KELSO, SARAH, see "Nicholas R. Moore," q.v.

KELSO, THOMAS (Baltimore Town), patriot and merchant who enrolled in Capt. John Sterrett's Independent Mercantile Company by February, 1777, at which time they were mustered into regular service with the continental army to repress loyalist activities in the Eastern Shore counties of Somerset and Worcester. {Ref: J. Thomas Scharf's *History of Baltimore City and County*, Part I, p. 77}

KEMP, FREDERICK (Frederick County), patriot who took the Oath of Fidelity and Allegiance and furnished supplies to the army in 1778; born 11 Feb 1742 in Maryland, married Dorothy Hershberger (1765-1831), and died 17 Feb 1841; their children were: Gilbert Kemp (born 31 Dec 1784, married Rebecca Curfman); Elizabeth Kemp (born 13 May 1786, married Jacob Staley); Abraham Kemp (born 10 Oct 1786, married Mary Brunner); David Kemp (born 21 Jan 1791, married Ruth S. Lakin); Frederick Kemp, Jr. (born 23 Nov 1793); Eva Kemp (married John Shaffer); Mary Kemp (married John Brunner); and, Joseph Kemp (married Magdalene Staley). {Ref: Maryland State Society DAR Directory, 1892-1965, p. 435}

KEMP, FREDERICK, SR. (Frederick County), patriot buried in Mount Olivet Cemetery; served as a member of the Committee of Observation in 1775; born 1725 in Germany, married Dorothy Kemp, and died 1804; their children were: John Peter Kemp (born 28 Jun 1749, married Mary Leaman); Maria Kemp; Sophia Kemp (married a Dern); Ludwig Kemp; David Kemp (died in infancy); Anna Maria Kemp (married Conrad Eyler); and, David Kemp. {Ref: Burial information compiled by Dr. Donald Wolf in Maryland Society SAR Newsletter circa 1996; Maryland State Society DAR Directory, 1892-1965, p. 435}

KEMP, GEORGE (Maryland Navy), sailor or seaman on 7 Jan 1780. {Ref: Calendar of Maryland State Papers, The Brown Books, p. 57}

KENDERDINE, JOHN (Maryland Navy), marine on the State Ship *Defence* in 1777. {Ref: Archives of Maryland Vol. 18, p. 657}

KENLY, ELIZABETH, see "Nathaniel Bayless," q.v.

KENLY, LEMUEL, see "Nathaniel Bayless," q.v.

KENNEDY, HENRIETTA, see "Henry Hill," q.v.

KENNEDY, J. F. (Baltimore Town), patriot and merchant who enrolled in Capt. John Sterrett's Independent Mercantile Company by February, 1777, at which time they were mustered into regular service with the continental army to repress loyalist activities in the Eastern Shore counties of Somerset and Worcester. {Ref: J. Thomas Scharf's *History of Baltimore City and County*, Part I, p. 77}

KENNEDY, JOHN (Baltimore County), private, aged 26, labourer, born in Ireland, enlisted 19 Feb 1776 in Capt. John Fulford's Company of Matrosses. {Ref: Maryland Historical Magazine, Vol. 69, No. 1, p. 95}

KENNEDY, JOHN (Baltimore Town), patriot and merchant who enrolled in Capt. John Sterrett's Independent Mercantile Company by February, 1777, at which time they were mustered into regular service with the continental army to

repress loyalist activities in the Eastern Shore counties of Somerset and Worcester. {Ref: J. Thomas Scharf's *History of Baltimore City and County*, Part I, p. 77}

KENNEDY, SARAH, see "Francis Lang," q.v.

KENNER, JAMES (Maryland Privateer), commander of the schooner *Eagle*, navigated by 30 men and mounting 4 carriage guns, 4 swivel guns, and 2 howitz guns, was issued Letters of Marque & Reprisal by the Council of Maryland on 26 Aug 1780; commissioned captain of the schooner *Eagle* on 20 Nov 1780. {Ref: Archives of Maryland Vol. 43, pp. 263-264, and Vol. 45, p. 219}

KENNER, NATHANIEL, JR. (Baltimore County), patriot who supplied provisions to the State of Maryland between June and September, 1780. {Ref: Archives of Maryland Vol. 45, p. 84}

KENT, HENRY (Baltimore County), private who enlisted in Pulaski's Legion on 22 Apr 1778 in Baltimore. {Ref: Maryland Historical Magazine, Vol. 13, No. 3, p. 222}

KENT, ISAAC (Calvert County), private (substitute) in the Maryland Continental Line by 1781, was discharged on 8 Dec 1781. {Ref: Archives of Maryland Vol. 48, p. 10}

KERR, ELIZABETH, see "John Adams," q.v.

KERR, JOHN (Harford County), private who was enrolled by 15 Apr 1776 in Militia Company No. 20 under Capt. Robert Glenn. {Ref: George W. Archer Collection and Revolutionary War File, Historical Society of Harford County Archives}

KEY, ELIZABETH, see "John E. Howard," q.v.

KEY, JAMES (Harford County), private (substitute) in the Maryland Continental Line by 1781, was discharged on 8 Dec 1781. {Ref: Archives of Maryland Vol. 48, p. 11}

KEY, JOHN ROSS (Frederick County), lieutenant and patriot buried in Mount Olivet Cemetery; born 19 Sep 1754 in Cecil County, Maryland, married Ann Phoebe Penn Dagworthy Charloton, and died 13 Oct 1821 in Frederick County; their son Francis Scott Key married Mary Tayloe Lloyd; also see "John Lainey" and "Frederick Clabaugh," q.v. {Ref: Burial information compiled by Dr. Donald Wolf in Maryland Society SAR Newsletter circa 1996; Maryland State Society DAR Directory, 1892-1965, p. 438}

KEY, PHILIP, see "Aquila Hall," q.v.

KEY, REBECCA, see "John E. Howard," q.v.

KIDD, JAMES (Harford County), private who was enrolled 9 Dec 1775 in Militia Company No. 14 under Capt. William McComas; James Kidd died intestate by 14 Feb 1809 (date of final distribution) and his heirs were: Pensely Kidd (widow, still living in 1836); sons John Kidd (deceased by 1836), James Kidd (deceased by 1836), and Joshua H. Kidd (resided in Baltimore County by 1836); and, daughters Rachel Kidd (married James Ward by 1809 and moved to Tennessee before 1836), Sarah or Sally Kidd (married Henry Scarff by 1809 and died by 1836), Elizabeth or Betsey Kidd (married ---- Thompson by 1809 and Andrew Hope by 1836), Rhoda or Rhode Kidd (married ---- Tarman and was a widow by 1836), and Lettecia or Letitia Kidd (deceased by 1836). {Ref: George W. Archer Collection and Revolutionary War File, Historical Society of Harford County Archives; Henry C. Peden, Jr.'s *Heirs & Legatees of Harford County, 1802-1846*, p. 14; Harford County Equity Court Case (Kidd vs. Kidd), 1836}

KIDD, WILLIAM (Harford County), private who was enrolled 9 Dec 1775 in Militia Company No. 14 under Capt. William McComas. {Ref: George W. Archer Collection and Revolutionary War File, Historical Society of Harford County Archives}

KIERSTED, JAMES (Baltimore Privateer), commander of the schooner *Nautilus*, navigated by 20 men and mounting 8 carriage guns, was issued Letters of Marque & Reprisal by the Council of Maryland on 13 Jan 1781. {Ref: Archives of Maryland Vol. 45, p. 274}

KIERSTED, LUKE (Baltimore Privateer), commander of the brigantine *Fair American*, navigated by 26 men and mounting 8 carriage guns, was issued Letters of Marque & Reprisal by the Council of Maryland on 15 Sep 1780. {Ref: Archives of Maryland Vol. 43, p. 291}

KILLPATRICK, WILLIAM (St. Mary's County), private (substitute) in the Maryland Continental Line by 1781, was discharged on 8 Dec 1781. {Ref: Archives of Maryland Vol. 48, p. 11}

KILTY (KELTY), WILLIAM (Annapolis?), patriot and doctor who received payment for his services to the 5th Maryland Continental Line in the amount of "1900 Dollars & £3.10s" on 12 Sep 1780. {Ref: Archives of Maryland Vol. 45, p. 98}

KING, BENJAMIN (Maryland Privateer), commander of the brigantine *Maryland*, mounting 16 carriage guns, 2 swivel guns and 25 small arms, was issued Letters of Marque & Reprisal by the Council of Maryland on 30 Sep 1779. {Ref: Archives of Maryland Vol. 21, p. 541}

KING, CHARLES (Charles County), private (substitute) in the Maryland Continental Line by 1781, was discharged on 8 Dec 1781. {Ref: Archives of Maryland Vol. 48, p. 11}

KING, DANIEL (Harford County), private who was enrolled by Capt. Praul in the Regiment Extraordinary and sent to Annapolis with Capt. Thompson on board the sloop *Liberty* on 17 Aug 1780; reported as a deserter sent off before by Capt. Praul, deserted from him and taken again. {Ref: Archives of Maryland Vol. 45, p. 50}

KING, HANNAH, see "Charles Close," q.v.

KING, JOHN (St. Mary's County), private who was drafted into the Maryland Continental Line, was discharged on 8 Dec 1781. {Ref: Archives of Maryland Vol. 48, p. 10}

KING, MR. (Maryland Continental Line, Staff and P. Officer), A.C.I., received payment for his services in the amount of "1900 Dollars & £3.10s" on 12 Sep 1780. {Ref: Archives of Maryland Vol. 45, p. 98}

KING, UPSHER (Baltimore County), patriot who supplied provisions to the State of Maryland between June and September, 1780. {Ref: Archives of Maryland Vol. 45, p. 84}

KING, WILLIAM (Baltimore Town), patriot who was appointed Quartermaster of the Troops of Horse raised in this State and ordered into actual service on 9 Jun 1781. {Ref: Archives of Maryland Vol. 45, p. 467}

KING, WILLIAM (Maryland Navy), ordinary sailor on the State Ship *Defence* in 1777. {Ref: Archives of Maryland Vol. 18, p. 657}

KINNAMON, SOLOMON (Maryland Navy), enlisted as a marine on the galley *Chester* and, being incapable of duty because of a sore leg, was discharged from the service on 2 Jun 1778. {Ref: Archives of Maryland Vol. 21, p. 119}

KINSEY, DAVID (Baltimore County), private, aged 33, weaver, born in Maryland, enlisted (made his "X" mark) on 4 Mar 1776 in Capt. John Fulford's Company of Matrosses. {Ref: Maryland Historical Magazine, Vol. 69, No. 1, p. 96}

KINSEY, THOMAS (Maryland Navy), midshipman on the State Ship *Defence* in 1777. {Ref: Archives of Maryland Vol. 18, p. 658}

KINZER, HENRY, see "Daniel Smith," q.v.

KIRBY, JOSHUA (Baltimore Town), patriot and merchant who enrolled in Capt. John Sterrett's Independent Mercantile Company by February, 1777, at which time they were mustered into regular service with the continental army to repress loyalist activities in the Eastern Shore counties of Somerset and Worcester. {Ref: J. Thomas Scharf's *History of Baltimore City and County*, Part I, p. 77}

KIRBY, NICHOLAS (Maryland Navy), sailor or seaman on 7 Jan 1780. {Ref: Calendar of Maryland State Papers, The Brown Books, p. 57}

KIRK, DANIEL (Maryland Navy), marine on the State Ship *Defence* in 1777. {Ref: Archives of Maryland Vol. 18, p. 658}

KIRKWOOD, JANE, see "Richard Hope," q.v.

KIRKWOOD, NANCY, see "Richard Hope," q.v.

KIRKWOOD, RICHARD, see "Richard Hope," q.v.

KISSEY, WILLIAM, see "Frederick Hook," q.v.

KNAP, NERO (Anne Arundel County), private (substitute) in the Maryland Continental Line by 1781, was discharged on 8 Dec 1781. {Ref: Archives of Maryland Vol. 48, p. 11}

KNIGHT, JACOB (Frederick County), private (substitute) in the Maryland Continental Line, Price's Regiment, enrolled in May, 1778 for 3 years or duration of the war. {Ref: Maryland Historical Magazine, Vol. 6, No. 3, p. 260}

KNIGHT, JOHN (Maryland Navy), marine on the State Ship *Defence* in 1777. {Ref: Archives of Maryland Vol. 18, p. 658}

KNIGHT, WILLIAM (Harford County, Susquehannah Hundred), private who was enrolled 23 Apr 1776 in Militia Company No. 21 under Capt. George Patterson. {Ref: George W. Archer Collection and Revolutionary War File, Historical Society of Harford County Archives}

KNOTT, WILLIAM (Harford County), private who was enrolled 10 Mar 1776 in Militia Company No. 18 under Capt. John Jolly. {Ref: George W. Archer Collection and Revolutionary War File, Historical Society of Harford County Archives}

KNOWELL, JOHN (Anne Arundel County), private (substitute) in the Maryland Continental Line by 1781, was discharged on 8 Dec 1781. {Ref: Archives of Maryland Vol. 48, p. 11}

KOFFEL, SAMUEL, see "Ichabod Davis," q.v.

KRAUSER, ADAM (Baltimore County), private who enlisted in Pulaski's Legion on 8 May 1778 and still in service in November, 1779. {Ref: Maryland Historical Magazine, Vol. 13, No. 3, p. 223}

KREMS, CHRISTIANNA, see "William Clemm," q.v.

KRICK, JACOB (Washington County), soldier who lived in Berks County, Pennsylvania at the time of his enlistment and applied for pension in Washington County, Maryland on 23 Apr 1839, aged 78, under the Act of June 7, 1832, but the claim was rejected because he did not serve six months. {Ref: *Rejected or Suspended Applications for Revolutionary War Pensions* (1850 Report), p. 229; Research by Virgil D. White, citing Federal Pension Application R6058}

KUYKENDALL, ELIJAH (Western Maryland), private in Capt. Michael Cresap's Company in 1775. {Ref: Howard L. Leckey's *The Tenmile Country and Its Pioneer Families*, p. 16}

KUYKENDALL, JACOB (Western Maryland), private in Capt. Michael Cresap's Company in 1775. {Ref: Howard L. Leckey's *The Tenmile Country and Its Pioneer Families*, p. 16}

LACEMAN, LODAWICK (Baltimore County), private who was enrolled to serve as a substitute in the Maryland Continental Line until 10 Dec 1781, but *"being represented unfit for the service for which he was intended"* was discharged on 30 Oct 1781. {Ref: Archives of Maryland Vol. 45, p. 657}

LAINEY, JOHN (Frederick County), patriot and farmer in Pipe Creek Hundred whose wagon and horses were impressed into the service of the State of Virginia in 1781 to take loads from Philadelphia to Stemtown in Virginia and, in their behalf, John Ross Key presented to the Governor and Council of Maryland that it could not be legal for Virginia to impress Maryland wagons and horses for their use and requested said property should be returned. {Ref: Archives of Maryland Vol. 47, pp. 502-503}

LAKIN, RUTH, see "Frederick Kemp," q.v.

LAMAR, WILLIAM (Frederick, Washington, and Allegany Counties), lieutenant in the 1st Maryland Continental Line and later captain in the 7th Maryland Continental Line, received payment for his services in the amount of "1900 Dollars & £3.10s" on 12 Sep 1780; born 1755 in Maryland, married Margaret Worthington in 1784, and their children were: John Lamar (born 1785); Sarah Lamar (born 1787); Louisa Lamar (born 1789, married Col. Frisby Tilghman on or about 23 Sep 1819); William Lynch Lamar (born 1792, married Maria

Briscoe); Mary Lamar (born 1794, married Michael Cresap Sprigg); Richard Lamar (born 1796); Thomas Lamar (born 1798); Ann Eliza Lamar (born 1800, married George Tilghman on or about 21 Dec 1819); and, Marine Lamar (born 1802, married first to a Hamilton and second to a Worthington). *"Col. William Lamar died 8 Jan 1838 in Allegany County of which he had long been a resident, at an advanced age, an officer during the Revolutionary War."* {Ref: Archives of Maryland Vol. 18, p. 388 and Vol. 45, p. 98; *The Times and Democractic Advocate,* 25 Jan 1838; Maryland State Society DAR Directory, 1892-1965, p. 447; Robert Barnes' *Maryland Marriages, 1801-1820,* p. 183}

LAMB, JOHN (Anne Arundel County), patriot who was paid £5.10.0 by the Maryland Council of Safety for boatage on 8 Oct 1776. {Ref: Archives of Maryland Vol. 12, p. 326}

LAMBERT, CHRISTOPHER or CHRISTIAN (Baltimore City), private in the Maryland Continental Line who applied for pension in Baltimore on 28 Apr 1818, aged 65; in 1820 he had a wife (not named, aged 55) and children Elizabeth Lambert (aged 18), Michael Lambert (aged 13), Maria Lambert (aged 11), and William Lambert (aged 9); he again applied for pension under the Act of June 7, 1832, but the claim was rejected because he was *"already pensioned under the Act of March 18, 1818."* His daughter Susan Cook made an affidavit on 6 May 1850 in Baltimore and stated her father had died on 24 Apr 1846. {Ref: Research by Virgil D. White, citing Federal Pension Application R6096; *Rejected or Suspended Applications for Revolutionary War Pensions* (1850 Report), p. 229}

LAMPREY, JOHN (Harford County), private who was enrolled 25 Mar 1776 in Militia Company No. 19 under Capt. William Morgan. {Ref: George W. Archer Collection and Revolutionary War File, Historical Society of Harford County Archives}

LANCASTER, MARY, see "John Parsons," q.v.

LANCASTER, REBECCA, see "John Parsons," q.v.

LANCASTER, SAMUEL (Cecil County), private (substitute) in the Maryland Continental Line, who enlisted to serve until 10 Dec 1781, was discharged on 29 Nov 1781. {Ref: Archives of Maryland Vol. 48, p. 7}

LANCE, THOMAS (Anne Arundel County), private by 5 Oct 1776 in Capt. Richard Chew's Militia Company, Weems' Battalion. {Ref: Archives of Maryland Vol. 12, p. 323}

LAND, WILLIAM (Maryland Navy), marine on the State Ship *Defence* in 1777. {Ref: Archives of Maryland Vol. 18, p. 658}

LANDERS, ROGER (Frederick County), private (substitute) in the Maryland Continental Line, Price's Regiment, enrolled in April, 1778 for 3 years or duration of the war. {Ref: Maryland Historical Magazine, Vol. 6, No. 3, p. 257}

LANDRAGAN, MICHAEL (Baltimore County), private, aged 21, bricklayer, born in Virginia, enlisted (made his "W" mark) on 24 Jun 1776 in Capt. John Fulford's Company of Matrosses, deserted 11 Dec 1776 and took his jacket, breeches and blanket with him. {Ref: Maryland Historical Magazine, Vol. 69, No. 1, pp. 96, 97}

LANG, FRANCIS (Charles County), private who enlisted in the 1st Maryland Continental Line in Charles County and applied for pension in Floyd County, Indiana on 8 Sep 1819, aged 59; in 1820 he had a wife (not named, aged 42) and these children: Nancy Lang (aged 17), Nehemiah Lang (aged 14), Stansbury Lang (aged 13), Sarah Lang (aged 11), and James Lang (aged 9), plus his wife's daughter Sarah Kennedy (aged 7); Francis married second to widow Susanna Phillips (her maiden name was Hunter) on 18 Sep 1828 in Lawrence County, Indiana, and died on 19 Jul 1847; his widow applied for pension in Greene County, Indiana on 14 Jul 1857, aged 65. {Ref: Archives of Maryland Vol. 18, pp. 355, 441; Research by Virgil D. White, citing Federal Pension Application W10188}

LANGRALE, LEVIN (Maryland Navy), sailor on the State Ship *Defence* in 1777. {Ref: Archives of Maryland Vol. 18, p. 658}

LANHAM, JOHN (Charles County), soldier in the Maryland troops who received disability payments beginning 4 Sep 1789; he died in 1801 and his widow Susannah Lanham died in 1838; her heirs, John Lanham and Betsy Bier, applied for pension in Baltimore under the Act of July 7, 1838, but their claim was rejected because *"both parties died before the passage of the act."* {Ref: *Rejected or Suspended Applications for Revolutionary War Pensions* (1850 Report), p. 235; Research by Virgil D. White, citing Federal Pension Application S25073}

LANNIN, JANE, see "Richard Donovan," q.v.

LARAVURE, JEAN (Baltimore County?), private in the 1st Maryland Continental Line who was recruited by 28 Feb 1780 at which time he was issued clothing due him. {Ref: Archives of Maryland Vol. 43, p. 98}

LARKIN, DENNIS (Maryland Navy), seaman on the State Ship *Defence* in 1777. {Ref: Archives of Maryland Vol. 18, p. 658}

LARKINS, JAMES (Frederick County), private in the Maryland troops who lived in Frederick County at the time of his enlistment and married Catharine Gerlinger on 3 Jul 1783 in Lancaster, Pennsylvania; applied for pension in Harrison County, Ohio on 4 Feb 1819, aged 63, but on 31 Jul 1820 he gave his age as 62, his wife as age 60, and they had 3 children (names not given) living at home: a son aged 21 on 17 Oct 1820, a son aged 20 on 5 Aug 1820, and a daughter aged 14; James died in Harrison County, Ohio on 12 Jul 1828 and his wife died on 27 Apr 1837 in Tuscarawas County, Ohio; daughter Betsey Cook (aged 56) lived in Wyandott County, Ohio on 5 Jan 1856. {Ref: Research by Christopher T. Smithson, citing Federal Pension Application R6167}

LARKINS, WILLIAM (Anne Arundel County), private by 5 Oct 1776 (made his "X" mark) in Capt. Richard Chew's Militia Company, Weems' Battalion. {Ref: Archives of Maryland Vol. 12, p. 323}

LARMAR, SAMUEL (Washington County), private who was enrolled to serve as a substitute in the Maryland Continental Line until 10 Dec 1781, but *"being represented unfit for the service for which he was intended"* was discharged on 30 Oct 1781. {Ref: Archives of Maryland Vol. 45, p. 657}

LAROCHE, GILBERT (Maryland Privateer), commander of the schooner *Young Neptune*, navigated by 30 men and mounting 10 carriage guns and 6 swivel guns, was issued Letters of Marque & Reprisal by the Council of Maryland on 9 Sep 1780. {Ref: Archives of Maryland Vol. 43, p. 282}

LATHIM, AARON (Cecil County), private in the Maryland Continental Line who was drafted to serve until 10 Dec 1781, was discharged on 29 Nov 1781. {Ref: Archives of Maryland Vol. 48, pp. 6-7}

LAUGHLIN, WILLIAM (Harford County), private who was enrolled 10 Mar 1776 in Militia Company No. 18 under Capt. John Jolly. {Ref: George W. Archer Collection and Revolutionary War File, Historical Society of Harford County Archives}

LAURENCE, JOHN (Harford County, Susquehannah Hundred), private who was enrolled 23 Apr 1776 in Militia Company No. 21 under Capt. George Patterson. {Ref: George W. Archer Collection and Revolutionary War File, Historical Society of Harford County Archives}

LAUTHERBACK, JOHN (Baltimore County), private who enlisted in Pulaski's Legion on 28 Mar 1778 and still in service in November, 1779. {Ref: Maryland Historical Magazine, Vol. 13, No. 3, p. 223}

LAWRENCE, JOSHUA (Maryland Navy), seaman on the State Ship *Defence* in 1777. {Ref: Archives of Maryland Vol. 18, p. 658}

LAWRENTS (LAWRENTZ), WENDAL (Harford County), soldier in the Maryland Continental Line who married Ann ---- on 28 Feb 1797 and applied for pension in Baltimore on 23 May 1818, aged 59; he was living in Harford County on 30 Aug 1820 at which time documents were filed in the 6th Judicial District, Harford County Court, stating in part: *"Wendal Lawrents, aged 61 years, resident in Harford County ... does on oath declare that he served in the Revolutionary War as follows: That he enlisted for three years in Baltimore in the State of Maryland in July 1776 in the company commanded by Capt. Philip Graybill of the German Regiment commanded first by Colonel Howsecker and afterwards by Colonel Weltner and served untill July 1779 when he was honorably discharged at Fort Wiomi now called Wilkesbury in Pennsylvania and was on the revolutionary pension list of the Maryland Agency as will appear by his certificate dated the 28th of July 1818. And I do solemlily swear that I was a resident citizen of the United States on the 18th of March 1818 and that I have not since that time by gift, sale or in any manner disposed of my property or any part thereof with intent thereby so as to diminish it as to bring myself within the provision of an Act of Congress entitled an act to provide for certain persons engaged in the land and naval service of the United States in* *the Revolutionary War passed on the 18th day of March 1818 and that I have not, nor has any person in trust for me, any property or securities, contracts or debts due me nor have I any income other than what is contained in the schedule hereto annexed and by me subscribed. Schedule referred to within namely two feather beds and covering $30; one bureau $8; six chairs $4; one table $2; [total] $44. Wendal Lawrents is by trade a brickmaker, greatly disabled by infirmity, his family consists of a sickly wife named Ann, four daughters namely Rachel age 19 years, Elizabeth age 14 years, Ann age 7 years and Mary age 4 years, and two sons namely George Washington age 10 years and Jacob age 2 years."* Signed: Wendal Lawrents (made his "+" mark). He died on 15 Mar 1823 and his widow applied for pension in Baltimore County on 21 Sep 1848, aged 77. {Ref: Historical Society of Harford County, Court Records File 25.14; Research by Virgil D. White, citing Federal Pension Application W9113}

LAYCOCK, ---- (Annapolis), private in the Maryland Continental Line before 27 Aug 1782 at which time permission was given by the Council of Maryland *"to Mary Laycock, late the wife of a Private soldier taken at the Reduction of York in Virginia who died in this City, to Return to New York in the Trimmer Captain Cox a Flag of Truce now lying in the Harbour."* {Ref: Archives of Maryland Vol. 48, p. 246}

LAZENBY, WILLIAM (Kent County), private (substitute) in the Maryland Continental Line by 1781, was discharged on 8 Dec 1781. {Ref: Archives of Maryland Vol. 48, p. 11}

LEALAND, JOHN (Baltimore County), private who enlisted in Pulaski's Legion on 28 Mar 1778 and still in service in November, 1779. {Ref: Maryland Historical Magazine, Vol. 13, No. 3, p. 223}

LEAMAN, MARY, see "Frederick Kemp," q.v.

LEARNER, ROBERT (Harford County), private who was enrolled 25 Mar 1776 in Militia Company No. 19 under Capt. William Morgan. {Ref: George W. Archer Collection and Revolutionary War File, Historical Society of Harford County Archives}

LEATH, ALEXANDER (Caroline County), private who was enrolled to serve as a substitute in the Maryland Continental Line until 10 Dec 1781, but *"being represented unfit for the service for which he was intended"* was discharged on 30 Oct 1781. {Ref: Archives of Maryland Vol. 45, p. 657}

LEATH, JOHN (Caroline County), private (substitute) in the Maryland Continental Line by 1781, was discharged on 8 Dec 1781. {Ref: Archives of Maryland Vol. 48, p. 10}

LEAVE, LUDWIC (Baltimore or Frederick County), private who enlisted in Pulaski's Legion on 6 Apr 1778 or 1779. {Ref: Maryland Historical Magazine, Vol. 13, No. 3, p. 224}

LEE, CASSANDRA, see "William Morgan," q.v.

LEE, CHRISTOPHER (Maryland Navy), marine on the State Ship *Defence* in 1777. {Ref: Archives of Maryland Vol. 18, p. 658}

LEE, ELIZABETH, see "George Zimmerman," q.v.

LEE, HENRY, see "James McCracken," q.v.

LEE, JAMES, OF SAMUEL (Harford County), private who was enrolled 25 Mar 1776 in Militia Company No. 19 under Capt. William Morgan. {Ref: George W. Archer Collection and Revolutionary War File, Historical Society of Harford County Archives}

LEE, JOSIAH (Harford County), private who was enrolled 25 Mar 1776 in Militia Company No. 19 under Capt. William Morgan. {Ref: George W. Archer Collection and Revolutionary War File, Historical Society of Harford County Archives}

LEE, MARK (Western Maryland), private in Capt. Michael Cresap's Company in 1775. {Ref: Howard L. Leckey's *The Tenmile Country and Its Pioneer Families*, p. 16}

LEE, PETER (Western Maryland), private in Capt. Michael Cresap's Company in 1775. {Ref: Howard L. Leckey's *The Tenmile Country and Its Pioneer Families*, p. 16}

LEE, RICHARD (Western Maryland), private in Capt. Michael Cresap's Company in 1775. {Ref: Howard L. Leckey's *The Tenmile Country and Its Pioneer Families*, p. 16}

LEE, SAMUEL, see "James Lee," q.v.

LEE, WILLIAM (Queen Anne's County), private (substitute) in the Maryland Continental Line by 1781, was discharged on 8 Dec 1781. {Ref: Archives of Maryland Vol. 48, p. 10}

LEECH, PHILIP (Baltimore County), private who was drafted to serve in the Maryland Continental Line until 10 Dec 1781, but *"being represented unfit for the duty for which he was intended"* was discharged on 30 Oct 1781. {Ref: Archives of Maryland Vol. 45, p. 656}

LEGGETT, JOHN (Baltimore Town), patriot and merchant who enrolled in Capt. John Sterrett's Independent Mercantile Company by February, 1777, at which time they were mustered into regular service with the continental army to repress loyalist activities in the Eastern Shore counties of Somerset and Worcester. {Ref: J. Thomas Scharf's *History of Baltimore City and County*, Part I, p. 77}

LEIGH, CHRISTOPHER (Maryland Navy), marine on the State Ship *Defence* in 1777. {Ref: Archives of Maryland Vol. 18, p. 658}

LEIGH, WILLIAM (Maryland Navy), surgeon's mate on the State Ship *Defence* in 1777. {Ref: Archives of Maryland Vol. 18, p. 658}

LEKENS, JAMES (Harford County), private who was enrolled by 15 Apr 1776 in Militia Company No. 20 under Capt. Robert Glenn. {Ref: George W. Archer Collection and Revolutionary War File, Historical Society of Harford County Archives}

LEMER, ROBERT (Harford County), private who was enrolled 9 Dec 1775 in Militia Company No. 14 under Capt. William McComas. {Ref: George W. Archer Collection and Revolutionary War File, Historical Society of Harford County Archives}

LEMMON, JOHN (Maryland Navy), marine on the State Ship *Defence* in 1777. {Ref: Archives of Maryland Vol. 18, p. 658}

LEMMON (LEMMEN), MOSES (Baltimore County), private, 31 May 1779, Capt. Benjamin Talbott's Militia Company, Cockey's Battalion. {Ref: Maryland Historical Magazine, Vol. 7, No. 1, p. 90}

LETHERMAN, MICHAEL (Washington County), private who was enrolled to serve as a substitute in the Maryland Continental Line until 10 Dec 1781, but *"being represented unfit for the service for which he was intended"* was discharged on 30 Oct 1781. {Ref: Archives of Maryland Vol. 45, p. 656}

LETTIGG, PETER (Baltimore County), contractor for State Arms in Baltimore County in 1781. {Ref: Archives of Maryland Vol. 47, p. 14}

LEWIN, SAMUEL (Anne Arundel County), private by 5 Oct 1776 in Capt. Richard Chew's Militia Company, Weems' Battalion. {Ref: Archives of Maryland Vol. 12, p. 323}

LEWIS, ISAAC (Baltimore County), private (substitute) in the Maryland Continental Line by 1781, was discharged on 8 Dec 1781. {Ref: Archives of Maryland Vol. 48, p. 11}

LEWIS, JONATHAN (Anne Arundel County), private in the 3rd Maryland Continental Line by 1 Dec 1781 at which time he was on duty guarding the magazine at the Head of Severn River. {Ref: Archives of Maryland Vol. 48, p. 8}

LEWIS, JOSEPH (Harford County), second lieutenant, commissioned 26 Apr 1776 in Militia Company No. 24 under Capt. Samuel Calwell. {Ref: George W. Archer Collection and Revolutionary War File, Historical Society of Harford County Archives}

LEWIS, THOMAS (Anne Arundel County), private who was a 9 month soldier in the 3rd Maryland Continental Line in 1778-1779, reenlisted on 22 Apr 1779 and received £2.14.4 in clothing. {Ref: Archives of Maryland Vol. 21, p. 360}

LEWIS, WILLIAM (Washington County), captain in the Maryland Continental Line who *"died on May 21, 1827 in the 72nd year of his age; deceased was in the battles of Trenton, Princeton, Brandywine, Germantown, and Monmouth, and engaged in several skirmishes; he also served under Gen. Wayne in the Indian campaign and was at the battle of Miami in 1793."* For additional information see Peden's *Revolutionary Patriots of Washington County, 1776-1783* (p. 211). {Ref: J. Thomas Scharf's *History of Western Maryland*, Vol. II, p. 1051}

LIDSINGER, HENRY (Baltimore County), private, aged 30, mason, born in Germany, enlisted (made his "X" mark) on 2 Mar 1776 in Capt. John Fulford's Company of Matrosses. {Ref: Maryland Historical Magazine, Vol. 69, No. 1, p. 96}

LIGHT, WILLIAM (Harford County), private (substitute) in the Maryland Continental Line by 1781, was discharged on 8 Dec 1781. {Ref: Archives of Maryland Vol. 48, p. 11}

LILBURN (LILBON), WALTER (Maryland Navy), midshipman on the State Ship *Defence* in 1777. {Ref: Archives of Maryland Vol. 18, p. 658}

LILLEY, WILLIAM (Harford County), private who was enrolled 25 Mar 1776 in Militia Company No. 19 under Capt. William Morgan. {Ref: George W. Archer Collection and Revolutionary War File, Historical Society of Harford County Archives}

LIMER, PETER (Baltimore or Frederick County), waggoner in Pulaski's Legion before July, 1782. {Ref: Maryland Historical Magazine, Vol. 13, No. 3, p. 225}

LINCH, WILLIAM (Baltimore County), private, 31 May 1779, Capt. Benjamin Talbott's Militia Company, Cockey's Battalion. {Ref: Maryland Historical Magazine, Vol. 7, No. 1, p. 90}

LINDSAY, JOHN (Prince George's County), private in the 2nd and 4th Maryland Continental Lines from 23 Dec 1776 to 16 Aug 1780; born 15 Mar 1758, married Rachel Dorsey in 1779, and died in 1840; their children were: Rachel Lindsay (born 1780, married Samuel Moreland); Anthony Lindsay (born 1781, married ---- Dorsey); Sarah Lindsay (born 1783, married Rev. Elder); Elizabeth Lindsay (born 1785, married Anthony Anderson); Samuel Dorsey Lindsay (born 1787, married Susan Underwood); and, John G. Lindsay (born 1791). {Ref: Archives of Maryland Vol. 18, p. 7; Maryland State Society DAR Directory, 1892-1965, pp. 464-465}

LINGAN, JAMES MACCUBBIN (Prince George's County), patriot who was appointed captain *"of a Company of Cavalry directed to be raised by the Act for the Defence of the Bay"* on 25 Apr 1781. {Ref: Archives of Maryland Vol. 45, p. 414}

LINK, ADAM (Frederick County), patriot buried in Mount Olivet Cemetery. {Ref: Information compiled by Dr. Donald Wolf in Maryland Society SAR Newsletter circa 1996}

LINTON, GEORGE (Anne Arundel County), private in the Maryland Continental Line by 1 Dec 1781 at which time he was on duty guarding the magazine at the Head of Severn River. {Ref: Archives of Maryland Vol. 48, p. 8}

LITSINGER, GEORGE (Baltimore County), matross soldier by 7 May 1779 at which time he gave a deposition about his enlistment terms. {Ref: Maryland State Archives Record MdHR 6636-14-83}

LITTLE, JOHN (Maryland Navy), marine on the State Ship *Defence* in 1777. {Ref: Archives of Maryland Vol. 18, p. 658}

LLOYD, EDWARD (Talbot County), patriot who was appointed by the Council of Maryland on 27 Jan 1776 as one of three persons in Talbot County to collect all gold and silver coin that can be procured in said county. {Ref: Archives of Maryland Vol. 11, p. 132}

LOAGAN, WILLIAM (Harford County), private who was enrolled 9 Dec 1775 in Militia Company No. 14 under Capt. William McComas. {Ref: George W. Archer Collection and Revolutionary War File, Historical Society of Harford County Archives}

LOCK, JOSEPH (Western Maryland), private in Capt. Michael Cresap's Company in 1775. {Ref: Howard L. Leckey's *The Tenmile Country and Its Pioneer Families*, p. 16}

LOCKER, PHILIP (Prince George's County), private who was drafted into the Maryland Continental Line, was discharged on 8 Dec 1781. {Ref: Archives of Maryland Vol. 48, p. 10}

LOGMAN, JAMES (Baltimore or Frederick County), corporal in Pulaski's Legion before July, 1782. {Ref: Maryland Historical Magazine, Vol. 13, No. 3, p. 225}

LONGFELLOW, ARNOLD (Queen Anne's County), private (substitute) in the Maryland Continental Line, who enlisted to serve until 10 Dec 1781, was discharged on 29 Nov 1781. {Ref: Archives of Maryland Vol. 48, p. 7}

LONGFELLOW, GEDION (Queen Anne's County), private (substitute) in the Maryland Continental Line by 1781, was discharged on 8 Dec 1781. {Ref: Archives of Maryland Vol. 48, p. 10}

LONGFELLOW, THOMAS (Queen Anne's and Caroline Counties), private who enlisted in the 5th Maryland Continental Line on 4 Jun 1778, fought in the Battle of Camden in South Carolina on 16 Aug 1780 and died from wounds on 18 Aug 1780 (although one muster roll reported him "missing" after the battle); born 6 Jun 1754, married Nancy Reed, and their son Jonathan was born 1 Dec 1778(?) and married Esther Griffith (although one source stated he was born in 1788 which is incorrect since his father died in 1780). Additional research may be necessary before drawing conclusions. {Ref: Maryland State Society DAR Directory, 1892-1965, p. 471; Archives of Maryland Vol. 18, p. 224}

LOVE, CORNELIUS (Baltimore or Frederick County), private who enlisted in Pulaski's Legion on 28 Nov 1779. {Ref: Maryland Historical Magazine, Vol. 13, No. 3, p. 224}

LOVE, SAMUEL (Charles County), patriot who was appointed by the Council of Maryland on 27 Jan 1776 as one of three persons in Charles County to collect all gold and silver coin that can be procured in said county. {Ref: Archives of Maryland Vol. 11, p. 132}

LOVELL, MARTHA, see "William Kelley," q.v.

LOVELY, JOSHUA (Baltimore County), private, aged 31, shoemaker, born in Hull, England, enlisted (made his "X" mark) on 15 Feb 1776 in Capt. John Fulford's Company of Matrosses. {Ref: Maryland Historical Magazine, Vol. 69, No. 1, p. 95}

LOVELY, WILLIAM (Charles County), private who was drafted into the Maryland Continental Line, was discharged on 8 Dec 1781. {Ref: Archives of Maryland Vol. 48, p. 10}

LOWE, BAZIL (Baltimore or Frederick County), private in Pulaski's Legion before July, 1782. {Ref: Maryland Historical Magazine, Vol. 13, No. 3, p. 225}

LOWE, CHARLES (Baltimore County), private, aged 25, linen weaver, born in Dublin, enlisted 13 Feb 1776 in Capt. John Fulford's Company of Matrosses. {Ref: Maryland Historical Magazine, Vol. 69, No. 1, p. 94}

LOWE, JACOB, SR. (Frederick County), patriot buried in Mount Olivet Cemetery. {Ref: Information compiled by Dr. Donald Wolf in Maryland Society SAR Newsletter circa 1996}

LOWE, JOHN TOLSON (Prince George's County), ensign in the 2nd Maryland Continental Line who was issued clothing *"due him from the Continent"* on 31 Jan 1780 and received payment for his services in the amount of "1900 Dollars & £3.10s" on 12 Sep 1780. For additional information see Peden's *Revolutionary Patriots of Prince George's County, 1775-1783* (p. 192). {Ref: Archives of Maryland Vol. 43, p. 73, and Vol. 45, p. 97}

LOWE, MICHAEL (Prince George's County), captain who served on a General Court-Martial on 6 Jul 1776. {Ref: Archives of Maryland Vol. 11, p. 553}

LOWE, NEHEMIAH (Prince George's County), soldier who allegedly served in the Maryland militia [no military record was found in *Archives of Maryland*]; born in 1756 in Prince George's County and stated he lived there at the time of his enlistment and married Amelia Macbee on 22 Nov 1791 [no marriage record was found in extant Maryland records]; removed to Montgomery County; applied for pension on 20 Nov 1844 under the Act of June 7, 1832, but the claim was suspended pending proof from the Register of the Land Office at Annapolis; his widow applied for pension on 15 Apr 1851, aged 81. {Ref: *Rejected or Suspended Applications for Revolutionary War Pensions* (1850 Report), p. 231; Research by Virgil D. White, citing Federal Pension Application R6489}

LOWNDES, CHRISTOPHER (Prince George's County), patriot who was commissioned one of the three persons in Prince George's County by the Council of Maryland on 19 Aug 1779 to receive subscriptions for use of the State. {Ref: Archives of Maryland Vol. 21, p. 499}

LOXLEY, BENJAMIN (Baltimore Privateer), commander of the ship *Fanny*, mounting 12 carriage guns, 7 howitz guns and 23 small arms, was issued Letters of Marque & Reprisal by the Council of Maryland on 14 Jun 1779. {Ref: Archives of Maryland Vol. 21, p. 453}

LOYAL, JOHN (Maryland Navy), marine on the State Ship *Defence* in 1777. {Ref: Archives of Maryland Vol. 18, p. 658}

LUCAS, JOHN (Southern Maryland), lieutenant, commissioned on 27 Jul 1780 to serve in the Regiment Extra by order of the Council of Maryland. {Ref: Archives of Maryland Vol. 43, p. 234}

LUCAS, THOMAS (Maryland Navy), sailor or seaman on 7 Jan 1780. {Ref: Calendar of Maryland State Papers, The Brown Books, p. 57}

LUCKETT, DAVID (Charles County), ensign in the 1st Maryland Continental Line who received payment for his services in the amount of "1900 Dollars & £3.10s" on 12 Sep 1780. {Ref: Archives of Maryland Vol. 45, p. 97}

LUCKETT, SAMUEL (Charles County), ensign, commissioned on 27 Jul 1780 to serve in the Regiment Extra by order of the Council of Maryland; recommended as captain in the 26th Battalion of Militia of Charles County on 20 Mar 1781. {Ref: Archives of Maryland Vol. 43, p. 234, and Vol. 47, p. 136}

LUCKETT, WILLIAM, JR. (Frederick County), patriot who was commissioned one of the three persons in Frederick County by the Council of Maryland on 19 Aug 1779 to receive subscriptions for use of the State. {Ref: Archives of Maryland Vol. 21, p. 499}

LUFF, JOHN (Frederick County), private (substitute) in the Maryland Continental Line, Williams' Regiment, enrolled in May, 1778 for 3 years or duration of the war. {Ref: Maryland Historical Magazine, Vol. 6, No. 3, p. 258}

LUKE, FOLIUS (Maryland Navy), seaman or marine on the State Ship *Defence* in 1777. {Ref: Archives of Maryland Vol. 18, p. 658}

LUKENS, TACE, see "John Parsons," q.v.

LUNDERGAN, DENNIS (Cecil County), private (substitute) in the Maryland Continental Line, who enlisted to serve until 10 Dec 1781, was discharged on 29 Nov 1781. {Ref: Archives of Maryland Vol. 48, p. 7}

LUNN, JOSHUA (Baltimore County), captain by 22 Oct 1778 at which time the Council of Maryland recorded, in part, that *"he hath been absent in parts beyond the Seas for about 11 months last past and hath lately that is to say within 3 months last past, returned into this State, appeared before the Governor & Council, and before them did take, repeat and Subscribe the Oath of Fidelity and Support to this State contained in th Act entitled An Act to punish certain Crimes and Misdemeanors and to prevent the Growth of Toryism."* {Ref: Archives of Maryland Vol. 21, p. 221}

LUSBY, HENRY (Maryland Navy), midshipman on the State Ship *Defence* from 15 Oct to 13 Nov 1777 and lieutenant of marines from 13 Nov to 31 Dec 1777. {Ref: Archives of Maryland Vol. 18, p. 658}

LUX, ROBERT (Maryland Navy), midshipman on the State Ship *Defence* in 1777. {Ref: Archives of Maryland Vol. 18, p. 658}

LUX, WILLIAM (Baltimore County), patriot who was appointed by the Council of Maryland on 27 Jan 1776 as one of three persons in Baltimore County to collect all gold and silver coin that can be procured in said county. {Ref: Archives of Maryland Vol. 11, p. 132}

LYDAY, SIMON (Washington County), private who was enrolled to serve as a substitute in the Maryland Continental Line until 10 Dec 1781, but *"being represented unfit for the service for which he was intended"* was discharged on 30 Oct 1781. {Ref: Archives of Maryland Vol. 45, p. 656}

LYDEN, SHADRACK, see "John Hooper," q.v.

LYNCH, JOHN (Queen Anne's County), captain in the 5th Maryland Continental Line who received payment for his services in the amount of "1900 Dollars & £3.10s" on 12 Sep 1780. {Ref: Archives of Maryland Vol. 45, p. 98}

LYNCH, JOHN (Baltimore County), private, aged 27, labourer, born in Ireland, enlisted (made his "X" mark) on 10 Aug 1776 in Capt. John Fulford's Company of Matrosses. {Ref: Maryland Historical Magazine, Vol. 69, No. 1, p. 96}

LYNCH, JOHN (Baltimore County), private, aged 23, carpenter, born in Ireland, enlisted 16 Sep 1776 in Capt. John Fulford's Company of Matrosses. {Ref: Maryland Historical Magazine, Vol. 69, No. 1, p. 96}

LYNCH, JOHN (Frederick County), patriot buried in Mount Olivet Cemetery. {Ref: Information compiled by Dr. Donald Wolf in Maryland Society SAR Newsletter circa 1996}

LYNCH, JOHN (Harford County), private who was enrolled 10 Mar 1776 in Militia Company No. 18 under Capt. John Jolly. {Ref: George W. Archer Collection and Revolutionary War File, Historical Society of Harford County Archives}

LYNCH, WILLIAM (Harford County), private who was enrolled 10 Mar 1776 in Militia Company No. 18 under Capt. John Jolly. {Ref: George W. Archer Collection and Revolutionary War File, Historical Society of Harford County Archives}

LYNCH, WILLIAM (Harford County), private who was enrolled 25 Mar 1776 in Militia Company No. 19 under Capt. William Morgan. {Ref: George W. Archer Collection and Revolutionary War File, Historical Society of Harford County Archives}

LYNN (LINN), DAVID (Frederick County), ensign and lieutenant in 1776 and captain in the 7th Maryland Continental Line in 1779; received payment for his services in the amount of "1900 Dollars & £3.10s" on 12 Sep 1780; born 15 Jul 1758, married Mary Galloway in 1794, and died 11 Apr 1834; their children were: Henry Galloway Lynn (born 27 Mar 1796); Francina Cheston Lynn (born 28 Jan 1798, married Frederick A. Schley); Mary Galloway Lynn (born 12 Nov 1799, married Jonathan W. Magruder); William Lynn (born 9 Sep 1801, married Jane Johns); John Galloway Lynn (born 1 Oct 1803, married Rebecca Singleton); George Lynn (born 8 Aug 1805, married Virginia Moss); Anna Brooke Lynn (born 3 Aug 1802, married George Tilghman); James Galloway Lynn (born 24 Jul 1809); Joseph Galloway Lynn (born 28 Mar 1811); and, Ellen Jane Lynn (born 7 Jan 1813, married James L. Willoughby). {Ref: Archives of Maryland Vol. 45, p. 98; Maryland State Society DAR Directory, 1892-1965, p. 478}

LYNN (LINN), JOHN (Frederick County), lieutenant in the 6th Maryland Continental Line who received payment for his services in the amount of "1900 Dollars & £3.10s" on 12 Sep 1780; Col. John Lynn died 30 Mar 1813 *"in Allegany County after 4 days illness of a pleurisy; his patriotic services were displayed throughout the Southern Campaigns in the Revolutionary War; he distinguished himself in the battles of Camden, Guilford, and Eutaw, in which last he received a dangerous wound which disabled him"* (buried in Mount Olivet Cemetery in Frederick). {Ref: Archives of Maryland Vol. 45, p. 98; *Frederick-Town Herald*, 3 Apr 1813; Burial information compiled by Dr. Donald Wolf in Maryland Society SAR Newsletter circa 1996}

LYON, JOHN (Western Maryland), private in Capt. Michael Cresap's Company in 1775. {Ref: Howard L. Leckey's *The Tenmile Country and Its Pioneer Families*, p. 16}

LYONS, JOHN (Queen Anne's County), private (substitute) in the Maryland Continental Line by 1781, was discharged on 8 Dec 1781. {Ref: Archives of Maryland Vol. 48, p. 11}

LYTLE, WILLIAM (Harford County), soldier who was reported in the August term, 1777 of the county court as follows: *"We the Grand Jurours for Harford County on our oaths do present James McAnair [McNear], one of the lieutenants of the State of Pennsylvania, for inlisting William Lytle of the State of Maryland."* {Ref: Historical Society of Harford County Court Records File 2.15(6)}

MACBEE, AMELIA, see "Nehemiah Lowe," q.v.

MACKALL, BENJAMIN IV (Calvert County), patriot who was appointed by the Council of Maryland on 27 Jan 1776 as one of three persons in Calvert County to collect all gold and silver coin that can be procured in said county. {Ref: Archives of Maryland Vol. 11, p. 132}

MACKETTEE, LEONARD (Prince George's or Montgomery County), private in the 3rd Maryland Continental Line who was a 9 month soldier in the 3rd Maryland Regiment in 1778-1779, was discharged on 17 May 1779 and received £15.15.6 in clothing. {Ref: Archives of Maryland Vol. 21, p. 395}

MACKETTEE, THOMAS (Prince George's or Montgomery County), private in the 3rd Maryland Continental Line who was a 9 month soldier in the 3rd Maryland Regiment in 1778-1779, was discharged on 17 May 1779 and received £15.15.6 in clothing. {Ref: Archives of Maryland Vol. 21, p. 395}

MACKEY (MACKAY), THOMAS (Anne Arundel County), private in the Maryland Continental Line who enlisted at Annapolis; applied for pension in Washington, D.C. on 19 Oct 1820, moved to Baltimore, and lived among friends in Virginia (county not stated) in 1826; he died on 16 Mar 1836. {Ref: Research by Virgil D. White, citing Federal Pension Application S38169}

MACRELL, THOMAS (Frederick County), private (substitute) in the Maryland Continental Line, German Regiment, enrolled in May, 1778 for 3 years or duration of the war. {Ref: Maryland Historical Magazine, Vol. 6, No. 3, p. 259}

MADDIN, JAMES (Harford County), private who was enrolled by 15 Apr 1776 in Militia Company No. 20 under Capt. Robert Glenn. {Ref: George W. Archer Collection and Revolutionary War File, Historical Society of Harford County Archives}

MADDIN, PHILIP (Harford County), private who was enrolled 9 Dec 1775 in Militia Company No. 14 under Capt. William McComas. {Ref: George W. Archer Collection and Revolutionary War File, Historical Society of Harford County Archives}

MADDIN, SAMUEL (Talbot County?), private in the 5th Maryland Continental Line who was a 9 month soldier in 1779, was discharged on 25 Oct 1779 and received £29.10.0 in clothing. {Ref: Archives of Maryland Vol. 21, p. 566}

MADDOX, JOHN (Maryland Navy), marine on the State Ship *Defence* in 1777. {Ref: Archives of Maryland Vol. 18, p. 658}

MADDUX, JOHN (St. Mary's County), private who was drafted into the Maryland Continental Line, was discharged on 8 Dec 1781. {Ref: Archives of Maryland Vol. 48, p. 10}

MADERN, ADAM (Frederick County), private (substitute) in the Maryland Continental Line, German Regiment, enrolled in May, 1778 for 3 years or duration of the war. {Ref: Maryland Historical Magazine, Vol. 6, No. 3, p. 259}

MADKIN, JOHN (Dorchester County), private (substitute) in the Maryland Continental Line, who enlisted to serve until 10 Dec 1781, was discharged on 29 Nov 1781. {Ref: Archives of Maryland Vol. 48, p. 7}

MAFFIT, THOMAS (Anne Arundel County), private (substitute) in the Maryland Continental Line, who enlisted to serve until 10 Dec 1781, was discharged on 29 Nov 1781. {Ref: Archives of Maryland Vol. 48, p. 7}

165

MAGEN, HENRY (Baltimore County), private, aged 26, labourer, born in Ireland, enlisted (made his "X" mark) on 24 Feb 1776 in Capt. John Fulford's Company of Matrosses. {Ref: Maryland Historical Magazine, Vol. 69, No. 1, p. 95}

MAGIN, CHARLES (Western Maryland), private in Capt. Michael Cresap's Company in 1775. {Ref: Howard L. Leckey's *The Tenmile Country and Its Pioneer Families*, p. 16}

MAGRAH, JAMES (Baltimore County), private, aged 22, labourer, born in Ireland, enlisted 2 Mar 1776 in Capt. John Fulford's Company of Matrosses. {Ref: Maryland Historical Magazine, Vol. 69, No. 1, p. 96}

MAGRUDER, CHARLES (Southern Maryland), lieutenant, commissioned on 27 Jul 1780 to serve in the Regiment Extra by order of the Council of Maryland. {Ref: Archives of Maryland Vol. 43, p. 234}

MAGRUDER, JONATHAN, see "David Lynn," q.v.

MAGRUDER, NATHANIEL (Southern Maryland), lieutenant, commissioned on 27 Jul 1780 to serve in the Regiment Extra by order of the Council of Maryland. {Ref: Archives of Maryland Vol. 43, p. 234}

MAGRUDER, NATHANIEL B. (Prince George's County), lieutenant in the Maryland Continental Line by 1 May 1781 at which time he received payment due in the amount of £22.8.10. {Ref: Archives of Maryland Vol. 45, p. 421}

MAHAN, JOHN (Harford County, Susquehannah Hundred), private who was enrolled 23 Apr 1776 in Militia Company No. 21 under Capt. George Patterson. {Ref: George W. Archer Collection and Revolutionary War File, Historical Society of Harford County Archives}

MAIN (MEHN), JOHN FREDERICK (Frederick County), associator in 1775; born 9 Aug 1754 (son of Johann George Mehn, 1722-1773) and married Susanna Beckenbach (or Pickenpaugh); took the Oath of Allegiance and Fidelity in 1778; died in 1833. His brother Johannes Mehn, born 11 Feb 1756, married Susannah ----, and died 16 Apr 1832. Since the name of the patriot was listed as John (not as Johannes or John Frederick), additional research will be necessary before drawing conclusions as to which brother this service applied. {Ref: Maryland Historical Magazine, Vol. 9 and Vol. 12; Research by Glenn A. Main, Jr. of Lutherville, Maryland (a direct descendant) in 2000}

MAIN (MEHN), JOHN GEORGE (Frederick County), patriot who took the Oath of Allegiance and Fidelity in 1780; born circa 1744 (son of Johann George Mehn, 1722-1773), married first to Catharine ---- and second to Mrs. Mary Madgalena ----, and died in 1822. His brother George Adam Mehn was born 15 May 1746, married Apollonia Weil, and died 17 May 1822. Since the name of the patriot was listed as George (not as John George or George Adam), additional research will be necessary before drawing conclusions as to which brother this service applied. {Ref: *Maryland Genealogical Society Bulletin* (Vol. 27, No. 1, Winter, 1986, p. 101) and research by Glenn A. Main, Jr. of Lutherville, Maryland (a direct descendant) in 2000}

MAKEMSON, JOHN (Harford County), private who was enrolled by 15 Apr 1776 in Militia Company No. 20 under Capt. Robert Glenn. {Ref: George W. Archer Collection and Revolutionary War File, Historical Society of Harford County Archives}

MAKEMSON, JOSEPH (Harford County), private who was enrolled by 15 Apr 1776 in Militia Company No. 20 under Capt. Robert Glenn. {Ref: George W. Archer Collection and Revolutionary War File, Historical Society of Harford County Archives}

MAKEMSON, THOMAS (Harford County), private who was enrolled by 15 Apr 1776 in Militia Company No. 20 under Capt. Robert Glenn. {Ref: George W. Archer Collection and Revolutionary War File, Historical Society of Harford County Archives}

MAKEMSON, WILLIAM (Harford County), private who was enrolled by 15 Apr 1776 in Militia Company No. 20 under Capt. Robert Glenn. {Ref: George W. Archer Collection and Revolutionary War File, Historical Society of Harford County Archives}

MAKIN, NICHOLAS (Western Maryland), private in Capt. Michael Cresap's Company in 1775. {Ref: Howard L. Leckey's *The Tenmile Country and Its Pioneer Families*, p. 16}

MALADY, JOHN (Frederick County), private (substitute) in the Maryland Continental Line, German Regiment, enrolled in May, 1778 for 3 years or duration of the war. {Ref: Maryland Historical Magazine, Vol. 6, No. 3, p. 258}

MALTS, JOHN (Baltimore County), private, aged 22, labourer, born in Bristol, enlisted 23 Feb 1776 in Capt. John Fulford's Company of Matrosses. {Ref: Maryland Historical Magazine, Vol. 69, No. 1, p. 95}

MANGER (MANGERS), NICHOLAS (St. Mary's County), lieutenant in the 3rd Maryland Continental Line before 18 Mar 1780 at which time he received $3000 to be expended in recruiting troops; also received payment for his services in the amount of "1900 Dollars & £3.10s" on 12 Sep 1780. {Ref: Archives of Maryland Vol. 43, p. 115 and Vol. 45, p. 97}

MANLEY, JOHN (Cecil County), soldier in the Maryland Continental Line who served in Lee's Legion, 1780-1783; lived in Cecil County at the time of his enlistment and there he married Susanna Cox on 13 Apr 1790; he died in Fairfield County, Ohio on 13 or 14 Feb 1814 and his widow applied for pension in Walnut Township on 20 May 1844, aged 74 years and 6 months. {Ref: Archives of Maryland Vol. 18, pp. 587-588; Research by Christopher T. Smithson, citing Federal Pension Application W5339}

MANLY, JOHN (Baltimore County), soldier whose widow Martha Manly's heirs applied for pension under the Act of July 4, 1836, but the claim was rejected because *"the case was not properly presented -- papers incomplete"* (noted also that the widow was deceased, but no date was given). {Ref: *Rejected or Suspended Applications for Revolutionary War Pensions* (1850 Report), p. 233}

MANNING, JOHN (Caroline County), private in the Maryland Continental Line who was drafted to serve until 10 Dec 1781, was discharged on 29 Nov 1781. {Ref: Archives of Maryland Vol. 48, p. 7}

MANSPIKER, HENRY (Baltimore County), private (substitute) in the Maryland Continental Line by 1781, was discharged on 8 Dec 1781. {Ref: Archives of Maryland Vol. 48, p. 11}

MANTZ, FRANCIS (Frederick County), patriot buried in Mount Olivet Cemetery. {Ref: Information compiled by Dr. Donald Wolf in Maryland Society SAR Newsletter circa 1996}

MANTZ, PETER (Frederick County), captain and patriot buried in Mount Olivet Cemetery. {Ref: Information compiled by Dr. Donald Wolf in Maryland Society SAR Newsletter circa 1996}

MAR, WILLIAM (Baltimore County), private (substitute) in the Maryland Continental Line by 1781, was discharged on 8 Dec 1781. {Ref: Archives of Maryland Vol. 48, p. 11}

MARATA, MATTHEW (Maryland Navy), midshipman on 7 Jan 1780. {Ref: Calendar of Maryland State Papers, The Brown Books, p. 57}

MARBURY, JOSEPH (Prince George's County), captain in the 3rd Maryland Continental Line who received payment for his services in the amount of "1900 Dollars & £3.10s" on 12 Sep 1780. {Ref: Archives of Maryland Vol. 45, p. 97}

MARBURY, LUKE (Prince George's County), captain who served on a General Court-Martial on 6 Jul 1776. {Ref: Archives of Maryland Vol. 11, p. 553}

MARCH, ELIZABETH, see "Aquila Norris," q.v.

MARKLAND, EDWARD (Maryland Navy), first lieutenant of marines on the galley *Baltimore*, commissioned on 18 May 1778; married first to Ann ---- (died 21 Sep 1784) and married second to Alice ---- on 29 May 1790; a daughter by his first marriage was Ann Markland (died in August, 1782); children by his second marriage were: John Markland (died 29 Sep 1792, aged 11 months and 29 days); Charles Wesley Markland (died 3 Aug 1793); John Markland (died 5 Aug 1799, aged 4 weeks and 2 days); Anna Maria Markland (died in 1818); William S. Markland (living in 1847); Penelope S. Markland (living in 1847); Mary E. Worthington (wife of Charles Worthington, living in 1847); and, Charles E. Markland (living in 1853); Edward Markland, the soldier, died 7 Oct 1827, aged 71; widow Alice Markland, of Darlington, Harford County, applied for pension on 16 Jul 1844, aged 72, under the Act of July 7, 1838, but the claim was suspended because of *"claims for service as lieutenant on board the Dolphin, but the period and length of service is not given."* She died on 13 Nov 1847. {Ref: Archives of Maryland Vol. 21, p. 91; *Rejected or Suspended Applications for Revolutionary War Pensions* (1850 Report), p. 236; Research by Virgil D. White, citing Federal Pension Application W4019}

MARLOW, BUTLER (Prince George's County), private (substitute) in the Maryland Continental Line by 1781, was discharged on 8 Dec 1781. {Ref: Archives of Maryland Vol. 48, p. 10}

MARR, JAMES (Calvert County), private who enlisted in the Maryland Continental Line by 9 Jun 1778 at which time the Council of Maryland was informed and in turn directed *"that James Marr who is inlisted into the Service and his Brother who was drafted in Calvert County (the said James Marr having as it is said obtained a furlough from Sergeant Gordon) have purchased Horses with the Declared Intention of going to Carolina. It is therefore ordered that they be apprehended and brought to Annapolis by any Persons who may have an Opportunity of doing it."* {Ref: Archives of Maryland Vol. 21, p. 127}

MARSH, JOSHUA (Baltimore County), captain in Gunpowder Upper Battalion of Militia in 1780; married Temperance Harryman on 9 Dec 1783 or 11 Dec 1785 and their children were Achsah Marsh, William Marsh, Stephen Marsh, Rebecca Marsh, Elijah Marsh, Sarah Marsh, Grafton Marsh, Dennis Marsh, Josiah Marsh, Ellen Marsh, Joshua Marsh, Beal Marsh, Nelson Marsh, and Benedict Marsh; Joshua, the soldier, died on 5 Nov 1825 or 1828 and his widow Temperance Marsh applied for pension on 5 May 1844, aged 81, under the Act of July 7, 1838, but the claim was suspended *"for further proof of marriage and service."* For additional information see Peden's *Revolutionary Patriots of Baltimore Town and Baltimore County, 1775-1783.* {Ref: *Rejected or Suspended Applications for Revolutionary War Pensions* (1850 Report), p. 236; Research by Virgil D. White, citing Federal Pension Application R6924}

MARSH, LLOYD (Harford County), private who was enrolled 31 Oct 1775 in Militia Company No. 8 under Capt. Greenberry Dorsey. {Ref: George W. Archer Collection and Revolutionary War File, Historical Society of Harford County Archives}

MARTIN, EDWARD (Harford County, Susquehannah Hundred), private who was enrolled 23 Apr 1776 in Militia Company No. 21 under Capt. George Patterson. {Ref: George W. Archer Collection and Revolutionary War File, Historical Society of Harford County Archives}

MARTIN, GEORGE (Somerset County), private (substitute) in the Maryland Continental Line by 1781, was discharged on 8 Dec 1781. {Ref: Archives of Maryland Vol. 48, p. 11}

MARTIN, JAMES (Harford County, Susquehannah Hundred), private who was enrolled 23 Apr 1776 in Militia Company No. 21 under Capt. George Patterson. {Ref: George W. Archer Collection and Revolutionary War File, Historical Society of Harford County Archives}

MARTIN, JOHN (Baltimore Privateer), commander of the sloop *Swallow*, mounting 6 carriage guns, 6 swivel guns and 12 small arms, was issued Letters of Marque & Reprisal by the Council of Maryland on 17 Jul 1779; commander of the brigantine *Tom Johnson*, mounting 12 carriage guns, 4 swivel guns and 16 small arms, was issued Letters of Marque & Reprisal by the Council of Maryland on 8 Oct 1779. {Ref: Archives of Maryland Vol. 21, pp. 475, 552}

MARTIN, JOHN (Baltimore County), private, aged 28, labourer, born in England, enlisted (made his "X" mark) on 20 Feb 1776 in Capt. John Fulford's Company of Matrosses; he was probably the John Martin who was a matross in Capt. Gale's Company who was deemed unfit for further service and discharged on

28 Jan 1780. {Ref: Maryland Historical Magazine, Vol. 69, No. 1, p. 95; Archives of Maryland Vol. 43, p. 72}

MARTIN, NICHOLAS (Annapolis Privateer), commander of the sloop *Morris and Wallace*, navigated by 15 men and mounting 4 carriage guns and 4 swivel guns, was issued Letters of Marque & Reprisal by the Council of Maryland on 28 Mar 1778; commander of the sloop *Porpus*, mounting 6 carriage guns, 4 howitz guns and 8 small arms, was issued Letters of Marque & Reprisal by the Council of Maryland on 23 Apr 1779; commander of the brigantine *Nesbitt*, navigated by 30 men and mounting 14 carriage guns, was issued Letters of Marque & Reprisal by the Council of Maryland on 15 Mar 1781. {Ref: Archives of Maryland Vol. 16, p. 557, Vol. 21, p. 362, and Vol. 45, p. 350}

MARTIN, SAMUEL (St. Mary's County), soldier who applied for pension under the Act of June 7, 1832, but the claim was suspended because he did not serve six months. {Ref: *Rejected or Suspended Applications for Revolutionary War Pensions* (1850 Report), p. 232}

MARTIN, SARAH, see "William Morgan," q.v.

MASON, ABEL (St. Mary's County), ordinary sailor on the State Ship *Defence* in 1777. {Ref: Archives of Maryland Vol. 18, p. 658}

MASON, CALEB (Charles County?), ensign in the 2nd Maryland Continental Line issued clothing *"due him from the Continent"* on 31 Jan 1780 and received payment for his services in the amount of "1900 Dollars & £3.10s" on 12 Sep 1780. {Ref: Archives of Maryland Vol. 43, p. 74, and Vol. 45, p. 97}

MASON, JAMES (Annapolis), private by 16 Jun 1778 at which time he called upon the Council of Maryland who in turn sent a message to Gen. Smallwood, stating, in part: *"James Mason the Bearer of this of the second Maryland Regiment has called here on his way to Camp and solicited a Discharge from the Service; he says that he was inlisted in Watkings's Company and has Received no Bounty or since inlisted, that Col. Price agreed, if he would procure another Man to inlist in his Stead, that he would discharge him and that, accordingly, he procured one William Norton to inlist in his Stead, for which he gave him £5; That notwithstanding he, as well as Norton, have served ever since, and that Capt. Brown of the Artillery is acquainted with those Facts."* {Ref: Archives of Maryland Vol. 21, pp. 137-138}

MASON, THOMAS (Queen Anne's County), captain in the 7th Maryland Continental Line who received payment for his services in the amount of "1900 Dollars & £3.10s" on 12 Sep 1780. {Ref: Archives of Maryland Vol. 45, p. 98}

MASON, THOMAS (Western Maryland), private in Capt. Michael Cresap's Company in 1775. {Ref: Howard L. Leckey's *The Tenmile Country and Its Pioneer Families*, p. 16}

MASSENBACH, FELIX LEWIS (Baltimore County), patriot who was appointed second lieutenant in Capt. John Fulford's Artillery Company on 9 Feb 1776. {Ref: Archives of Maryland Vol. 11, p. 148}

MASSEY, HENRY LEE or LEIGH (Maryland Navy), midshipman on the State Ship *Defence* from 10 May to 31 Dec 1777; boat captain by 31 Jul 1778 at which time the Council of Maryland directed the Treasurer to pay him *"£94.11.4 for Wages due himself and the Crew of the Amelia per Account passed by the Auditor General."* {Ref: Archives of Maryland Vol. 18, p. 658 and Vol. 21, p. 171}

MASSON, NICOLAS (Baltimore or Frederick County), private who enlisted in Pulaski's Legion on 28 Nov 1779. {Ref: Maryland Historical Magazine, Vol. 13, No. 3, p. 224}

MASTERS, WATTERLY (Maryland Navy), marine on the State Ship *Defence* in 1777. {Ref: Archives of Maryland Vol. 18, p. 658}

MATCHET, JOHN (Baltimore County), private (substitute) in the Maryland Continental Line by 1781, was discharged on 8 Dec 1781. {Ref: Archives of Maryland Vol. 48, p. 11}

MATHEW, THOMAS (Western Maryland), private in Capt. Michael Cresap's Company in 1775. {Ref: Howard L. Leckey's *The Tenmile Country and Its Pioneer Families*, p. 16}

MATTHEWMAN, LUKE (Baltimore Privateer), commander of the brigantine *Snake*, mounting 14 carriage guns, 6 swivel guns and 18 small arms, was issued Letters of Marque & Reprisal by the Council of Maryland on 28 Apr 1769. {Ref: Archives of Maryland Vol. 21, p. 369}

MATTHEWS, GEORGE (Baltimore Town), patriot and Cannon Founder by 30 Jan 1776 at which time he was *"requested to attend the Council of Safety and give what Information he could with Regard to casting a Cannon, and the Cannon now in that place"* [with which he comply]. {Ref: Archives of Maryland Vol. 11, p. 122}

MATTHEWS, JOHN (Maryland Navy), sweeper on the State Ship *Defence* in 1777. {Ref: Archives of Maryland Vol. 18, p. 658}

MATTHEWS, ROBERT (Frederick County), private (substitute) in the Maryland Continental Line, Williams' Regiment, enrolled in May, 1778 for 3 years or duration of the war. {Ref: Maryland Historical Magazine, Vol. 6, No. 3, p. 259}

MATTHEWS, WILLIAM (Maryland Navy), corporal of marines on the State Ship *Defence* in 1777. {Ref: Archives of Maryland Vol. 18, p. 658}

MATTINGLY, IGNATIUS (St. Mary's County), private who was enrolled to serve as a substitute in the Maryland Continental Line until 10 Dec 1781, but *"being represented unfit for the service for which he was intended"* was discharged on 30 Oct 1781. {Ref: Archives of Maryland Vol. 45, p. 657}

MATTINGLY, LUKE (St. Mary's County), patriot who supplied 800 lbs. of beef on the hoof to the State of Maryland on 13 Oct 1780. {Ref: Archives of Maryland Vol. 45, p. 156}

MAULEGE, SAMUEL (Baltimore County), private (substitute) in the Maryland Continental Line by 1781, was discharged on 8 Dec 1781. {Ref: Archives of Maryland Vol. 48, p. 11}

MAULZ, PETER (Frederick County), captain and patriot buried in Mount Olivet Cemetery. {Ref: Information compiled by Dr. Donald Wolf in Maryland Society SAR Newsletter circa 1996}

MAXWELL, WILLIAM, JR. (Kent County), second major of the 27th Battalion of Militia, commissioned 8 May 1777; one William Maxwell, farmer, died testate in Kent County by 15 Jun 1792. {Ref: Archives of Maryland Vol. 16, p. 243; Kent County Wills Liber 7, p. 360}

McADAMS, JOHN (Maryland Navy), armorer on the State Ship *Defence* in 1777. {Ref: Archives of Maryland Vol. 18, p. 658}

McANAIR, JAMES, see "William Lytle," q.v.

McAVOY, PATRICK (Frederick County), private in the Maryland Continental Line by 1778, was retained in the service on 22 Jun 1778 and sent on board the galleys. {Ref: Archives of Maryland Vol. 21, p. 144}

McBRIDE, JAMES, see "Gabriel Williams," q.v.

McC---ORN(?), JAMES (Baltimore County), private, aged 32, born in New York, enlisted 15 Feb 1776 in Capt. John Fulford's Company of Matrosses. {Ref: Maryland Historical Magazine, Vol. 69, No. 1, p. 95}

McCAIN, MARMADUKE (Frederick County), private in the Maryland Continental Line who had enlisted to serve until 10 Dec 1781, having served the term for which he became a substitute, was discharged on 16 Feb 1782. {Ref: Archives of Maryland Vol. 48, p. 78}

McCALLISTER, ARCHIBALD (Frederick County), captain in the 1st Maryland Continental Line who received payment for his services in the amount of "1900 Dollars & £3.10s" on 12 Sep 1780. {Ref: Archives of Maryland Vol. 45, p. 97}

McCARTY, JAMES (Baltimore County), private (substitute) in the Maryland Continental Line by 1781, was discharged on 8 Dec 1781. {Ref: Archives of Maryland Vol. 48, p. 11}

McCARTY, FLORENCE (Maryland Navy), seaman on the State Ship *Defence* in 1777. {Ref: Archives of Maryland Vol. 18, p. 658}

McCARTY, TIMOTHY (Frederick County), private (substitute) in the Maryland Continental Line, Price's Regiment, enrolled in May, 1778 for 3 years or duration of the war. {Ref: Maryland Historical Magazine, Vol. 6, No. 3, p. 259}

McCAY, HUGH (Frederick County), private (substitute) in the Maryland Continental Line, German Regiment, enrolled in May, 1778 for 3 years or duration of the war. {Ref: Maryland Historical Magazine, Vol. 6, No. 3, p. 260}

McCLAIN, FRANCIS (Harford County), private who was enrolled by Capt. Praul in the Regiment Extraordinary and sent to Annapolis with Capt. Thompson on board the sloop *Liberty* on 17 Aug 1780. {Ref: Archives of Maryland Vol. 45, p. 50}

McCLAND, ROBERT (Frederick County), private (substitute) in the Maryland Continental Line, Williams' Regiment, enrolled in May, 1778 for 3 years or duration of the war. {Ref: Maryland Historical Magazine, Vol. 6, No. 3, p. 258}

McCLASKEY, JOSEPH (Harford County), private who was enrolled 9 Dec 1775 in Militia Company No. 14 under Capt. William McComas. {Ref: George W. Archer Collection and Revolutionary War File, Historical Society of Harford County Archives}

McCLELLAND, JOHN, JR. (Baltimore Town), patriot and merchant who enrolled in Capt. John Sterrett's Independent Mercantile Company by February, 1777, at which time they were mustered into regular service with the continental army to repress loyalist activities in the Eastern Shore counties of Somerset and Worcester. {Ref: J. Thomas Scharf's *History of Baltimore City and County*, Part I, p. 77}

McCLENAN (McCLELAND), ROBERT (Maryland Navy), marine on the State Ship *Defence* in 1777. {Ref: Archives of Maryland Vol. 18, p. 658}

McCLINTOCK, MATTHEW (Harford County), first lieutenant, commissioned -- Feb 1777, Militia Company No. 32. {Ref: George W. Archer Collection and Revolutionary War File, Historical Society of Harford County Archives}

McCLUNG, ADAM (Harford County), private who was enrolled by 15 Apr 1776 in Militia Company No. 20 under Capt. Robert Glenn. {Ref: George W. Archer Collection and Revolutionary War File, Historical Society of Harford County Archives}

McCLURE, JOHN (Harford County), private who was enrolled 9 Dec 1775 in Militia Company No. 14 under Capt. William McComas. {Ref: George W. Archer Collection and Revolutionary War File, Historical Society of Harford County Archives}

McCOARD, ARTHUR (Harford County), private who was enrolled by 15 Apr 1776 in Militia Company No. 20 under Capt. Robert Glenn. {Ref: George W. Archer Collection and Revolutionary War File, Historical Society of Harford County Archives}

McCOLLOCH, JAMES (Baltimore Town), patriot and merchant who enrolled in Capt. John Sterrett's Independent Mercantile Company by February, 1777, at which time they were mustered into regular service with the continental army to repress loyalist activities in the Eastern Shore counties of Somerset and Worcester. {Ref: J. Thomas Scharf's *History of Baltimore City and County*, Part I, p. 77}

McCOMAS, AARON (Harford County), private who was enrolled 30 Sep 1775 in Militia Company No. 13 under Capt. William Bradford; born in 1760 in Baltimore County and lived in Harford County at the time of his enlistment; married Martha Gilbert on 19 Feb 1798; applied for pension on 7 Aug 1833 under the Act of June 7, 1832, but the claim was rejected because he did not serve six months; he died in 1845. {Ref: *Rejected or Suspended Applications for Revolutionary War Pensions* (1850 Report), p. 229; Research by Virgil D. White, citing Federal Pension Application R6638; Maryland Society SAR Application 3143}

McCOMAS, DANIEL, OF DANIEL (Harford County), private who was enrolled 9 Dec 1775 in Militia Company No. 14 under Capt. William McComas. {Ref: George W. Archer Collection and Revolutionary War File, Historical Society of Harford County Archives}

McCOMAS, DANIEL, OF JOHN (Harford County), private who was enrolled 9 Dec 1775 in Militia Company No. 14 under Capt. William McComas. {Ref: George W. Archer Collection and Revolutionary War File, Historical Society of Harford County Archives}

McCOMAS, DANIEL, OF WILLIAM (Harford County), private who was enrolled 9 Dec 1775 in Militia Company No. 14 under Capt. William McComas. {Ref: George W. Archer Collection and Revolutionary War File, Historical Society of Harford County Archives}

McCOMAS, ELIZABETH, see "Alexander Norris," q.v.

McCOMAS, JAMES (Harford County), captain, commissioned 28 Apr 1776 in Militia Company No. 23. {Ref: George W. Archer Collection and Revolutionary War File, Historical Society of Harford County Archives}

McCOMAS, MARY, see "Parker Gilbert," q.v.

McCOMAS, MORDECAI (Harford County), private who was enrolled 9 Dec 1775 in Militia Company No. 14 under Capt. William McComas. {Ref: George W. Archer Collection and Revolutionary War File, Historical Society of Harford County Archives}

McCOMAS, WILLIAM (Harford County), captain, 9 Dec 1775 in Militia Company No. 14. {Ref: George W. Archer Collection and Revolutionary War File, Historical Society of Harford County Archives}

McCORD, ELIZABETH, see "Benjamin Moore," q.v.

McCORD, RUTH, see "Ichabod Davis," q.v.

McCOWEN, ANDREW (Baltimore County), private who enlisted in Pulaski's Legion on 28 Mar 1778 and still in service in November, 1779. {Ref: Maryland Historical Magazine, Vol. 13, No. 3, p. 223}

McCOY, GEORGE (Maryland Navy), seaman or marine on the State Ship *Defence* in 1777. {Ref: Archives of Maryland Vol. 18, p. 658}

McCOY, JAMES (Baltimore Privateer), commander of the brigantine *Trooper*, navigated by 40 men and mounting 12 carriage guns, 2 swivel guns and 14 small arms, was issued Letters of Marque & Reprisal by the Council of Maryland on 24 Jul 1780. {Ref: Archives of Maryland Vol. 43, p. 227}

McCOY, JOHN (Maryland Continental Line, Staff Officer), ensign and forage master who received payment for his services in the amount of "1900 Dollars & £3.10s" on 12 Sep 1780. {Ref: Archives of Maryland Vol. 45, p. 98}

McCOY (McKOY), JOHN (St. Mary's County), maimed soldier who stated that he *"has no money and has received no pay for between two and three years"* and petitioned the Council of Maryland on 15 Aug 1780 for relief; they in turn ordered the Treasurer to *"pay to John McCoy who served faithfully in the 3rd Maryland Regiment and has had the misfortune to loose his Leg, £150 to enable him to return to his Friends in St. Mary's"* on 16 Aug 1780. {Ref: Archives of Maryland Vol. 43, p. 256, and Vol. 45, p. 48}

McCOY, WILLIAM (Frederick County), private (substitute) in the Maryland Continental Line, Price's Regiment, enrolled in April, 1778 for 3 years or duration of the war. {Ref: Maryland Historical Magazine, Vol. 6, No. 3, p. 258}

McCRACKEN, CYRUS (Western Maryland), sergeant in Capt. Michael Cresap's Company in 1775. {Ref: Howard L. Leckey's *The Tenmile Country and Its Pioneer Families*, p. 15}

McCRACKEN (McCRAKIN), JAMES (Cecil and Harford Counties), soldier who was living in Harford County on 11 Aug 1824 at which time documents were filed in Harford County Court, stating in part: *"James McCracken, aged 72 years, resident in Harford County ... does on his oath declare that he served in the Revolutionary War as follows: That he enlisted at Charles Town in Cecil County and State aforesaid [Maryland] in the spring of the year 1778, for during the war, in the 3rd Company of Dragoons commanded by Joseph Eagleston [Eccleston], Esquire, in Col. Henry Lee's Legion - Continued in the service in said company until the close of the war when he was dismounted at Charleston in South Carolina, horses sold, and himself with some hundred others sent by water to Hampton Roads, from thence put on board a schooner and conveyed to the head of Elk where he received a written discharge from Capt. Michael Rudolph - That he was heretofore placed on the pension list roll of the State of Maryland at the rate of $80 per month as will appear by reference to a certificate granted by the Secretary of War dated the 9th of June 1818 and numbered 4663, but was discontinued and stricken off on the alteration of the law of 1 May 1820 which required the exhibition of a schedule of property, he then having in his possession one negro man, one negro woman and one small girl which were erroniously returned as slaves, and their term of service recently sold by the sheriff under feiri facias to satisfy a debt previously owing. And I do solemnly swear that I was a resident citizen of the United States on the 18th of March 1818 and that I have not since that time by gift, sale or in any manner disposed of my property or any part thereof with intent thereby so as to diminish it as to bring myself within the provision of an Act of Congress entitled An Act to provide for certain persons engaged in the land and naval service of the United States in the Revolutionary War passed on the 18th day of March 1818 and that I have not, nor has any person in trust for me, any property or securities, contracts or debts due me nor have I any income other than what is contained in the schedule hereto annexed and by me subscribed. Schedule referred to vizt., one female negro child 7 years of age, valued at about $30; two cows, which would not sell for $10 each, $20; four hogs, supposed to be worth about 150 cents each, $6; three pots, two kettles, two common tables, six common chairs, one cupboard with sundry cupboard* *furniture, etc., not worth the whole, $15; no other property save necessary wearing apparel and bedding; [total] $71. That his family consists of himself age 72 years, his wife Mary age 53 years and in delicate health, an orphan child named Eliza Smith age 4 years, and the little negro above mentioned. That he formerly followed fishing and going by water for hire but from advanced age and various infirmities is now incapable of performing manual labour so as to procure a living for himself and is actually in such indigent circumstances as to be unable to support himself without the assistance of his country." Witness: Thomas Bailey.* Earlier, on 1 Sep 1820, James McCracken had filed papers outlining his military service and listing his property which included at that time one yellow woman age 37 years worth $50, one black boy named Vincent, aged 16 years, worth $150, one black boy named Hamp, aged 14 years, worth $150, one black girl named Jince, aged 10 years, worth $150, and one black boy named Jerry, aged 2 years, worth $50; he also stated *"my occupation was a farmer. I have no family except a wife."* Subsequently, on 14 Aug 1826, he filed more papers outlining his military service and listing his property which included at that time *"negro Lewis, aged 2 years, worth $20, negro Vincent, to serve 8 months, $30, and negro Jenny, aged 18 years and infirm, $20."* He further stated *"that his family consisted of himself, his wife age about 58, negro Lewis, negro Vincent, and negro Jenny, and that from his great age and the infirmities of himself and his wife that he is unable to support himself without assistance of his country, and that he is unable from infirmity to pursue any employment except netting seines which he can only get to do occasionally in the winter."* Signed: James McCracken (made his mark that resembled a "D" or an "O"). {Ref: Historical Society of Harford County, Court Records File 25.14}

McCRACKEN, WILLIAM (Baltimore or Harford County), soldier in the Maryland Continental Line who applied for pension in Baltimore under the Act of June 7, 1832, but the claim was rejected because he did not serve six months; however, Federal Pension Application R6665 indicates he lived in Chester County, Pennsylvania at the time of his enlistment in the Pennsylvania Line and he applied for pension in Harford County on 20 Jan 1834, aged 88. {Ref: *Rejected or Suspended Applications for Revolutionary War Pensions* (1850 Report), p. 229}

McCULLOCH, DAVID (Harford County), private who was enrolled by 15 Apr 1776 in Militia Company No. 20 under Capt. Robert Glenn. {Ref: George W. Archer Collection and Revolutionary War File, Historical Society of Harford County Archives}

McCULLOCH, JAMES H. (Baltimore Town), patriot and merchant who enrolled in Capt. John Sterrett's Independent Mercantile Company by February, 1777, at which time they were mustered into regular service with the continental army to repress loyalist activities in the Eastern Shore counties of Somerset and Worcester. {Ref: J. Thomas Scharf's *History of Baltimore City and County*, Part I, p. 77}

McCURDY, HUGH (Baltimore Town), patriot and merchant who enrolled in Capt. John Sterrett's Independent Mercantile Company by February, 1777, at which time they were mustered into regular service with the continental army to repress loyalist activities in the Eastern Shore counties of Somerset and Worcester. {Ref: J. Thomas Scharf's *History of Baltimore City and County*, Part I, p. 77}

McDANIEL, JOHN (Harford County), private who was enrolled 9 Dec 1775 in Militia Company No. 14 under Capt. William McComas. {Ref: George W. Archer Collection and Revolutionary War File, Historical Society of Harford County Archives}

McDANIEL, PETER (Western Maryland), private in Capt. Michael Cresap's Company in 1775. {Ref: Howard L. Leckey's *The Tenmile Country and Its Pioneer Families*, p. 16}

McDOLE, JESSE (Cecil County), private who was enrolled to serve as a substitute in the Maryland Continental Line until 10 Dec 1781, but *"being represented unfit for the service for which he was intended"* was discharged on 30 Oct 1781. {Ref: Archives of Maryland Vol. 45, p. 657}

McDONALD, ---- (Anne Arundel County?), soldier in the Maryland Continental Line *"now remaining in Annapolis"* on 24 Jul 1780 at which time his wife Mary McDonald was entitled to rations under the laws of the State. {Ref: Archives of Maryland Vol. 43, p. 227}

McDONALD, JOHN (Harford County), private who was enrolled by 15 Apr 1776 in Militia Company No. 20 under Capt. Robert Glenn. {Ref: George W. Archer Collection and Revolutionary War File, Historical Society of Harford County Archives}

McDONALD, MARY, see "---- McDonald," q.v.

McDONALD, ROBERT (Maryland Navy), ordinary seaman on the State Ship *Defence* in 1777. {Ref: Archives of Maryland Vol. 18, p. 658}

McELDERY, THOMAS (Baltimore Town), patriot and merchant who enrolled in Capt. John Sterrett's Independent Mercantile Company by February, 1777, at which time they were mustered into regular service with the continental army to repress loyalist activities in the Eastern Shore counties of Somerset and Worcester. {Ref: J. Thomas Scharf's *History of Baltimore City and County*, Part I, p. 77}

McELROY, PATRICK (Western Maryland), ensign in Capt. Michael Cresap's Company in 1775. {Ref: Howard L. Leckey's *The Tenmile Country and Its Pioneer Families*, p. 16}

McELVIN, BENJAMIN (Cecil County), private who was enrolled to serve as a substitute in the Maryland Continental Line until 10 Dec 1781, but *"being represented unfit for the service for which he was intended"* was discharged on 30 Oct 1781. {Ref: Archives of Maryland Vol. 45, p. 657}

McFADDEN, ELIZABETH, see "Archibald Harvey," q.v.

McFADDEN, JOSEPH (Harford County, Susquehannah Hundred), private who was enrolled 23 Apr 1776 in Militia Company No. 21 under Capt. George Patterson. {Ref: George W. Archer Collection and Revolutionary War File, Historical Society of Harford County Archives}

McFADDEN, SAMUEL (Harford County, Susquehannah Hundred), private who was enrolled 23 Apr 1776 in Militia Company No. 21 under Capt. George Patterson. {Ref: George W. Archer Collection and Revolutionary War File, Historical Society of Harford County Archives}

McFADDON, FAITHFULL, see "Jesse Foster," q.v.

McFADON, JOHN (Baltimore Town), patriot and merchant who enrolled in Capt. John Sterrett's Independent Mercantile Company by February, 1777, at which time they were mustered into regular service with the continental army to repress loyalist activities in the Eastern Shore counties of Somerset and Worcester. {Ref: J. Thomas Scharf's *History of Baltimore City and County*, Part I, p. 77}

McFARLAND, MARCUS (Baltimore Town), patriot and merchant who enrolled in Capt. John Sterrett's Independent Mercantile Company by February, 1777, at which time they were mustered into regular service with the continental army to repress loyalist activities in the Eastern Shore counties of Somerset and Worcester. {Ref: J. Thomas Scharf's *History of Baltimore City and County*, Part I, p. 77}

McGAW, JAMES (Harford County), private who was enrolled by 15 Apr 1776 in Militia Company No. 20 under Capt. Robert Glenn. {Ref: George W. Archer Collection and Revolutionary War File, Historical Society of Harford County Archives}

McGILL, JAMES (Maryland Navy), marine on the State Ship *Defence* in 1777. {Ref: Archives of Maryland Vol. 18, p. 658}

McGILL, THOMAS (Montgomery County), private who was drafted into the Maryland Continental Line, was discharged on 8 Dec 1781. {Ref: Archives of Maryland Vol. 48, p. 10}

McGUIRE, JOHN (Montgomery County?), ensign in the 3rd Maryland Continental Line who received payment for his services in the amount of "1900 Dollars & £3.10s" on 12 Sep 1780. {Ref: Archives of Maryland Vol. 45, p. 97, which listed the name as "Ensign McGiven"}

McGLAMORY, ELIJAH (Worcester County), private (substitute) in the Maryland Continental Line by 1781, was discharged on 8 Dec 1781. {Ref: Archives of Maryland Vol. 48, p. 11}

McGRAW, JOHN (Frederick County), private (substitute) in the Maryland Continental Line, Price's Regiment, enrolled in May, 1778 for 3 years or duration of the war. {Ref: Maryland Historical Magazine, Vol. 6, No. 3, p. 258}

McGRAW, LEONARD (Dorchester County), private (substitute) in the Maryland Continental Line by 1781, was discharged on 8 Dec 1781. {Ref: Archives of Maryland Vol. 48, p. 10}

McGRAW, STEPHEN (Frederick County), private (substitute) in the Maryland Continental Line, German Regiment, enrolled in April, 1778 for 3 years or duration of the war. {Ref: Maryland Historical Magazine, Vol. 6, No. 3, p. 257}

McGUIRE, NICHOLAS (Frederick County), private (substitute) in the Maryland Continental Line by 1781, was discharged on 8 Dec 1781. {Ref: Archives of Maryland Vol. 48, p. 11}

178

McHENRY, JOHN, see "John Eager Howard" and "Aquila Hall," q.v.

McKEEN, WILLIAM, see "Nicholas R. Moore," q.v.

McKENNA, FRANCIS (Baltimore Town), patriot and merchant who enrolled in Capt. John Sterrett's Independent Mercantile Company by February, 1777, at which time they were mustered into regular service with the continental army to repress loyalist activities in the Eastern Shore counties of Somerset and Worcester. {Ref: J. Thomas Scharf's *History of Baltimore City and County*, Part I, p. 77}

McKENNA, THOMAS (Baltimore Town), patriot and merchant who enrolled in Capt. John Sterrett's Independent Mercantile Company by February, 1777, at which time they were mustered into regular service with the continental army to repress loyalist activities in the Eastern Shore counties of Somerset and Worcester. {Ref: J. Thomas Scharf's *History of Baltimore City and County*, Part I, p. 77}

McKENNY, SAMUEL (Western Maryland), private in Capt. Michael Cresap's Company in 1775. {Ref: Howard L. Leckey's *The Tenmile Country and Its Pioneer Families*, p. 16}

McKIM, JOHN, JR. (Baltimore Town), patriot and merchant who enrolled in Capt. John Sterrett's Independent Mercantile Company by February, 1777, at which time they were mustered into regular service with the continental army to repress loyalist activities in the Eastern Shore counties of Somerset and Worcester. {Ref: J. Thomas Scharf's *History of Baltimore City and County*, Part I, p. 77}

McKINNEY, JOHN (Frederick County), private (substitute) in the Maryland Continental Line, Price's Regiment, enrolled in April, 1778 for 3 years or duration of the war. {Ref: Maryland Historical Magazine, Vol. 6, No. 3, p. 256}

McKINSEY, JOSHUA (Frederick County), private (substitute) in the Maryland Continental Line, German Regiment, enrolled in April, 1778 for 3 years or duration of the war. {Ref: Maryland Historical Magazine, Vol. 6, No. 3, p. 257}

McKINSEY, MOSES (Frederick County), private (substitute) in the Maryland Continental Line, German Regiment, enrolled in April, 1778 for 3 years or duration of the war. {Ref: Maryland Historical Magazine, Vol. 6, No. 3, p. 257}

McKIRDY, JOHN (Baltimore Privateer), commander of the schooner *Dove*, navigated by 13 men and mounting 4 swivel guns, was issued Letters of Marque & Reprisal by the Council of Maryland on 13 Mar 1780. {Ref: Archives of Maryland Vol. 43, p. 110}

McKISSON, JOHN (Harford County), private who was enrolled 10 Mar 1776 in Militia Company No. 18 under Capt. John Jolly. {Ref: George W. Archer Collection and Revolutionary War File, Historical Society of Harford County Archives}

McKISSON, SAMUEL (Harford County), private who was enrolled 10 Mar 1776 in Militia Company No. 18 under Capt. John Jolly. {Ref: George W. Archer Collection and Revolutionary War File, Historical Society of Harford County Archives}

McKOY, JOHN, see "John McCoy," q.v.

McLANE, SAMUEL (Southern Maryland), lieutenant, commissioned on 27 Jul 1780 to serve in the Regiment Extra by order of the Council of Maryland. {Ref: Archives of Maryland Vol. 43, p. 234}

McLAUGHLAN, MARK (Maryland Navy), carpenter on the State Ship *Defence* in 1777. {Ref: Archives of Maryland Vol. 18, p. 658}

McNABB, JAMES (Harford County), private who was enrolled 10 Mar 1776 in Militia Company No. 18 under Capt. John Jolly; James McNabb died by 10 Jun 1806 (date of final distribution) and his heirs were Alse McNabb (widow), sons Isaac, John, James, Robert, and Daniel McNabb, and daughters Catharine and Susanna McNabb. {Ref: George W. Archer Collection and Revolutionary War File, Historical Society of Harford County Archives; Henry C. Peden, Jr.'s *Heirs & Legatees of Harford County, 1802-1846*, p. 10}

McNALEY, JOHN (Frederick County), private (substitute) in the Maryland Continental Line, Gunby's Regiment, enrolled in April, 1778 for 3 years or duration of the war. {Ref: Maryland Historical Magazine, Vol. 6, No. 3, p. 257}

McNASS, GEORGE (Charles County), private (substitute) in the Maryland Continental Line by 1781, was discharged on 8 Dec 1781. {Ref: Archives of Maryland Vol. 48, p. 17}

McNEALE, JOHN (Washington County), private who was drafted to serve in the Maryland Continental Line until 10 Dec 1781, but *"being represented unfit for the duty for which he was intended"* was discharged on 30 Oct 1781. {Ref: Archives of Maryland Vol. 45, p. 656}

McNEALIS, CHARLES (Maryland Navy), marine on the State Ship *Defence* in 1777. {Ref: Archives of Maryland Vol. 18, p. 658}

McNEAR, JAMES, see "William Lytle," q.v.

McNUTT, ---- (Harford County), first sergeant, enrolled by 15 Apr 1776 in Militia Company No. 20 under Capt. Robert Glenn. {Ref: George W. Archer Collection and Revolutionary War File, Historical Society of Harford County Archives}

McPHERSON, JOHN, SR. (Frederick County), colonel and patriot buried in Mount Olivet Cemetery. {Ref: Information compiled by Dr. Donald Wolf in Maryland Society SAR Newsletter circa 1996}

McPHERSON, SAMUEL (Anne Arundel County), captain in the 1st and 2nd Maryland Continental Lines who received payment for his services in the amount of "1900 Dollars & £3.10s" on 12 Sep 1780. {Ref: Archives of Maryland Vol. 45, p. 97}

McPHERSON, WILLIAM HANSON (Annapolis), patriot who was appointed Assistant Clerk to the Auditor General and qualified before the Council of Maryland by taking the several required oaths on 5 May 1778. {Ref: Archives of Maryland Vol. 21, p. 67}

McWILLIAMS, THOMAS (Maryland Navy), captain of marines on board the sloop *Molly*, commissioned by the Maryland Council of Safety on 14 Dec 1776. {Ref: Archives of Maryland Vol. 12, p. 527}

180

MEADS, JAMES (Harford County), private who was enrolled by 15 Apr 1776 in Militia Company No. 20 under Capt. Robert Glenn. {Ref: George W. Archer Collection and Revolutionary War File, Historical Society of Harford County Archives}

MEDLEY, ENOCH (Maryland Navy), seaman on the State Ship *Defence* in 1777. {Ref: Archives of Maryland Vol. 18, p. 658}

MEDTART, JACOB (Frederick County), patriot buried in Mount Olivet Cemetery. {Ref: Information compiled by Dr. Donald Wolf in Maryland Society SAR Newsletter circa 1996}

MEEK, ABNER (Frederick County), soldier who served in the New Jersey and Pennsylvania Lines; born in Pennsylvania, enlisted at Amboy, New Jersey and again at Chambersburg, Pennsylvania; after the war he moved to Maryland and worked on the Potomac River for several years; in 1806 he became overseer of Mr. Garrott's farm near Berlin in Frederick County; applied for pension on 7 Dec 1835, aged 75 or 76, under the Act of June 7, 1832, but the claim was suspended *"pending further proof and specification."* {Ref: *Rejected or Suspended Applications for Revolutionary War Pensions* (1850 Report), p. 232; Research by Virgil D. White, citing Federal Pension Application R7093}

MEEK, ANDREW (Harford County, Susquehannah Hundred), private who was enrolled 23 Apr 1776 in Militia Company No. 21 under Capt. George Patterson. {Ref: George W. Archer Collection and Revolutionary War File, Historical Society of Harford County Archives}

MEEK, JACOB (Baltimore or Anne Arundel County), soldier in the Pennsylvania Line who was born in March, 1755 at Elkridge near Baltimore and lived in Westmoreland County, Pennsylvania at the time of his enlistment; after the war he moved to Shelby and Henry Counties, Kentucky for about 19 years; in 1807 he moved to Wayne County, Indiana where he applied for pension on 31 Aug 1832. {Ref: Research by Virgil D. White, citing Federal Pension Application S16480}

MEEKINS, ROBERT (Dorchester County), private (substitute) in the Maryland Continental Line by 1781, was discharged on 8 Dec 1781. {Ref: Archives of Maryland Vol. 48, p. 10}

MEHN, JOHN, see "John Main," q.v.

MELLEN, JOHN (Baltimore County), private, aged 16, weaver, born in Quebec, enlisted 22 Oct 1776 in Capt. John Fulford's Company of Matrosses. {Ref: Maryland Historical Magazine, Vol. 69, No. 1, p. 97}

MERCER, RICHARD (Western Maryland), private in Capt. Michael Cresap's Company in 1775. {Ref: Howard L. Leckey's *The Tenmile Country and Its Pioneer Families*, p. 16}

MERCER, STEPHEN (Maryland Navy), seaman or marine on the State Ship *Defence* in 1777. {Ref: Archives of Maryland Vol. 18, p. 658}

MERCERLY, CONRAD (Western Maryland), private in Capt. Michael Cresap's Company in 1775. {Ref: Howard L. Leckey's *The Tenmile Country and Its Pioneer Families*, p. 16}

MERRICK, JOHN (Talbot County), private who was drafted into the Maryland Continental Line, was discharged on 8 Dec 1781. {Ref: Archives of Maryland Vol. 48, p. 10}

MERRICK, WILLIAM (Talbot County), private (substitute) in the Maryland Continental Line by 1781, was discharged on 8 Dec 1781. {Ref: Archives of Maryland Vol. 48, p. 11}

MERRIMAN, ELIZABETH, see "Luke Merryman," q.v.

MERRIWITHER, REUBEN (Anne Arundel County), patriot who was commissioned one of the three persons in Anne Arundel County by the Council of Maryland on 19 Aug 1779 to receive subscriptions for use of the State. {Ref: Archives of Maryland Vol. 21, p. 499}

MERRYMAN, JOSHUA (Baltimore Town), patriot and merchant who enrolled in Capt. John Sterrett's Independent Mercantile Company by February, 1777, at which time they were mustered into regular service with the continental army to repress loyalist activities in the Eastern Shore counties of Somerset and Worcester. {Ref: J. Thomas Scharf's *History of Baltimore City and County*, Part I, p. 77}

MEY, JAMES (Harford County), contractor for State Arms in Harford County in 1781. {Ref: Archives of Maryland Vol. 47, p. 14}

MERRYMAN, LUKE (Baltimore County), private in the 3rd Maryland Continental Line in 1781; married Elizabeth Gorsuch on 29 Jan 1794 and had three children: first child (name not given) born in 1795; second child (Caleb) born in 1797 (aged 52 in 1849); and, third child (name and birth date not given); Luke died in Baltimore County on 14 Feb 1813 and his widow Elizabeth Merriman *[sic]* applied for pension on 20 Aug 1836, aged 69, in Baltimore under the Act of July 4, 1836, but the claim was suspended *"for further proof and specification."* {Ref: Archives of Maryland Vol. 18, pp. 392, 448; *Rejected or Suspended Applications for Revolutionary War Pensions* (1850 Report), p. 234; Research by Virgil D. White, citing Federal Pension Application W2648; Dawn B. Smith's *Baltimore County Marriage Licenses, 1777-1798*, p. 130}

MICKLE, ROBERT (Baltimore Town), patriot and merchant who enrolled in Capt. John Sterrett's Independent Mercantile Company by February, 1777, at which time they were mustered into regular service with the continental army to repress loyalist activities in the Eastern Shore counties of Somerset and Worcester. {Ref: J. Thomas Scharf's *History of Baltimore City and County*, Part I, p. 77}

MIDDLETON, GILBERT (Maryland Navy), captain of the State Ship *Plater* in 1780. {Ref: Archives of Maryland Vol. 45, p. 218}

MIDDLETON, JOSEPH (Maryland Privateer), captain of a schooner [not named] which was impressed into service by order of the Council of Maryland on 27 Apr 1780 *"to go to the Head of Elk to Transport Troops from thence to Virginia, but as she is at present engaged in the Public Service she is to return from Baltimore to Annapolis."* {Ref: Archives of Maryland Vol. 43, p. 155}

MIDDLETON, THEO. (Southern Maryland), ensign, commissioned on 27 Jul 1780 to serve in the Regiment Extra by order of the Council of Maryland. {Ref: Archives of Maryland Vol. 43, p. 234}

MIDDLETON, WILLIAM (Maryland Navy), captain of the State Schooner *Dolphin* in 1780. {Ref: Archives of Maryland Vol. 43, p. 207, and Vol. 45, p. 218}

MILCAKEY, DANIEL (Queen Anne's County), private who was drafted into the Maryland Continental Line, was discharged on 8 Dec 1781. {Ref: Archives of Maryland Vol. 48, p. 10}

MILES, JOSHUA (Baltimore County), private, aged 22, labourer, born in Maryland, enlisted (made his "X" mark) on 13 Feb 1776 in Capt. John Fulford's Company of Matrosses; see "Thomas Ellis," q.v. {Ref: Maryland Historical Magazine, Vol. 69, No. 1, p. 94}

MILES, NICHOLAS (Charles County), private (substitute) in the Maryland Continental Line by 1781, was discharged on 8 Dec 1781. {Ref: Archives of Maryland Vol. 48, p. 11}

MILES, WILLIAM (Maryland Navy), sailor or seaman on 7 Jan 1780. {Ref: Calendar of Maryland State Papers, The Brown Books, p. 57}

MILHOLLAND, ARTHUR (Frederick County), private (substitute) in the Maryland Continental Line, Price's Regiment, enrolled in May, 1778 for 3 years or duration of the war. {Ref: Maryland Historical Magazine, Vol. 6, No. 3, p. 260}

MILLER, JACOB (Frederick County), private in the 1st Maryland Continental Line who had enlisted for 9 months and was discharged on 11 Mar 1779 at which time he received £14.5.6 in clothing. {Ref: Archives of Maryland Vol. 21, p. 320}

MILLER, JOHN (Frederick County), private who was enrolled to serve as a substitute in the Maryland Continental Line until 10 Dec 1781, but *"being represented unfit for the service for which he was intended"* was discharged on 30 Oct 1781. {Ref: Archives of Maryland Vol. 45, p. 657}

MILLER, JOSIAS (Southern Maryland), ensign, commissioned on 27 Jul 1780 to serve in the Regiment Extra by order of the Council of Maryland; lieutenant by 22 Feb 1782 at which time he was paid £159.4.5 by the State Treasurer. {Ref: Archives of Maryland Vol. 43, p. 234, and Vol. 48, p. 83}

MILLER, MARTIN (Baltimore or Frederick County), corporal, enlisted in Pulaski's Legion on 12 Mar 1778 (apparently from Pennsylvania). {Ref: Maryland Historical Magazine, Vol. 13, No. 3, p. 224}

MILLER, PHILIP (Maryland Navy), seaman on the State Ship *Defence* in 1777. {Ref: Archives of Maryland Vol. 18, p. 658}

MILLER, SAMUEL (Frederick County), patriot buried in Mount Olivet Cemetery. {Ref: Information compiled by Dr. Donald Wolf in Maryland Society SAR Newsletter circa 1996}

MILLER, SAMUEL (Harford County, Susquehannah Hundred), private who was enrolled 23 Apr 1776 in Militia Company No. 21 under Capt. George Patterson. {Ref: George W. Archer Collection and Revolutionary War File, Historical Society of Harford County Archives}

MILLER, WILLIAM (Maryland Navy), ship's steward on the State Ship *Defence* from 2 Jun to 11 Jul 1777, seaman from 11 Jul to 15 Oct 1777 and gunner's mate from 15 Oct to 31 Dec 1777. {Ref: Archives of Maryland Vol. 18, p. 658}

MILLS, CORNELIUS (Anne Arundel County), lieutenant who was paid £120 by the Committee of Claims on 2 Apr 1778 for recruiting services; possibly a captain by 1782. {Ref: Archives of Maryland Vol. 16, p. 467, Vol. 18, p. 417, and Vol. 21, p. 4}

MILLS, JONATHAN (Maryland Navy), seaman or marine on the State Ship *Defence* in 1777. {Ref: Archives of Maryland Vol. 18, p. 658}

MILLS, JAMES (St. Mary's County), patriot who supplied 650 lbs. of beef on the hoof to the State of Maryland on 9 Oct 1780. {Ref: Archives of Maryland Vol. 45, p. 156}

MILLS, JOSEPH (Frederick County), private who was enrolled to serve as a substitute in the Maryland Continental Line until 10 Dec 1781, but *"being represented unfit for the service for which he was intended"* was discharged on 30 Oct 1781. {Ref: Archives of Maryland Vol. 45, p. 657}

MINOR, LEVIN (Caroline County), private (substitute) in the Maryland Continental Line by 1781, was discharged on 8 Dec 1781. {Ref: Archives of Maryland Vol. 48, p. 10}

MITCHELL, ABRAHAM (Cecil County), patriot and doctor who took the Oath of Fidelity and Allegiance in 1778 and converted his home at Fair Hill near Elkton into a temporary hospital for wounded soldiers of the Maryland Continental Line; born 1733/4 in Lancaster County, Pennsylvania, moved to Cecil County, Maryland at age 25, married Mary Thompson on 19 Nov 1772, and died 30 Sep 1818; their children were: George Edward Mitchell (born 3 Mar 1781, married Mary Hooper); Ephraim Thompson Mitchell (born 17 Nov 1783); and, Abraham David Mitchell (born 1 Dec 1786, married Jane Evans). {Ref: Maryland State Society DAR Directory, 1892-1965, p. 521; George Johnston's *History of Cecil County*, p. 496}

MITCHELL, CHARLOTTE, see "John H. Hughes," q.v.

MITCHELL, DELIA, see "William Arnold," q.v.

MITCHELL, ISAAC (Worcester County), ensign in the militia in Capt. John Pope Mitchell's Company; born 1729, married Jannett ----, and died in 1787; their children were: Nannie Mitchell (born 26 Jul 1751); John Mitchell (born 8 Oct 1753); Mary Mitchell (born 9 Apr 1755, died in infancy); Josiah Mitchell (born 30 Mar 1756); James Mitchell (born 16 May 1758); Isaac Mitchell (born 10 Aug 1760); and, Mary Mitchell (born 20 Sep 1764). {Ref: Maryland State Society DAR Directory, 1892-1965, p. 521}

MITCHELL, JAMES (Harford County, Susquehannah Hundred), private who was enrolled 23 Apr 1776 in Militia Company No. 21 under Capt. George Patterson. {Ref: George W. Archer Collection and Revolutionary War File, Historical Society of Harford County Archives}

MITCHELL, JOHN (Charles County), captain in the 1st Maryland Continental Line who received payment for his services in the amount of "1900 Dollars & £3.10s" on 12 Sep 1780; born 1760, married first to Lucy Stoddard and second to Catherine Barnes, and died in October, 1812; his sons were Walter H. J. Mitchell (born 1801, married Mary Ferguson) and Richard Henry Barnes Mitchell (married Lucinda Compton). {Ref: Archives of Maryland Vol. 45, p. 97; Maryland State Society DAR Directory, 1892-1965, p. 522}

MITCHELL, JOHN (Maryland Privateer), commander of the schooner *Polly Sudler*, navigated by 25 men and mounting 6 swivel guns and 10 small arms, was issued Letters of Marque & Reprisal by the Council of Maryland on 12 Sep 1778. {Ref: Archives of Maryland Vol. 21, p. 201}

MITCHELL, JOHN (Maryland Privateer), lieutenant on the schooner *Decoy* "fitted out to Cruise in this Bay" under Capt. Richard Harrison on 11 May 1781. {Ref: Archives of Maryland Vol. 45, p. 432}

MITCHELL, JOHN (Harford County), private who was enrolled 25 Mar 1776 in Militia Company No. 19 under Capt. William Morgan. {Ref: George W. Archer Collection and Revolutionary War File, Historical Society of Harford County Archives}

MITCHELL, JOHN P., see "Isaac Mitchell," q.v.

MITCHELL, MARY, see "William Arnold," q.v.

MITCHELL, MICAJAH (Harford County, Susquehannah Hundred), private who was enrolled 23 Apr 1776 in Militia Company No. 21 under Capt. George Patterson; served as a deputy sheriff in 1781 and was charged as follows: *"State vs. Micajah Mitchell. Harford County ss: The jurors for the State of Maryland for Harford County upon their oath present that Micajah Mitchell, late of Harford County, yeoman, being one of the Deputy Sheriffs of the said county, on the 26th day of August in the year of our Lord 1781, at the county aforesaid, by colour(?) of his said office, unlawfully and unjustly did demand, extort, receive and take of and from one George Hollingsworth the sum of two State dollars and six shillings and three pence specie under pretence that the said sums were due from the said George for substitute money and fees of execution for the same, where in truth no such sums were due then and there from the said George, to the evil example of all others in ---- [ink blot] like manner offending and against the peace, government and dignity of the State. Signed: Luther Martin, Attorney General."* {Ref: George W. Archer Collection and Revolutionary War File in the Historical Society of Harford County Archives and Court Records File 5.05(4)}

MITCHELL, PRISCILLA, see "Parker Gilbert," q.v.

MITTINGER, JACOB (Baltimore Town), patriot who enrolled in the Mechanical Company of Baltimore on 4 Nov 1775 and possibly the "Lieutenant Mitinger" who had *"resigned his Commission in the Artillery Service of this Service with intent of going into the Dragoons in Continental Service"* on 12 Aug 1778. {Ref: Margaret R. Hodges' *Unpublished Revolutionary Records of Maryland*, Vol. 2, p. 298; Archives of Maryland Vol. 21, p. 182}

MIXDORFF, SAMUEL (Frederick County), patriot buried in Mount Olivet Cemetery. {Ref: Information compiled by Dr. Donald Wolf in Maryland Society SAR Newsletter circa 1996}

MOALE, JOHN (Baltimore County), patriot who was appointed by the Council of Maryland on 27 Jan 1776 as one of three persons in Baltimore County to collect all the gold and silver coin that can be procured in said county; he also supplied provisions to the State of Maryland between June and September, 1780. {Ref: Archives of Maryland Vol. 11, p. 131, and Vol. 45, p. 84, which listed his name as "John Moles"}

MOALE, ROBERT (Baltimore Town), patriot and merchant who enrolled in Capt. John Sterrett's Independent Mercantile Company by February, 1777, at which time they were mustered into regular service with the continental army to repress loyalist activities in the Eastern Shore counties of Somerset and Worcester. {Ref: J. Thomas Scharf's History of Baltimore City and County, Part I, p. 77}

MOLEDGE, SAMUEL (Baltimore County), private (substitute) in the Maryland Continental Line by 1781, was discharged on 8 Dec 1781. {Ref: Archives of Maryland Vol. 48, p. 11}

MOLOHON, WILLIAM (St. Mary's County), patriot who was paid £4.17.6 for expenses incurred in bringing recruits from St. Mary's County to Annapolis on 8 Jun 1778. {Ref: Archives of Maryland Vol. 21, p. 125}

MOLNIX, WILLIAM (Frederick County), private (substitute) in the Maryland Continental Line, German Regiment, enrolled in April, 1778 for 3 years or duration of the war. {Ref: Maryland Historical Magazine, Vol. 6, No. 3, p. 257}

MONCREIFT (MOUCREIFT), ARCHIBALD (Baltimore Town), patriot and merchant who enrolled in Capt. John Sterrett's Independent Mercantile Company by February, 1777, at which time they were mustered into regular service with the continental army to repress loyalist activities in the Eastern Shore counties of Somerset and Worcester. {Ref: J. Thomas Scharf's History of Baltimore City and County, Part I, p. 77}

MONGOMERY, ---- (Maryland Continental Line, Staff and P. Officer), doctor who received payment for his services in the amount of "1900 Dollars & £3.10s" on 12 Sep 1780. {Ref: Archives of Maryland Vol. 45, p. 98}

MONTGOMERY, IGNATIUS (Charles County), private (substitute) in the Maryland Continental Line, who enlisted to serve until 10 Dec 1781, was discharged on 29 Nov 1781. {Ref: Archives of Maryland Vol. 48, p. 7}

MONTGOMERY, JOHN (Harford County), first lieutenant on 10 Mar 1776 in Militia Company No. 18 under Capt. John Jolly. {Ref: George W. Archer Collection and Revolutionary War File, Historical Society of Harford County Archives}

MONTGOMERY, JOHN (Maryland Navy), ship's tender on the State Ship Defence in 1777. {Ref: Archives of Maryland Vol. 18, p. 658}

MONTGOMERY, ROBERT (Baltimore Privateer), commander of the schooner Holker, navigated by 14 men and mounting 6 carriage guns and 4 swivel guns, was issued Letters of Marque & Reprisal by the Council of Maryland on 15 Sep 1780. {Ref: Archives of Maryland Vol. 43, p. 291}

MONTGOMERY, WILLIAM (Harford County), private who was enrolled 10 Mar 1776 in Militia Company No. 18 under Capt. John Jolly. {Ref: George W. Archer Collection and Revolutionary War File, Historical Society of Harford County Archives}

MOOMAW, CELIA, see "John Adams," q.v.

MOORE, CAMMILLA, see "Nicholas R. Moore," q.v.

MOORE, BENJAMIN (Baltimore City), soldier in the Pennsylvania Line who enlisted in Lebanon County and married Magdalena ---- circa 1791; known children were Mary or Polly Thomas (aged 52 in 1845) and Elizabeth McCord (died 4 Mar 1835, aged 46 years, 2 months and 20 days); Benjamin died in 1830 and widow Magdalena Moore applied for pension in Baltimore on 3 Mar 1845, aged 78, under the Act of July 7, 1838, but the claim was suspended *"for further proof of marriage and service."* {Ref: *Rejected or Suspended Applications for Revolutionary War Pensions* (1850 Report), p. 236; Research by Virgil D. White, citing Federal Pension Application R3745}

MOORE, GAY, see "Nicholas R. Moore," q.v.

MOORE, GEORGE (Frederick County), private who served in Rawlings' Regiment, appeared before a Justice of the Peace in Jasper County, Indiana on 22 Jun 1848 and stated, in part: *"I am the son of George and Phoebe Moore and was born in Frederick County, Maryland on 10 Oct 1749. I was a weaver by trade. When in my 26th year I enlisted in the service of the United States in the 2nd Maryland Regiment on 15 Apr 1775 at Old Town or Skipton on the north branch of the Potomac about 2 miles from the forks. Said enlistment was for 1 year and in the company of Capt. Michael Crissop [Cresap] ... I took the bounty of $10 and was promised 100 acres of land per year. On 16 April we started to Keysertown, Fredericktown, Baltimore and Havre de Grace to Boston where we arrived toward the end of May ... That he lay at Boston until he thinks about 16 June when the Battle of Bunker Hill was fought in which engagement he was. That he was in the Rifle Regiment of Gen. Warren and they flanked in the right wing. Our orders were be still boys until you see the white of their eyes. We did to and as this enemy approached we fairly mowed them down ... In the engagement Michael Crissop was wounded in the leg and afterward died in New York ... When the British left Boston we entered and remained until ordered to New York in February or March 1776. We arrived in New York in April, where I was discharged 15 Apr 1776 ... About an hour after my discharge I again enlisted in New York in the 3rd Maryland Regiment, Col. James Smith, Capt. Joseph Smith, for two years. Took the bounty of $15 and was again promised 100 acres of land each year ... We fought the Battle of Long Island [27 Aug 1776]. In this battle the Americans were beaten. The password was Beware of what you are after ... In the night Washington had* *peat fires kindled along the river and before morning had crossed the whole army into New York ... Went up river to a place called White Plains. Here a battle was fought ... We retreated into the Jersey ... We crossed the Delaware in December .... took about 1000 prisoners at Trenton ... the password was New York at the Battle of Trenton I think ... we went to Morristown where we encamped. This I think was in the spring of 1777 ... A great many had the small pox .... I had it before I joined the Army .... From there we went to Middlebrook ... Quibbletown ... retreated to Middlebrook ... in July to Philadelphia ... and to place called Brandywine. Here we fought a battle ... I was under Wayne and stationed at a place called Chadsford ... The password I think was Philadelphia ... I was at the Paoli Tavern Massacre. From this we went to Germantown and we fought that battle ... From this we went to Whitemarsh and from there to Valley Forge to spend the winter ... In the month of June [1778] we left Valley Forge and crossed into Jersey. In this month we fought the Battle of Monmouth ... Here I was wounded in the head ... From this we went to White Plains where my time being out I was discharged ... I then went home and finding that my brother in law Obadiah Forshay had been drafted I took his place and released him ... I enlisted at Hancock Town, took the $20 bounty and sent to Fort Frederick. From this to Middlebrook, New Jersey ... In July 1779 Wayne was ordered to take Stoney Point. I was with him at that time. The password was Remember the Paoli boys. After this we returned to Fort Frederick where I was discharged. This enlistment was for one year ... I then went home and my brother William was drafted to go to Fort Frederick to guard the prisoners. I took his place and served his time out 6 months and was discharged. I then returned home and remained over night and took my brother John's place who had been drafted for 4 months. I served his time out and was not in the Army afterwards. On 24 Oct 1780 I married Nancy Ball who bore me 21 children, 5 of whom now live. I left Maryland in 1791 and removed to Kentucky in 1792 and settled near Washington Mason County. In 1806 I removed to Champagne County, Ohio and in 1842 with my son William where I now live to Jasper County, Indiana ... my knapsack and papers were stolen ... I have no way of proving my service but had I in 1832 been a few weeks earlier in Kentucky might have proved it by two of my messmates Isaac Naylor and Arthur Davenport who died there ... I never got any land although promised 100 acres per year each enlistment ... I have no property of any kind and have been dependent for 17 years on my son William for support ..."* The soldier George Moore and his wife Nancy (whom he referred to as Ann in 1826) had 21 children, but the only names of children given were: William Moore (lived in Indiana in 1848); George Moore (died 7 Jun 1855); John Moore (died in Feb 18--?); Mahala Moore (married John Woodfield and died about 15 Feb 185-?);

Nancy Moore (married a Dowden); Phoebe Moore (died without issue); and, Mary Moore (married a Standage). On 20 Jul 1855 the only surviving children were Nancy Dowden and William Moore. Reference was also made to grandchildren George Fitch (aged about 15 in 1826), and George and Nancy Standage, children of Mary Moore Standage. {Ref: Research by Christopher T. Smithson, citing Federal Pension Application S33116}

MOORE, HEZEKIAH (Charles County), ensign in the 2nd Maryland Continental Line who received payment for his services in the amount of "1900 Dollars & £3.10s" on 12 Sep 1780. {Ref: Archives of Maryland Vol. 45, p. 97}

MOORE, HUGH (Frederick County), private (substitute) in the Maryland Continental Line, German Regiment, enrolled in May, 1778 for 3 years or duration of the war. {Ref: Maryland Historical Magazine, Vol. 6, No. 3, p. 259}

MOORE, JOHN (Maryland Navy), marine on the State Ship *Defence* in 1777. {Ref: Archives of Maryland Vol. 18, p. 658}

MOORE, JOHN, see "George Moore," q.v.

MOORE (MOOR), JOHN (Harford County), private who was enrolled 10 Mar 1776 in Militia Company No. 18 under Capt. John Jolly. {Ref: George W. Archer Collection and Revolutionary War File, Historical Society of Harford County Archives}

MOORE, JOSEPH (St. Mary's County), private in the Maryland Continental Line by 1778 and *"appearing to be altogether incapable of service"* was discharged on 22 Jun 1778. {Ref: Archives of Maryland Vol. 21, p. 144}

MOORE, MAGDALENA, see "Benjamin Moore," q.v.

MOORE, MAHALA, see "George Moore," q.v.

MOORE, MARY, see "George Moore," q.v.

MOORE, NANCY, see "George Moore," q.v.

MOORE, NICHOLAS RUXTON (Baltimore County), second lieutenant by 22 Jun 1776 at which time he was paid *"for Expences incurred in marching the Train of Artillery from Baltimore to Annapolis"* by the Council of Maryland; promoted to first lieutenant on 2 Feb 1777 and captain on 15 Mar 1778; commissioned captain of horse troops on 26 Jul 1780 by the Council of Maryland, as follows: *"We have appointed and commissioned you Captain of the voluntier Troop of Light Horse, raised in Baltimore Town, Thomas Russel Lieutenant and Mark Pringle Cornet. We cannot too much applaud that martial and patriotic Spirit which influenced yourself and the Gentlemen who compose your Troop, to make so noble and disinterested an Offer of your Services to your Country at a Time when the Aspect of our Affairs is far from being flattering or inviting. Your laudable Example cannot fail to excite an Emulation in the Gentlemen of the respective Counties, that will render the Militia of this State much more respectable."* Nicholas Ruxton Moore was born on 21 Jul 1756, married Sarah Kelso on 25 Dec 1793, and died on 7 or 11 Oct 1816; their children were: Cammilla Hammond Moore (married William Swan McKeen);

Gay Moore (married Sarah Chalmers); Rebecca Moore; and, Smith Hollings Moore. In spite of his valiant service during the war, it is interesting to note that when his widow Sarah Moore applied for pension in Baltimore in November, 1839, aged 72, under the Act of July 7, 1838, the claim was suspended, stating Nicholas was *"a lieutenant in 1776, promoted to captain in 1780, company mounted militia, and the Land Office Register certifies to the grade and to two tours of service, but the length thereof is not given."* {Ref: Archives of Maryland Vol. 11, p. 506 and Vol. 43, p. 233; Maryland State Society DAR Directory, 1892-1965, pp. 527-528; *Rejected or Suspended Applications for Revolutionary War Pensions* (1850 Report), p. 237; Research by Virgil D. White, citing Federal Pension Application W26275}

MOORE, PHOEBE, see "George Moore," q.v.

MOORE, REBECCA, see "Nicholas R. Moore," q.v.

MOORE, SAMUEL (Western Maryland), private in Capt. Michael Cresap's Company in 1775. {Ref: Howard L. Leckey's *The Tenmile Country and Its Pioneer Families*, p. 16}

MOORE, SARAH, see "Nicholas R. Moore," q.v.

MOORE, SHILES (Anne Arundel County?), patriot who was paid £5 by the Maryland Council of Safety for boatage on 2 Oct 1776. {Ref: Archives of Maryland Vol. 12, p. 316}

MOORE, SMITH, see "Nicholas R. Moore," q.v.

MOORE, THOMAS (Baltimore Privateer), commander of the brigantine *Columbus*, mounting 12 carriage guns, was issued Letters of Marque & Reprisal by the Council of Maryland on 5 Dec 1778. {Ref: Archives of Maryland Vol. 21, p. 259}

MOORE, THOMAS (Maryland Navy), ordinary sailor on the State Ship *Defence* in 1777. {Ref: Archives of Maryland Vol. 18, p. 658}

MOORE, WILLIAM (Frederick County), private in the Maryland Continental Line who was drafted to serve until 10 Dec 1781, was discharged on 29 Nov 1781. {Ref: Archives of Maryland Vol. 48, p. 7}

MOORE, WILLIAM, see "George Moore," q.v.

MOORES, JAMES R. (Maryland Navy), purser on the State Ship *Defence* in 1777. {Ref: Archives of Maryland Vol. 18, p. 658}

MOOSER, FRANCIS (Frederick County), private (substitute) in the Maryland Continental Line by 1781, was discharged on 8 Dec 1781. {Ref: Archives of Maryland Vol. 48, p. 11}

MOREAU, MOSES (Baltimore Town), patriot and merchant who enrolled in Capt. John Sterrett's Independent Mercantile Company by February, 1777, at which time they were mustered into regular service with the continental army to repress loyalist activities in the Eastern Shore counties of Somerset and Worcester. {Ref: J. Thomas Scharf's *History of Baltimore City and County*, Part I, p. 77}

MORELAND, SAMUEL, see "John Lindsay," q.v.

MORFORD, ANN, see "John Parsons," q.v.

MORGAN, CHARLES (Western Maryland), private in Capt. Michael Cresap's Company in 1775. {Ref: Howard L. Leckey's *The Tenmile Country and Its Pioneer Families*, p. 16}

MORGAN, JOEL, see "William Norris," q.v.

MORGAN, JOHNSEY (Frederick County), private (substitute) in the Maryland Continental Line, Price's Regiment, enrolled in April, 1778 for 3 years or duration of the war. {Ref: Maryland Historical Magazine, Vol. 6, No. 3, p. 256}

MORGAN, THOMAS (Dorchester County), private (substitute) in the Maryland Continental Line by 1781, was discharged on 8 Dec 1781. {Ref: Archives of Maryland Vol. 48, p. 10}

MORGAN, THOMAS (Talbot County), private (substitute) in the Maryland Continental Line by 1781, was discharged on 8 Dec 1781. {Ref: Archives of Maryland Vol. 48, p. 11}

MORGAN, WILLIAM (Harford County), signer of the Bush Declaration on 22 Mar 1775 and captain of Militia Company No. 19 on 25 Mar 1776; born 1744 at Trappe in Baltimore County, married Cassandra Lee in 1760, and died testate on Deer Creek in Harford County before 23 Nov 1795; their children were: Elizabeth Morgan (married Thomas Sheredine Chew); Sarah Morgan (married Joseph Hopkins); Cassandra Morgan (married Zaccheus O. Bond); Edward Morgan; Ellinor Morgan (married John Hopkins); James L. Morgan; Mary Morgan (married Ephraim Hopkins); Martha Morgan; and, Margaret Morgan. {Ref: George W. Archer Collection and Revolutionary War File, Historical Society of Harford County Archives; Maryland State Society DAR Directory, 1892-1965, p. 532; Harford County Wills AJ No. 2, p. 463}

MORRIS, JONATHAN (Frederick and Washington Counties), lieutenant and later captain in the 7th Maryland Continental Line who received payment for his services in the amount of "1900 Dollars & £3.10s" on 12 Sep 1780. {Ref: Archives of Maryland Vol. 45, p. 98}

MORRIS, JOHN (Harford County), private (substitute) in the Maryland Continental Line by 1781, was discharged on 8 Dec 1781. {Ref: Archives of Maryland Vol. 48, p. 11}

MORRIS, WILLIAM (Kent County), first lieutenant in the county militia, commissioned 22 Jun 1776. {Ref: Archives of Maryland Vol. 11, p. 506}

MORRIS, WILLIAM (Maryland Navy), lieutenant of marines on the State Ship *Defence* in 1777. {Ref: Archives of Maryland Vol. 18, p. 658}

MORRISON, DANIEL (Frederick County), soldier in the Pennsylvania Line and privateer service whose widow Anna Morrison applied for pension under the Act of July 7, 1838, but the claim was suspended because she was *"not a widow at the date of the act -- not pensioned under the Act of 1832."* For additional family information see Federal Pension Application R7416 for Daniel Morris or Morrison. {Ref: *Rejected or Suspended Applications for Revolutionary War Pensions* (1850 Report), p. 237}

MORTON, JAMES (Western Maryland), private in Capt. Michael Cresap's Company in 1775. {Ref: Howard L. Leckey's *The Tenmile Country and Its Pioneer Families*, p. 16}

MORVALL (MORWALL), WILLIAM (Baltimore County), private, aged 28, labourer, born in Flanders, enlisted 16 Sep 1776 in Capt. John Fulford's Company of Matrosses, deserted 25 Oct 1776 and took his hunting shirt and trousers with him. {Ref: Maryland Historical Magazine, Vol. 69, No. 1, pp. 96-97}

MOSELEY, ROBERT (Western Maryland), private in Capt. Michael Cresap's Company in 1775. {Ref: Howard L. Leckey's *The Tenmile Country and Its Pioneer Families*, p. 16}

MOSER, JACOB (Frederick County), private (substitute) in the Maryland Continental Line, German Regiment, enrolled in May, 1778 for 3 years or duration of the war. {Ref: Maryland Historical Magazine, Vol. 6, No. 3, p. 259}

MOSER, VALENTINE (Frederick County), private who neglected to march with the militia under Lt. Col. Wood in June, 1782, petitioned the Council of Maryland on 22 Aug 1782 stating, in part, *"that your Petitioner was last Summer ordered to march to George Town with the Militia of Frederick County. He having a large and helpless Family, and himself being above 50 years of age, did not go according to said order, Whereupon he was fined £20 by a Court Martial, owing as he believes to the matter not fully investigated."* On 29 Aug 1782 a board or panel verified before a county magistrate that *"Valentine Moser was more than 52 years of age and could not be legally fined as he at the time he was ordered to march with the Militia was above 50 Years of Age & therefore exempt from all Militia duty."* It appears that he and the fine were subsequently discharged. {Ref: Archives of Maryland Vol. 48, p. 248}

MOSS, ---- (Anne Arundel County?), soldier in the Maryland Continental Line *"now remaining in Annapolis"* on 24 Jul 1780 at which time his wife Eve Moss was entitled to rations under the laws of the State. {Ref: Archives of Maryland Vol. 43, p. 227}

MOSS, NICHOLAS (Frederick County), private (substitute) from Frederick Town in the Maryland Continental Line who was *"sent from camp by General Smallwood as unfit for the service"* and was discharged on 22 Jun 1778. {Ref: Archives of Maryland Vol. 21, p. 144}

MOSS, VIRGINIA, see "David Lynn," q.v.

MOTHERSPAW, PHILIP (Washington County), private who was enrolled to serve as a substitute in the Maryland Continental Line until 10 Dec 1781, but *"being represented unfit for the service for which he was intended"* was discharged on 30 Oct 1781. {Ref: Archives of Maryland Vol. 45, p. 656}

MOTTER, C., see "Daniel Smith," q.v.

MOUND, WILLIAM (Washington County), private who was enrolled to serve as a substitute in the Maryland Continental Line until 10 Dec 1781, but *"being*

represented unfit for the service for which he was intended" was discharged on 30 Oct 1781. {Ref: Archives of Maryland Vol. 45, p. 657}

MUCKLEROY, PATRICK (Western Maryland), private, later ensign, in Capt. Michael Cresap's Company in 1775. {Ref: Howard L. Leckey's *The Tenmile Country and Its Pioneer Families*, p. 16}

MUDD, HEZEKIAH (Charles County), private (substitute) in the Maryland Continental Line by 1781, was discharged on 8 Dec 1781. {Ref: Archives of Maryland Vol. 48, p. 11}

MUIR, JOHN (Anne Arundel County), captain in the Maryland Continental Line, Gist's Regiment, who received payment for his services in the amount of "1900 Dollars & £3.10s" on 12 Sep 1780; appointed Purchaser of Clothing for Anne Arundel County on 16 Jun 1781. {Ref: Archives of Maryland Vol. 45, pp. 98, 476}

MUMMERT, WILLIAM (Frederick County), private (substitute) in the Maryland Continental Line, German Regiment, enrolled in April, 1778 for 3 years or duration of the war. {Ref: Maryland Historical Magazine, Vol. 6, No. 3, p. 257}

MUNROE, JOHN, see "Frederick Hook," q.v.

MUNSEL, JAMES (Baltimore County), private, aged 26, weaver, born in Ireland, enlisted (made his "X" mark) on 27 Apr 1776 in Capt. John Fulford's Company of Matrosses. {Ref: Maryland Historical Magazine, Vol. 69, No. 1, p. 96}

MURDOCH, GEORGE S. (Frederick County), patriot buried in Mount Olivet Cemetery. {Ref: Information compiled by Dr. Donald Wolf in Maryland Society SAR Newsletter circa 1996}

MURDOCK, ADDISON (Prince George's County), patriot who served on the Committee of Correspondence (elected in 1774 and 1775) and Committee of Observation (elected 1775); born 1731, probably never married, and died testate in 1793; brother of "John Murdock," q.v. {Ref: Edward C. Papenfuse's *A Biographical Dictionary of the Maryland Legislature, 1635-1789*, p. 605}

MURDOCK, BENJAMIN (Frederick County), captain, commissioned on 27 Jul 1780 to serve in the Regiment Extra by order of the Council of Maryland. {Ref: Archives of Maryland Vol. 43, p. 234}

MURDOCK, ELEANOR, see "Richard Potts," q.v.

MURDOCK, JOHN (Montgomery County), colonel and lieutenant of the county in 1781; born 1733, married ----, and died testate in Georgetown by 27 Aug 1790, leaving a son William Murdock and a brother Addison Murdock. {Ref: Archives of Maryland Vol. 45, p. 384; Montgomery County Wills Liber L#B, p. 423}

MURDOCK, WILLIAM (Prince George's County), ensign in the 6th Maryland Continental Line who received payment for his services in the amount of "1900 Dollars & £3.10s" on 12 Sep 1780; see "John Murdock," q.v. {Ref: Archives of Maryland Vol. 45, p. 98}

MURE, THOMAS (Somerset County), private (substitute) in the Maryland Continental Line by 1781, was discharged on 8 Dec 1781. {Ref: Archives of Maryland Vol. 48, p. 11}

MURET, CHARLES (Baltimore County), private, aged 26, labourer, born in London, enlisted 22 Feb 1776 in Capt. John Fulford's Company of Matrosses. {Ref: Maryland Historical Magazine, Vol. 69, No. 1, p. 95}

MURPHY, ---- (Anne Arundel County?), soldier in the 2nd Maryland Continental Line *"now remaining in Annapolis"* on 24 Jul 1780 at which time his wife Elizabeth Murphy was entitled to rations under the laws of the State; she also received rations on 26 Sep 1781. {Ref: Archives of Maryland Vol. 43, p. 227, and Vol. 45, p. 626}

MURPHY, ELIZABETH, see "---- Murphy," q.v.

MURPHY, JAMES (Frederick County), private (substitute) in the Maryland Continental Line, German Regiment, enrolled in April, 1778 for 3 years or duration of the war. {Ref: Maryland Historical Magazine, Vol. 6, No. 3, p. 257}

MURPHY (MURPHEY), JAMES (Montgomery County), private in the 1st Maryland Continental Line in 1776 and on 25 Oct 1779 the Council of Maryland ordered *"that the western shore Treasurer pay to James Murphey a soldier, late of Capt. Lucas's Company of the old Maryland Regiment who lost one of his Legs in Consequence of a Wound received in the Battle on Long Island in 1776, £250 so much allowed him up to the first Day of next Month by this Board by Virtue of the Resolution of the General Assembly of the 9th of August last."* {Ref: Archives of Maryland Vol. 18, p. 632, and Vol. 21, p. 566}

MURPHY, MORGAN (Maryland Navy), marine on the State Ship *Defence* in 1777. {Ref: Archives of Maryland Vol. 18, p. 658}

MURPHY, SAMUEL (Maryland Navy), marine on the State Ship *Defence* in 1777. {Ref: Archives of Maryland Vol. 18, p. 658}

MURPHY, WILLIAM (Charles County), private (substitute) in the Maryland Continental Line by 1781, was discharged on 8 Dec 1781. {Ref: Archives of Maryland Vol. 48, p. 11}

MURPHY, WILLIAM (Dorchester County), private (substitute) in the Maryland Continental Line by 1781, was discharged on 8 Dec 1781. {Ref: Archives of Maryland Vol. 48, p. 10}

MURRAY (MURRY), ALEXANDER (Baltimore Privateer), commander of the brigantine *Saratoga*, navigated by 20 men and mounting 12 carriage guns and 8 swivel guns, was issued Letters of Marque & Reprisal by the Council of Maryland on 3 Apr 1778; commander of the brigantine *Columbus*, mounting 10 carriage guns, 6 howitz guns and 12 small arms, was issued Letters of Marque & Reprisal by the Council of Maryland on 5 Apr 1779; commander of the brigantine *Revenge*, navigated by 32 men and mounting 12 carriage guns, was issued Letters of Marque & Reprisal by the Council of Maryland on 24 Jun 1780. {Ref: Archives of Maryland Vol. 21, pp. 62, 336, and Vol. 43, p. 203}

MURRAY, JAMES (Dorchester County), patriot who was appointed by the Council of Maryland on 27 Jan 1776 as one of three persons in Dorchester

194

County to collect all gold and silver coin that can be procured in said county. {Ref: Archives of Maryland Vol. 11, p. 132}

MURRAY, JAMES (Baltimore County), private who enlisted in Pulaski's Legion in July, 1778 in Baltimore. {Ref: Maryland Historical Magazine, Vol. 13, No. 3, p. 223}

MURRAY, MATTHEW (Maryland Navy), marine on the State Ship *Defence* in 1777. {Ref: Archives of Maryland Vol. 18, p. 658}

MURRAY, MATTHIAS (Baltimore or Frederick County), private in Pulaski's Legion before July, 1782. {Ref: Maryland Historical Magazine, Vol. 13, No. 3, p. 225}

MURSON, GASPARD (Baltimore County), private who enlisted in Pulaski's Legion on 28 Aug 1779 and still in service in November, 1779. {Ref: Maryland Historical Magazine, Vol. 13, No. 3, p. 224}

MUSE, WALKER (Baltimore County), captain in the 1st Maryland Continental Line who received payment for his services in the amount of "1900 Dollars & £3.10s" on 12 Sep 1780. {Ref: Archives of Maryland Vol. 45, p. 97}

MUSGROVE, NATHAN (Montgomery County), private in the Lower Battalion of Militia in Frederick (now Montgomery) County in 1776; born 7 Mar 1758, married Ann Conner, and died 4 Jul 1823 at Unity, Maryland; their children were: Sarah Ann Musgrove (married Thomas I. Hobbs); Ara Musgrove (married Philemon Smith); Rebecca Musgrove (married Caleb Gartrell); Mary Musgrove (married a Carter); Eliza Musgrove (married a Duvall); and, Amelia Musgrove (married a Stutson). {Ref: Archives of Maryland Vol. 18, p. 42; Maryland State Society DAR Directory, 1892-1965, pp. 538-539;

MUSHLER, ADAM (Frederick County), private (substitute) in the Maryland Continental Line, German Regiment, enrolled in April, 1778 for 3 years or duration of the war. {Ref: Maryland Historical Magazine, Vol. 6, No. 3, p. 257}

MYER, PHILIP (Frederick County), private in the Maryland Continental Line who was drafted to serve until 10 Dec 1781, was discharged on 29 Nov 1781. {Ref: Archives of Maryland Vol. 48, p. 7}

MYHAN, DENNIS (Baltimore County), private, aged 22, tailor, born in Ireland, enlisted (made his "X" mark) on 29 Oct 1776 in Capt. John Fulford's Company of Matrosses. {Ref: Maryland Historical Magazine, Vol. 69, No. 1, p. 97}

MYSS, NICHOLAS (Frederick County), private (substitute) in the Maryland Continental Line, Price's Regiment, enrolled in April, 1778 for 3 years or duration of the war. {Ref: Maryland Historical Magazine, Vol. 6, No. 3, p. 256}

NAGILL (NAGALE), MICHAEL (Maryland Navy), marine on the State Ship *Defence* in 1777. {Ref: Archives of Maryland Vol. 18, p. 658}

NASH, THOMAS (Maryland Navy), boatswain's mate on the State Ship *Defence* from 28 Apr to 15 Aug 1777 and marine from 15 Aug to 11 Dec 1777. {Ref: Archives of Maryland Vol. 18, p. 658}

NAVY, MATTHEW (Dorchester County), private (substitute) in the Maryland Continental Line, who enlisted to serve until 10 Dec 1781, was discharged on 30 Nov 1781. {Ref: Archives of Maryland Vol. 48, p. 8}

NAYLOR, ISAAC, see "George Moore," q.v.

NEAL, JOHN (Charles County), lieutenant in the militia at Port Tobacco in Charles County in 1778; moved to New Jersey and married Margaret ---- on 27 Feb 1780 at Boundbrook; applied for pension in Ovid, New York on 18 May 1818, aged 61; son Benjamin was born 17 Mar 1781 and lived in Seneca County, New York in 1847; daughter Theodosia was aged 18 in 1820 and had a child (not named); John died on 22 Jul 1825 and his widow married Benjamin Smith who died on 9 Oct 1847; Margaret (Neal) Smith applied for pension at Hector, New York on 4 Nov 1847, aged 81. {Ref: Research by Virgil D. White, citing Federal Pension Application W19054}

NEEDHAM, MICHAEL (Worcester County), private who was drafted into the Maryland Continental Line, was discharged on 8 Dec 1781. {Ref: Archives of Maryland Vol. 48, p. 10}

NEEPER, REBECCA, see "Richard Sappington," q.v.

NEGLE, RICHARD (Frederick County), private (substitute) in the Maryland Continental Line by 1781, was discharged on 8 Dec 1781. {Ref: Archives of Maryland Vol. 48, p. 11}

NEGRO MICHAL (Maryland Navy), sailor or seaman on 7 Jan 1780. {Ref: Calendar of Maryland State Papers, The Brown Books, p. 57}

NEGRO THOMAS (Maryland Navy), sailor or seaman on 7 Jan 1780. {Ref: Calendar of Maryland State Papers, The Brown Books, p. 57}

NEGRO YORK (Maryland Navy), sailor or seaman on 7 Jan 1780. {Ref: Calendar of Maryland State Papers, The Brown Books, p. 57}

NEGUIRE, PETER (Baltimore County), private who enlisted in Pulaski's Legion on 9 May 1778 in Baltimore. {Ref: Maryland Historical Magazine, Vol. 13, No. 3, p. 222}

NEILE, WILLIAM (Baltimore Privateer), captain of the schooner *Nancy* by 25 May 1776 at which time he was compensated for its loss, *"insured by this Province, and captured at St. Eustatia."* {Ref: Archives of Maryland Vol. 11, p. 443}

NEISTER, FREDERICK (Washington County), private who was drafted to serve in the Maryland Continental Line until 10 Dec 1781, but *"being represented unfit for the duty for which he was intended"* was discharged on 30 Oct 1781. {Ref: Archives of Maryland Vol. 45, p. 656}

NELSON, HANNAH, see "Thomas Hope," q.v.

NELSON, JOHN (Baltimore or Frederick County?), ensign in the 1st Maryland Continental Line who received payment for his services in the amount of "1900 Dollars & £3.10s" on 12 Sep 1780. {Ref: Archives of Maryland Vol. 45, p. 97}

NELSON, JOHN (Frederick County), doctor who was appointed surgeon of the 6th Maryland Continental Line on 9 May 1777; general and patriot buried in Mount Olivet Cemetery. {Ref: Archives of Maryland Vol. 16, p. 245; Burial information compiled by Dr. Donald Wolf in Maryland Society SAR Newsletter circa 1996}

NELSON, JOHN (Cecil County), private who was enrolled to serve as a substitute in the Maryland Continental Line until 10 Dec 1781, but *"being represented unfit for the service for which he was intended"* was discharged on 30 Oct 1781. {Ref: Archives of Maryland Vol. 45, p. 657}

NELSON, ROBERT (Harford County), private who was enrolled by 15 Apr 1776 in Militia Company No. 20 under Capt. Robert Glenn. {Ref: George W. Archer Collection and Revolutionary War File, Historical Society of Harford County Archives}

NELSON, ROGER (Frederick County), patriot and officer in the Maryland Continental Line who subsequently became a brigadier general; buried in Mount Olivet Cemetery, having *"died in Frederick on June 7, 1815 after a long and incredible suffering; he participated in the battle of Camden and received several bayonet wounds; he later practiced law and represented the county in the State Legislature."* {Ref: *Frederick-Town Herald*, 10 Jun 1815; Burial information compiled by Dr. Donald Wolf in Maryland Society SAR Newsletter circa 1996}

NERVELL, WILLIAM (Washington County), private who was enrolled to serve as a substitute in the Maryland Continental Line until 10 Dec 1781, but *"being represented unfit for the service for which he was intended"* was discharged on 30 Oct 1781. {Ref: Archives of Maryland Vol. 45, p. 656}

NESBIT, THOMAS (Maryland Navy), seaman on the State Ship *Defence* in 1777. {Ref: Archives of Maryland Vol. 18, p. 659}

NEVEN, DANIEL (Maryland Navy), ordinary seaman on the State Ship *Defence* in 1777. {Ref: Archives of Maryland Vol. 18, p. 659}

NEVIN, HUGH (Harford County), private who was enrolled 9 Dec 1775 in Militia Company No. 14 under Capt. William McComas. {Ref: George W. Archer Collection and Revolutionary War File, Historical Society of Harford County Archives}

NEVIN, WILLIAM (Frederick County), private (substitute) in the Maryland Continental Line, German Regiment, enrolled in May, 1778 for 3 years or duration of the war. {Ref: Maryland Historical Magazine, Vol. 6, No. 3, p. 260}

NEWBY, JOHN (Cecil County), private who was enrolled to serve as a substitute in the Maryland Continental Line until 10 Dec 1781, but *"being represented unfit for the service for which he was intended"* was discharged on 30 Oct 1781. {Ref: Archives of Maryland Vol. 45, p. 657}

NEWLAND, JACOB (Western Maryland), private, later sergeant, in Capt. Michael Cresap's Company in 1775. {Ref: Howard L. Leckey's *The Tenmile Country and Its Pioneer Families*, p. 15}

NEWTON, THOMAS (Baltimore County), private, aged 24, labourer, born in Maryland, enlisted (made his "X" mark) on 19 Apr 1776 in Capt. John Fulford's Company of Matrosses. {Ref: Maryland Historical Magazine, Vol. 69, No. 1, p. 96}

NEWTON, WILLIAM (Baltimore Privateer), commander of the sloop *Bennington*, mounting 6 carriage guns, 4 howitz guns and 10 small arms, was issued Letters of Marque & Reprisal by the Council of Maryland on 16 Dec 1778. {Ref: Archives of Maryland Vol. 21, p. 266}

NICHODEMUS, HENRY (Washington County), private who was drafted to serve in the Maryland Continental Line until 10 Dec 1781, but *"being represented unfit for the duty for which he was intended"* was discharged on 30 Oct 1781. {Ref: Archives of Maryland Vol. 45, p. 656}

NICHOLAS, JOHN (Western Maryland), lieutenant in Capt. Michael Cresap's Company in 1775. {Ref: Howard L. Leckey's *The Tenmile Country and Its Pioneer Families*, p. 15}

NICHOLAS, JOHN (Frederick County), private who was a 9 month soldier in the 7th Maryland Continental Line in 1778-1779, was discharged on 12 Aug 1779 and received £29.10.0 in clothing. {Ref: Archives of Maryland Vol. 21, p. 491}

NICHOLLS, ACE (Cecil County), private who was drafted into the Maryland Continental Line, was discharged on 8 Dec 1781. {Ref: Archives of Maryland Vol. 48, p. 10}

NICHOLLS, JOHN (Talbot County), captain and patriot *"in the State of Maryland who hath been absent therefrom for about eight or nine Months last past and hath lately, that is to say within three Months now last past, returned into this State, appeared before the Council and before them did take, repeat and Subscribe the Oath of Fidelity and Support to this State contained in the Act to Punish certain Crimes and Misdemeanors and to prevent the Growth of Toryism"* on 23 Sep 1778. {Ref: Archives of Maryland Vol. 21, p. 209}

NICHOLLS, SIMON (Montgomery County), elected sheriff of Montgomery County and commissioned on 20 Oct 1779. {Ref: Archives of Maryland Vol. 21, p. 563}

NICHOLS, JEREMIAH (Kent County), quartermaster of the 13th Battalion of Militia, commissioned 8 May 1777; one Jeremiah Nicols *[sic]* died testate in Kent County by 2 Dec 1806. {Ref: Archives of Maryland Vol. 16, p. 243; Kent County Wills Liber 8, p. 317}

NICHOLS, JOHN (Maryland Privateer), commander of the schooner *Betsey*, navigated by 11 men and mounting 6 carriage guns and 6 swivel guns, was issued Letters of Marque & Reprisal by the Council of Maryland on 30 Oct 1779. {Ref: Archives of Maryland Vol. 43, p. 6}

NICHOLS, WALTER (Maryland Navy), quarter gunner on the State Ship *Defence* in 1777. {Ref: Archives of Maryland Vol. 18, p. 659}

NICHOLSON, ALEXANDER (Maryland Navy), sailor and quartermaster on the State Ship *Defence* in 1777. {Ref: Archives of Maryland Vol. 18, p. 659}

NICHOLSON, JAMES (Maryland Navy), captain of the State Ship *Defence* in 1777. {Ref: Archives of Maryland Vol. 18, p. 659}

NICHOLSON, JOHN (Maryland Navy), first lieutenant on the State Ship *Defence*, commissioned 5 Apr 1776 and still serving on said ship in 1777. {Ref: Archives of Maryland Vol. 11, p. 312 and Vol. 18, p. 659}

NICKS, WILLIAM (Frederick County), private (substitute) in the Maryland Continental Line, Gunby's Regiment, enrolled in May, 1778 for 3 years or duration of the war. {Ref: Maryland Historical Magazine, Vol. 6, No. 3, p. 258}

NICOLLS, JAMES (Baltimore Town), patriot and merchant who enrolled in Capt. John Sterrett's Independent Mercantile Company by February, 1777, at which time they were mustered into regular service with the continental army to repress loyalist activities in the Eastern Shore counties of Somerset and Worcester. {Ref: J. Thomas Scharf's *History of Baltimore City and County*, Part I, p. 77}

NIXON, CATHARINE (Anne Arundel or Baltimore County), patriot who was paid for her services on 25 Sep 1776 *"for attending Hospital"* by order of the Council of Maryland. {Ref: Archives of Maryland Vol. 12, p. 298}

NOORE, SAMUEL (Western Maryland), private in Capt. Michael Cresap's Company in 1775. {Ref: Howard L. Leckey's *The Tenmile Country and Its Pioneer Families*, p. 16}

NORMAN, ELIZABETH, see "John Woodfield," q.v.

NORMAN, JOHN, see "Acquilla Randall," q.v.

NORMAN, WILLIAM, see "John Woodfield," q.v.

NORRINGTON, HANNAH, see "Thomas Norris," q.v.

NORRIS, AARON, see "Thomas Norris," q.v.

NORRIS, ABRAHAM, see "Thomas Norris," q.v.

NORRIS, ALEXANDER (Harford County), private who was enrolled by 15 Apr 1776 in Militia Company No. 20 under Capt. Robert Glenn; born 9 Dec 1744, son of Thomas Norris and Elizabeth McComas. {Ref: George W. Archer Collection and Revolutionary War File, Historical Society of Harford County Archives; Thomas M. Myers' *The Norris Family of Maryland*, p. 74}

NORRIS, ALEXANDRIA, see "Thomas Norris," q.v.

NORRIS, AMANDA, see "Jacob Norris," q.v.

NORRIS, AMELIA, see "Benjamin B. Norris," q.v.

NORRIS, ANN, see "Thomas Norris," q.v.

NORRIS, AQUILA, OF EDWARD (Harford County), captain in the 8th Battalion of Militia on 9 Apr 1778; born 13 Jun 1754 in Baltimore County, married first to cousin Sarah Norris on 25 Nov 1778 and second to Mary (Waltham) Dutton on 23 Dec 1804, and died testate on 18 May 1825 in Harford County; all children were by his first wife Sarah, viz.: Lloyd Norris (born 1779, married Jane Peterkin on 7 Nov 1799); Rhesa Norris (born 21 Aug 1781, married Susannah Dutton on 30 Oct 1804); Cardiff Norris (born 1 Feb 1784, died 1801); Silas Norris (born 29 Sep 1786, died in infancy); Mary Norris (born 13 Aug 1789, died 1793); Susan Norris (born 19 Mar 1792, married Daniel Cunningham on 1 Feb 1815); Silas C. Norris (born 18 Apr 1795, married Elizabeth March on 30 Apr 1817); and, Gabriel Norris (born 10 Mar 1798). {Ref: Archives of Maryland Vol. 21, p. 24; Maryland State Society DAR Directory, 1892-1965, p. 546 (which contains some errors); Thomas M. Myers' *The Norris Family of Maryland*, pp. 25-26}

NORRIS, AQUILA, see "Thomas Norris," q.v.

NORRIS, ARNOLD (St. Mary's County), private who was drafted into the Maryland Continental Line, was discharged on 8 Dec 1781. {Ref: Archives of Maryland Vol. 48, p. 10}

NORRIS, BENJAMIN BRADFORD (Harford County), signer of the Bush Declaration on 22 Mar 1775, commissioned captain of Militia Company No. 29 on 8 Oct 1776, and served in the 6th Maryland Continental Line under his brother Capt. Jacob Norris in the New Jersey campaign; born 16 Aug 1745 in Baltimore County, married Elizabeth Richardson on 3 Apr 1768, and died intestate in April, 1790 in Harford County; their children were: Martha Norris (born 1770, married Enoch Churchman on 2 Feb 1792); Sarah Norris (married William Bradford); William Lee Norris; Amelia Norris; Susan Norris; Harriet Norris (married Thomas Wharton); Provey Norris (married John Gadsby); and, Benjamin Bradford Norris, Jr. {Ref: George W. Archer Collection and Revolutionary War File, Historical Society of Harford County Archives; Harford County Estate File No. 493; Maryland State Society DAR Directory, 1892-1965, p. 546 (which contains some errors); Thomas M. Myers' *The Norris Family of Maryland*, p. 27}

NORRIS, CATHERINE, see "Jacob Norris," q.v.

NORRIS, CLARISSA, see "Jacob Norris," q.v.

NORRIS, DANIEL (Kent County), private (substitute) in the Maryland Continental Line by 1781, was discharged on 8 Dec 1781. {Ref: Archives of Maryland Vol. 48, p. 11}

NORRIS, EDWARD, see "Aquila Norris," q.v.

NORRIS, ELEANOR, see "Thomas Norris," q.v.

NORRIS, ELIJAH, see "Thomas Norris," q.v.

NORRIS, ELIZABETH, see "William Norris" and "Thomas Norris," q.v.

NORRIS, ELLEN, see "William Norris," q.v.

NORRIS, GEORGE, see "Jacob Norris," q.v.

NORRIS, HANNAH, see "Thomas Norris," q.v.

NORRIS, HARRIET, see "Benjamin B. Norris," q.v.

NORRIS, HENRY (St. Mary's County), private who was drafted to serve in the Maryland Continental Line until 10 Dec 1781, but *"being represented unfit for the duty for which he was intended"* was discharged on 30 Oct 1781. {Ref: Archives of Maryland Vol. 45, p. 656}

NORRIS, ISAAC, see "Thomas Norris," q.v.

NORRIS, JACOB (Harford County), second lieutenant in the 6th Maryland Continental Line on 10 Oct 1777; first lieutenant, 26 Nov 1778; served in the New Jersey campaign; wounded and taken prisoner at the Battle of Camden, South Carolina on 16 Aug 1780; received payment for his services in the amount of "1900 Dollars & £3.10s" on 12 Sep 1780; transferred to 5th Maryland Continental Line on 1 Jan 1781 (prisoner on parole until the close of the war); captain, 9th U. S. Infantry, 8 Jan 1799 (honorably discharged 15 Jun 1800); born 10 May 1753 in Baltimore County, married Avarilla Gallion on 30

Mar 1785, and died in Bel Air, Harford County, in March, 1807 and was buried in the Methodist Church Cemetery; their children were: Sophia Norris (married John Johnson on 8 Jan 1827); Clarissa Norris (died unmarried in 1822); George Alexander Norris; Matilda Norris; Luther Augustus Norris (married Mary Hollis on 22 Jul 1819); John Calvin Norris (married Caroline S. Calwell on 26 Nov 1827); Amanda A. Norris (married William B. Norris on 25 Jun 1827); Catherine Theresa Norris (married Richard Frisby Hollis on 21 Oct 1813); and, Otho Norris (married Cornelia Wright on 31 Dec 1824). {Ref: Archives of Maryland Vol. 45, p. 98; Thomas M. Myers' *The Norris Family of Maryland*, pp. 29-30}

NORRIS, JACOB, see "Benjamin B. Norris" and "William Norris" and "James Sloan," q.v.

NORRIS, JAMES, see "Thomas Norris," q.v.

NORRIS, JAMES, OF JAMES (Harford County), private who was enrolled 9 Sep 1775 in Militia Company No. 7 under Capt. John Taylor; born circa 1747, second son of James Norris and Elizabeth Davis, and died after 1798 (named in father's will). {Ref: George W. Archer Collection and Revolutionary War File, Historical Society of Harford County Archives; Thomas M. Myers' *The Norris Family of Maryland*, p. 75}

NORRIS, JESSIE, see "Thomas Norris," q.v.

NORRIS, JOHN (Maryland Navy), sailor or seaman on 7 Jan 1780. {Ref: Calendar of Maryland State Papers, The Brown Books, p. 57}

NORRIS, JOHN (St. Mary's County), private (substitute) in the Maryland Continental Line by 1781, was discharged on 8 Dec 1781. {Ref: Archives of Maryland Vol. 48, p. 11}

NORRIS, JOHN, see "William Norris" and "Thomas Norris," q.v.

NORRIS, LUTHER, see "Jacob Norris," q.v.

NORRIS, MARTHA, see "Benjamin B. Norris" and "William Norris," q.v.

NORRIS, MARY, see "William Norris" and "Thomas Norris," q.v.

NORRIS, MATILDA, see "Jacob Norris," q.v.

NORRIS, MOSES, see "Thomas Norris," q.v.

NORRIS, OTHO, see "Jacob Norris," q.v.

NORRIS, PROVEY, see "Benjamin B. Norris," q.v.

NORRIS, SARAH, see "Aquila Norris" and "Benjamin B. Norris," q.v.

NORRIS, SOPHIA, see "Jacob Norris," q.v.

NORRIS, SUSAN, see "Benjamin B. Norris" and "William Norris," q.v.

NORRIS, THOMAS (Harford County), private who was enrolled by 15 Apr 1776 in Militia Company No. 20 under Capt. Robert Glenn; born circa 1743 in Baltimore County, married Hannah Norrington on 4 May 1762, and their children were: Jesse Norris (born 4 Apr 1763); Elijah Norris (born 25 Jul 1764); Aaron Norris (born 13 Jan 1766); Elizabeth Norris (born 11 Feb 1767); John Norris (born 12 Oct 1768); Abraham Norris (born 14 May 1770); Mary Norris (born 11 Oct 1771); Alexandria Norris (born 16 May 1773); Ann Norris (born 16 Sep 1774); Aquila Norris (born 4 Jul 1776 in Harford County, married Eleanor Norris, and died 4 Mar 1856 in Sangamon County, Illinois); Thomas Norris (born 12 Oct 1777); Hannah Norris (born 14 Oct 1778); James Norris (born 19 Feb 1780); Moses Norris (born 18 Apr 1782); and, Isaac Norris (born 25 Jun 1783, married Charity Ann Conley on 5 Aug 1805, and moved to Zanesville, Ohio in 1811). {Ref: George W. Archer Collection and Revolutionary War File, Historical Society of Harford County Archives; Thomas M. Myers' *The Norris Family of Maryland*, pp. 76-77}

NORRIS, THOMAS, see "William Norris" and "Thomas Norris" and "Alexander Norris," q.v.

NORRIS, WILLIAM (Harford County), private in Militia Company No. 13 in 1776; born 26 Mar 1749 in Baltimore County, married Martha Amos on 24 Dec 1780, and died testate in August, 1837 in Harford County; their children were: Thomas Amos Norris (unmarried); William Norris, Jr. (married Sarah H. Martin on 7 Aug 1806 and pre-deceased his father); Elizabeth Norris (married Joel Morgan on 16 Nov 1797); Susan Norris (unmarried); Martha Norris (unmarried); Jacob Norris (married Henrietta or Harriet Frick on 24 May 1803 and pre-deceased his father); Mary Norris (unmarried); Ellen Norris (unmarried); and, John Bradford Norris. {Ref: Maryland State Society DAR Directory, 1892-1965, pp. 546-547; Thomas M. Myers' *The Norris Family of Maryland*, pp. 28-29}

NORRIS, WILLIAM (Frederick County), private (substitute) in the Maryland Continental Line, German Regiment, enrolled in May, 1778 for 3 years or duration of the war. {Ref: Maryland Historical Magazine, Vol. 6, No. 3, p. 258}

NORRIS, WILLIAM, see "Jacob Norris" and "Benjamin B. Norris" and "William Norris," q.v.

NORTON, ----CK (Baltimore County), private, aged 24, labourer, born in Ireland, enlisted (made his "X" mark) on 4 Mar 1776 in Capt. John Fulford's Company of Matrosses. {Ref: Maryland Historical Magazine, Vol. 69, No. 1, p. 96}

NORTON, WILLIAM, see "James Mason," q.v.

NORWOOD, EDWARD, see "Michael O'Connor," q.v.

NOTTINGHAM, JOHN (Anne Arundel County), private in the Maryland Continental Line by 24 Jun 1776 at which time he was reported as being *"a young English lad about 18 who had run away from his master, joined the military, and then deserted from Capt. Scott while a soldier in the service of this province."* {Ref: Archives of Maryland Vol. 11, p. 512}

NOWELL, ELLIAS (Baltimore County), private who enlisted in Pulaski's Legion on 22 Mar 1778 and still in service in November, 1779. {Ref: Maryland Historical Magazine, Vol. 13, No. 3, p. 223}

NUGEN, PATRICK (Baltimore County), private, aged 22, born in Dublin, enlisted 17 Feb 1776 in Capt. John Fulford's Company of Matrosses. {Ref: Maryland Historical Magazine, Vol. 69, No. 1, p. 95}

O'BRIAN, DENNIS (Anne Arundel County), private in the Maryland Continental Line who enlisted in Anne Arundel County and applied for pension in Hampshire County, Virginia on 3 Aug 1818, aged 61; in 1820 his wife (not named) was aged 61. {Ref: Research by Virgil D. White, citing Federal Pension Application S38274}

O'BRIAN, JAMES (Harford County), private who was recruited, but twice deserted, was enrolled by Richard Dallam in the Regiment Extraordinary and sent to Annapolis with Capt. Thompson on board the sloop *Liberty* on 17 Aug 1780. {Ref: Archives of Maryland Vol. 45, pp. 50-51}

O'BRIEN, JOSEPH (Queen Anne's County), private (substitute) in the Maryland Continental Line by 1781, was discharged on 8 Dec 1781. {Ref: Archives of Maryland Vol. 48, p. 10}

O'BRIEN, MICHAEL (Baltimore County), private, aged 23, labourer, born in Ireland, enlisted (made his "X" mark) on 19 Feb 1776 in Capt. John Fulford's Company of Matrosses. {Ref: Maryland Historical Magazine, Vol. 69, No. 1, p. 95}

O'BRYAN, JAMES (Queen Anne's County), second major of the 20th Battalion of Militia, commissioned 8 May 1777. {Ref: Archives of Maryland Vol. 16, p. 244}

O'BRYAN, JAMES (Caroline County), private by 12 May 1778 at which time the Council of Maryland informed Col. William Richardson that *"James O'Bryan of your Regiment who obtained a Furlough, was, after the Time expired, taken up as a Deserter and escaped from Prison, has surrendered himself to Col. Burkhead; he has been useful in assisting the Recruiting Service. Col. Burkhead is very desirous and we join in our Request to his Solicitation, that O'Bryan's late Conduct may wipe off his former ill Behaviour."* {Ref: Archives of Maryland Vol. 21, p. 78}

O'CONNOR, MICHAEL (Harford County), soldier in the Maryland Continental Line who was living in Harford County on 12 Mar 1821 at which time documents were filed in Harford County Court stating, in part: *"Simon Fitzgerald, resident in Harford County, aged 65 years ... does on his oath declare that he served in the Revolutionary War, as follows: That he enlisted under Lt. John W. Dorsey in Capt. Edward Norwood's Company of Infantry in Flying Camp, served out the period of his enlistment and returned to Baltimore after the Battle of White Plains, and in the spring of 1777 entered into Capt. Alexander Furnival's Company of Artillery, stationed at Pt. Whetstone (point now called Fort McHenry) in the State of Maryland for the term of three years, from thence enlisted into Capt. Richard Dorsey's Company of Artillery for 3 years and was attached to Col. Charles Harrison's Artillery Regiment and after the Battle of Monmouth reenlisted for during the war, served out the period of his enlistment and was discharged at Annapolis after returning from James Island. That he made his original declaration at Baltimore before the Honorable Judge Brice on or about the 8th of July 1818 and was placed on the*

Revolutionary Pension List of the Maryland Agency as will appear by his certificate dated 27th of January 1819 and numbered 5829. And I do solemnly swear that I was a resident citizen of the United States on the 18th March 1818 and that I have not since that time by gift, sale or in any manner disposed of my property or any part thereof with intent thereby so as to diminish it as to bring myself within the provision of an Act of Congress entitled An Act to provide for certain persons engaged in the land and naval service of the United States in the Revolutionary War passed on the 18th day of March 1818 and that I have not, nor has any person in trust for me, any property or securities, contracts or debts due me nor have I any income other than what is contained in the schedule hereto annexed and by me subscribed. That he hath no property of any kind or nature whatsoever, neither hath he any family. That he formerly obtained his support by common labouring work through the country, but now from advanced age and debility depends solely on his pension and the assistance of Friends. That in consequence of his reduced circumstances stands in need of the assistance of his country for support, not being able to support himself without public or private charity." Signed: Michael O'Connor (made his "X" mark). {Ref: Historical Society of Harford County, Court Records File 25.14}

ODLE, RIGDON (Prince George's County), private (substitute) in the Maryland Continental Line by 1781, was discharged on 8 Dec 1781. {Ref: Archives of Maryland Vol. 48, p. 10}

O'DONOVAN, WILLIAM, see "Richard Donovan," q.v.

OFFUTT, MARY, see "Martin and Philip Houser," q.v.

OFFUTT, NATHANIEL (Montgomery County), private who was drafted into the Maryland Continental Line and discharged on 8 Dec 1781. {Ref: Archives of Maryland Vol. 48, p. 10}

OFIELD, JOHN (Harford County), private who was enrolled by Capt. Praul in the Regiment Extraordinary and sent to Annapolis with Capt. Thompson on board the sloop *Liberty* on 17 Aug 1780; although committed as a deserter from the 1st Maryland Regiment, he *"had a pass from Gen. Smallwood to continue till his wound got well."* {Ref: Archives of Maryland Vol. 45, p. 50}

OGDEN, JOHN (Prince George's County), private who was drafted into the Maryland Continental Line, was discharged on 8 Dec 1781. {Ref: Archives of Maryland Vol. 48, p. 10}

OGDEN, JOHN (Frederick County), private (substitute) in the Maryland Continental Line by 1781, was discharged on 8 Dec 1781. {Ref: Archives of Maryland Vol. 48, p. 11}

OGLE, JAMES (Frederick County), private who was drafted to serve in the Maryland Continental Line until 10 Dec 1781, but *"being represented unfit for the duty for which he was intended"* was discharged on 30 Oct 1781. {Ref: Archives of Maryland Vol. 45, p. 656}

OGLE, WILLIAM (Western Maryland), private, later ensign, in Capt. Michael Cresap's Company in 1775. {Ref: Howard L. Leckey's *The Tenmile Country and Its Pioneer Families*, p. 15}

OGLESBY, CHARLES (Kent County), private (substitute) in the Maryland Continental Line by 1781, was discharged on 8 Dec 1781. {Ref: Archives of Maryland Vol. 48, p. 11}

O'KELL, CHARLES (Harford County), private who was drafted into the Maryland Continental Line, was discharged on 8 Dec 1781. {Ref: Archives of Maryland Vol. 48, p. 10}

OLDEN, JOHN (Frederick Town), private in the Maryland Continental Line who was *"sent from camp by General Smallwood as unfit for the service"* and was discharged on 22 Jun 1778. {Ref: Archives of Maryland Vol. 21, p. 144}

OLDHAM, EDWARD (Baltimore County), captain in the 4th Maryland Continental Line who received payment for his services in the amount of "1900 Dollars & £3.10s" on 12 Sep 1780. For additional information see Peden's *Revolutionary Patriots of Baltimore Town and Baltimore County, 1775-1783*. {Ref: Archives of Maryland Vol. 45, p. 98}

OLDHAM, JACOB (Cecil County), soldier in the Maryland troops who was born 16 Apr 1759 at East Nottingham in Cecil County and lived there at the time of his enlistment; he later moved to Baltimore where he applied for pension on 23 May 1832; affidavit was also given by his cousin James Oldham, aged 74; see "James Oldham," q.v. {Ref: Research by Virgil D. White, citing Federal Pension Application S8908}

OLDHAM, JAMES (Baltimore or Cecil County), soldier in the Pennsylvania troops who applied for pension in Baltimore on 7 Mar 1845, aged 87, under the Act of June 7, 1832, but the claim was suspended because he did not serve six months; see "Jacob Oldham," q.v. {Ref: *Rejected or Suspended Applications for Revolutionary War Pensions* (1850 Report), p. 232; Research by Virgil D. White, citing Federal Pension Application R7783}

OLLMAN, ANDREW (Baltimore County), private who enlisted in Pulaski's Legion on 28 Mar 1778 and still in service in November, 1779. {Ref: Maryland Historical Magazine, Vol. 13, No. 3, p. 223}

O'NEAL, JOHN (Harford County), private (substitute) in the Maryland Continental Line who had enlisted to serve until 10 Dec 1781, was not discharged until 27 Dec 1781. {Ref: Archives of Maryland Vol. 48, p. 34}

O'NEAL, JOHN (Western Maryland), private in Capt. Michael Cresap's Company in 1775. {Ref: Howard L. Leckey's *The Tenmile Country and Its Pioneer Families*, p. 16}

O'NEILL, MARY, see "Richard Sappington," q.v.

ONSTUTT, GEORGE (Frederick County), private (substitute) in the Maryland Continental Line by 1781, was discharged on 8 Dec 1781. {Ref: Archives of Maryland Vol. 48, p. 11}

ORAM, COOPER (Maryland and Pennsylvania), private in the 3rd Maryland Continental Line who also served in the Pennsylvania Line; born 13 Jul 1759 in Port Oram, New Jersey, married Abigail ---- on 25 Jul 1779 and had 13 children, but the only ones named in the record were sons John Oram (born in July, 1780, married Mary Field), Cooper Oram, Jr., William Oram, and Samuel Oram; he applied for pension in Philadelphia County on 13 Dec 1824, aged 64 years and 5 months, and died on 7 May 1832 in Bristol, Pennsylvania; his widow applied for pension on 5 Sep 1836, aged 74. {Ref: Research by Virgil D. White, citing Federal Pension Application W5452; Maryland State Society DAR Directory, 1892-1965, p. 550}

ORAM, DARBY (Baltimore County), soldier who was born in 1755 at Baltimore and enlisted in the continental line at Providence, Rhode Island; after the revolution he moved to New Brunswick, New Jersey where he applied for a pension on 31 Mar 1818; in 1820 he had a wife aged 58 (not named) and a son aged 16 (not named); Darby's mother (not named) lived in Baltimore in 1802 and died before 1832; he died on 24 Apr 1841. {Ref: Research by Virgil D. White, citing Federal Pension Application S1067}

ORAM, SPEDDEN (Talbot County), sailor or waterman in the Maryland Navy who served on the barge *Intrepid* for 3 months in 1781; applied for pension on 22 Jun 1838, aged 77, under the Act of June 7, 1832, but the claim was rejected because he did not serve six months. {Ref: *Rejected or Suspended Applications for Revolutionary War Pensions* (1850 Report), p. 229; Research by Virgil D. White, citing Federal Pension Application R7809}

ORME, ROBERT (Prince George's County), private who was drafted for 9 months in the Continental Army in 1778, but procured George Ennis to serve in his stead and was discharged on 25 Jun 1778; born in 1744 in Prince George's County, married Priscilla Edmonston in February, 1769, and died 13 Sep 1820; their children were: Deborah Orme (born 4 Nov 1769, married Brooks Edmonston); James B. Orme (born 24 Nov 1770, married Rebecca ----); Dorothy E. Orme (born 21 Sep 1772); Robert Orme (born 21 Jun 1774); Nathan Orme (born 5 Mar 1776); Anne Henrietta Orme (born 27 Jan 1778, married Basil Belt); Eli Orme (born 10 Jan 1779); Elizabeth Orme (born 6 Nov 1781); and, Archibald E. Orme (born 25 Jul 1785, married Sarah Engle). {Ref: Archives of Maryland Vol. 21, p. 150; Maryland State Society DAR Directory, 1892-1965, p. 551}

ORNDORFF, CHRISTOPHER (Washington County), major in the Maryland troops who *"was of German extraction and lived in great state on his plantation near Sharpsburg; he was a handsome man of commanding presence and very free and genial in his manners; he kept open house and dispensed a generous but by no means ostentatious hospitality; he reared twelve children, all of whom were educated with unusual care; he served as an officer in the Revolutionary War, attaining the rank of major, and all the officers of the*

206

Continental Army passing to and fro the theatre of war were received and entertained at his house with the utmost cordiality." {Ref: J. Thomas Scharf's *History of Western Maryland*, Vol. II, p. 1013}

ORR, JAMES (Harford County), private who was enrolled 9 Dec 1775 in Militia Company No. 14 under Capt. William McComas. {Ref: George W. Archer Collection and Revolutionary War File, Historical Society of Harford County Archives}

OSBORNE, SAMUEL GROOME (Harford County), second lieutenant, commissioned 26 Apr 1776 in Militia Company No. 22 under Capt. Alexander Cowan. {Ref: George W. Archer Collection and Revolutionary War File, Historical Society of Harford County Archives}

OTT, ADAM (Washington County), officer in the revolution: *"Col. Adam Ott died 10 Aug 1827 in his 74th year; he was commissioned an officer of the Pennsylvania Line in January, 1776, and served with credit in the war; afterwards he became sheriff of Washington County, in addition to which he occupied other civil positions of honor and trust."* {Ref: J. Thomas Scharf's *History of Western Maryland*, Vol. II, p. 1053}

OUTTEN, THOMAS (Worcester County), second lieutenant in the county militia, commissioned 21 Jun 1776. {Ref: Archives of Maryland Vol. 11, p. 506}

OWENS, ARTHUR (Harford County), private who was enrolled 25 Mar 1776 in Militia Company No. 19 under Capt. William Morgan. {Ref: George W. Archer Collection and Revolutionary War File, Historical Society of Harford County Archives}

OWENS, BENJAMIN (Maryland Navy), marine on the sloop *Lincoln* who was taken prisoner and confined in New York before 17 Jan 1781 and was subsequently exchanged. {Ref: Archives of Maryland Vol. 45, p. 277}

OWENS, HENRY (Maryland Navy), marine on the sloop *Lincoln* who was taken prisoner and confined in New York before 17 Jan 1781 and was subsequently exchanged. {Ref: Archives of Maryland Vol. 45, p. 277}

OWENS, ISAAC (Somerset County), private (substitute) in the Maryland Continental Line by 1781, was discharged on 8 Dec 1781. {Ref: Archives of Maryland Vol. 48, p. 11}

OWENS, JOSEPH (Charles County), private in the 1st Maryland Continental Line who had enlisted for 9 months and was discharged on 11 Mar 1779 at which time he received £14.5.6 in clothing. {Ref: Archives of Maryland Vol. 21, p. 320}

OWINGS, CALEB (Baltimore County), private, 31 May 1779, Capt. Benjamin Talbott's Militia Company, Cockey's Battalion. {Ref: Maryland Historical Magazine, Vol. 7, No. 1, p. 90}

OWINGS, CATHERINE, see "George Zimmerman," q.v.

OWINGS, ROGER (Baltimore County), private who enlisted in Pulaski's Legion on 27 Apr 1778 in Baltimore. {Ref: Maryland Historical Magazine, Vol. 13, No. 3, p. 222}

OX, GEORGE (Baltimore County), private who enlisted in Pulaski's Legion on 1 Jun 1778 and still in service in November, 1779. {Ref: Maryland Historical Magazine, Vol. 13, No. 3, p. 223}

OYSTER, HENRY (Frederick County), private (substitute) in the Maryland Continental Line, Price's Regiment, enrolled in April, 1778 for 3 years or duration of the war. {Ref: Maryland Historical Magazine, Vol. 6, No. 3, p. 257}

PACA, AQUILA (Harford County), patriot who was appointed by the Council of Maryland on 27 Jan 1776 as one of three persons in Harford County to collect all gold and silver coin that can be procured in said county. {Ref: Archives of Maryland Vol. 11, p. 132}

PACK, JAMES (Frederick County), private (substitute) in the Maryland Continental Line, Williams' Regiment, enrolled in April, 1778 for 3 years or duration of the war. {Ref: Maryland Historical Magazine, Vol. 6, No. 3, p. 257}

PAGE, JOHN (Kent County), second major of the 13th Battalion of Militia, commissioned 8 May 1777; one John Page died testate in Kent County by 12 Mar 1792. {Ref: Archives of Maryland Vol. 16, p. 243; Kent County Wills Liber 7, p. 346}

PAINE, WILLIAM (Dorchester County), private in the Maryland troops who was born in England and came to America in 1763; applied for pension in Belmont County, Ohio on 20 Jul 1818, aged 81 on 14 Dec 1817; in 1820 he had a wife aged about 60 and eleven grown children (no names were given). {Ref: Archives of Maryland Vol. 18, p. 411; Research by Christopher T. Smithson, citing Federal Pension Application S40240}

PAINTER, HENRY (Washington County), private (substitute) in the Maryland Continental Line by 1781, was discharged on 10 Dec 1781. {Ref: Archives of Maryland Vol. 48, p. 17}

PAINTER, MELCHER (Washington County), private in the Maryland Continental Line, German Regiment; married Mary ---- in 1779 and died circa 1823; applied for pension in Washington County on 16 Jun 1818, aged 79; in 1820 he again gave his age as 79 and had a wife Mary Painter (aged 58) and children Christianna Painter (aged 33), George Painter (aged 25), John Painter (aged 23), and Richard Painter (aged 17 and "moon struck"); his widow applied for pension on 12 Feb 1839, aged 72. {Ref: Research by Virgil D. White, citing Federal Pension Application W9226}

PALMER, THOMAS (Maryland Navy), marine on the State Ship *Defence* in 1777. {Ref: Archives of Maryland Vol. 18, p. 659}

PARKER, EDWARD, see "Jesse Bussey," q.v.

PARKER, HUGH (Western Maryland), private in Capt. Michael Cresap's Company in 1775. {Ref: Howard L. Leckey's *The Tenmile Country and Its Pioneer Families*, p. 16}

PARKER, JOHN (Frederick County), private (substitute) in the Maryland Continental Line, Price's Regiment, enrolled in April, 1778 for 3 years or duration of the war. {Ref: Maryland Historical Magazine, Vol. 6, No. 3, p. 256}

PARKER, JONATHAN (Annapolis), patriot who was paid for riding express for the Council of Maryland on 17 Nov 1778. {Ref: Maryland State Archives Record MdHR 6636-12-63}

PARKER, THOMAS (Maryland Privateer), captain and master of the brigantine *Friendship* who was granted permission by the Council of Maryland *"to load with Flour and Grain within this State for the consumption of the Eastern States"* on 16 Sep 1778. {Ref: Archives of Maryland Vol. 21, p. 204}

PARKIN, THOMAS (Baltimore Town), patriot and merchant who enrolled in Capt. John Sterrett's Independent Mercantile Company by February, 1777, at which time they were mustered into regular service with the continental army to repress loyalist activities in the Eastern Shore counties of Somerset and Worcester. {Ref: J. Thomas Scharf's *History of Baltimore City and County*, Part I, p. 77}

PARKINSON, MARTIN (Maryland Privateer), commander of the sloop *Jane*, navigated by 25 men and mounting 6 carriage guns and 12 small arms, was issued Letters of Marque & Reprisal by the Council of Maryland on 10 May 1780. {Ref: Archives of Maryland Vol. 43, p. 170}

PARMER, JACOB (Frederick County), private in the Maryland Continental Line who was drafted to serve until 10 Dec 1781, was discharged on 29 Nov 1781. {Ref: Archives of Maryland Vol. 48, p. 7}

PARNELL, STEPHEN (Anne Arundel County), private in the Maryland Continental Line who applied for pension in Decatur County, Indiana on 13 Nov 1832, aged 70. {Ref: Research by Virgil D. White, citing Federal Pension Application R7976}

PARNHAM, JOHN (Anne Arundel County), patriot and doctor who was paid *"for Militia utensils"* on 17 Sep 1776 by order of the Council of Maryland. {Ref: Archives of Maryland Vol. 12, p. 276}

PARSONS, JOHN (Harford County), private who was enrolled 9 Dec 1775 in Militia Company No. 14 under Capt. William McComas and took the Oath of Fidelity and Allegiance on 18 Mar 1778; born circa 1735, married Rebecca ---- and died by 3 Nov 1807 (date of distribution); their children were: Mary Parsons (married a Lancaster); John Parsons, Jr.; Rebecca Parsons (married a Lancaster); Ruth Parsons (married a Smith); Ann Parsons (married a Morford); Abner Parsons; Abraham Parsons; Amos Parsons; and, Tace Parsons (married a Lukens, probably Jacob). {Ref: George W. Archer Collection and Revolutionary War File, Historical Society of Harford County Archives; Maryland State Society DAR Directory, 1892-1965, p. 560; Henry C. Peden, Jr.'s *Heirs & Legatees of Harford County, 1802-1846*, p. 12}

PARSONS, JOHN (Washington County), convicted in county court in August, 1780 of horse stealing, he was pardoned on 2 Feb 1781 *"on Condition that he forthwith join the Regiment to which he belongs and do not desert there from during the present war, and further that he do not return to the said County of Washington during the term aforesaid."* He was probably the John Parsons who enlisted to serve 3 years in the 7th Maryland Continental Line on 15 Feb 1780. {Ref: Archives of Maryland Vol. 45, p. 297, and Vol. 18, p. 312}

PARSONS, JONATHAN (Baltimore Privateer), commander of the sloop *Fly*, navigated by 6 men and mounting 2 swivel guns, was issued Letters of Marque

& Reprisal by the Council of Maryland on 25 Jun 1778. {Ref: Archives of Maryland Vol. 21, p. 150}

PARSONS, WILLIAM (Maryland Navy), marine on the State Ship *Defence* in 1777. {Ref: Archives of Maryland Vol. 18, p. 659}

PATRICK, JOHN (Harford County), signer of the Bush Declaration on 22 Mar 1775 and captain of Militia Company No. 17 on 1 Apr 1776; born in 1735 in Baltimore County, married Elizabeth Cummings on 11 Mar 1765, and died 16 Oct 1805 in Harford County; their known children were: twins Elizabeth and Mary Patrick (born 12 Jul 1775); Mary Patrick (married Basil Brook); Martha Patrick (born 1780, married William Thomas); and, Samuel Patrick. {Ref: Maryland State Society DAR Directory, 1892-1965, p. 562; C. Milton Wright's *Our Harford Heritage*, p. 355}

PATTEN, THOMAS (Baltimore Privateer), commander of the schooner *Rover*, navigated by 10 men and mounting 6 carriage guns, 4 swivel guns and 10 muskets, was issued Letters of Marque & Reprisal by the Council of Maryland on 5 Sep 1780. {Ref: Archives of Maryland Vol. 43, p. 276}

PATTERSON, GEORGE (Harford County, Susquehannah Hundred), captain of Militia Company No. 21 on 23 Apr 1776. {Ref: George W. Archer Collection and Revolutionary War File, Historical Society of Harford County Archives}

PATTERSON, JAMES (Harford County), private who was enrolled by 15 Apr 1776 in Militia Company No. 20 under Capt. Robert Glenn. {Ref: George W. Archer Collection and Revolutionary War File, Historical Society of Harford County Archives}

PATTERSON, SAMUEL (Harford County), private who was enrolled by 15 Apr 1776 in Militia Company No. 20 under Capt. Robert Glenn. {Ref: George W. Archer Collection and Revolutionary War File, Historical Society of Harford County Archives}

PATTERSON, THOMAS (Prince George's County), private in the Maryland Continental Line who was *"sent from camp by General Smallwood as unfit for the service"* and was discharged on 22 Jun 1778. {Ref: Archives of Maryland Vol. 21, p. 144}

PATTERSON, WILLIAM (Harford County), private who was enrolled by 15 Apr 1776 in Militia Company No. 20 under Capt. Robert Glenn. {Ref: George W. Archer Collection and Revolutionary War File, Historical Society of Harford County Archives}

PAWSON, MATTHEW (Caroline County), patriot who took the Oath of Fidelity and Support to the State of Maryland on 9 Apr 1778. {Ref: Archives of Maryland Vol. 21, p. 22}

PAYNE, BARNEY (St. Mary's County), private (substitute) in the Maryland Continental Line by 1781, was discharged on 8 Dec 1781. {Ref: Archives of Maryland Vol. 48, p. 11}

PAYNE, IGNATIUS (St. Mary's County), private (substitute) in the Maryland Continental Line by 1781, was discharged on 8 Dec 1781. {Ref: Archives of Maryland Vol. 48, p. 11}

PAYNE, JOHN (Maryland Navy), sailor or seaman on 7 Jan 1780. {Ref: Calendar of Maryland State Papers, The Brown Books, p. 57}

PAYNE, JOHN, JR. (Maryland Navy), sailor or seaman on 7 Jan 1780. {Ref: Calendar of Maryland State Papers, The Brown Books, p. 57}

PAYNE (PAINE), MICHAEL (Calvert County), patriot who was noted by the Council of Maryland on 9 Sep 1779 in a letter to Capt. Gale stating that *"John Chain has offered Michael Paine who says he was born in Calvert County and that he came hither in a Boat with one Copper in his stead. If on enquiry of Copper you find Paine is at Liberty you may inlist him instead of John Chain to whom on its being done give a Discharge hereon."* {Ref: Archives of Maryland Vol. 21, p. 517}

PAYNE, WILLIAM (Harford County), private (substitute) in the Maryland Continental Line by 1781, was discharged on 8 Dec 1781. {Ref: Archives of Maryland Vol. 48, p. 11}

PAYSON, HENRY (Baltimore Town), patriot and merchant who enrolled in Capt. John Sterrett's Independent Mercantile Company by February, 1777, at which time they were mustered into regular service with the continental army to repress loyalist activities in the Eastern Shore counties of Somerset and Worcester. {Ref: J. Thomas Scharf's *History of Baltimore City and County*, Part I, p. 77}

PEACOCK, NEALE (Washington County), private in the 7th Maryland Continental Line, enlisted 24 Dec 1776 for 3 years. *"Neale Peacock, formerly of Washington County, died 17 Aug 1827 near Cadiz, Ohio, and for many years a soldier in the Revolutionary Maryland Continental Line."* {Ref: Archives of Maryland Vol. 18, pp. 239, 307; J. Thomas Scharf's *History of Western Maryland*, Vol. II, p. 1053}

PEALE, ST. GEORGE, see "John Callahan," q.v.

PEARCE, HENRY WARD (Cecil County), patriot who was appointed by the Council of Maryland on 27 Jan 1776 as one of three persons in Cecil County to collect all gold and silver coin that can be procured in said county. {Ref: Archives of Maryland Vol. 11, p. 132}

PEARCE, HUGH (Kent County), private (substitute) in the Maryland Continental Line by 1781, was discharged on 8 Dec 1781. {Ref: Archives of Maryland Vol. 48, p. 11}

PEARCE, JOHN (Kent County), private (substitute) in the Maryland Continental Line by 1781, was discharged on 8 Dec 1781. {Ref: Archives of Maryland Vol. 48, p. 11}

PEARCE, PHILLIP G. (Baltimore County), lieutenant in the militia on 31 May 1779 in Capt. Benjamin Talbott's Company, Cockey's Battalion. {Ref: Maryland Historical Magazine, Vol. 7, No. 1, p. 90}

PEARSEFALL, JOHN (Western Maryland), private in Capt. Michael Cresap's Company in 1775. {Ref: Howard L. Leckey's *The Tenmile Country and Its Pioneer Families*, p. 16}

PEARSON, ABEL (Harford County, Susquehannah Hundred), private who was enrolled 23 Apr 1776 in Militia Company No. 21 under Capt. George Patterson.

{Ref: George W. Archer Collection and Revolutionary War File, Historical Society of Harford County Archives}

PEARSON, THOMAS (Baltimore County), matross soldier by 7 May 1779 at which time he gave a deposition about his enlistment terms. {Ref: Maryland State Archives Record MdHR 6636-14-83}

PECK, GEORGE (Western Maryland), private in Capt. Michael Cresap's Company in 1775. {Ref: Howard L. Leckey's *The Tenmile Country and Its Pioneer Families*, p. 16}

PECKINPAUGH, MICHAEL, see "Leonard Backenbaugh," q.v.

PEDDICOARD, ELIZABETH, see "George Zimmerman," q.v.

PENCHEY, WILLIAM T. (Baltimore Town), patriot and merchant who enrolled in Capt. John Sterrett's Independent Mercantile Company by February, 1777, at which time they were mustered into regular service with the continental army to repress loyalist activities in the Eastern Shore counties of Somerset and Worcester. {Ref: J. Thomas Scharf's *History of Baltimore City and County*, Part I, p. 77}

PENDERGAST, WILLIAM (Anne Arundel County), ensign in the 3rd and 5th Maryland Continental Lines who received payment for his services in the amount of "1900 Dollars & £3.10s" on 12 Sep 1780. For additional information see Peden's *Revolutionary Patriots of Maryland, 1775-1783: A Supplement* (p. 168). {Ref: Archives of Maryland Vol. 45, p. 98}

PENFOLD, GEORGE (Queen Anne's County), private (substitute) in the Maryland Continental Line by 1781, was discharged on 8 Dec 1781. {Ref: Archives of Maryland Vol. 48, p. 10}

PENNEWELL, ELIAS (Worcester County), private who was drafted into the Maryland Continental Line, was discharged on 8 Dec 1781. {Ref: Archives of Maryland Vol. 48, p. 10}

PEOPLES, GEORGE (Western Maryland), private in Capt. Michael Cresap's Company in 1775. {Ref: Howard L. Leckey's *The Tenmile Country and Its Pioneer Families*, p. 16}

PERCIFIELD, SAMUEL (Anne Arundel County), patriot who took the Oath of Fidelity and Support to the State of Maryland on 1 Apr 1778. {Ref: Archives of Maryland Vol. 21, p. 1}

PERCIVAL, JOSEPH F. (Baltimore Town), patriot and merchant who enrolled in Capt. John Sterrett's Independent Mercantile Company by February, 1777, at which time they were mustered into regular service with the continental army to repress loyalist activities in the Eastern Shore counties of Somerset and Worcester. {Ref: J. Thomas Scharf's *History of Baltimore City and County*, Part I, p. 77}

PERES, ANTHONY (Maryland Navy), seaman on the State Ship *Defence* in 1777. {Ref: Archives of Maryland Vol. 18, p. 659}

PERKINS, JOHN (Kent County), private (substitute) in the Maryland Continental Line by 1781, was discharged on 8 Dec 1781. {Ref: Archives of Maryland Vol. 48, p. 11}

PERKINS, WILLIAM (Harford County, Susquehannah Hundred), private who was enrolled 23 Apr 1776 in Militia Company No. 21 under Capt. George Patterson. {Ref: George W. Archer Collection and Revolutionary War File, Historical Society of Harford County Archives}

PERRY, JAMES (Harford County, Susquehannah Hundred), private who was enrolled 23 Apr 1776 in Militia Company No. 21 under Capt. George Patterson. {Ref: George W. Archer Collection and Revolutionary War File, Historical Society of Harford County Archives}

PETERKIN, JANE, see "Aquila Norris," q.v.

PETERS, EDWARD (Maryland Privateer), commander of the schooner *Return*, navigated by 17 men and mounting 6 carriage guns, was issued Letters of Marque & Reprisal by the Council of Maryland on 28 Aug 1782. {Ref: Archives of Maryland Vol. 48, p. 247}

PETERS, NICHOLAS (Maryland Navy), marine on the State Ship *Defence* in 1777. {Ref: Archives of Maryland Vol. 18, p. 659}

PHERILL (FERROL), JOSEPH (Montgomery County), private in the 7th Maryland Continental Line, enlisted 8 Jun 1780; having been convicted of rape by the county court, he had been pardoned on 10 May 1780 *"on condition that he forthwith inlist himself into some one of the Regiments of the Quota of this State in the Continental Army during the War and that he do not desert therefrom."* {Ref: Archives of Maryland Vol. 43, pp. 170-171, and Vol. 18, p. 312}

PHILIPS, JOSEPH (Baltimore County), private who enlisted in Pulaski's Legion on 28 Mar 1778 and still in service in November, 1779. {Ref: Maryland Historical Magazine, Vol. 13, No. 3, p. 223}

PHILIPS, WILLIAM (Frederick County), private (substitute) in the Maryland Continental Line, Price's Regiment, enrolled in May, 1778 for 3 years or duration of the war. {Ref: Maryland Historical Magazine, Vol. 6, No. 3, p. 258}

PHILLIPS, JAMES (Maryland Privateer), commander of the sloop *General Lee*, mounting 10 carriage guns and 8 swivel guns, commissioned by the Council of Maryland on 17 Dec 1776; see "Henry Stump," q.v. {Ref: Archives of Maryland Vol. 12, p. 534}

PHILLIPS, JOHN (Western Maryland), private in Capt. Michael Cresap's Company in 1775. {Ref: Howard L. Leckey's *The Tenmile Country and Its Pioneer Families*, p. 16}

PHILLIPS, SUSANNA, see "Francis Lang," q.v.

PHILLIPS, WILLIAM (Baltimore County), private, 31 May 1779, Capt. Benjamin Talbott's Militia Company, Cockey's Battalion. {Ref: Maryland Historical Magazine, Vol. 7, No. 1, p. 90}

PHILPOT, THOMAS (Anne Arundel County), private (substitute for Jonathan Brashears), enlisted to serve in the Maryland Continental Line until 10 Dec 1781 and was discharged on 21 Feb 1782 *"having as he says served to the 21 of November the time he got home."* {Ref: Archives of Maryland Vol. 48, p. 83}

PICKENBAUGH, SUSANNA, see "John F. Main," q.v.

PIERCY, GEORGE (St. Mary's County), patriot who took the Oath of Fidelity and Allegiance to the State of Maryland on 31 Mar 1778. {Ref: Archives of Maryland Vol. 16, p. 559}

PIERCY, WILLIAM (Maryland Navy), midshipman on the State Ship *Defence* in 1777. {Ref: Archives of Maryland Vol. 18, p. 659}

PIGMAN, JESSE (Western Maryland), private in Capt. Michael Cresap's Company in 1775. {Ref: Howard L. Leckey's *The Tenmile Country and Its Pioneer Families*, p. 16}

PIKE, JOHN (Maryland Navy), marine on the State Ship *Defence* in 1777. {Ref: Archives of Maryland Vol. 18, p. 659}

PIKE, WILLIAM (St. Mary's County), private (substitute) in the Maryland Continental Line by 1781, was discharged on 8 Dec 1781. {Ref: Archives of Maryland Vol. 48, p. 11}

PINDLE (PINDELL), RICHARD (Anne Arundel County), doctor in the 4th Maryland Continental Line who received payment for his services in the amount of "1900 Dollars & £3.10s" on 12 Sep 1780. {Ref: Archives of Maryland Vol. 45, p. 98}

PINNIX, JOHN (Harford County), private who was enrolled 10 Mar 1776 in Militia Company No. 18 under Capt. John Jolly. {Ref: George W. Archer Collection and Revolutionary War File, Historical Society of Harford County Archives}

PINTER, THOMAS (Worcester County), private (substitute) in the Maryland Continental Line by 1781, was discharged on 8 Dec 1781. {Ref: Archives of Maryland Vol. 48, p. 11}

PITT, MARY, see "Thomas Adams," q.v.

PITT, THOMAS (Dorchester County), patriot who was appointed Inspector of Ennalls Ferry Warehouse on 27 Oct 1780 by the Council of Maryland in the room of Joseph Ennalls who had resigned. {Ref: Archives of Maryland Vol. 43, p. 342}

PLANT, JOHN (Southern Maryland), ensign, commissioned on 27 Jul 1780 to serve in the Regiment Extra by order of the Council of Maryland. {Ref: Archives of Maryland Vol. 43, p. 234}

PLATER, ELIZABETH, see "James Tootell," q.v.

PLATER, GEORGE (St. Mary's County), colonel and patriot who was appointed by the Council of Maryland on 27 Jan 1776 as one of three persons in St. Mary's County to collect all gold and silver coin that can be procured in said county. {Ref: Archives of Maryland Vol. 11, p. 132}

PLUMBLY, GEORGE (Anne Arundel County), private in the Maryland Continental Line by 1 Dec 1781 at which time he was on duty guarding the magazine at the Head of Severn River. {Ref: Archives of Maryland Vol. 48, p. 8}

PLUMMER, JOHN (Anne Arundel County), patriot who took the Oath of Fidelity and Support to the State of Maryland on 9 Apr 1778. {Ref: Archives of Maryland Vol. 21, p. 22}

POAK, SAMUEL (Harford County), private who was enrolled 25 Mar 1776 in Militia Company No. 19 under Capt. William Morgan. {Ref: George W. Archer Collection and Revolutionary War File, Historical Society of Harford County Archives}

POE, DAVID (Baltimore City), soldier in the Maryland militia who died circa 1817 and his widow Elizabeth died in 1835 (son David Poe, Jr. was the father of Edgar Allen Poe); their heirs applied for pension on 8 May 1837 under the Act of July 4, 1836, but the claim was rejected because the soldier and his widow had died before the passage of the act. For additional information see Peden's *Revolutionary Patriots of Baltimore Town and Baltimore County, 1775-1783.* {Ref: *Rejected or Suspended Applications for Revolutionary War Pensions* (1850 Report), p. 233; Research by Virgil D. White, citing Federal Pension Application R8293}

POGUE, CHARLES (Western Maryland), private in Capt. Michael Cresap's Company in 1775. {Ref: Howard L. Leckey's *The Tenmile Country and Its Pioneer Families*, p. 16}

POLAND, JOHN (Baltimore or Frederick County), private who enlisted in Pulaski's Legion on 2 May 1778 or 1779. {Ref: Maryland Historical Magazine, Vol. 13, No. 3, p. 224}

POLAND (POLLAND), WILLIAM (Maryland Navy), marine on the State Ship *Defence* in 1777. {Ref: Archives of Maryland Vol. 18, p. 659}

POLK, ROBERT (Maryland Privateer), commander of the sloop *Black Joke*, navigated by 25 men and mounting 10 carriage guns and 2 swivel guns, was issued Letters of Marque & Reprisal by the Council of Maryland on 21 Jun 1777. {Ref: Archives of Maryland Vol. 16, p. 297}

POLSTON, JOSEPH (Cecil County), private who was enrolled to serve as a substitute in the Maryland Continental Line until 10 Dec 1781, but *"being represented unfit for the service for which he was intended"* was discharged on 30 Oct 1781. {Ref: Archives of Maryland Vol. 45, p. 657}

POPE, ---- (Anne Arundel County?), soldier in the Maryland Continental Line *"now remaining in Annapolis"* on 24 Jul 1780 at which time his wife Sarah Pope was entitled to rations under the laws of the State. {Ref: Archives of Maryland Vol. 43, p. 227}

POPE, JAMES (Somerset County), a blind soldier in the 3rd Maryland Continental Line who was issued clothing on 9 Dec 1780, apparently after he was discharged from the service. {Ref: Archives of Maryland Vol. 45, p. 239}

POPE, SARAH, see "---- Pope," q.v.

POPE, WILLIAM (Frederick County), private (substitute) in the Maryland Continental Line, German Regiment, enrolled in May, 1778 for 3 years or duration of the war. {Ref: Maryland Historical Magazine, Vol. 6, No. 3, p. 261}

POPHAM, BENJAMIN (Anne Arundel County), private (substitute) in the Maryland Continental Line by 1781, was discharged on 8 Dec 1781. {Ref: Archives of Maryland Vol. 48, p. 11}

PORTER, DAVID (Baltimore Privateer), commander of the sloop *Delight*, navigated by 8 men and mounting 6 carriage guns and 6 carbines, was issued Letters of Marque & Reprisal by the Council of Maryland on 1 May 1778. {Ref: Archives of Maryland Vol. 21, p. 62}

PORTER, ROBERT (Frederick County), private (substitute) in the Maryland Continental Line, German Regiment, enrolled in May, 1778 for 3 years or duration of the war. {Ref: Maryland Historical Magazine, Vol. 6, No. 3, p. 259}

PORTER, SUSANNA, see "Acquilla Randall," q.v.

PORTER, WILLIAM (Maryland Navy), marine on the State Ship *Defence* in 1777. {Ref: Archives of Maryland Vol. 18, p. 659}

PORTER, WILLIAM (Maryland Navy), sailor on the State Ship *Defence* in 1777. {Ref: Archives of Maryland Vol. 18, p. 659}

POSEY, HUMPHREY (Charles County), recommended as second lieutenant in the 26th Battalion of Militia of Charles County on 20 Mar 1781. {Ref: Archives of Maryland Vol. 47, p. 136}

POTEET, THOMAS (Harford County), private who was enrolled 9 Dec 1775 in Militia Company No. 14 under Capt. William McComas. {Ref: George W. Archer Collection and Revolutionary War File, Historical Society of Harford County Archives}

POTTER, NATHANIEL (Caroline County), patriot who was commissioned one of the three persons in Caroline County by the Council of Maryland on 19 Aug 1779 to receive subscriptions for use of the State; appointed Commissary of Purchases on 8 Jul 1780. {Ref: Archives of Maryland Vol. 21, p. 499, and Vol. 43, p. 215}

POTTS, RICHARD (Frederick County), patriot who served as clerk to the Committee of Observation and aide to Gen. Thomas Johnson in 1777; born 19 Jul 1753, married Eleanor Murdock (1774-1842) on 19 Dec 1799, died 26 Nov 1808 and buried in Mount Olivet Cemetery; their daughter Mary J. F. Potts married Worthington Johnson. {Ref: Burial information compiled by Dr. Donald Wolf in Maryland Society SAR Newsletter circa 1996; Maryland State Society DAR Directory, 1892-1965, p. 586}

POWEL, WILLIAM (Anne Arundel County?), private in the 1st Maryland Continental Line by 31 Jan 1780 at which time he was issued clothing *"due him from the Continent."* {Ref: Archives of Maryland Vol. 43, p. 73}

POWER, JOHN (Maryland Navy), marine on the State Ship *Defence* in 1777. {Ref: Archives of Maryland Vol. 18, p. 659}

POWER, SAMUEL (Harford County, Susquehannah Hundred), private who was enrolled 23 Apr 1776 in Militia Company No. 21 under Capt. George Patterson. {Ref: George W. Archer Collection and Revolutionary War File, Historical Society of Harford County Archives}

POWLET, SEVERN (Maryland Navy), seaman or marine on the State Ship *Defence* in 1777. {Ref: Archives of Maryland Vol. 18, p. 659}

POYMARAT, ANDREW (Baltimore County?), private in the 1st Maryland Continental Line who was recruited by 28 Feb 1780 at which time he was issued clothing due him. {Ref: Archives of Maryland Vol. 43, p. 98}

PRANGLEY, WILLIAM (Frederick County), private (substitute) in the Maryland Continental Line, Gunby's Regiment, enrolled in May, 1778 for 3 years or duration of the war. {Ref: Maryland Historical Magazine, Vol. 6, No. 3, p. 261}

PRATHER, ANN, see "James Higgins," q.v.

PRATHER, SARAH, see "James Higgins," q.v.

PRATT, JOHN (St. Mary's County), private in the 5th Maryland Continental Line in Capt. Thomas' Company before 22 Nov 1776 at which time he was classified as an invalid and a request was made to the Council of Maryland that he be discharged from the service. {Ref: Archives of Maryland Vol. 12, p. 471}

PRAY(?), WILLIAM (Maryland Navy), sailor or seaman on 7 Jan 1780. {Ref: Calendar of Maryland State Papers, The Brown Books, p. 57}

PRESBURY, ISABELLA, see "Aquila Hall," q.v.

PRESBURY, SOPHIA, see "Aquila Hall," q.v.

PRESTON, ANDREW (Frederick County), private (substitute) in the Maryland Continental Line, Price's Regiment, enrolled in May, 1778 for 3 years or duration of the war. {Ref: Maryland Historical Magazine, Vol. 6, No. 3, p. 260}

PRESTON, BARNARD, OF DANIEL (Harford County), private who was enrolled 25 Mar 1776 in Militia Company No. 19 under Capt. William Morgan. {Ref: George W. Archer Collection and Revolutionary War File, Historical Society of Harford County Archives}

PRESTON, BENJAMIN, see "Martin Preston," q.v.

PRESTON, CLEMENCY, see "Martin Preston," q.v.

PRESTON, ELIZABETH, see "Martin Preston," q.v.

PRESTON, GRAFTON (Harford County), ensign, 6th Maryland Regiment of Continental Troops, commissioned 10 Dec 1779. {Ref: Archives of Maryland Vol. 43, p. 34}

PRESTON, JAMES, see "Martin Preston," q.v.

PRESTON, MARTHA, see "Martin Preston," q.v.

PRESTON, MARTIN (Harford County), second lieutenant, commissioned 28 Apr 1776 in Militia Company No. 23 under Capt. James McComas; Martin Preston died by 10 Jun 1806 (date of final distribution) and his heirs were Rebecca Preston (widow), sons Benjamin, Scott, and James T. Preston, and daughters Elizabeth, Clemency, and Martha Preston. {Ref: George W. Archer Collection and Revolutionary War File, Historical Society of Harford County Archives; Henry C. Peden, Jr.'s *Heirs & Legatees of Harford County, 1802-1846*, p. 10}

PRESTON, REBECCA, see "Martin Preston," q.v.

PRESTON, SCOTT, see "Martin Preston," q.v.

PRESTON, THOMAS (Anne Arundel County), soldier before 27 Dec 1781 at which time his wife Mary Preston petitioned General Smallwood and informed him that *"her husband Thomas Preston has been now about three years to the Southward Having left your Petitioner with three small Children And no ways provided for, so that we all are in a very distressed & destitute way ... Your Petitioner's husband being now Almost Six Years in the Service."* {Ref: Archives of Maryland Vol. 47, p. 580}

PREW, WILLIAM (Maryland Navy), ship's steward on the State Ship *Defence* in 1777. {Ref: Archives of Maryland Vol. 18, p. 659}

PRICE, BENJAMIN (Baltimore or Cecil County?), captain in the 2nd Maryland Continental Line who received payment for his services in the amount of "1900 Dollars & £3.10s" on 12 Sep 1780. {Ref: Archives of Maryland Vol. 45, pp. 97, 354}

PRICE, HANNAH, see "William Price," q.v.

PRICE, HENRY (Maryland Navy), marine on the State Ship *Defence* in 1777. {Ref: Archives of Maryland Vol. 18, p. 659}

PRICE, JOHN (Baltimore County), private who enlisted in Pulaski's Legion on 6 May 1778 in Baltimore. {Ref: Maryland Historical Magazine, Vol. 13, No. 3, p. 222}

PRICE, THOMAS (Montgomery County), lieutenant and paymaster in the 3rd Maryland Continental Line who received payment for his services in the amount of "1900 Dollars & £3.10s" on 12 Sep 1780. {Ref: Archives of Maryland Vol. 45, p. 98}

PRICE, THOMAS (Frederick County), colonel who was appointed Commissary of Purchases by the Council of Maryland on 8 Jul 1780. {Ref: Archives of Maryland Vol. 43, p. 215}

PRICE, WILLIAM (Baltimore City), soldier in the Maryland troops whose widow Hannah Price applied for pension under the Act of July 7, 1838, but the claim was suspended because *"company and regiment and duration of service must be set forth."* {Ref: *Rejected or Suspended Applications for Revolutionary War Pensions* (1850 Report), p. 237}

PRICHARD, JESSE (Harford County), ensign, 9 Dec 1775 in Militia Company No. 14 under Capt. William McComas. {Ref: George W. Archer Collection and Revolutionary War File, Historical Society of Harford County Archives}

PRICKETT, JOSIAH (Baltimore County), private in the Pennsylvania Line who was born in Maryland in 1764 at the forks of Gunpowder River about 20 miles from Baltimore; moved with his father (not named) and family (none named except brother Richard Prickett) to Berkeley County, Virginia and then to Washington County, Pennsylvania where he enlisted in the war; married Sarah Van Camp (born 9 Sep 1761, daughter of Larance Van Camp) on 4 Jul 1783; Josiah applied for pension in Clermont County, Ohio on 10 Aug 1832, died on 3 Dec 1845 and his widow Sarah Prickett applied for pension on 8 Jun 1846. {Ref: Research by Christopher T. Smithson, citing Federal Pension Application W5584}

PRICKETT, NICHOLAS (Baltimore County), private, aged 26, labourer, born in Maryland, enlisted 23 Feb 1776 in Capt. John Fulford's Company of Matrosses. {Ref: Maryland Historical Magazine, Vol. 69, No. 1, p. 95}

PRICKETT, RICHARD, see "Josiah Prickett," q.v.

PRICKETT, SARAH, see "Josiah Prickett," q.v.

PRIGG, EDWARD (Harford County), private who was enrolled 25 Mar 1776 in Militia Company No. 19 under Capt. William Morgan. {Ref: George W. Archer Collection and Revolutionary War File, Historical Society of Harford County Archives}

PRIGG, JOSEPH, see "William Prigg," q.v.

PRIGG, SUSAN, see "William Prigg," q.v.

PRIGG, WILLIAM (Harford County), ensign in Militia Company No. 19 under Capt. William Morgan on 25 Mar 1776; married Susan ---- in November, 1776 and died on 23 Sep 1833; yet, when widow Susan Prigg applied for pension on 11 May 1842, aged 88, under the Act of July 7, 1838, the claim was suspended because it *"claims an ensign in the Maryland militia and the Register of the Loan Office at Annapolis must be referred to for proof."* The applicant also mentioned soldier's brother Joseph Prigg (aged 77) and his sister Martha Gover (aged 78) in 1842; one source called him "William Prigg, Jr." {Ref: George W. Archer Collection and Revolutionary War File, Historical Society of Harford County Archives; *Rejected or Suspended Applications for Revolutionary War Pensions* (1850 Report), p. 237; Research by Virgil D. White, citing Federal Pension Application R8485}

PRIMROSE, DAVID (Maryland Navy), sailor on the State Ship *Defence* in 1777. {Ref: Archives of Maryland Vol. 18, p. 659}

PRINCE, WILLIAM (Maryland Navy), marine on the State Ship *Defence* in 1777. {Ref: Archives of Maryland Vol. 18, p. 659}

PRINGLE, MARK (Baltimore County), cornet in a Troop of Light Horse, commissioned 26 Jul 1780; see "Nicholas R. Moore," q.v. {Ref: Archives of Maryland Vol. 43, p. 233}

PRIOR, BENJAMIN (Baltimore County), private who enlisted in Pulaski's Legion in July, 1778 or 1779 in Baltimore. {Ref: Maryland Historical Magazine, Vol. 13, No. 3, p. 222}

PRITCHARD, ELEAZER (Harford County, Susquehannah Hundred), private who was enrolled 23 Apr 1776 in Militia Company No. 21 under Capt. George Patterson. {Ref: George W. Archer Collection and Revolutionary War File, Historical Society of Harford County Archives}

PRITCHARD, HARMON (Harford County, Susquehannah Hundred), private who was enrolled 23 Apr 1776 in Militia Company No. 21 under Capt. George Patterson. {Ref: George W. Archer Collection and Revolutionary War File, Historical Society of Harford County Archives}

PRITCHARD, JAMES (Harford County, Susquehannah Hundred), private who was enrolled 23 Apr 1776 in Militia Company No. 21 under Capt. George Patterson. {Ref: George W. Archer Collection and Revolutionary War File, Historical Society of Harford County Archives}

PRITCHARD, OBEDIAH (Harford County, Susquehannah Hundred), second lieutenant on 23 Apr 1776 in Militia Company No. 21 under Capt. George

Patterson. {Ref: George W. Archer Collection and Revolutionary War File, Historical Society of Harford County Archives}

PROCTER, WILLIAM (Dorchester County), private who was drafted to serve in the Maryland Continental Line until 10 Dec 1781, but *"being represented unfit for the duty for which he was intended"* was discharged on 30 Oct 1781. {Ref: Archives of Maryland Vol. 45, p. 656}

PROCTOR, HENRY (Charles County), private who was drafted into the Maryland Continental Line, was discharged on 8 Dec 1781. {Ref: Archives of Maryland Vol. 48, p. 10}

PROUT, JOHN (Baltimore County), private, aged 30, farmer, born in Maryland, enlisted (made his "X" mark) on 31 Oct 1776 in Capt. John Fulford's Company of Matrosses. {Ref: Maryland Historical Magazine, Vol. 69, No. 1, p. 97}

PRY, PETER (Washington County), private (substitute) in the Maryland Continental Line, who enlisted to serve until 10 Dec 1781, was discharged on 29 Nov 1781. {Ref: Archives of Maryland Vol. 48, p. 7}

PUGH, HUMPHREY (Cecil County), corporal in the 2nd Maryland Continental Line, drafted to serve until 10 Dec 1781, was discharged on 29 Nov 1781; born circa 1751 in Carlisle, Pennsylvania, married first to Francina Crow and second to Ann Cheek, and died circa 1824 at Bohemia Manor, Cecil County; his daughter Francina Miriam Pugh married Noble Biddle. {Ref: Archives of Maryland Vol. 48, p. 6; Maryland State Society DAR Directory, 1892-1965, p. 592}

PURCELL, JOHN (Maryland Navy), sailor or seaman on 7 Jan 1780. {Ref: Calendar of Maryland State Papers, The Brown Books, p. 57}

PURTLE, ROBERT (St. Mary's or Baltimore County), soldier in the Maryland troops who married Catherine Sitler on 4 Aug 1796 in Baltimore and died in 1797 in Baltimore County or 1802 in St. Mary's County (different dates and places given in two different statements); his widow married second to William Wistel (no date was given) who also died; Catherine applied for pension in Baltimore on 1 Aug 1849, aged 81, under the Act of July 7, 1838, but the claim was suspended and indicated as *"no claim -- married in 1796; she can apply under the Act of July 29, 1848 by proving herself the widow of the soldier Robert Purtle, whose service is certified by the Register of the Land Office at Annapolis, and proving that she was married prior to 1800."* Catherine Sitler married Robert Purtel *[sic]* by license dated 4 Aug 1796 in Baltimore; no marriage license found for William Wistel and Catherine Purtle; she was still living in 1856. {Ref: *Rejected or Suspended Applications for Revolutionary War Pensions* (1850 Report), p. 237; Research by Virgil D. White, citing Federal Pension Application W4397; Dawn B. Smith's *Baltimore County Marriage Licenses, 1777-1798*, p. 154}

PURVIANCE, J. H. (Baltimore Town), patriot and merchant who enrolled in Capt. John Sterrett's Independent Mercantile Company by February, 1777, at which time they were mustered into regular service with the continental army to

repress loyalist activities in the Eastern Shore counties of Somerset and Worcester. {Ref: J. Thomas Scharf's *History of Baltimore City and County*, Part I, p. 77}

PURVIANCE, JAMES (Baltimore Town), patriot and merchant who enrolled in Capt. John Sterrett's Independent Mercantile Company by February, 1777, at which time they were mustered into regular service with the continental army to repress loyalist activities in the Eastern Shore counties of Somerset and Worcester. {Ref: J. Thomas Scharf's *History of Baltimore City and County*, Part I, p. 77}

PURVIANCE, SAMUEL (Baltimore County), patriot who was appointed by the Council of Maryland on 27 Jan 1776 as one of three persons in Baltimore County to collect all gold and silver coin that can be procured in said county. {Ref: Archives of Maryland Vol. 11, p. 132}

QUAY, JAMES (Maryland Navy), ordinary seaman on the State Ship *Defence* in 1777. {Ref: Archives of Maryland Vol. 18, p. 659}

QUIN, RICHARD (Frederick County), private (substitute) in the Maryland Continental Line, German Regiment, enrolled in May, 1778 for 3 years or duration of the war. {Ref: Maryland Historical Magazine, Vol. 6, No. 3, p. 258}

QUYNN, WILLIAM (Maryland Navy), doctor, commissioned surgeon of the brigantine *Cato* on 20 Nov 1780. {Ref: Archives of Maryland Vol. 45, p. 219}

RADCLIFFE, JOHN (Baltimore County), private, aged 47, barber, born in England, enlisted 19 Feb 1776 in Capt. John Fulford's Company of Matrosses. {Ref: Maryland Historical Magazine, Vol. 69, No. 1, p. 95}

RAGAN, RODERICK (Maryland Navy), marine on the State Ship *Defence* in 1777. {Ref: Archives of Maryland Vol. 18, p. 659}

RAISON, WILLIAM, see "William B. Rasin," q.v.

RAMSAY, NATHANIEL, see "Aquila Hall," q.v.

RAMSBURG, CHRISTIAN (Frederick County), patriot buried in Mount Olivet Cemetery. {Ref: Information compiled by Dr. Donald Wolf in Maryland Society SAR Newsletter circa 1996}

RAMSBURG, JOHN (Frederick County), patriot buried in Mount Olivet Cemetery. {Ref: Information compiled by Dr. Donald Wolf in Maryland Society SAR Newsletter circa 1996}

RAMSBURG, JOHN, SR. (Frederick County), patriot buried in Mount Olivet Cemetery. {Ref: Information compiled by Dr. Donald Wolf in Maryland Society SAR Newsletter circa 1996}

RANDALL, ACQUILLA (Anne Arundel County), patriot who took the Oath of Fidelity and Allegiance on 2 Mar 1778; born 5 Oct 1723 (son of Christopher Randall and Anne Chew), married Margaret Browne (daughter of Joshua Browne and Margaret Chew), and died in 1801; their children were: Christopher Randall (married Ann Crandall on 15 Nov 1788); John Randall; Acquilla Randall, Jr. (married Rebecca Cord on 8 Jun 1779); Nathan Randall (married Ruth Gaither Davis, mother of Ichabod Davis, on 21 Oct 1790); Brice

Randall (married Susanna Porter on 21 Feb 1795); Delilah Randall (married Ichabod Davis on 25 Jan 1785 in Baltimore); Ruth Randall (married Michael Cramblett on 14 Oct 1795); Hannah Randall (married John Norman); and, Margaret Randall (married Amos Debworth); also see "Ichabod Davis," q.v. {Ref: *For King or Country*, Vol. II, p. 226; Walter Arps' *Heirs & Orphans of Anne Arundel County, Distributions, 1788-1838*, p. 27}

RANDALL, RICHARD (Anne Arundel County), private by 5 Oct 1776 in Capt. Richard Chew's Militia Company, Weems' Battalion. {Ref: Archives of Maryland Vol. 12, p. 323}

RANKIN, ROBERT (Baltimore Town), patriot and merchant who enrolled in Capt. John Sterrett's Independent Mercantile Company by February, 1777, at which time they were mustered into regular service with the continental army to repress loyalist activities in the Eastern Shore counties of Somerset and Worcester. {Ref: J. Thomas Scharf's *History of Baltimore City and County*, Part I, p. 77}

RASIN, WILLIAM BLACKISTON (Kent County), private in the 5th Maryland Continental Line, enlisted 10 Jan 1777; promoted to corporal, to sergeant, and then to ensign on 26 Jan 1780; distinguished himself at the Battle of Camden in South Carolina; received payment for his services in the amount of "1900 Dollars & £3.10s" on 12 Sep 1780 (listed as "Ensign Raison"); promoted to lieutenant in the 1st Maryland Continental Line on 1 Jan 1781; became a captain in the militia after the war. It should be noted that Peden's *Revolutionary Patriots of Kent and Queen Anne's Counties, 1775-1783* contains incorrect information about this man that has been corrected as follows: *"The Capt. William Rasin and the Lt. William B. Rasin are the same person. Also Capt. William B. Rasin did not have a son Philip Freeman Rasin as the DAR directory indicated. Philip F. Rasin was a son of Philip Rasin and Hannah Freeman. Also Capt. William B. Rasin was married to Martha Wroth, not Sarah Freeman. There was a William Rasin who married Sarah Freeman in 1776 but he was a Quaker and never served in the military. I have seen many articles especially the Baltimore Histories done in the late 1800's that said Philip Freeman Rasin was a son of William Rasin but they are incorrect. The Daughters of the American Revolution had accepted an application years ago that was incorrect too. They have been made aware of the rror and this past month a legitimate descendant of Capt. William B. Rasin, John A. Barnhouser, has been accepted into the Children of the American Revolution through the captain's son Philip R. Rasin. Because of the many errors about the life of William B. Rasin (m. Martha Wroth), William Rasin (m. Sarah Freeman) and Philip F. Rasin, I have submitted an article to the Maryland Genealogical Society that will be published in their next bulletin regarding William B. Rasin ... with proofs for the information I have given above."* {Ref: Research by Christos Christou, Jr., of Baltimore, Maryland in 1995, whose article was published in the *Maryland*

Genealogical Society Bulletin (Vol. 36, No. 2, Spring, 1995, pp. 299-303); Archives of Maryland Vol. 45, p. 98}

RATIKEN, PETER (Harford County), private (substitute) in the Maryland Continental Line by 1781, was discharged on 8 Dec 1781. {Ref: Archives of Maryland Vol. 48, p. 11}

RAVENEAU, FRANCIS (Baltimore Privateer), commander of the ship *Polacre Peter*, navigated by 14 men and mounting 4 carriage guns, was issued Letters of Marque & Reprisal by the Council of Maryland on 14 Aug 1780. {Ref: Archives of Maryland Vol. 43, p. 248}

RAWARK (RUARK?), MICHAEL (Worcester County?), private who was a 9 month soldier in the 4th Maryland Regiment in 1779, was discharged on 19 Oct 1779 and received £6.15.0 in clothing. {Ref: Archives of Maryland Vol. 21, p. 562}

RAWEN, PATRICK (Frederick County), private (substitute) in the Maryland Continental Line, Price's Regiment, enrolled in May, 1778 for 3 years or duration of the war. {Ref: Maryland Historical Magazine, Vol. 6, No. 3, p. 258}

RAWLINGS, ISAAC (Baltimore County), private, aged 27, farmer, born in Maryland, enlisted 16 Feb 1776 in Capt. John Fulford's Company of Matrosses; lieutenant in the Maryland Artillery who received payment for his services in the amount of "1900 Dollars & £3.10s" on 12 Sep 1780. {Ref: Archives of Maryland Vol. 45, p. 98; Maryland Historical Magazine, Vol. 69, No. 1, p. 95, which listed the name as "Isaac Rawluy(?)"}

RAWLINGS, MOSES (Washington County), colonel, appointed Commissary of Purchases by the Council of Maryland on 8 Jul 1780. {Ref: Archives of Maryland Vol. 43, p. 215}

RAY, BENJAMIN (Anne Arundel County), private who was drafted into the Maryland Continental Line, was discharged on 8 Dec 1781; applied for pension under the Act of June 7, 1832, but the claim was rejected because he did not serve six months; he died on 4 Nov 1835, leaving no widow and only one child Benjamin Ray, Jr. {Ref: Archives of Maryland Vol. 48, p. 10; *Rejected or Suspended Applications for Revolutionary War Pensions* (1850 Report), p. 229; Research by Virgil D. White, citing Federal Pension Application R8609}

RAY, JAMES (Maryland Navy), marine on the State barge *Revenge* on 16 Jun 1781 under Commodore Grason. {Ref: Archives of Maryland Vol. 45, p. 477}

RAY, NANCY, see "Charles Close," q.v.

READ, CORNELIA, see "John E. Howard," q.v.

READ, PEREGRINE (Kent County), private (substitute) in the Maryland Continental Line by 1781, was discharged on 8 Dec 1781. {Ref: Archives of Maryland Vol. 48, p. 11}

READ, WILLIAM, see "John E. Howard," q.v.

READY, JAMES (Maryland Navy), marine on the State Ship *Defence* in 1777. {Ref: Archives of Maryland Vol. 18, p. 659}

READY, LAWRENCE (Maryland Navy), marine on the State Ship *Defence* in 1777. {Ref: Archives of Maryland Vol. 18, p. 659}

REAMER (RAYMER), MICHAEL (Frederick County), patriot who was appointed by the Council of Maryland on 27 Jan 1776 as one of three persons in Frederick County to collect all the gold and silver coin that can be procured in said county; buried in Mount Olivet Cemetery. {Ref: Archives of Maryland Vol. 11, p. 132; Burial information compiled by Dr. Donald Wolf in Maryland Society SAR Newsletter circa 1996}

REASER, JACOB (Frederick County), contractor for State Arms in Frederick County in 1781. {Ref: Archives of Maryland Vol. 47, p. 14}

RECORDS, ANN (Somerset County), by order of the Council of Maryland on 3 Dec 1782, was *"to be paid £19.18.3 specie due her for Provision found the Recruits in Somerset County on a Certificate issued agreeable to the Act to adjust the Debts due from this State issued 13 August 1782."* It is unclear whether Ann was the wife or widow of a soldier or if she was paid for some patriotic service she had rendered to the State. {Ref: Archives of Maryland Vol. 48, p. 312}

REDDING, JAMES (Queen Anne's County), private (substitute) in the Maryland Continental Line by 1781, was discharged on 8 Dec 1781. {Ref: Archives of Maryland Vol. 48, p. 11}

REDDLEY, DRUE (Frederick County), private (substitute) in the Maryland Continental Line, Gunby's Regiment, enrolled in April, 1778 for 3 years or duration of the war. {Ref: Maryland Historical Magazine, Vol. 6, No. 3, p. 257}

REDMAN, JAMES (Cecil County), private who was enrolled to serve as a substitute in the Maryland Continental Line until 10 Dec 1781, but *"being represented unfit for the service for which he was intended"* was discharged on 30 Oct 1781. {Ref: Archives of Maryland Vol. 45, p. 657}

REE, GEORGE (Harford County, Susquehannah Hundred), private who was enrolled 23 Apr 1776 in Militia Company No. 21 under Capt. George Patterson. {Ref: George W. Archer Collection and Revolutionary War File, Historical Society of Harford County Archives}

REED, ANDREW (Washington County), private who was drafted to serve in the Maryland Continental Line until 10 Dec 1781, but *"being represented unfit for the duty for which he was intended"* was discharged on 30 Oct 1781. {Ref: Archives of Maryland Vol. 45, p. 656}

REED, JOHN (Prince George's County), captain in the Maryland Continental Line by 1 May 1781 at which time he received payment due in the amount of £22.8.10. {Ref: Archives of Maryland Vol. 45, p. 421}

REED, JOHN (Caroline County), private in Col. Richardson's Regiment in 1776 who was recommended for promotion. {Ref: Archives of Maryland Vol. 18, p. 74}

REED, NANCY, see "Thomas Longfellow," q.v.

REED (REID), PHILIP (Kent County), lieutenant and later captain in the 5th Maryland Continental Line who received payment for his services in the amount of "1900 Dollars & £3.10s" on 12 Sep 1780. For additional information see Papenfuse's *A Biographical Dictionary of the Maryland Legislature, 1635-1789* (pp. 674-675). {Ref: Archives of Maryland Vol. 45, p. 98}

REEDER, HENRY (St. Mary's County), patriot who was commissioned one of the three persons in St. Mary's County by the Council of Maryland on 19 Aug 1779 to receive subscriptions for use of the State. {Ref: Archives of Maryland Vol. 21, p. 499}

REESE, SOLOMON (Harford County, Susquehannah Hundred), private who was enrolled 23 Apr 1776 in Militia Company No. 21 under Capt. George Patterson. {Ref: George W. Archer Collection and Revolutionary War File, Historical Society of Harford County Archives}

REEVES, NOAH (Harford County), private who was a 9 month soldier in the 6th Maryland Continental Line in 1779, was discharged on 19 Oct 1779 and received £12 in clothing. {Ref: Archives of Maryland Vol. 21, p. 562}

REFO, JOHN ADAM (Frederick County), patriot buried in Mount Olivet Cemetery. {Ref: Information compiled by Dr. Donald Wolf in Maryland Society SAR Newsletter circa 1996}

REITH, RICHARD (Annapolis), messenger to the Governor and Council of Maryland by 1 Aug 1780 at which time he was paid £125 for one month's salary; died before 6 Feb 1781 at which time he was replaced by Jubb Fowler. {Ref: Archives of Maryland Vol. 43, p. 244}

RENSHAW, JAMES (Harford County), private who was enrolled 25 Mar 1776 in Militia Company No. 19 under Capt. William Morgan. {Ref: George W. Archer Collection and Revolutionary War File, Historical Society of Harford County Archives}

RENSHAW, JOSEPH, JR. (Harford County), private who was enrolled 25 Mar 1776 in Militia Company No. 19 under Capt. William Morgan. {Ref: George W. Archer Collection and Revolutionary War File, Historical Society of Harford County Archives}

RENTFORD, HENRY (Maryland Navy), sailor on the State Ship *Defence* in 1777. {Ref: Archives of Maryland Vol. 18, p. 659}

RESSICK, JOSEPH (St. Mary's County), private who was drafted to serve in the Maryland Continental Line until 10 Dec 1781, but *"being represented unfit for the duty for which he was intended"* was discharged on 30 Oct 1781. {Ref: Archives of Maryland Vol. 45, p. 656}

REVELEY, FRANCIS (Baltimore County?), lieutenant in the 3rd Maryland Continental Line who received payment for his services in the amount of "1900 Dollars & £3.10s" on 12 Sep 1780. {Ref: Archives of Maryland Vol. 45, p. 97}

REYNER (REYNOL), CHRISTOPHER (Harford County), soldier in the 4th Maryland Continental Line who was transferred on account of his wounds to the Corps of Invalids by 25 Apr 1781 at which time he was issued clothing. {Ref: Archives of Maryland Vol. 18, p. 661, and Vol. 45, p. 414}

REYNOLDS, JOHN (Anne Arundel County), patriot who took the Oath of Fidelity and Allegiance to the State of Maryland on 31 Mar 1778. {Ref: Archives of Maryland Vol. 16, p. 559}

REYNOLDS (RENOLDS), THOMAS (Harford County), private who was reportedly a deserter enrolled or captured by Capt. Praul for the Regiment Extraordinary and sent to Annapolis with Capt. Thompson on board the sloop *Liberty* on 17 Aug 1780. {Ref: Archives of Maryland Vol. 45, p. 50}

RICE, JOSEPH (Baltimore Town), patriot and merchant who enrolled in Capt. John Sterrett's Independent Mercantile Company by February, 1777, at which time they were mustered into regular service with the continental army to repress loyalist activities in the Eastern Shore counties of Somerset and Worcester. {Ref: J. Thomas Scharf's *History of Baltimore City and County*, Part I, p. 77}

RICE, WALTER (Harford County), private who was enrolled 9 Dec 1775 in Militia Company No. 14 under Capt. William McComas. {Ref: George W. Archer Collection and Revolutionary War File, Historical Society of Harford County Archives}

RICH, VILETT, (Queen Anne's County), private (substitute) in the Maryland Continental Line by 1781, was discharged on 8 Dec 1781. {Ref: Archives of Maryland Vol. 48, p. 11}

RICHARDS, JANE, see "Daniel Root," q.v.

RICHARDS, JOHN (Frederick County), private (substitute) in the Maryland Continental Line, German Regiment, enrolled in May, 1778 for 3 years or duration of the war. {Ref: Maryland Historical Magazine, Vol. 6, No. 3, p. 261}

RICHARDS, SAMUEL (Montgomery County), private who was drafted into the Maryland Continental Line and discharged on 8 Dec 1781. {Ref: Archives of Maryland Vol. 48, p. 10}

RICHARDSON, ALEXANDER (Maryland Navy), seaman or marine on the State Ship *Defence* in 1777. {Ref: Archives of Maryland Vol. 18, p. 659}

RICHARDSON, ANN, see "Samuel Calwell," q.v.

RICHARDSON, BENJAMIN, see "John B. Howard," q.v.

RICHARDSON, DANIEL (Baltimore County), patriot who along with John Cannon contracted with the Council of Maryland to make 250 pairs of shoes for use of the State on 25 Nov 1776. {Ref: Archives of Maryland Vol. 12, pp. 477-478}

RICHARDSON, ELIZABETH, see "Benjamin B. Norris," q.v.

RICHARDSON, JONATHAN (Cecil County), private who was enrolled to serve as a substitute in the Maryland Continental Line until 10 Dec 1781, but *"being represented unfit for the service for which he was intended"* was discharged on 30 Oct 1781. {Ref: Archives of Maryland Vol. 45, p. 657}

RICHARDSON, THOMAS (Montgomery County), patriot who was appointed Commissary of Purchases by the Council of Maryland on 8 Jul 1780. {Ref: Archives of Maryland Vol. 43, p. 215}

RICHARDSON, WILLIAM (Caroline County), patriot who was appointed by the Council of Maryland on 27 Jan 1776 as one of three persons in Caroline County to collect all gold and silver coin that can be procured in said county; see "James O'Bryan," q.v. {Ref: Archives of Maryland Vol. 11, p. 132}

RICHARDSON, WILLIAM (Harford County), soldier in the Maryland Continental Line who was living in Harford County on 18 Aug 1824 at which time documents were filed in open court in Harford County stating, in part: *"William Richardson, aged 72 years ... does on his oath make the following declaration in order to obtain the provision made by the acts of Congress of the 18th of March of 1818 and the 1st of May 1820 that he the said William Richardson enlisted for and during the war in the State of Maryland in the company then commanded by Capt. Lee attached to the Eighth Maryland Regiment on the continental establishment, that he continued to serve in the said corps until the third day of February in the year 1780 when he was discharged from the said service at Philadelphia in the State of Pennsylvania. That he was at the seige of Stony Point under Genl. Wane [General Wayne] and he had no other evidence now in his power of his service. And in pursuance of the act of the 1st of May 1820 I do solemnly swear that I was a resident citizen of the United States on the 18th of March 1818 and that I have not since that time by gift, sale or in any manner disposed of my property or any part thereof with intent thereby so as to diminish it as to bring myself within the provision of an Act of Congress entitled an act to provide for certain persons engaged in the land and naval service of the United States in the Revolutionary War passed on the 18th day of March 1818 and that I have not, nor has any person in trust for me, any property or securities, contracts or debts due me nor have I any income other than what is contained in the schedule hereto annexed and by me subscribed. Schedule: 8½ acres of land with a small house at $5 per acre, $42.50; one old horse $15; two cows and a calf $25; house hold furniture $15; one old coat $8; [total] $105.50."* Signed: Wm. Richardson. {Ref: Historical Society of Harford County, Court Records File 25.14}

RICHEY, WILLIAM (Frederick County), private (substitute) in the Maryland Continental Line, Price's Regiment, enrolled in April, 1778 for 3 years or duration of the war. {Ref: Maryland Historical Magazine, Vol. 6, No. 3, p. 256}

RICHMOND, CHR. (Baltimore County?), lieutenant and paymaster in the 1st Maryland Continental Line who received payment for his services in the amount of "1900 Dollars & £3.10s" on 12 Sep 1780. {Ref: Archives of Maryland Vol. 45, p. 97}

RICKETTS, NICHOLAS (Baltimore County), second lieutenant in the Maryland Artillery, commissioned 31 Dec 1777; first lieutenant who received payment for his services in the amount of "1900 Dollars & £3.10s" on 12 Sep 1780. For additional information see Peden's *Revolutionary Patriots of Baltimore Town and Baltimore County, 1775-1783* (pp. 226, 323). {Ref: Archives of Maryland Vol. 18, pp. 365, 477, and Vol. 45, p. 98}

RIDER, WILLIAM (Frederick County), private (substitute) in the Maryland Continental Line, German Regiment, enrolled in May, 1778 for 3 years or duration of the war. {Ref: Maryland Historical Magazine, Vol. 6, No. 3, p. 260}

RIDGELY, NICHOLAS G. (Baltimore Town), patriot and merchant who enrolled in Capt. John Sterrett's Independent Mercantile Company by February, 1777, at which time they were mustered into regular service with the continental army to repress loyalist activities in the Eastern Shore counties of Somerset and Worcester. {Ref: J. Thomas Scharf's *History of Baltimore City and County*, Part I, p. 77}

RIDGELY, PRUDENCE, see "John E. Howard," q.v.

RIDGELY, SOPHIA, see "John E. Howard," q.v.

RIDLEY, MATTHEW (Baltimore County), patriot who was noted by the Council of Maryland on 21 Jul 1779 stating, in part, that *"he was a native of Great Britain who left this State about the year 1775 and hath since been absent in parts beyond the Sea and is now lately that is to say within three months last past, returned into this State, appeared before the Governor and Council, and before them did take, repeat and Subscribe the Oath of Fidelity and Support to this State contained in the Act entitled An Act to punish certain Crimes and Misdemeanors and to prevent the Growth of Toryism."* {Ref: Archives of Maryland Vol. 21, p. 477}

RIEMAN, SAMUEL, see "Daniel Smith," q.v.

RIGDON, GEORGE (Harford County), private who was enrolled 14 Sep 1775 in Militia Company No. 10 under Capt. John Love. {Ref: George W. Archer Collection and Revolutionary War File, Historical Society of Harford County Archives}

RIGGINS, EBENEZER (Baltimore County), private who enlisted in Pulaski's Legion on 20 Mar 1778 and still in service in November, 1779. {Ref: Maryland Historical Magazine, Vol. 13, No. 3, p. 223}

RIGHT, ELIJAH (Washington County), private who was enrolled to serve as a substitute in the Maryland Continental Line until 10 Dec 1781, but *"being represented unfit for the service for which he was intended"* was discharged on 30 Oct 1781. {Ref: Archives of Maryland Vol. 45, p. 656}

RIGHTMYER, CONRAD (Frederick County), soldier in the Maryland Continental Line who applied for pension under the Act of June 7, 1832, but the claim was rejected because he did not serve six months. {Ref: *Rejected or Suspended Applications for Revolutionary War Pensions* (1850 Report), p. 230}

RILEY, MICHAEL (Maryland Navy), marine on the State Ship *Defence* in 1777. {Ref: Archives of Maryland Vol. 18, p. 659}

RILEY, PATRICK (Frederick County), private (substitute) in the Maryland Continental Line, Williams' Regiment, enrolled in May, 1778 for 3 years or duration of the war. {Ref: Maryland Historical Magazine, Vol. 6, No. 3, p. 258}

RILEY, TIM (Maryland Navy), ordinary sailor on the State Ship *Defence* in 1777. {Ref: Archives of Maryland Vol. 18, p. 659}

RILEY (REILY), WILLIAM (Baltimore County), captain in the 4th Maryland Continental Line who received payment for his services in the amount of "1900 Dollars & £3.10s" on 12 Sep 1780. {Ref: Archives of Maryland Vol. 45, p. 98}

RINGER, MATTHIAS (Washington County), soldier in the Maryland Continental Line who applied for pension on 12 Apr 1836, aged 73, under the Act of June 7, 1832, but the claim was rejected because he did not serve six months. {Ref: *Rejected or Suspended Applications for Revolutionary War Pensions* (1850 Report), p. 230; Research by Virgil D. White, citing Federal Pension Application R8831}

RINGGOLD, THOMAS (Kent County), patriot who was appointed by the Council of Maryland on 27 Jan 1776 as one of three persons in Kent County to collect all gold and silver coin that can be procured in said county. {Ref: Archives of Maryland Vol. 11, p. 132}

RINGGOLD, WILLIAM, JR. (Kent County), lieutenant colonel of the 13th Battalion of Militia, commissioned 8 May 1777; appointed by the Council of Maryland on 27 Jan 1776 as one of three persons in Kent County to collect all gold and silver coin that can be procured in said county; one William Ringgold died testate in Kent County by 1 Nov 1808 and a William Ringgold, Jr. of Bayside in Kent County died testate by 29 Jan 1812. {Ref: Archives of Maryland Vol. 11, p. 132 and Vol. 16, p. 243; Kent County Wills Liber 9, pp. 39, 155}

RISTEAU, ---- (Baltimore County), soldier in the Maryland Continental Line by 13 Apr 1776 at which time the Council of Maryland contacted the Committee of Safety in Virginia stating, in part, that *"Mr. Risteau the Bearer has the Misfortune of having a Brother in Captivity taken by Lord Dunmore and entertains some Hopes of obtaining his Release if he can gain Access to him. He is a Native of this Province and well known to some of us to be a warm Friend to American Liberty."* {Ref: Archives of Maryland Vol. 11, p. 330}

RISTEAU, ABRAHAM (Baltimore County), patriot who was appointed Commissary of Purchases by the Council of Maryland on 8 Jul 1780. {Ref: Archives of Maryland Vol. 43, p. 215}

RITCHIE, WILLIAM (Frederick County), soldier from York County, Pennsylvania who enlisted as a substitute at Frederick Town *"for the war, blind"* and a private in the Maryland Continental Line who was *"sent from camp by General Smallwood as unfit for the service"* and discharged on 22 Jun 1778. {Ref: Archives of Maryland Vol. 21, p. 144}

RITCHIE, WILLIAM (Frederick County), patriot who was commissioned one of the three persons in Frederick County by the Council of Maryland on 19 Aug 1779 to receive subscriptions for use of the State. {Ref: Archives of Maryland Vol. 21, p. 499}

RITTER, TOBIAS (Frederick County), private who was drafted to serve in the Maryland Continental Line until 10 Dec 1781, but *"being represented unfit for the duty for which he was intended"* was discharged on 30 Oct 1781. {Ref: Archives of Maryland Vol. 45, p. 656}

ROBERTS, ARCHIBALD (Frederick County), private who was enrolled to serve as a substitute in the Maryland Continental Line until 10 Dec 1781, but *"being represented unfit for the service for which he was intended"* was discharged on 30 Oct 1781. {Ref: Archives of Maryland Vol. 45, p. 657}

ROBERTS, BASIL, see "Thomas Bounds," q.v.

ROBERTS, BENJAMIN (Caroline County), officer in Col. Richardson's Regiment in 1776 who was recommended for promotion to second lieutenant. {Ref: Archives of Maryland Vol. 18, p. 74}

ROBERTS, THOMAS (Maryland Navy), marine on the State Ship *Defence* in 1777. {Ref: Archives of Maryland Vol. 18, p. 659}

ROBERTS, WILLIAM (Anne Arundel County), private (substitute) in the Maryland Continental Line, who enlisted to serve until 10 Dec 1781, was discharged on 29 Nov 1781. {Ref: Archives of Maryland Vol. 48, p. 7}

ROBERTS, WILLIAM (Dorchester County), private (substitute) in the Maryland Continental Line by 1781, was discharged on 8 Dec 1781. {Ref: Archives of Maryland Vol. 48, p. 10}

ROBERTS, WILLIAM (Montgomery County), private who was drafted into the Maryland Continental Line and discharged on 8 Dec 1781. {Ref: Archives of Maryland Vol. 48, p. 10}

ROBERTSON, CHARLES (Prince George's County), private who was drafted into the Maryland Continental Line, was discharged on 8 Dec 1781. {Ref: Archives of Maryland Vol. 48, p. 10}

ROBERTSON, GEORGE (Maryland Navy), surgeon on the State Ship *Defence* in 1777. {Ref: Archives of Maryland Vol. 18, p. 659}

ROBERTSON, WILLIAM (Maryland Navy), captain's clerk on the State Ship *Defence* in 1777. {Ref: Archives of Maryland Vol. 18, p. 659}

ROBINSON, ABRAM (Harford County, Susquehannah Hundred), private who was enrolled 23 Apr 1776 in Militia Company No. 21 under Capt. George Patterson. {Ref: George W. Archer Collection and Revolutionary War File, Historical Society of Harford County Archives}

ROBINSON, JAMES (Harford County), private who was enrolled 10 Mar 1776 in Militia Company No. 18 under Capt. John Jolly. {Ref: George W. Archer Collection and Revolutionary War File, Historical Society of Harford County Archives}

ROBINSON, JOHN (Baltimore County), private, aged 40, labourer, born in England, enlisted 12 Mar 1776 in Capt. John Fulford's Company of Matrosses. {Ref: Maryland Historical Magazine, Vol. 69, No. 1, p. 96}

ROBINSON, SOLOMON (Baltimore Town), patriot and merchant who enrolled in Capt. John Sterrett's Independent Mercantile Company by February, 1777, at which time they were mustered into regular service with the continental army to repress loyalist activities in the Eastern Shore counties of Somerset and Worcester. {Ref: J. Thomas Scharf's *History of Baltimore City and County*, Part I, p. 77}

ROBINSON, THOMAS, see "Richard Goodwin," q.v.

ROBINSON, THOMAS, OF CHRISTOPHER (Anne Arundel County), patriot who took the Oath of Fidelity and Allegiance to the State of Maryland on 31 Mar 1778. {Ref: Archives of Maryland Vol. 16, p. 559}

ROBINSON, WALTER (Harford County), private who was enrolled 10 Mar 1776 in Militia Company No. 18 under Capt. John Jolly. {Ref: George W. Archer Collection and Revolutionary War File, Historical Society of Harford County Archives}

ROBINSON, WILLIAM (Harford County), private who was enrolled 10 Mar 1776 in Militia Company No. 18 under Capt. John Jolly. {Ref: George W. Archer Collection and Revolutionary War File, Historical Society of Harford County Archives}

ROBINSON, WILLIAM (Western Maryland), private in Capt. Michael Cresap's Company in 1775. {Ref: Howard L. Leckey's *The Tenmile Country and Its Pioneer Families*, p. 16}

ROBOSSON, ELIJAH (Anne Arundel County), lieutenant colonel of the Severn Battalion of Militia, commissioned 26 Jan 1777 by the Maryland Council of Safety; died by 20 Jun 1799 (date of distribution), leaving a widow Mary Robosson and children Elijah Robosson, Elizabeth Robosson, and Ann Ghiselin (wife of Dr. Reverdy Ghiselin). {Ref: Archives of Maryland Vol. 16, p. 77; Anne Arundel County Administration Account JG No. 2, p. 55}

RODGERS, JOHN, see "Nathaniel Chew," q.v.

ROGERS, ALEXANDER (Harford County), private who was enrolled by 15 Apr 1776 in Militia Company No. 20 under Capt. Robert Glenn. {Ref: George W. Archer Collection and Revolutionary War File, Historical Society of Harford County Archives}

ROGERS, BENJAMIN (Harford County), private who was enrolled 25 Mar 1776 in Militia Company No. 19 under Capt. William Morgan. {Ref: George W. Archer Collection and Revolutionary War File, Historical Society of Harford County Archives}

ROGERS, JOHN (Maryland Navy), second lieutenant of marines on the State Ship *Defence* in 1777. {Ref: Archives of Maryland Vol. 18, p. 659}

ROGERS, JOHN (Maryland Privateer), commander of the schooner *General Smallwood*, navigated by 10 men and mounting 4 carriage guns, was issued Letters of Marque & Reprisal by the Council of Maryland on 28 Jan 1778; commander of the brigantine *Black Prince*, navigated by 40 men and mounting 12 carriage guns, 4 swivel guns and 18 small arms, was issued Letters of Marque & Reprisal by the Council of Maryland on 13 Mar 1780. {Ref: Archives of Maryland Vol. 16, p. 476 and Vol. 43, p. 109}

ROHR, JOHN (Montgomery County), patriot and possible soldier who was born in 1761 in Frederick County and applied for pension on 21 Dec 1840, aged 79, under the Act of June 7, 1832, but the claim was rejected because his service was *"not under military authority."* {Ref: *Rejected or Suspended Applications for Revolutionary War Pensions* (1850 Report), p. 230; Research by Virgil D. White, citing Federal Pension Application R8934}

ROHR, PHILIP (Frederick County), soldier who served in the Maryland troops and applied for pension under the Act of June 7, 1832, but the claim was rejected because he did not serve six months. {Ref: *Rejected or Suspended Applications for Revolutionary War Pensions* (1850 Report), p. 230; Research by Virgil D. White, citing Federal Pension Application R8936}

ROLLINGS, BENJAMIN (Maryland Navy), sailor or seaman on 7 Jan 1780. {Ref: Calendar of Maryland State Papers, The Brown Books, p. 57}

ROLLINS, ELIAS (Charles County), private who was drafted to serve in the Maryland Continental Line until 10 Dec 1781, but *"being represented unfit for the duty for which he was intended"* was discharged on 30 Oct 1781. {Ref: Archives of Maryland Vol. 45, p. 656}

ROLLINS, ISAAC (Baltimore County), private who enlisted in Pulaski's Legion on 28 Mar 1778 and still in service in November, 1779. {Ref: Maryland Historical Magazine, Vol. 13, No. 3, p. 223}

ROLPH, WILLIAM (Baltimore County), private who enlisted in Pulaski's Legion on 22 Apr 1778 in Baltimore. {Ref: Maryland Historical Magazine, Vol. 13, No. 3, p. 222}

ROLSTON, ALEXANDER (Harford County), private who was enrolled 25 Mar 1776 in Militia Company No. 19 under Capt. William Morgan. {Ref: George W. Archer Collection and Revolutionary War File, Historical Society of Harford County Archives}

ROOT, ANN, see "Daniel Root," q.v.

ROOT, DANIEL (Harford County), second lieutenant in Militia Company No. 19 under Capt. William Morgan on 25 Mar 1776; second lieutenant, Deer Creek Battalion, on 9 Apr 1778, who reportedly *"left State"* but he actually moved to Frederick County; Daniel was born in 1750 (aged 26 in 1776), a son of Daniel and Ann Root who resided on Deer Creek in Baltimore (now Harford) County by 1755; he lived in Susquehanna Hundred in 1774 and served in the militia as noted above; Daniel Root, Jr. moved to Frederick County by 1781 at which time his name appeared in a court record regarding a business fee; Daniel Root, Sr. followed circa 1785 at which time his name had appeared on a return of collections made by John Taylor, former sheriff, for the Rev. Mr. William West in Harford County (he was assessed and/or paid 4 shillings); Daniel, Sr. died testate in 1808 and Daniel, Jr. died in 1813; Elizabeth Root was administratrix of the latter estate and she apparently died soon thereafter because a local newspaper reported the following on 26 Apr 1817: *"Notice is given to Jane Richards and Sarah Davis of payment on legacies left them by their deceased father Daniel Root, Sr., of Frederick County, and George Fox, administrator de bonis non of Daniel Root, Jr., who was executor of said Daniel Root, Sr."* Their descendants settled in Clay and Laurel Counties, Kentucky. {Ref: George W. Archer Collection in the Historical Society of Harford County Archives, and Court Records File 8.0A(F); 1776 Census of Harford County; Henry C. Peden, Jr.'s *Early Harford Countians*, p. 405; Margaret R. Hodges' *Unpublished Revolutionary Records of Maryland*, Vol. 1, pp. 34, 44; *Frederick-Town Herald*, 6 Feb 1813 and 26 Apr 1817; Research by Ruth Hale Freitag of San Marino, California (a direct descendant) in 2001}

ROOT, ELIZABETH, see "Daniel Root," q.v.

ROOT, JAMES (Harford County), private who was enrolled 25 Mar 1776 in Militia Company No. 19 under Capt. William Morgan; born circa 1760 (aged about 15 or 16 in 1776) and a brother of "Daniel Root," q.v. {Ref: George W. Archer Collection and Revolutionary War File, Historical Society of Harford County Archives; 1776 Census of Harford County}

ROOT, JOHN (Harford County), private who was enrolled 25 Mar 1776 in Militia Company No. 19 under Capt. William Morgan; born circa 1757 (aged about 19 in 1776) and a brother of "Daniel Root," q.v. {Ref: George W. Archer Collection and Revolutionary War File, Historical Society of Harford County Archives; 1776 Census}

ROSE, JOSEPH (Dorchester County), private (substitute) in the Maryland Continental Line by 1781, was discharged on 10 Dec 1781. {Ref: Archives of Maryland Vol. 48, p. 17}

ROSE, TAVENOR (Western Maryland), private in Capt. Michael Cresap's Company in 1775. {Ref: Howard L. Leckey's *The Tenmile Country and Its Pioneer Families*, p. 16}

ROSS, CATHERINE, see "John E. Howard," q.v.

ROSS, GEORGE (Maryland Navy), first lieutenant of marines on the State Ship *Defence* in 1777. {Ref: Archives of Maryland Vol. 18, p. 659}

ROSS, GEORGE (Queen Anne's County), private (substitute) in the Maryland Continental Line by 1781, was discharged on 8 Dec 1781. {Ref: Archives of Maryland Vol. 48, p. 10}

ROSS, JOHN (Baltimore Town), patriot and merchant who enrolled in Capt. John Sterrett's Independent Mercantile Company by February, 1777, at which time they were mustered into regular service with the continental army to repress loyalist activities in the Eastern Shore counties of Somerset and Worcester. {Ref: J. Thomas Scharf's *History of Baltimore City and County*, Part I, p. 77}

ROSS, JOHN (Baltimore County), doctor and surgeon's mate in the 4th Maryland Continental Line and stationed at Camp Buttermilk Falls on 13 Oct 1779; received payment for his services to the Maryland Regiment in the amount of "1900 Dollars & £3.10s" on 12 Sep 1780. {Ref: Maryland State Archives Record MdHR 6636-15-75; Archives of Maryland Vol. 45, p. 98}

ROSS, LEVIN (Dorchester County), private (substitute) in the Maryland Continental Line by 1781, was discharged on 8 Dec 1781. {Ref: Archives of Maryland Vol. 48, p. 10}

ROSS, NATHAN (Maryland Navy), seaman or marine on the State Ship *Defence* in 1777. {Ref: Archives of Maryland Vol. 18, p. 659}

ROSS, NATHANIEL (Maryland Privateer), captain of the schooner *Planters Friend* which was impressed into service by order of the Council of Maryland on 27 Apr 1780 *"to go to the Head of Elk for the Purpose of Transporting a Detachment of the American Army to the State of Virginia."* {Ref: Archives of Maryland Vol. 43, p. 155}

ROWE, JOHN (Maryland Navy), seaman or marine on the State Ship *Defence* in 1777. {Ref: Archives of Maryland Vol. 18, p. 659}

ROWEN, GEORGE (Maryland Navy), master at arms on the State Ship *Defence* in 1777. {Ref: Archives of Maryland Vol. 18, p. 659}

ROWNS, JAMES (Maryland Navy), midshipman on the State Ship *Defence* in 1777. {Ref: Archives of Maryland Vol. 18, p. 659}

ROWNTREE, THOMAS (Harford County), private who was enrolled 25 Mar 1776 in Militia Company No. 19 under Capt. William Morgan. {Ref: George W. Archer Collection and Revolutionary War File, Historical Society of Harford County Archives}

ROXBURGH, ALEXANDER (Frederick County?), major in the 4th and 7th Maryland Continental Line received payment for his services in the amount of "1900 Dollars & £3.10s" on 12 Sep 1780. {Ref: Archives of Maryland Vol. 45, p. 98}

RUDOLPH, JOHN (Cecil County), captain, Maryland Continental Line, Staff Officer, Lee's Regiment, who received payment for his services in the amount of "1900 Dollars & £3.10s" on 12 Sep 1780. {Ref: Archives of Maryland Vol. 18, p. 586, and Vol. 45, p. 98}

RUDOLPH, MICHAEL (Cecil County), captain, Maryland Continental Line, Staff Officer, Lee's Regiment, who received payment for his services in the amount of "1900 Dollars & £3.10s" on 12 Sep 1780; see "James McCracken," q.v. {Ref: Archives of Maryland Vol. 18, p. 587, and Vol. 45, p. 98}

RUMMAGE, DAVID (Harford County), private who was enrolled 10 Mar 1776 in Militia Company No. 18 under Capt. John Jolly. {Ref: George W. Archer Collection and Revolutionary War File, Historical Society of Harford County Archives}

RUMSEY, CHARLOTTE, see "John B. Howard," q.v.

RUMSEY, WILLIAM (Cecil County), patriot who was appointed by the Council of Maryland on 27 Jan 1776 as one of three persons in Cecil County to collect all gold and silver coin that can be procured in said county. {Ref: Archives of Maryland Vol. 11, p. 132}

RUSSELL, ELIZABETH, see "Thomas Johnson, Jr.," q.v.

RUSSELL, J. (Baltimore Town), patriot and merchant who enrolled in Capt. John Sterrett's Independent Mercantile Company by February, 1777, at which time they were mustered into regular service with the continental army to repress loyalist activities in the Eastern Shore counties of Somerset and Worcester. {Ref: J. Thomas Scharf's *History of Baltimore City and County*, Part I, p. 77}

RUSSELL, JOHN (Washington County), private who was drafted to serve in the Maryland Continental Line until 10 Dec 1781, but *"being represented unfit for the duty for which he was intended"* was discharged on 30 Oct 1781. {Ref: Archives of Maryland Vol. 45, p. 656}

RUSSELL, THOMAS (Harford County), private who was enrolled by 15 Apr 1776 in Militia Company No. 20 under Capt. Robert Glenn. {Ref: George W. Archer Collection and Revolutionary War File, Historical Society of Harford County Archives}

RUSSELL (RUSSEL), THOMAS (Baltimore County), lieutenant in a Troop of Light Horse, commissioned on 26 Jul 1780; see "Nicholas R. Moore," q.v. {Ref: Archives of Maryland Vol. 43, p. 233}

RUTH, JOSEPH (Harford County, Susquehannah Hundred), private who was enrolled 23 Apr 1776 in Militia Company No. 21 under Capt. George Patterson. {Ref: George W. Archer Collection and Revolutionary War File, Historical Society of Harford County Archives}

RUTLEDGE, JOSHUA (Harford County), ensign and later lieutenant in the 4th Maryland Continental Line who received payment for his services in the amount of "1900 Dollars & £3.10s" on 12 Sep 1780; he became an original member of the Society of the Cincinnati in 1783. For additional information see Peden's *Revolutionary Patriots of Harford County, 1775-1783* (p. 197). {Ref: Archives of Maryland Vol. 45, p. 98}

RUTTER, JOHN (Baltimore Town), patriot and merchant who enrolled in Capt. John Sterrett's Independent Mercantile Company by February, 1777, at which time they were mustered into regular service with the continental army to repress loyalist activities in the Eastern Shore counties of Somerset and Worcester. {Ref: J. Thomas Scharf's *History of Baltimore City and County*, Part I, p. 77}

RUTTER, RICHARD (Harford County, Susquehannah Hundred), private who was enrolled 23 Apr 1776 in Militia Company No. 21 under Capt. George Patterson. {Ref: George W. Archer Collection and Revolutionary War File, Historical Society of Harford County Archives}

RYLAND, NICHOLAS (Baltimore County), private who enlisted in Pulaski's Legion on 8 May 1778 in Baltimore. {Ref: Maryland Historical Magazine, Vol. 13, No. 3, p. 222}

SACK, JOSEPH (Baltimore or Frederick County), trumpeter, enlisted in Pulaski's Legion on 20 Mar 1778. {Ref: Maryland Historical Magazine, Vol. 13, No. 3, p. 224}

SADLER, SAMUEL (Baltimore County), patriot who was appointed a Recruiting Sergeant for the Artillery Service on 8 May 1777. {Ref: Archives of Maryland Vol. 16, p. 243}

SADLER, THOMAS (Prince George's County), private who was drafted into the Maryland Continental Line, was discharged on 8 Dec 1781. {Ref: Archives of Maryland Vol. 48, p. 10}

SALLIDAY, JOHN M. (Western Maryland), private in Capt. Michael Cresap's Company in 1775. {Ref: Howard L. Leckey's *The Tenmile Country and Its Pioneer Families*, p. 16}

SALMON, EDWARD (Frederick County), captain and patriot buried in Mount Olivet Cemetery. {Ref: Information compiled by Dr. Donald Wolf in Maryland Society SAR Newsletter circa 1996}

SALMON, GEORGE, see "Daniel Smith," q.v.

SAMINE, ---- (Anne Arundel County?), soldier in the Maryland Continental Line *"now remaining in Annapolis"* on 24 Jul 1780 at which time his wife Mary

Samine was entitled to rations under the laws of the State. {Ref: Archives of Maryland Vol. 43, p. 227}

SAMPSON, JOHN (Harford County), private who was reportedly a deserter enrolled (or captured and re-enrolled) by Capt. Praul for the Regiment Extraordinary and sent to Annapolis with Capt. Thompson on board the sloop *Liberty* on 17 Aug 1780. {Ref: Archives of Maryland Vol. 45, p. 50}

SAMUEL, MASHACK (Baltimore County), private, aged 29, chairmaker, born in Pennsylvania, enlisted 19 Feb 1776 in Capt. John Fulford's Company of Matrosses. {Ref: Maryland Historical Magazine, Vol. 69, No. 1, p. 95}

SANDERS, JOHN, see "William Sanders," q.v.

SANDERS, THOMAS (Baltimore Privateer), commander of the brigantine *Queen of France*, navigated by 40 men and mounting 12 carriage guns, 6 swivel guns and 24 small arms, was issued Letters of Marque & Reprisal by the Council of Maryland on 25 Oct 1779. {Ref: Archives of Maryland Vol. 21, p. 566}

SANDERS, VINCENT, see "Henry Young," q.v.

SANDERS, WILLIAM (Anne Arundel County), quartermaster for the West River Battalion of Militia by 26 Apr 1781 at which time he received provisions from the Commissary of Stores; one William Sanders died by 8 Feb 1804 (date of distribution), leaving a widow Elizabeth Gassaway Sanders (now wife of Richard Contee), and sons William and John Sanders. {Ref: Archives of Maryland Vol. 45, p. 416; Anne Arundel County Administration Account JG No. 2, p. 61}

SANDSBERY, JOHN (Maryland Navy), sailor or seaman on 7 Jan 1780. {Ref: Calendar of Maryland State Papers, The Brown Books, p. 57}

SANFORD, JOHN (Maryland Privateer), commander of the schooner *St. Patrick*, navigated by 18 men and mounting 6 carriage guns, was issued Letters of Marque & Reprisal by the Council of Maryland on 12 Mar 1781. {Ref: Archives of Maryland Vol. 45, p. 349}

SAPPINGTON, FRANCIS BROWN (Frederick County), doctor and patriot buried in Mount Olivet Cemetery. {Ref: Information compiled by Dr. Donald Wolf in Maryland Society SAR Newsletter circa 1996}

SAPPINGTON, HARTLEY (Cecil County), private who was enrolled to serve as a substitute in the Maryland Continental Line until 10 Dec 1781, but *"being represented unfit for the service for which he was intended"* was discharged on 30 Oct 1781. {Ref: Archives of Maryland Vol. 45, p. 657}

SAPPINGTON, RICHARD (Harford County), doctor and surgeon's assistant in the 3rd Maryland Regiment in 1777; issued clothing by the Commissary of Stores on 25 Jun 1778; appointed surgeon in August, 1780 and served until 1782; born 27 Sep 1755 in Anne Arundel County, married first to Margaret Hamilton and second to Cassandra Frances Durbin, and died 18 Apr 1828 in Harford County; his children were: William Sappington; Gerard Sappington; Robert Sappington; Mary Sappington; John K. Sappington (born 1791, married Rebecca Neeper);

Edward Sappington; Thomas Sappington; Frederick Sappington; and, John Sappington (born 1801, married first to Lavinia Bagley and second to Mary O'Neill). {Ref: Archives of Maryland Vol. 21, p. 150; Maryland State Society, DAR Directory, 1892-1965, pp. 628-629}

SAUNDERS, PHILLIP (Western Maryland), private in Capt. Michael Cresap's Company in 1775. {Ref: Howard L. Leckey's *The Tenmile Country and Its Pioneer Families*, p. 16}

SCARBOROUGH, JOSEPH (Harford County), private who was enrolled 25 Mar 1776 in Militia Company No. 19 under Capt. William Morgan. {Ref: George W. Archer Collection and Revolutionary War File, Historical Society of Harford County Archives}

SCARBOROUGH, WILLIAM (Harford County), private who was enrolled 25 Mar 1776 in Militia Company No. 19 under Capt. William Morgan. {Ref: George W. Archer Collection and Revolutionary War File, Historical Society of Harford County Archives}

SCARFF, HENRY, see "James Kidd," q.v.

SCARFF, SARAH, see "James Kidd," q.v.

SCHLEY, FREDERICK, see "David Lynn," q.v.

SCHLEY, JACOB (Frederick County), contractor for State Arms in Frederick County in 1781. *"Capt. George Jacob Schley died 27 May 1811, after a long and painful illness, in his 72nd year."* {Ref: Archives of Maryland Vol. 47, p. 14; *Frederick-Town Herald*, 1 Jun 1811}

SCHNEBLY, HENRY (Washington County), doctor and officer in the revolution, died 24 Jul 1805, aged 77: *"Dr. Schnebly was prominent during the Revolution and was one of the most highly respected citizens in the county."* {Ref: J. Thomas Scharf's *History of Western Maryland*, Vol. II, p. 1055}

SCHRADER, JACOB (Frederick County), soldier who allegedly served in the Maryland or Pennsylvania Line and applied for pension under the Act of June 7, 1832, but the claim was suspended *"pending further action awaited for the completion of the papers"* (which was never done and no papers had been received in the pension office by 1849). {Ref: *Rejected or Suspended Applications for Revolutionary War Pensions* (1850 Report), p. 232; Research by Virgil D. White, citing Federal Pension Application R9271}

SCHUELER, JAMES (Queen Anne's County), private (substitute) in the Maryland Continental Line by 1781, was discharged on 8 Dec 1781. {Ref: Archives of Maryland Vol. 48, p. 11}

SCHULTZE, CATHARINE, see "William Clemm," q.v.

SCONE, CHARLES (Maryland Navy), seaman or marine on the State Ship *Defence* in 1777. {Ref: Archives of Maryland Vol. 18, p. 659}

SCOTT, ANDREW (Harford County), private who was enrolled 25 Mar 1776 in Militia Company No. 19 under Capt. William Morgan. {Ref: George W. Archer Collection and Revolutionary War File, Historical Society of Harford County Archives}

SCOTT, BENJAMIN (Harford County), first lieutenant, commissioned 28 Apr 1776 in Militia Company No. 23 under Capt. James McComas. {Ref: George W. Archer Collection and Revolutionary War File, Historical Society of Harford County Archives}

SCOTT, CHARLES (Charles County), private in the 1st Maryland Continental Line by 29 Nov 1779 at which time he was issued clothing due him; private in the 2nd Maryland Continental Line by 31 Jan 1780 at which time he was issued clothing *"due him from the Continent."* {Ref: Archives of Maryland Vol. 43, pp. 25, 74}

SCOTT, JAMES (Maryland Navy), sailor or seaman on 7 Jan 1780. {Ref: Calendar of Maryland State Papers, The Brown Books, p. 57}

SCOTT, JAMES (Harford County), private who was enrolled by Capt. Praul in the Regiment Extraordinary and sent to Annapolis with Capt. Thompson on board the sloop *Liberty* on 17 Aug 1780. {Ref: Archives of Maryland Vol. 45, p. 50}

SCOTT, JAMES (Harford County), private who was enrolled 9 Dec 1775 in Militia Company No. 14 under Capt. William McComas. {Ref: George W. Archer Collection and Revolutionary War File, Historical Society of Harford County Archives}

SCOTT, MOSES (Baltimore County), marine on the State Ship *Defence* in 1777. {Ref: Archives of Maryland Vol. 18, p. 659, which misspelled his name as "Mores Scott"}

SCOTT, PETER (Harford County), private who was enrolled by Capt. Praul in the Regiment Extraordinary and sent to Annapolis with Capt. Thompson on board the sloop *Liberty* on 17 Aug 1780. {Ref: Archives of Maryland Vol. 45, p. 50}

SCOTT, ROBERT (Cecil County), private who was enrolled to serve as a substitute in the Maryland Continental Line until 10 Dec 1781, but *"being represented unfit for the service for which he was intended"* was discharged on 30 Oct 1781. {Ref: Archives of Maryland Vol. 45, p. 657}

SCOTT, SAMUEL (Queen Anne's County), private (substitute) in the Maryland Continental Line by 1781, was discharged on 8 Dec 1781. {Ref: Archives of Maryland Vol. 48, p. 10}

SCOTT, THOMAS (Western Maryland), private in Capt. Michael Cresap's Company in 1775. {Ref: Howard L. Leckey's *The Tenmile Country and Its Pioneer Families*, p. 16}

SCOTT, WILLIAM (Montgomery County), private (substitute) in the Maryland Continental Line by 1781, was discharged on 8 Dec 1781. {Ref: Archives of Maryland Vol. 48, p. 11}

SEABROOK, RICHARD (Frederick County), private who was drafted to serve in the Maryland Continental Line until 10 Dec 1781, but *"being represented unfit for the duty for which he was intended"* was discharged on 30 Oct 1781. {Ref: Archives of Maryland Vol. 45, p. 656}

SEAGRAVE, PATRICK (Maryland Navy), seaman or marine on the State Ship *Defence* in 1777. {Ref: Archives of Maryland Vol. 18, p. 659}

SEARLES, DANIEL (Anne Arundel County), private by 5 Oct 1776 in Capt. Richard Chew's Militia Company, Weems' Battalion. {Ref: Archives of Maryland Vol. 12, p. 323}

SEARS, GEORGE (Baltimore Town), patriot and merchant who enrolled in Capt. John Sterrett's Independent Mercantile Company by February, 1777, at which time they were mustered into regular service with the continental army to

repress loyalist activities in the Eastern Shore counties of Somerset and Worcester. {Ref: J. Thomas Scharf's *History of Baltimore City and County*, Part I, p. 77}

SEARS, JOHN (Anne Arundel County), ensign in the 2nd Maryland Continental Line who received payment for his services in the amount of "1900 Dollars & £3.10s" on 12 Sep 1780. {Ref: Archives of Maryland Vol. 45, p. 97}

SEBREE, SPENCER (Baltimore County), private, aged 26, tailor, born in Virginia, enlisted 25 Aug 1776 in Capt. John Fulford's Company of Matrosses. {Ref: Maryland Historical Magazine, Vol. 69, No. 1, p. 96}

SEEA, JOHN (Maryland Navy), marine on the State Ship *Defence* in 1777. {Ref: Archives of Maryland Vol. 18, p. 659}

SELBY, JOHN (Worcester County), patriot who was commissioned one of the three persons in Worcester County by the Council of Maryland on 19 Aug 1779 to receive subscriptions for use of the State. {Ref: Archives of Maryland Vol. 21, p. 499}

SELBY, JOSEPH (Worcester County), patriot who contracted with the Council of Safety on 24 Sep 1776 to make 2,000 cartouch boxes, bayonet belts, and gun slings. {Ref: Archives of Maryland Vol. 12, p. 297}

SELLMAN, JOHN, see "William Fisher," q.v.

SELLMAN (SELMAN), JOHN (Prince George's County), private who was drafted into the Maryland Continental Line, was discharged on 8 Dec 1781. {Ref: Archives of Maryland Vol. 48, p. 10}

SELLMAN (SELMAN), JONATHAN (Anne Arundel County), captain in the 4th Maryland Continental Line who received payment for his services in the amount of "1900 Dollars & £3.10s" on 12 Sep 1780. {Ref: Archives of Maryland Vol. 45, p. 98}

SELLMAN, THOMAS (Maryland Navy), marine on the sloop *Lincoln* who was taken prisoner and confined in New York before 17 Jan 1781 and was subsequently exchanged. {Ref: Archives of Maryland Vol. 45, p. 277}

SELLS, ANTHONY (Western Maryland), private in Capt. Michael Cresap's Company in 1775. {Ref: Howard L. Leckey's *The Tenmile Country and Its Pioneer Families*, p. 16}

SENEY, JOHN (Queen Anne's County), lieutenant colonel of the 5th Battalion of Militia, commissioned 8 May 1777. {Ref: Archives of Maryland Vol. 16, p. 243}

SENEY (SENCY?), WILLIAM (Maryland Navy), seaman or marine on the State Ship *Defence* in 1777. {Ref: Archives of Maryland Vol. 18, p. 659}

SEPT, WILLIAM (Baltimore or Frederick County), corporal in Pulaski's Legion before July, 1782. {Ref: Maryland Historical Magazine, Vol. 13, No. 3, p. 225}

SERMON, LEONARD (Maryland Navy), seaman or marine on the State Ship *Defence* in 1777. {Ref: Archives of Maryland Vol. 18, p. 659}

SETH, WILLIAM (Baltimore County), private who enlisted in Pulaski's Legion in 1778; sergeant, discharged 15 Nov 1783. {Ref: Maryland Historical Magazine, Vol. 13, No. 3, p. 223}

SHAFFER, JOHN, see "Frederick Kemp," q.v.

SHARPE, ELIZA (Anne Arundel County), patriot who was paid 40 shillings by the Maryland Council of Safety for attending hospital on 5 Oct 1776. {Ref: Archives of Maryland Vol. 12, p. 321}

SHARPE (SHARP), PETER (Maryland Navy and Baltimore Privateer), midshipman on the State Ship *Defence* in 1777; commander of the schooner *Luzerne*, navigated by 17 men and mounting 6 carriage guns, was issued Letters of Marque & Reprisal by the Council of Maryland on 11 Sep 1780. {Ref: Archives of Maryland Vol. 18, p. 659 and Vol. 43, p. 285}

SHAVER, GEORGE (Frederick and Washington Counties), private who was enrolled to serve as a substitute in the Maryland Continental Line until 10 Dec 1781, but *"being represented unfit for the service for which he was intended"* was discharged on 30 Oct 1781. {Ref: Archives of Maryland Vol. 45, p. 657}

SHAVER, PETER (Frederick and Washington Counties), private in the 7th Maryland Continental Line who was a 9 month soldier in the 7th Maryland Regiment in 1778-1779, was discharged on 12 Aug 1779 and received £26 in clothing. {Ref: Archives of Maryland Vol. 21, p. 491}

SHAW, JOHN (Baltimore County), private who enlisted in Pulaski's Legion on 22 Mar 1778 and still in service in November, 1779. {Ref: Maryland Historical Magazine, Vol. 13, No. 3, p. 223}

SHEAN, JAMES (Frederick County), private in the 2nd Maryland Continental Line by 1 Dec 1781 at which time he was on duty guarding the magazine at the Head of Severn River. {Ref: Archives of Maryland Vol. 18, p. 630, and Vol. 48, p. 8}

SHEAN, PATRICK (Frederick County), private (substitute) in the Maryland Continental Line, Williams' Regiment, enrolled in May, 1778 for 3 years or duration of the war. {Ref: Maryland Historical Magazine, Vol. 6, No. 3, p. 260}

SHEE, JOHN (Frederick County), private who enlisted in Pulaski's Legion on 1 Jul 1779. {Ref: Maryland Historical Magazine, Vol. 13, No. 3, p. 224}

SHELLMAN, JACOB (Frederick County), patriot who loaned money to the State in 1780; buried in Mount Olivet Cemetery. {Ref: Archives of Maryland Vol. 43, p. 520; Burial information compiled by Dr. Donald Wolf in Maryland Society SAR Newsletter circa 1996}

SHELMERDINE, STEPHEN (Baltimore County), first lieutenant in the Baltimore Town Battalion of Militia, commissioned 12 Apr 1781. {Ref: Archives of Maryland Vol. 45, p. 393}

SHELLMIRE, ---- (Frederick or Baltimore County?), soldier in the 4th Maryland Continental Line by 15 Aug 1780 at which time his wife Mary Shelmire or Shellmire was entitled to *"one ration per day until further orders"* from the Issuing Commissary. {Ref: Archives of Maryland Vol. 43, p. 255; Maryland State Archives Record MdHR 4598-89}

SHENCK, JACOB (Frederick and Carroll Counties), soldier who allegedly served in the Maryland troops; his widow Magdalena Shenck applied for pension under the Act of July 4, 1836, but the claim was suspended and requiring *"each tour to be specified as to period, length, grade, localities and commanding officers."* {Ref: *Rejected or Suspended Applications for Revolutionary War Pensions* (1850 Report), p. 234}

SHEPARD, FRANCIS (Southern Maryland), lieutenant, commissioned on 27 Jul 1780 to serve in the Regiment Extra by order of the Council of Maryland. {Ref: Archives of Maryland Vol. 43, p. 234}

SHEPHERD, JOHN (Talbot County), private (substitute) in the Maryland Continental Line by 1781, was discharged on 8 Dec 1781. {Ref: Archives of Maryland Vol. 48, p. 11}

SHEPPERD, CAPTAIN, see "William Simmons," q.v.

SHERIDAN, BEN W. (Baltimore County), private, aged 25, barber, born in Ireland, enlisted 26 Feb 1776 in Capt. John Fulford's Company of Matrosses. {Ref: Maryland Historical Magazine, Vol. 69, No. 1, p. 95}

SHERWOOD, HUGH (Maryland Privateer), commander of the schooner *Oxford*, navigated by 10 men and mounting 6 carriage guns and 6 small arms, was issued Letters of Marque & Reprisal by the Council of Maryland on 23 May 1780. {Ref: Archives of Maryland Vol. 43, p. 180}

SHIELDS, MARTIN (Maryland Navy), marine on the sloop *Lincoln* who was taken prisoner and confined in New York before 17 Jan 1781 and was subsequently exchanged. {Ref: Archives of Maryland Vol. 45, p. 277}

SHINE, ADAM (Frederick County), private in the Maryland Continental Line who was drafted to serve until 10 Dec 1781, was discharged on 29 Nov 1781. {Ref: Archives of Maryland Vol. 48, p. 7}

SHIPLEY, ROBERT (Baltimore County), private, aged 18, farmer, born in Maryland, enlisted 3 Nov 1776 in Capt. John Fulford's Company of Matrosses. {Ref: Maryland Historical Magazine, Vol. 69, No. 1, p. 97}

SHIRCLIFF, WILLIAM (Prince George's County), ensign in Capt. Hezekiah Wheeler's Company of Select Militia, commissioned 8 Jun 1781. {Ref: Archives of Maryland Vol. 45, p. 466}

SHIVELY, JOHN (Frederick County), private (substitute) in the Maryland Continental Line, Williams' Regiment, enrolled in May, 1778 for 3 years or duration of the war. {Ref: Maryland Historical Magazine, Vol. 6, No. 3, p. 258}

SHOAN (SHEAN?), JAMES (Frederick County?), private in the 2nd Maryland Continental Line by 9 Apr 1781 at which time he was issued clothing by the Commissary of Stores. {Ref: Archives of Maryland Vol. 18, p. 630, and Vol. 45, p. 384}

SHOCKLEY, JONATHAN (Worcester County), private (substitute) in the Maryland Continental Line by 1781, was discharged on 8 Dec 1781. {Ref: Archives of Maryland Vol. 48, p. 11}

SHOEMAKER, JACOB (Frederick County), lieutenant in the 4th Maryland Continental Line who received payment for his services in the amount of "1900 Dollars & £3.10s" on 12 Sep 1780. {Ref: Archives of Maryland Vol. 45, p. 98}

SHOEMAKER, GIDEON (Anne Arundel County), private by 5 Oct 1776 in Capt. Richard Chew's Militia Company, Weems' Battalion. {Ref: Archives of Maryland Vol. 12, p. 322}

SHOEMAKER, PETER (Frederick County), private (substitute) in the Maryland Continental Line, Gunby's Regiment, enrolled in May, 1778 for 3 years or duration of the war. {Ref: Maryland Historical Magazine, Vol. 6, No. 3, p. 260}

SHORES, RICHARD (Harford County), private who was enrolled 10 Mar 1776 in Militia Company No. 18 under Capt. John Jolly. {Ref: George W. Archer Collection and Revolutionary War File, Historical Society of Harford County Archives}

SHORT, CHRISTOPHER (Maryland Navy), sailor on the State Ship *Defence* in 1777. {Ref: Archives of Maryland Vol. 18, p. 659}

SHOVER, PHILLIP (Western Maryland), private in Capt. Michael Cresap's Company in 1775. {Ref: Howard L. Leckey's *The Tenmile Country and Its Pioneer Families*, p. 16}

SHROYER, CATHARINE, see "Leonard Backenbaugh," q.v.

SHRYOCK, HENRY (Frederick and Washington Counties), officer and patriot who supplied provisions to the State of Maryland between June and September, 1780, and *"in politics he was a follower of Washington and after the revolution he settled in Hagerstown; though at one time rich, he died poor"* on 19 May 1814. *"Col. Henry Shryock, late of Washington County, Maryland, aged 78, died at his residence in Shendandoah County, Virginia after an illness of about 3 weeks; he served as a soldier in the wars preceding the revolution and was high sheriff of Washington County."* {Ref: Archives of Maryland Vol. 45, p. 84; F. Edward Wright's *Newspaper Abstracts of Frederick County, 1811-1815*, p. 144, citing *Bartgis's Republican Gazette*, 18 Jun 1814; J. Thomas Scharf's *History of Western Maryland*, Vol. II, p. 1054}

SHULER, ANDREW (Frederick County), private (substitute) in the Maryland Continental Line, German Regiment, enrolled in May, 1778 for 3 years or duration of the war. {Ref: Maryland Historical Magazine, Vol. 6, No. 3, p. 259}

SHULL, AMELIA, see "Daniel Smith," q.v.

SHUTTLEWORTH, JOHN (Annapolis), patriot and doctor in 1783 *"who hath lately arrived in this State from Great Britain, but last from New York, appeared before the Governor and Council and before them did make, repeat and Subscribe a Declaration of his Belief in the Christian Religion and took, repeated and Subscribed to the Oath of Fidelity and Support to this State directed by the Act to punish certain Crimes and Misdemeanors and to prevent the growth of Toryism and also the Oath directed to be taken in the Act for Naturalization ----"* on 4 Apr 1783. {Ref: Archives of Maryland Vol. 48, p. 394}

SHY, JOHN (Baltimore County), matross soldier by 7 May 1779 at which time he gave a deposition about his enlistment terms. {Ref: Maryland State Archives Record MdHR 6636-14-83}

SILVER, BENJAMIN (Harford County, Susquehannah Hundred), private who was enrolled 23 Apr 1776 in Militia Company No. 21 under Capt. George Patterson. {Ref: George W. Archer Collection and Revolutionary War File, Historical Society of Harford County Archives}

SILVER, WILLIAM (Harford County, Susquehannah Hundred), private who was enrolled 23 Apr 1776 in Militia Company No. 21 under Capt. George Patterson. {Ref: George W. Archer Collection and Revolutionary War File, Historical Society of Harford County Archives}

SIMMON, JOHN (Calvert County), private who was drafted to serve in the Maryland Continental Line until 10 Dec 1781, but *"being represented unfit for the duty for which he was intended"* was discharged on 30 Oct 1781. {Ref: Archives of Maryland Vol. 45, p. 656}

SIMMONS, THOMAS (Maryland or Virginia Privateer), captain of the brigantine *Ranger*, navigated by 20 men and mounting 7 carriage guns, which *"was attacked off St. Mary's near the mouth of the Potomac River on 5 Jul 1782 by two refugee barges commanded by Anderson and Barrett, with 30 men each, and after an obstinate engagement for 3 glasses, the latter was obliged to steer off with the loss of 15 men killed and 34 wounded, and the barges rowed off to St. George's Island with their mangled crew, where they buried two and left two others mortally wounded; Capt. Simmons was wounded in the leg and his second lieutenant in both arms, plus one private wounded and one killed; nothing could exceed the bravery of the captain and crew, having 3 men to 1 opposing, and the night being dark, the barges could not be discovered until they were nearly alongside, which gave them but a moment's warning; the brig returned to Alexandria on the 8th instant, having no surgeon on board."* {Ref: *Maryland Gazette*, 18 Jul 1782}

SIMMONS, WILLIAM (Harford County), private who was enrolled 10 Mar 1776 in Militia Company No. 18 under Capt. John Jolly; see "Jesse Dungan," q.v. {Ref: George W. Archer Collection and Revolutionary War File, Historical Society of Harford County Archives}

SIMMONS, WILLIAM (Kent and Harford Counties), soldier in the Maryland Continental Line who was living in Harford County on 28 Aug 1820 at which time documents were filed in Harford County Court stating, in part: *"William Simmons, aged 61 years, resident in Harford County ... does on his oath declare that he served in the Revolutionary War, as follows: That he was enlisted at Chester Town on the Eastern Shore of the State of Maryland by Col. Richard Boardly, first mustered under Capt. John Hawkins, ordered to Annapolis under Captain Shepperd, from thence sent on an expedition to Philadelphia with horses, returned to Annapolis, joined the 2nd Regiment Maryland Continental Line in Capt. Woolford Gray's Company, in which company and regiment continued to serve the U. States on the Continental Establishment to the end of the War when he was honorably discharged at*

Frederick Town in said State as will appear by reference to his Certificate of Discharge bearing date October --, 1783. That he hath been placed on the Revolutionary Pension List of the Maryland Agency as will more fully appear by his pension certificate bearing date the 9th of July 1818 and numbered on the back ---- [blank]. And I do solemnly swear that I was a resident citizen of the United States on the 18th March 1818 and that I have not since that time by gift, sale or in any manner disposed of my property or any part thereof with intent thereby so as to diminish it as to bring myself within the provision of an Act of Congress entitled An Act to provide for certain persons engaged in the land and naval service of the United States in the Revolutionary War passed on the 18th day of March 1818 and that I have not, nor has any person in trust for me, any property or securities, contracts or debts due me nor have I any income other than what is contained in the schedule hereto annexed and by me subscribed. Schedule referred to within, viz: That his property consists of one cow and yearling valued at $15, four shoats or pigs $10, one small plough, hoes, axe, etc. $5, half a dozen old rush bottom chairs $2, one pine table and one mahogany breakfast table, both old, $5, two iron pots, kettle, water bucket, baker, old andirons, etc. $5, some trifle of crockery ware, knives and forks, etc. $5; [total] $47. Applicant hath also purchased an old mare for which he hath promised to pay $20, also an old horse cart worth about $10, but neither of them being paid for does not conceive it to be correct from him to return them. That he hath no trade, rents about ten acres of poor land, for which he pays $50 per annum, by the cultivation of which and the pension he receives for his Revolutionary Services he makes out to live in a very frugal way. That his family consists of his wife named Elizabeth upwards of 30 years of age, son Joseph 10 years, James 7 years, and John 2 years of age, and were it not for the assistance of his pension aforesaid it would not be in his power to support himself except by private or public charity, as he is greatly afflicted with rheumatic pains, etc." Signed: William Simmons (made his "X" mark). {Ref: Historical Society of Harford County, Court Records File 25.14}

SIMPSON, BENJAMIN (Maryland Navy), boatswain's mate on the State Ship *Defence* in 1777. {Ref: Archives of Maryland Vol. 18, p. 659}

SIMPSON, GREENBERRY (Anne Arundel County), soldier who stated that *"he was drafted in the 47th Class under the Act to procure Recruits passed October sixteen 1781 and that he procured John Jordan to enlist for the War in his place to whom he gave £40 part gold and part paper of the value of Gold, that he has a Mother sixty odd years of Age and three sisters, the eldest about 14 who has not been able to do any thing for two years past, the next to her about 12 and the youngest about 10 years of Age, who depend on his Labour only for Support"* (petition signed by 12 associates who recommended his discharge from military service). {Ref: Archives of Maryland Vol. 47, p. 465}

SIMS, JAMES, JR. (Harford County), private who was enrolled 10 Mar 1776 in Militia Company No. 18 under Capt. John Jolly. {Ref: George W. Archer Collection and Revolutionary War File, Historical Society of Harford County Archives}

SIMS, RALPH (Harford County), private who was enrolled 10 Mar 1776 in Militia Company No. 18 under Capt. John Jolly. {Ref: George W. Archer Collection and Revolutionary War File, Historical Society of Harford County Archives}

SIMS, ROBERT (Harford County), private who was enrolled 10 Mar 1776 in Militia Company No. 18 under Capt. John Jolly. {Ref: George W. Archer Collection and Revolutionary War File, Historical Society of Harford County Archives}

SINCLARE, JAMES (Harford County), private who was enrolled 9 Dec 1775 in Militia Company No. 14 under Capt. William McComas. {Ref: George W. Archer Collection and Revolutionary War File, Historical Society of Harford County Archives}

SINCLARE, LESTER (Harford County), private who was enrolled 9 Dec 1775 in Militia Company No. 14 under Capt. William McComas. {Ref: George W. Archer Collection and Revolutionary War File, Historical Society of Harford County Archives}

SINCLARE, WILLIAM (Harford County), private who was enrolled 9 Dec 1775 in Militia Company No. 14 under Capt. William McComas. {Ref: George W. Archer Collection and Revolutionary War File, Historical Society of Harford County Archives}

SINGLETON, REBECCA, see "David Lynn," q.v.

SITLER, CATHERINE, see "Robert Purtle," q.v.

SITSLER, PHILIP (Baltimore County), matross soldier by 7 May 1779 at which time he gave a deposition about his enlistment terms. {Ref: Maryland State Archives Record MdHR 6636-14-83}

SKELLY, JOHN (Baltimore County), private (substitute) in the Maryland Continental Line by 1781, was discharged on 8 Dec 1781. {Ref: Archives of Maryland Vol. 48, p. 11}

SKERRETT, CLEMENT (Baltimore County), second lieutenant in the Maryland Artillery, commissioned 5 Feb 1778 and served at Valley Forge; received payment for his services in the amount of "1900 Dollars & £3.10s" on 12 Sep 1780. For additional information see Peden's *Revolutionary Patriots of Baltimore Town and Baltimore County, 1775-1783*, p. 246. {Ref: Archives of Maryland Vol. 18, p. 477, and Vol. 45, p. 98}

SKIFFINGTON, ROGER (Maryland Navy), marine on the State Ship *Defence* in 1777. {Ref: Archives of Maryland Vol. 18, p. 660}

SKILLIRN, WILLIAM (Maryland Privateer), commander of the schooner *Willey and Minta*, navigated by 7 men and mounting 4 carriage guns, was issued Letters of Marque & Reprisal by the Council of Maryland on 28 May 1778. {Ref: Archives of Maryland Vol. 21, p. 113}

SKINNER, FRANCIS (Maryland Navy), prize master on the State Ship *Defence* in 1777. {Ref: Archives of Maryland Vol. 18, p. 660}

SKINNER, FREDERICK (Calvert County), captain of a militia company on 16 Jun 1778. {Ref: Archives of Maryland Vol. 21, p. 137}

SKINNER, JAMES JOHN (Anne Arundel County), sergeant and later lieutenant in the 7th Maryland Continental Line who received payment for his services in the amount of "1900 Dollars & £3.10s" on 12 Sep 1780. {Ref: Archives of Maryland Vol. 45, p. 98}

SKINNER, JOHN (Anne Arundel County), private by 5 Oct 1776 in Capt. Richard Chew's Militia Company, Weems' Battalion. {Ref: Archives of Maryland Vol. 12, p. 323}

SKINNER, THOMAS (Talbot County), recruiting officer by 18 Jun 1780 at which time he was paid $3000 to be expended in the recruiting service in Talbot County for the Maryland Continental Line. {Ref: Archives of Maryland Vol. 43, p. 198}

SKINNER, TRUEMAN (Prince George's County), captain who served on a General Court-Martial on 6 Jul 1776. {Ref: Archives of Maryland Vol. 11, p. 553}

SKIRT, PATRICK (Baltimore County), private who enlisted in Pulaski's Legion on 22 Mar 1778 and still in service in November, 1779. {Ref: Maryland Historical Magazine, Vol. 13, No. 3, p. 223}

SKOOP, HENRY (Baltimore or Frederick County), private who enlisted in Pulaski's Legion on 1 Sep 1778. {Ref: Maryland Historical Magazine, Vol. 13, No. 3, p. 224}

SKOOP, JOHN (Baltimore or Frederick County), private who enlisted in Pulaski's Legion on 1 Sep 1778. {Ref: Maryland Historical Magazine, Vol. 13, No. 3, p. 224}

SLACK, HENRY (Baltimore County), soldier in Capt. Brown's Company of Artillery by 27 Nov 1781 at which time his wife Ann Slack received provisions from the Issuing Commissary. {Ref: Archives of Maryland Vol. 48, p. 5}

SLATER, WILLIAM (Baltimore Town), patriot and merchant who enrolled in Capt. John Sterrett's Independent Mercantile Company by February, 1777, at which time they were mustered into regular service with the continental army to repress loyalist activities in the Eastern Shore counties of Somerset and Worcester. {Ref: J. Thomas Scharf's History of Baltimore City and County, Part I, p. 77}

SLAYMAKER, JOHN (Maryland Navy), lieutenant on the State Ship Defence in 1777. {Ref: Archives of Maryland Vol. 18, p. 660}

SLAYTON, ELIZABETH, see "Ichabod Davis," q.v.

SLOAN, JAMES (Baltimore Town), patriot and merchant who enrolled in Capt. John Sterrett's Independent Mercantile Company by February, 1777, at which time they were mustered into regular service with the continental army to repress loyalist activities in the Eastern Shore counties of Somerset and Worcester; James married first to Elizabeth ---- and had seven children: James Sloan (born 28 Jan 1784, baptized 29 Sep 1784, died in infancy); James Sloan (born 5 Feb 1786, baptized 16 Apr 1786, died 31 Mar 1819); William Sloan (born 15 Feb 1788, baptized 23 Mar 1788, died 5 Apr 1819); Elizabeth Sloan (born 17 Mar 1793, baptized 9 Aug 1793, married John Buckler on 3 Jan 1820, died 3 Feb 1863); Mary Sloan (born 1 Oct 1795, baptized 14 Dec 1795, married

William Frick on 6 Jun 1816, died 6 Jun 1816); Charles Sloan (twin of Jane, born 18 Mar 1798, baptized 8 Apr 1798, died 15 Nov 1821); and, Jane Sloan (twin of Charles, born 18 Mar 1798, baptized 8 Apr 1798, date of death not stated); James Sloan married second to Harriet Frick (born 17 Feb 1786, died 20 May 1861, daughter of Peter Frick and Anna Barbara Breidenhart) on or after 7 Oct 1820 (date of license) and they had four children: Harriet Frick Sloan (born 13 Nov 1822, married Lucien Bonaparte Calwell on 14 Nov 1848, died 1 Nov 1907); James Sloan (born 1825, died 3 Sep 1891); Charles Sloan (born 1827, died 19 Nov 1890); and, William Fredrick Sloan (born 1830, died 4 Oct 1870); James Sloan was buried on 30 Jun 1833, aged 84, and his widow Harriet married Jacob Norris; see "William Norris," q.v. {Ref: J. Thomas Scharf's *History of Baltimore City and County*, Part I, p. 77, and research by J. Andrew Calwell of Baltimore, Maryland (a direct descendant) in 2001, citing Presbyterian Church Records in Maryland Historical Society Manuscript MS.2703}

SLONE, CHARLES (Frederick County), private (substitute) in the Maryland Continental Line, Price's Regiment, enrolled in May, 1778 for 3 years or duration of the war. {Ref: Maryland Historical Magazine, Vol. 6, No. 3, p. 259}

SMALL, ROBERT (Harford County, Susquehannah Hundred), private who was enrolled 23 Apr 1776 in Militia Company No. 21 under Capt. George Patterson. {Ref: George W. Archer Collection and Revolutionary War File, Historical Society of Harford County Archives}

SMALLWOOD, WILLIAM (Charles County), general of the 1st Maryland Continental Line who received payment for his services in the amount of "1900 Dollars & £3.10s" on 12 Sep 1780. For much more information on his life and times, see Papenfuse's *A Biographical Dictionary of the Maryland Legislature, 1635-1789* and Peden's *Revolutionary Patriots of Charles County, 1775-1783*; also see "James Bryant," q.v. {Ref: Archives of Maryland Vol. 45, p. 97}

SMATTER, JOHN (Frederick County), private (substitute) in the Maryland Continental Line, German Regiment, enrolled in April, 1778 for 3 years or duration of the war. {Ref: Maryland Historical Magazine, Vol. 6, No. 3, p. 257}

SMITH, ALEXANDER (Frederick County), private (substitute) in the Maryland Continental Line, German Regiment, enrolled in May, 1778 for 3 years or duration of the war. {Ref: Maryland Historical Magazine, Vol. 6, No. 3, p. 261}

SMITH, BASEL (St. Mary's County), patriot who supplied 400 lbs. of beef on the hoof to the State of Maryland on 6 Oct 1780. {Ref: Archives of Maryland Vol. 45, p. 156}

SMITH, BENJAMIN (Harford County, Susquehannah Hundred), private who was enrolled 23 Apr 1776 in Militia Company No. 21 under Capt. George Patterson. {Ref: George W. Archer Collection and Revolutionary War File, Historical Society of Harford County Archives}

SMITH, BENJAMIN, see "John Neal," q.v.

247

SMITH, CHARLES (Southern Maryland), captain, commissioned on 27 Jul 1780 to serve in the Regiment Extra by order of the Council of Maryland. {Ref: Archives of Maryland Vol. 43, p. 234}

SMITH, CHARLES (St. Michaels, Talbot County), sailor or marine in the Maryland Navy who was born 19 May 1763 in Talbot County; applied for pension on 27 Jul 1838 under the Act of June 7, 1832, but the claim was rejected because he did not serve six months. {Ref: *Rejected or Suspended Applications for Revolutionary War Pensions* (1850 Report), p. 230; Research by Virgil D. White, citing Federal Pension Application R9703}

SMITH, DANIEL (Frederick County), captain, Maryland Continental Line; born 21 Sep 1756 in York County, Pennsylvania and when only 2 or 3 months old his parents (not named) moved to Frederick County, Maryland; married Amelia Shull on 1 Jun 1783 and had these children: Catharine Smith (born 13 Oct 1784, died 26 Mar 1785); John Smith (born 29 Jan 1786, married Mary Willard); Elizabeth Smith (born 20 Sep 1787, married Henry Gordon); Daniel Smith (born 25 Aug 1780); Magdalin Smith (born 24 Mar 1791); Charles Smith (born 23 Dec 1792, married C. Motter); Joseph Smith (born 12 mar 1797, married Elizabeth Dorsey); Susanna Smith (born 6 Feb 1799, married Henry Kinzer and moved to Indiana); Catharine Smith (born 25 Jan 1801, married Hon. George Salmon); Ezra Smith (born 6 Feb 1803, died 29 May 1807); and, Seraphina Smith (born 28 Dec 1809, married first Samuel Rieman and second David Hammett); Daniel applied for pension on 31 Oct 1834 and *"died Thursday evening last [2 May 1839] in his 84th year at his residence on the farm where he was born in Harbaugh's Valley, Frederick County, and was buried by Captain Jones' Uniform Company with honors due a soldier."* {Ref: Maryland State Society DAR Directory, 1892-1965, p. 657; Research by Virgil D. White, citing Federal Pension Application S7568; *Political Examiner*, 8 May 1839}

SMITH, DRUCILLA, see "Elisha Jarvis," q.v.

SMITH, ELIZA, see "James McCracken," q.v.

SMITH, EMORY (Queen Anne's County), private (substitute) in the Maryland Continental Line by 1781, was discharged on 10 Dec 1781. {Ref: Archives of Maryland Vol. 48, p. 17}

SMITH, GILBERT HAMILTON (Anne Arundel County), private by 5 Oct 1776 in Capt. Richard Chew's Militia Company, Weems' Battalion. {Ref: Archives of Maryland Vol. 12, p. 322}

SMITH, HUGH (Harford County, Susquehannah Hundred), first lieutenant on 23 Apr 1776 in Militia Company No. 21 under Capt. George Patterson. {Ref: George W. Archer Collection and Revolutionary War File, Historical Society of Harford County Archives}

SMITH, ISAAC (Baltimore Town), patriot and merchant who enrolled in Capt. John Sterrett's Independent Mercantile Company by February, 1777, at which time they were mustered into regular service with the continental army to

repress loyalist activities in the Eastern Shore counties of Somerset and Worcester. {Ref: J. Thomas Scharf's *History of Baltimore City and County*, Part I, p. 77}

SMITH, JAMES (Frederick County), private (substitute) in the Maryland Continental Line, Gunby's Regiment, enrolled in May, 1778 for 3 years or duration of the war. {Ref: Maryland Historical Magazine, Vol. 6, No. 3, p. 260}

SMITH, JAMES (Frederick County), patriot buried in Mount Olivet Cemetery. {Ref: Information compiled by Dr. Donald Wolf in Maryland Society SAR Newsletter circa 1996}

SMITH, JAMES (Maryland Navy), marine on the State Ship *Defence* in 1777. {Ref: Archives of Maryland Vol. 18, p. 660}

SMITH, JAMES, see "George Moore" and "Thomas Adams," q.v.

SMITH, JOHN (Baltimore City), soldier who applied for pension under the Act of June 7, 1832, but the claim was suspended pending further proof. {Ref: *Rejected or Suspended Applications for Revolutionary War Pensions* (1850 Report), p. 232}

SMITH, JOHN (Baltimore County), private (substitute) in the Maryland Continental Line by 1781, was discharged on 8 Dec 1781. {Ref: Archives of Maryland Vol. 48, p. 11}

SMITH, JOHN (Frederick County), captain and patriot buried in Mount Olivet Cemetery. {Ref: Information compiled by Dr. Donald Wolf in Maryland Society SAR Newsletter circa 1996}

SMITH, JOHN (St. Mary's County), patriot who supplied 1000 lbs. of beef on the hoof to the State of Maryland on 5 Oct 1780. {Ref: Archives of Maryland Vol. 45, p. 156}

SMITH, JOHN (Harford County), private who was enrolled 10 Mar 1776 in Militia Company No. 18 under Capt. John Jolly. {Ref: George W. Archer Collection and Revolutionary War File, Historical Society of Harford County Archives}

SMITH, JOHN (Western Maryland), private in Capt. Michael Cresap's Company in 1775. {Ref: Howard L. Leckey's *The Tenmile Country and Its Pioneer Families*, p. 16}

SMITH, JOHN (Baltimore County?), ensign in the 3rd Maryland Continental Line who received payment for his services in the amount of "1900 Dollars & £3.10s" on 12 Sep 1780. {Ref: Archives of Maryland Vol. 45, p. 97}

SMITH, JOHN (Harford County), captain in the 3rd Maryland Continental Line who received payment for his services in the amount of "1900 Dollars & £3.10s" on 12 Sep 1780; original member of the Society of the Cincinnati in 1783. For additional information see Peden's *Revolutionary Patriots of Harford County, 1775-1783*. {Ref: Archives of Maryland Vol. 45, p. 97}

SMITH, JOHN (Frederick County), captain in the 6th Maryland Continental Line who received payment for his services in the amount of "1900 Dollars & £3.10s" on 12 Sep 1780. {Ref: Archives of Maryland Vol. 45, p. 98}

SMITH, JOHN ADDISON (Maryland Navy), gunner on the State Ship *Defence* in 1777. {Ref: Archives of Maryland Vol. 18, p. 660}

SMITH, JOSEPH (Baltimore County), private who enlisted in Pulaski's Legion in July, 1778 or 1779 in Baltimore. {Ref: Maryland Historical Magazine, Vol. 13, No. 3, p. 222}

SMITH, JOSEPH (Maryland Continental Line, Staff Officer, Gist's Regiment), captain who received payment for his services in the amount of "1900 Dollars & £3.10s" on 12 Sep 1780; see "George Moore," q.v. {Ref: Archives of Maryland Vol. 45, p. 98}

SMITH, JOSEPH (Maryland Navy), lieutenant of marines on the State Ship *Defence* in 1777. {Ref: Archives of Maryland Vol. 18, p. 660}

SMITH, LAMBERT (Baltimore Town), patriot and merchant who enrolled in Capt. John Sterrett's Independent Mercantile Company by February, 1777, at which time they were mustered into regular service with the continental army to repress loyalist activities in the Eastern Shore counties of Somerset and Worcester. {Ref: J. Thomas Scharf's *History of Baltimore City and County*, Part I, p. 77}

SMITH, LEONARD (Frederick County), patriot buried in Mount Olivet Cemetery. {Ref: Information compiled by Dr. Donald Wolf in Maryland Society SAR Newsletter circa 1996}

SMITH, MARGARET, see "John Neal," q.v.

SMITH, MARTHA, see "Samuel Griffith," q.v.

SMITH, MATHIAS (Frederick County), patriot buried in Mount Olivet Cemetery. {Ref: Information compiled by Dr. Donald Wolf in Maryland Society SAR Newsletter circa 1996}

SMITH, MATHIAS (Frederick County), private (substitute) in the Maryland Continental Line, German Regiment, enrolled in May, 1778 for 3 years or duration of the war. {Ref: Maryland Historical Magazine, Vol. 6, No. 3, p. 260}

SMITH, MICHAEL (Frederick County), private (substitute) in the Maryland Continental Line, German Regiment, enrolled in May, 1778 for 3 years or duration of the war. {Ref: Maryland Historical Magazine, Vol. 6, No. 3, p. 261}

SMITH, NATHAN (Charles County), private (substitute) in the Maryland Continental Line by 1781, was discharged on 8 Dec 1781. {Ref: Archives of Maryland Vol. 48, p. 11}

SMITH, NATHANIEL (Harford County), patriot who was appointed ensign in the 4th Maryland Regiment of Continental Troops by the Council of Maryland on 18 Nov 1779; lieutenant by 1780 and received payment for his services in the amount of "1900 Dollars & £3.10s" on 12 Sep 1780. {Ref: Archives of Maryland Vol. 43, p. 18, and Vol. 45, p. 98}

SMITH, PATRICK SIM (Calvert County), patriot who was appointed by the Council of Maryland on 27 Jan 1776 as one of three persons in Calvert County to collect all the gold and silver coin that can be procured in said county; appointed Commissary of Purchases on 8 Jul 1780. {Ref: Archives of Maryland Vol. 11, p. 132, and Vol. 43, p. 215}

SMITH, PHILEMON, see "Nathan Musgrove," q.v.

SMITH, RICHARD (Maryland Navy), sailor or seaman on 7 Jan 1780. {Ref: Calendar of Maryland State Papers, The Brown Books, p. 57}

SMITH, RICHARD (Baltimore County), private, aged 18, ship carpenter, born in Maryland, enlisted (made his "X" mark) on 16 Feb 1776 in Capt. John Fulford's Company of Matrosses; see "Richard Williams," q.v. {Ref: Maryland Historical Magazine, Vol. 69, No. 1, p. 95}

SMITH, ROBERT (Frederick County), private (substitute) in the Maryland Continental Line, German Regiment, enrolled in May, 1778 for 3 years or duration of the war; see "Richard Williams," q.v. {Ref: Maryland Historical Magazine, Vol. 6, No. 3, p. 260}

SMITH, RUTH, see "John Parsons," q.v.

SMITH, SAMUEL (Harford County), captain, commissioned 16 May 1776 in Militia Company No. 26. {Ref: George W. Archer Collection and Revolutionary War File, Historical Society of Harford County Archives}

SMITH, SILVANUS (Baltimore County), a matross in the late Capt. Edward Gale's Company of Maryland Artillery who *"being adjudged incapable of Service is hereby Discharged therefrom"* on 1 Feb 1780. {Ref: Archives of Maryland Vol. 43, p. 75}

SMITH, SOPHIA, see "John Adams," q.v.

SMITH, THOMAS (Maryland Navy), sailor or seaman on 7 Jan 1780. {Ref: Calendar of Maryland State Papers, The Brown Books, p. 57}

SMITH, WILLIAM (Harford County), first lieutenant, commissioned 8 Oct 1776 in Militia Company No. 29 under Capt. Benjamin Bradford Norris. {Ref: George W. Archer Collection and Revolutionary War File, Historical Society of Harford County Archives}

SMITH, WILLIAM (Harford County), private (substitute) in the Maryland Continental Line by 1781, was discharged on 8 Dec 1781. {Ref: Archives of Maryland Vol. 48, p. 11}

SMITH, WILLIAM (Baltimore County?), patriot and doctor in the 6th Maryland Continental Line who received payment for his services in the amount of "1900 Dollars & £3.10s" on 12 Sep 1780. {Ref: Archives of Maryland Vol. 45, p. 98}

SMITH, WILLIAM, OF ROBERT (Harford County), private who was enrolled 9 Dec 1775 in Militia Company No. 14 under Capt. William McComas. {Ref: George W. Archer Collection and Revolutionary War File, Historical Society of Harford County Archives}

SMITH, WILLIAM, JR. (Baltimore Town), patriot and merchant who enrolled in Capt. John Sterrett's Independent Mercantile Company by February, 1777, at which time they were mustered into regular service with the continental army to repress loyalist activities in the Eastern Shore counties of Somerset and Worcester. {Ref: J. Thomas Scharf's *History of Baltimore City and County*, Part I, p. 77}

SMITH, WILLIAM R. (Baltimore Town), patriot and merchant who enrolled in Capt. John Sterrett's Independent Mercantile Company by February, 1777, at which time they were mustered into regular service with the continental army to repress loyalist activities in the Eastern Shore counties of Somerset and Worcester. {Ref: J. Thomas Scharf's *History of Baltimore City and County*, Part I, p. 77}

SMOOT, MATTHEW (Charles County), private in the Maryland Continental Line who was drafted to serve until 10 Dec 1781 and was discharged on 8 Dec 1781. {Ref: Archives of Maryland Vol. 48, p. 17}

SMOOT (SMOOTE), WILLIAM (Charles County), ensign in the 1st Maryland Continental Line who received payment for his services in the amount of "1900 Dollars & £3.10s" on 12 Sep 1780. {Ref: Archives of Maryland Vol. 45, p. 97}

SMYTH, JOHN (Harford County), ensign by 15 Apr 1776 in Militia Company No. 20 under Capt. Robert Glenn. {Ref: George W. Archer Collection and Revolutionary War File, Historical Society of Harford County Archives}

SNIDER, FREDERICK (Washington County), private who was enrolled to serve as a substitute in the Maryland Continental Line until 10 Dec 1781, but *"being represented unfit for the service for which he was intended"* was discharged on 30 Oct 1781. {Ref: Archives of Maryland Vol. 45, p. 656}

SNIVELY, HENRY (Frederick County), patriot who supplied provisions to the State of Maryland between June and September, 1780. {Ref: Archives of Maryland Vol. 45, p. 84}

SNOWDEN, NED (Prince George's County), private who was drafted into the Maryland Continental Line, was discharged on 8 Dec 1781. {Ref: Archives of Maryland Vol. 48, p. 10}

SNOWDEN, THOMAS (Anne Arundel County), patriot who took the Oath of Fidelity and Support to the State of Maryland on 8 Apr 1778. {Ref: Archives of Maryland Vol. 21, p. 16}

SNYDER, JOSEPH (Baltimore or Frederick County), corporal, enlisted in Pulaski's Legion on 12 Mar 1778. {Ref: Maryland Historical Magazine, Vol. 13, No. 3, p. 224}

SOHAN, WILLIAM (Maryland Navy), marine on the State Ship *Defence* in 1777. {Ref: Archives of Maryland Vol. 18, p. 660}

SOLLERS, JOHN (Baltimore County), private, 31 May 1779, Capt. Benjamin Talbott's Militia Company, Cockey's Battalion. {Ref: Maryland Historical Magazine, Vol. 7, No. 1, p. 90}

SOLOMON, DAVID (Western Maryland), private in Capt. Michael Cresap's Company in 1775. {Ref: Howard L. Leckey's *The Tenmile Country and Its Pioneer Families*, p. 16}

SOMERVILL, ALEXANDER (Calvert County), patriot who was appointed by the Council of Maryland on 27 Jan 1776 as one of three persons in Calvert County to collect all gold and silver coin that can be procured in said county. {Ref: Archives of Maryland Vol. 11, p. 132}

SOMERVILLE, JAMES (Prince George's County), captain in the 6th Maryland Continental Line who received payment for his services in the amount of "1900 Dollars & £3.10s" on 12 Sep 1780. {Ref: Archives of Maryland Vol. 45, p. 98}

SOMMERS, ---- (Baltimore County), private, aged 22, backer *[sic]*, born in Philadelphia, enlisted 4 Mar 1776 in Capt. John Fulford's Company of Matrosses. {Ref: Maryland Historical Magazine, Vol. 69, No. 1, p. 96}

SOMMERS, JACOB (Maryland Navy), seaman or marine on the State Ship *Defence* in 1777. {Ref: Archives of Maryland Vol. 18, p. 660}

SOMMERS, JOHN (Maryland Navy), quartermaster on the State Ship *Defence* in 1777. {Ref: Archives of Maryland Vol. 18, p. 660}

SOPER, RENECKAH, see "James Higgins," q.v.

SOUDER, ADAM (Frederick County), private who was drafted to serve in the Maryland Continental Line until 10 Dec 1781, but *"being represented unfit for the duty for which he was intended"* was discharged on 30 Oct 1781. {Ref: Archives of Maryland Vol. 45, p. 656}

SOUTH(?), JOHN (Baltimore County), private, aged 22, brickmaker, born in Maryland, enlisted 15 Feb 1776 in Capt. John Fulford's Company of Matrosses. {Ref: Maryland Historical Magazine, Vol. 69, No. 1, p. 95}

SOWARD, RICHARD (Harford County, Susquehannah Hundred), private who was enrolled 23 Apr 1776 in Militia Company No. 21 under Capt. George Patterson. {Ref: George W. Archer Collection and Revolutionary War File, Historical Society of Harford County Archives}

SPEAR, JOSEPH (Baltimore Town), patriot and merchant who enrolled in Capt. John Sterrett's Independent Mercantile Company by February, 1777, at which time they were mustered into regular service with the continental army to repress loyalist activities in the Eastern Shore counties of Somerset and Worcester. {Ref: J. Thomas Scharf's *History of Baltimore City and County*, Part I, p. 77}

SPELLECY, DARBY (Baltimore County), private, aged 21, ropemaker, born in Ireland, enlisted 21 Feb 1776 in Capt. John Fulford's Company of Matrosses. {Ref: Maryland Historical Magazine, Vol. 69, No. 1, p. 95}

SPENCE, JAMES (Harford County, Susquehannah Hundred), private who was enrolled 23 Apr 1776 in Militia Company No. 21 under Capt. George Patterson. {Ref: George W. Archer Collection and Revolutionary War File, Historical Society of Harford County Archives}

SPENCE, JOHN (Harford County, Susquehannah Hundred), private who was enrolled 23 Apr 1776 in Militia Company No. 21 under Capt. George Patterson. {Ref: George W. Archer Collection and Revolutionary War File, Historical Society of Harford County Archives}

SPENCER, ISAAC (Kent County), colonel of the 27th Battalion of Militia, commissioned 8 May 1777; one Isaac Spencer died testate in Kent County by 21 Jul 1785 and he had a son named Isaac. {Ref: Archives of Maryland Vol. 16, p. 243; Kent County Wills Liber 7, p. 109}

SPENCER, TAMERLANE (Baltimore County), private, aged 26, ship carpenter, born in Talbot County, Maryland, enlisted 12 Mar 1776 in Capt. John Fulford's Company of Matrosses. {Ref: Maryland Historical Magazine, Vol. 69, No. 1, p. 96}

SPICER, WILLIAM (Anne Arundel County), patriot who took the Oath of Fidelity and Support to the State of Maryland on 7 Apr 1778. {Ref: Archives of Maryland Vol. 21, p. 13}

SPINKS, RAWLEIGH (Baltimore County), private, aged 28, carpenter, born in Virginia, enlisted 13 Feb 1776 in Capt. John Fulford's Company of Matrosses. {Ref: Maryland Historical Magazine, Vol. 69, No. 1, p. 95}

SPOOR, LUDWIC (Baltimore or Frederick County), sergeant, enlisted in Pulaski's Legion on 11 Jun 1778 or 1779. {Ref: Maryland Historical Magazine, Vol. 13, No. 3, p. 224}

SPRAY, JOHN (Frederick County), private (substitute) in the Maryland Continental Line, Price's Regiment, enrolled in April, 1778 for 3 years or duration of the war. {Ref: Maryland Historical Magazine, Vol. 6, No. 3, p. 257}

SPRIGG, MICHAEL, see "William Lamar," q.v.

SPRIGG, THOMAS (Washington County), officer and county lieutenant during the revolution, died 13 Dec 1809, aged 62: *"Gen. Sprigg resided in Washington County and was conspicuous in the Revolutionary War and as a member of Congress."* For additional information see Papenfuse's *A Biographical Dictionary of the Maryland Legislature, 1635-1789* (pp. 766-767). {Ref: J. Thomas Scharf's *History of Western Maryland*, Vol. II, p. 1055}

SPURRIER, EDWARD (Anne Arundel County), captain in the 4th Maryland Continental Line who received payment for his services in the amount of "1900 Dollars & £3.10s" on 12 Sep 1780. {Ref: Archives of Maryland Vol. 45, p. 98}

SQUIB, JOHN (Maryland Navy), marine on the State Ship *Defence* in 1777. {Ref: Archives of Maryland Vol. 18, p. 660}

ST. CLAIR, CAMPBELL, see "William St. Clair," q.v.

ST. CLAIR, NATHAN (Baltimore County), patriot who took the Oath of Fidelity and Support to the State of Maryland on 2 Apr 1778. {Ref: Archives of Maryland Vol. 21, p. 1}

ST. CLAIR, WILLIAM (Kent County), captain in the county militia, commissioned 22 Jun 1776; a William St. Clair died testate in Kent County by 10 Aug 1777 and named only his minor son Campbell St. Clair in his will. {Ref: Archives of Maryland Vol. 11, p. 506; Kent County County Wills Liber 6, p. 83}

ST. FALL, JOHN (Baltimore County), private, aged 25, labourer, born in Ireland, enlisted (made his "X" mark) on 24 Feb 1776 in Capt. John Fulford's Company of Matrosses. {Ref: Maryland Historical Magazine, Vol. 69, No. 1, p. 95}

STAFFORD, JAMES (Caroline County), patriot who was appointed second lieutenant in the 14th Militia Battalion by the Council of Maryland on 28 Jun 1780. {Ref: Archives of Maryland Vol. 43, p. 207}

STAINTON, BENTON (Caroline County), patriot who was appointed by the Council of Maryland on 27 Jan 1776 as one of three persons to collect all the gold and silver coin that can be procured in said county; commissioned on 19

Aug 1779 as one of the three persons to receive subscriptions for use of the State in said county. {Ref: Archives of Maryland Vol. 11, p. 132 and Vol. 21, p. 499}

STALEY, JACOB, see "Frederick Kemp," q.v.

STALEY, MAGDALENE, see "Frederick Kemp," q.v.

STALLINGS, ABRAHAM (Frederick County), private (substitute) in the Maryland Continental Line, Gunby's Regiment, enrolled in May, 1778 for 3 years or duration of the war. {Ref: Maryland Historical Magazine, Vol. 6, No. 3, p. 261}

STALLINGS, LANSLET (Anne Arundel County), private by 5 Oct 1776 (made his "X" mark) in Capt. Richard Chew's Militia Company, Weems' Battalion. {Ref: Archives of Maryland Vol. 12, p. 323}

STANDAGE, MARY, see "George Moore," q.v.

STANDIFORD, CLORINDA, see "Jonathan Ady," q.v.

STANLEY, FRANCIS (Baltimore County), private, aged 28, labourer, born in England, enlisted (made his "X" mark) on 5 Mar 1776 in Capt. John Fulford's Company of Matrosses, deserted 30 May 1776 and took his coat jacket, breeches and blanket with him. {Ref: Maryland Historical Magazine, Vol. 69, No. 1, pp. 96, 97}

STANSBURY, DANIEL (Baltimore County), private, 31 May 1779, Capt. Benjamin Talbott's Militia Company, Cockey's Battalion. {Ref: Maryland Historical Magazine, Vol. 7, No. 1, p. 90}

STANSBURY, DAVID (Baltimore County), private, 31 May 1779, Capt. Benjamin Talbott's Militia Company, Cockey's Battalion. {Ref: Maryland Historical Magazine, Vol. 7, No. 1, p. 90}

STANSBURY, TOBIAS (Baltimore Privateer), commander of the schooner *Dispatch*, navigated by 30 men and mounting 6 carriage guns, was issued Letters of Marque & Reprisal by the Council of Maryland on 7 Dec 1782. {Ref: Archives of Maryland Vol. 48, p. 316}

STANTON, ALEXANDER (Maryland Navy), armorer and master at arms on the State Ship *Defence* in 1777. {Ref: Archives of Maryland Vol. 18, p. 660}

STANTON, JOHN (Frederick County), private (substitute) in the Maryland Continental Line, German Regiment, enrolled in May, 1778 for 3 years or duration of the war. {Ref: Maryland Historical Magazine, Vol. 6, No. 3, p. 259}

STAR, OBEDIAH (Anne Arundel County), private who was drafted into the Maryland Continental Line, was discharged on 8 Dec 1781. {Ref: Archives of Maryland Vol. 48, p. 10}

STARCK, JOHN, JR. (Baltimore Town), patriot and merchant who enrolled in Capt. John Sterrett's Independent Mercantile Company by February, 1777, at which time they were mustered into regular service with the continental army to repress loyalist activities in the Eastern Shore counties of Somerset and Worcester. {Ref: J. Thomas Scharf's *History of Baltimore City and County*, Part I, p. 77}

STARK, RICHARD (Talbot County), soldier drafted into the Maryland Continental Line to serve until 10 Dec 1781, was discharged on 27 Nov 1781. {Ref: Archives of Maryland Vol. 48, p. 5}

STAUT, JOHN (Frederick County), private (substitute) in the Maryland Continental Line, German Regiment, enrolled in May, 1778 for 3 years or duration of the war. {Ref: Maryland Historical Magazine, Vol. 6, No. 3, p. 261}

STEARS, EARNEST (Baltimore County), private who enlisted in Pulaski's Legion on 12 Mar 1778 and still in service in November, 1779. {Ref: Maryland Historical Magazine, Vol. 13, No. 3, p. 223}

STEEL, JOHN (Baltimore County), private (substitute) in the Maryland Continental Line by 1781, was discharged on 8 Dec 1781. {Ref: Archives of Maryland Vol. 48, p. 11}

STEEL, JOHN (Baltimore or Frederick County), private in Pulaski's Legion before July, 1782. {Ref: Maryland Historical Magazine, Vol. 13, No. 3, p. 225}

STEEL, THOMAS (Baltimore Privateer), commander of the sloop *Irish Gimblet*, mounting 4 carriage guns, 2 swivel guns and 6 small arms, was issued Letters of Marque & Reprisal by the Council of Maryland on 9 Nov 1778; commander of the schooner *Tucker*, navigated by 21 men and mounting 10 carriage guns, was issued Letters of Marque & Reprisal by the Council of Maryland on 14 Aug 1780; commander of the brigantine *Fox*, navigated by 22 men and mounting 10 carriage guns and 4 swivel guns, was issued Letters of Marque & Reprisal by the Council of Maryland on 12 Jan 1781. {Ref: Archives of Maryland Vol. 21, p. 233, Vol. 43, p. 255, and Vol. 45, p. 273}

STEELE, ELISHA (Baltimore or Frederick County), private in Pulaski's Legion before July, 1782. {Ref: Maryland Historical Magazine, Vol. 13, No. 3, p. 225}

STEELE, HENRY (Dorchester County), patriot who was appointed by the Council of Maryland on 27 Jan 1776 as one of three persons in Dorchester County to collect all gold and silver coin that can be procured in said county. {Ref: Archives of Maryland Vol. 11, p. 132}

STEELE, JAMES (Harford County), ensign, commissioned 28 Apr 1776 in Militia Company No. 23 under Capt. James McComas. {Ref: George W. Archer Collection and Revolutionary War File, Historical Society of Harford County Archives}

STENSON, WILLIAM (Baltimore Town), patriot and merchant who enrolled in Capt. John Sterrett's Independent Mercantile Company by February, 1777, at which time they were mustered into regular service with the continental army to repress loyalist activities in the Eastern Shore counties of Somerset and Worcester. {Ref: J. Thomas Scharf's *History of Baltimore City and County*, Part I, p. 77}

STEPHENSON, EDWARD (Frederick County), patriot who took the Oath of Fidelity and Support to the State of Maryland on 9 Apr 1778. {Ref: Archives of Maryland Vol. 21, p. 22}

STEPHENSON, MATHEW (Western Maryland), private in Capt. Michael Cresap's Company in 1775. {Ref: Howard L. Leckey's *The Tenmile Country and Its Pioneer Families*, p. 16}

STERRETT, JOHN (Baltimore Town), patriot and merchant who was captain of an Independent Mercantile Company by February, 1777, at which time they were mustered into regular service with the continental army to repress loyalist activities in the Eastern Shore counties of Somerset and Worcester. {Ref: J. Thomas Scharf's *History of Baltimore City and County*, Part I, p. 77}

STERRETT, JOHN (Baltimore County), agent for purchasing provisions in Baltimore County until 9 Apr 1778 at which time he had *"lately removed into Anne Arundel County"* and was replaced by Benjamin Griffith. {Ref: Archives of Maryland Vol. 21, p. 22}

STERRETT (STERETT), JOSEPH (Baltimore Town), patriot and merchant who enrolled in Capt. John Sterrett's Independent Mercantile Company by February, 1777, at which time they were mustered into regular service with the continental army to repress loyalist activities in the Eastern Shore counties of Somerset and Worcester. {Ref: J. Thomas Scharf's *History of Baltimore City and County*, Part I, p. 77}

STERRETT, SAMUEL (Baltimore Town), patriot and merchant who enrolled in Capt. John Sterrett's Independent Mercantile Company by February, 1777, at which time they were mustered into regular service with the continental army to repress loyalist activities in the Eastern Shore counties of Somerset and Worcester. {Ref: J. Thomas Scharf's *History of Baltimore City and County*, Part I, p. 77}

STEUART, JOHN (Baltimore Privateer), commander of the schooner *Molly*, navigated by 13 men and mounting 4 carriage guns, was issued Letters of Marque & Reprisal by the Council of Maryland on 27 Jun 1780. {Ref: Archives of Maryland Vol. 43, p. 206}

STEVENS, ANNA, see "Levi Stevens," q.v.

STEVENS, BENTOL (Caroline County), first lieutenant in the 14th Militia Battalion, appointed by the Council of Maryland on 28 Jun 1780. {Ref: Archives of Maryland Vol. 43, p. 207}

STEVENS, BETSY, see "Levi Stevens," q.v.

STEVENS, DAVID, see "Levi Stevens," q.v.

STEVENS, HENRY, see "Levi Stevens," q.v.

STEVENS, JOHN, see "Levi Stevens," q.v.

STEVENS, JOSIAH, see "Levi Stevens," q.v.

STEVENS, JULY, see "Levi Stevens," q.v.

STEVENS, LEVI (Worcester County), private in the 2nd Maryland Continental Line from 8 Jan 1777 until discharged on 10 Jan 1780; married Mary Furniss in August, 1791 and their children were: John Stevens (born 23 Dec 1792 and died young); Sally Stevens (born 12 Aug 1794); Anna Stevens (born in July, 1796); William Stevens (born 21 Nov 1797); David Stevens (born 6 Nov

---

1799); Betsy Stevens (born 3 Oct 1802); Susey Stevens (born 20 Nov 1803); Josiah Stevens (born 20 Dec 1805); July Stevens (born 10 Nov 1808); and, Henry Stevens (born 6 Dec 1812); Levi applied for pension at Salisbury in July, 1833, under the Act of June 7, 1832, but the claim was suspended because of *"imperfect papers and if better ones have ever been on file it does not appear"* and his widow Mary Stevens applied for pension on 28 Apr 1841, aged 71, stating the soldier was born on 1 Jun 1757, lived in Worcester County during and after the war, and died on 16 Dec 1834. {Ref: Archives of Maryland Vol. 18, p. 161; *Rejected or Suspended Applications for Revolutionary War Pensions* (1850 Report), p. 232; Research by Virgil D. White, citing Federal Pension Application W25147}

STEVENS, LEWIS (Anne Arundel County), private by 5 Oct 1776 in Capt. Richard Chew's Militia Company, Weems' Battalion. {Ref: Archives of Maryland Vol. 12, p. 323}

STEVENS, MARY, see "Levi Stevens," q.v.

STEVENS, SALLY, see "Levi Stevens," q.v.

STEVENS, SUSEY, see "Levi Stevens," q.v.

STEVENS, WILLIAM (Frederick County), a substitute for Vachel Hammond, was a private in the Maryland Continental Line who was *"sent from camp by General Smallwood as unfit for the service"* and was discharged on 22 Jun 1778. {Ref: Archives of Maryland Vol. 21, p. 144}

STEVENS, WILLIAM, see "Levi Stevens," q.v.

STEVENSON, DANIEL (Frederick County), private soldier who had neglected to march with the militia, petitioned the Council of Maryland on 26 Sep 1782 stating, in part, that *"he was subject to Fits & totally unqualified for any Militia Duty ... fined £20 by a Court Martial for a neglect of Duty ... which will reduce him, his Wife and seven small Children to extreme distress."* Three of the witnesses were Edward Stevensom, Richard Stevenson, and brother Sater Stevenson. Daniel and the fine were both subsequently discharged. {Ref: Archives of Maryland Vol. 48, pp. 268-269}

STEVENSON, HENRY (Baltimore County), patriot who was appointed and commissioned sheriff of Baltimore County on 8 May 1777. {Ref: Archives of Maryland Vol. 16, p. 244}

STEVENSON, JOHN (Harford County), first lieutenant, commissioned 16 May 1776 in Militia Company No. 26 under Capt. Samuel Smith. {Ref: George W. Archer Collection and Revolutionary War File, Historical Society of Harford County Archives}

STEVENSON, JOSHUA (Baltimore County), patriot who supplied provisions to the State of Maryland between June and September, 1780. {Ref: Archives of Maryland Vol. 45, p. 84}

STEVENSON, ROBERT (Harford County), private who was enrolled by 16 Sep 1775 in Militia Company No. 2 under Capt. John Archer. {Ref: George W. Archer Collection and Revolutionary War File, Historical Society of Harford County Archives}

STEVENSON, STEVEN (Frederick County), private (substitute) in the Maryland Continental Line, Gunby's Regiment, enrolled in April, 1778 for 3 years or duration of the war. {Ref: Maryland Historical Magazine, Vol. 6, No. 3, p. 257}

STEVENSON, WILLIAM (Annapolis), patriot and *"a native of this State who hath long resided in Great Britain and is now lately, that is to say within three Months last past, returned into this State, appeared before the Governor and Council and before them did take, repeat and Subscribe the Oath of Fidelity and Support to this State contained in the Act to Punish certain Crimes and Misdemeanors and to prevent the Growth of Toryism"* on 16 Jun 1778. {Ref: Archives of Maryland Vol. 21, p. 136}

STEWARD, DAVID (Dorchester County), private (substitute) in the Maryland Continental Line by 1781, was discharged on 8 Dec 1781. {Ref: Archives of Maryland Vol. 48, p. 10}

STEWARD, GEORGE (Baltimore County), private, aged 26, labourer, born in London, enlisted 22 Feb 1776 in Capt. John Fulford's Company of Matrosses. {Ref: Maryland Historical Magazine, Vol. 69, No. 1, p. 95}

STEWARD, IGNATIUS (Charles County), private who was drafted into the Maryland Continental Line, was discharged on 8 Dec 1781. {Ref: Archives of Maryland Vol. 48, p. 10}

STEWARD, JOHN (Somerset County), patriot who was commissioned one of the three persons in Somerset County by the Council of Maryland on 19 Aug 1779 to receive subscriptions for use of the State; major in the 2nd Maryland Continental Line who received payment for his services in the amount of "1900 Dollars & £3.10s" on 12 Sep 1780. {Ref: Archives of Maryland Vol. 21, p. 499, and Vol. 45, p. 97}

STEWART, JAMES (Maryland Navy), commander on 7 Jan 1780. {Ref: Calendar of Maryland State Papers, The Brown Books, p. 57}

STEWART, JOHN THOMAS (Talbot County), captain in the Maryland troops whose widow Elizabeth Stewart applied for pension at Wye under the Act of July 7, 1838, but the claim was suspended because *"he was a captain in the militia, as certified by the Register of the Land Office at Annapolis, but the duration of his service is not established; if she was married before the termination of her husband's service, she should apply under the Act of July 4, 1836."* {Ref: *Rejected or Suspended Applications for Revolutionary War Pensions* (1850 Report), p. 237}

STEWART, RICHARD (Western Maryland), private in Capt. Michael Cresap's Company in 1775. {Ref: Howard L. Leckey's *The Tenmile Country and Its Pioneer Families*, p. 16}

STILES, SOLOMON (Maryland Navy), pilot on the State Ship *Defence* in 1777. {Ref: Archives of Maryland Vol. 18, p. 660}

STILES, THOMAS (Maryland Privateer), commander of the schooner *Beggars Benison*, navigated by 7 men and mounting 4 swivel guns, was issued Letters of Marque & Reprisal by the Council of Maryland on 22 Jun 1778. {Ref: Archives of Maryland Vol. 21, p. 144}

STINCHCOMB, AQUILLA (Baltimore City), soldier in the Maryland militia whose widow Catharine Stinchcomb applied for pension under the Act of July 7, 1838, but the claim was suspended *"for further proof"* (also noted that she was deceased, but no date was given). {Ref: *Rejected or Suspended Applications for Revolutionary War Pensions* (1850 Report), p. 237}

STINCHCOMB, MAGDALEN, see "George Zimmerman," q.v.

STITE, JAMES (Frederick County), private (substitute) in the Maryland Continental Line, German Regiment, enrolled in May, 1778 for 3 years or duration of the war. {Ref: Maryland Historical Magazine, Vol. 6, No. 3, p. 259}

STITLEY, FREDERICK (Frederick County), private who was enrolled to serve as a substitute in the Maryland Continental Line until 10 Dec 1781, but *"being represented unfit for the service for which he was intended"* was discharged on 30 Oct 1781. {Ref: Archives of Maryland Vol. 45, p. 657}

STOCKER, JAMES (Frederick County), private (substitute) in the Maryland Continental Line, who enlisted to serve until 10 Dec 1781, was discharged on 29 Nov 1781. {Ref: Archives of Maryland Vol. 48, p. 7}

STOCKWELL, WILLIAM (Western Maryland), private in Capt. Michael Cresap's Company in 1775. {Ref: Howard L. Leckey's *The Tenmile Country and Its Pioneer Families*, p. 16}

STODDARD, LUCY, see "John Mitchell," q.v.

STODDARD, WILLIAM TRUEMAN (Prince George's County), lieutenant in the 3rd Maryland Continental Line who received payment for his services in the amount of "1900 Dollars & £3.10s" on 12 Sep 1780. {Ref: Archives of Maryland Vol. 45, p. 98}

STODDERT, DAVID (Baltimore County), second lieutenant in Capt. George Hunter's Company of Matrosses, formed in the defense of the harbor of Baltimore, commissioned 30 Mar 1781. {Ref: Archives of Maryland Vol. 45, p. 368}

STONE, JOHN HOSKINS (Charles County), colonel who was appointed Auditor General by the Maryland Assembly and qualified before the Governor & Council by taking the several required oaths on 7 Apr 1778, but resigned by 11 Apr 1778. {Ref: Archives of Maryland Vol. 21, pp. 12, 29}

STONE, JOSEPH (Harford County), private who was enrolled 25 Mar 1776 in Militia Company No. 19 under Capt. William Morgan. {Ref: George W. Archer Collection and Revolutionary War File, Historical Society of Harford County Archives}

STORMENT, NATHAN (Cecil County), private who was drafted to serve in the Maryland Continental Line until 10 Dec 1781, but *"being represented unfit for the duty for which he was intended"* was discharged on 30 Oct 1781. {Ref: Archives of Maryland Vol. 45, p. 656}

STOUDER, JOHN (Frederick County), private who *"was fined £30 by a Militia Court Martial held at Frederick Town on September 21, 1781 for not doing duty as Guard to the British Convention Troops at Frederick Town"* and it was certified to the Council of Maryland by several named associates on 15 Mar 1783 *"that the said John Stouder was sick when he should be on Duty and continued so the best part of the Summer."* The Council therefore ordered that £29 of the £30 fine be remitted to him. {Ref: Archives of Maryland Vol. 48, p. 382}

STOUT, JOHN (Maryland Privateer), commander of the schooner *Humming Bird*, navigated by 13 men and mounting 4 carriage guns, 4 swivel guns and 6 small arms, was issued Letters of Marque & Reprisal by the Council of Maryland on 13 Mar 1780. {Ref: Archives of Maryland Vol. 43, p. 109}

STREETT, THOMAS, JR. (Harford County), private who was enrolled 9 Dec 1775 in Militia Company No. 14 under Capt. William McComas. {Ref: George W. Archer Collection and Revolutionary War File, Historical Society of Harford County Archives}

STREETT, THOMAS, SR. (Harford County), private who was enrolled 9 Dec 1775 in Militia Company No. 14 under Capt. William McComas. {Ref: George W. Archer Collection and Revolutionary War File, Historical Society of Harford County Archives}

STRICKER, JOHN (Baltimore Town), patriot and merchant who enrolled in Capt. John Sterrett's Independent Mercantile Company by February, 1777, at which time they were mustered into regular service with the continental army to repress loyalist activities in the Eastern Shore counties of Somerset and Worcester. {Ref: J. Thomas Scharf's *History of Baltimore City and County*, Part I, p. 77}

STRIDER, JOHN, see "Joshua Hickman," q.v.

STRIDER, MARGARET, see "Joshua Hickman," q.v.

STRINGER, RICHARD (Anne Arundel County), patriot who was paid £6 by the State Treasurer for the hire of his wagon on 15 Jun 1778. {Ref: Archives of Maryland Vol. 21, p. 135}

STRONG, ABRAM (Maryland Navy), marine on the State Ship *Defence* in 1777. {Ref: Archives of Maryland Vol. 18, p. 660}

STUART, ALEXANDER (Harford County, Susquehannah Hundred), private who was enrolled 23 Apr 1776 in Militia Company No. 21 under Capt. George Patterson. {Ref: George W. Archer Collection and Revolutionary War File, Historical Society of Harford County Archives}

STUMP, HENRY (Harford County), patriot for whom James Phillips was paid £44.9.0 by the State Treasurer for the hire of his wagon on 20 May 1778. {Ref: Archives of Maryland Vol. 21, p. 97}

STUMP, JOHN (Baltimore Town), patriot and merchant who enrolled in Capt. John Sterrett's Independent Mercantile Company by February, 1777, at which time they were mustered into regular service with the continental army to repress loyalist activities in the Eastern Shore counties of Somerset and Worcester. {Ref: J. Thomas Scharf's *History of Baltimore City and County*, Part I, p. 77}

STUMP, JOHN (Harford County, Susquehannah Hundred), private who was enrolled 23 Apr 1776 in Militia Company No. 21 under Capt. George Patterson.

{Ref: George W. Archer Collection and Revolutionary War File, Historical Society of Harford County Archives}

STURGEON, ROBERT (Harford County), private who was enrolled 9 Dec 1775 in Militia Company No. 14 under Capt. William McComas. {Ref: George W. Archer Collection and Revolutionary War File, Historical Society of Harford County Archives}

STUTSON, AMELIA, see "Nathan Musgrove," q.v.

SULLIVAN, BRIGHT (Maryland Navy), sailmaker on the State Ship *Defence* in 1777. {Ref: Archives of Maryland Vol. 18, p. 660}

SULLIVAN, JAMES (Maryland Navy), second lieutenant on the galley *Chester*, commissioned 16 Jul 1778. {Ref: Archives of Maryland Vol. 21, p. 160}

SULLIVANE, ---- (Baltimore County?), private in the 7th Maryland Continental Line by 10 May 1780 at which time his wife Mary Sullivane received 3 days' rations from the Issuing Commissary. {Ref: Archives of Maryland Vol. 43, p. 170}

SULLIVANE, SOLOMON (Anne Arundel County), private in the Maryland Continental Line by 1 Dec 1781 at which time he was on duty guarding the magazine at the Head of Severn River. {Ref: Archives of Maryland Vol. 48, p. 8}

SUTTON, BENJAMIN (Maryland Navy), marine on the State Ship *Defence* in 1777. {Ref: Archives of Maryland Vol. 18, p. 660}

SUTTON, JACOB (Maryland Navy), marine on the State Ship *Defence* in 1777. {Ref: Archives of Maryland Vol. 18, p. 660}

SUTTON, RICHARD (Maryland Navy), marine on the State Ship *Defence* in 1777. {Ref: Archives of Maryland Vol. 18, p. 660}

SWAILES, ROBERT (Maryland Navy), marine on the State Ship *Defence* in 1777. {Ref: Archives of Maryland Vol. 18, p. 660}

SWAN, FREDERICK (Harford County), private who was enrolled 9 Dec 1775 in Militia Company No. 14 under Capt. William McComas. {Ref: George W. Archer Collection and Revolutionary War File, Historical Society of Harford County Archives}

SWAN, JOHN (Baltimore County), major in the 1st Maryland Continental Line before 16 Feb 1782, at which time he was *"paid £30 in lieu of a Suit of Cloaths for the present Year."* For additional information see Peden's *Revolutionary Patriots of Baltimore Town and Baltimore County, 1775-1783* (p. 265). {Ref: Archives of Maryland Vol. 48, p. 78}

SWAN, JOSEPH (Baltimore Town), patriot and merchant who enrolled in Capt. John Sterrett's Independent Mercantile Company by February, 1777, at which time they were mustered into regular service with the continental army to repress loyalist activities in the Eastern Shore counties of Somerset and Worcester. {Ref: J. Thomas Scharf's *History of Baltimore City and County*, Part I, p. 77}

SWAN, MATHEW (Baltimore County), patriot who supplied provisions to the State of Maryland between June and September, 1780. {Ref: Archives of Maryland Vol. 45, p. 84}

SWART, SAMUEL (Harford County, Susquehannah Hundred), private who was enrolled 23 Apr 1776 in Militia Company No. 21 under Capt. George Patterson.

262

{Ref: George W. Archer Collection and Revolutionary War File, Historical Society of Harford County Archives}

SWEARINGEN, JOSEPH (Frederick County), general and patriot buried in Mount Olivet Cemetery. {Ref: Information compiled by Dr. Donald Wolf in Maryland Society SAR Newsletter circa 1996}

SWEARINGEN, SUSANNAH, see "James Higgins," q.v.

SWENEY, DAVID, JR. (Harford County), private who was enrolled 10 Mar 1776 in Militia Company No. 18 under Capt. John Jolly. {Ref: George W. Archer Collection and Revolutionary War File, Historical Society of Harford County Archives}

SWINK, HARDMAN (Cecil County), private in the Maryland Continental Line by 1778, was retained in the service on 22 Jun 1778 and sent on board the galleys. {Ref: Archives of Maryland Vol. 21, p. 144}

SYSAS, JAMES (Baltimore County), private who was drafted into the Maryland Continental Line, was discharged on 8 Dec 1781. {Ref: Archives of Maryland Vol. 48, p. 10}

TALBOTT, BENJAMIN (Baltimore County), captain, 31 May 1779, Militia Company, Cockey's Battalion. {Ref: Maryland Historical Magazine, Vol. 7, No. 1, p. 90}

TALBOTT, JOHN (Baltimore County), private, 31 May 1779, Capt. Benjamin Talbott's Militia Company, Cockey's Battalion. {Ref: Maryland Historical Magazine, Vol. 7, No. 1, p. 90}

TALBOTT, VINCENT (Baltimore County), sergeant, 31 May 1779, Capt. Benjamin Talbott's Militia Company, Cockey's Battalion. {Ref: Maryland Historical Magazine, Vol. 7, No. 1, p. 90}

TALBY, ZACH. (Harford County), private who was enrolled 16 Sep 1775 in Militia Company No. 6 under Capt. Benjamin Rumsey. {Ref: George W. Archer Collection and Revolutionary War File, Historical Society of Harford County Archives}

TANEY, CHARLES (St. Mary's County), private in the Maryland Continental Line who was drafted to serve until 10 Dec 1781, was discharged on 29 Nov 1781. {Ref: Archives of Maryland Vol. 48, p. 6}

TANNEHILL, JOSIAH, see "Jesse Dungan," q.v.

TANNEHILL, NINIAN (Western Maryland), private in Capt. Michael Cresap's Company in 1775. {Ref: Howard L. Leckey's *The Tenmile Country and Its Pioneer Families*, p. 16}

TARLTON, JOHN (St. Mary's County), patriot who supplied 320 lbs. of beef on the hoof to the State of Maryland on 8 Oct 1780. {Ref: Archives of Maryland Vol. 45, p. 156}

TARMAN, RHODA, see "James Kidd," q.v.

TARMAN, RICHARD, JR. (Calvert County), private (substitute) in the Maryland Continental Line by 1781, was discharged on 8 Dec 1781. {Ref: Archives of Maryland Vol. 48, p. 10}

TARMAN, RICHARD, SR. (Calvert County), private (substitute) in the Maryland Continental Line by 1781, was discharged on 8 Dec 1781. {Ref: Archives of Maryland Vol. 48, p. 10}

TATE, DAVID (Harford County), private who was enrolled 9 Dec 1775 in Militia Company No. 14 under Capt. William McComas; David Tate died by 22 Jun 1813 (date of final distribution) and his heirs were Elizabeth Tate (widow), sons Samuel and James Tate, and daughters Mary Vernay, Margaret Tate, and Martha Tate. {Ref: George W. Archer Collection and Revolutionary War File, Historical Society of Harford County Archives; Henry C. Peden, Jr.'s *Heirs & Legatees of Harford County, 1802-1846*, p. 18}

TATE, JAMES (Baltimore Privateer), commander of the sloop *Franklin*, mounting 10 carriage guns, 6 swivel guns and 10 small arms, was issued Letters of Marque & Reprisal by the Council of Maryland on 11 Mar 1779. {Ref: Archives of Maryland Vol. 21, p. 320}

TATEM, BENJAMIN (Baltimore Privateer), commander of the schooner *General Gates*, mounting 8 swivel guns and 9 small arms, was issued Letters of Marque & Reprisal by the Council of Maryland on 5 Apr 1779. {Ref: Archives of Maryland Vol. 21, p. 336}

TAYLOR, CATHARINE, see "Christopher Taylor," q.v.

TAYLOR, CHRISTOPHER (Baltimore City), surgeon's mate in the Pennsylvania Line who applied for pension at Baltimore in 1828, aged 63; he applied again under the Act of June 7, 1832, but the claim was suspended because he was *"already pensioned under Act of 1818 and his petition for increase is unfounded."* He died on 11 Jun 1839 and was survived by three daughters: Ann Amelung, Hannah Taylor, and Catharine L. Taylor. {Ref: *Rejected or Suspended Applications for Revolutionary War Pensions* (1850 Report), p. 232; Research by Virgil D. White, citing Federal Pension Application S42450}

TAYLOR, HANNAH, see "Christopher Taylor," q.v.

TAYLOR, JAMES (Baltimore County), private, aged 23, plaisterer, born in London, enlisted (made his "X" mark) on 31 Aug 1776 in Capt. John Fulford's Company of Matrosses. {Ref: Maryland Historical Magazine, Vol. 69, No. 1, p. 96}

TAYLOR, JAMES (Dorchester County), private (substitute) in the Maryland Continental Line by 1781, was discharged on 8 Dec 1781. {Ref: Archives of Maryland Vol. 48, p. 10}

TAYLOR, JAMES (Western Maryland), private in Capt. Michael Cresap's Company in 1775. {Ref: Howard L. Leckey's *The Tenmile Country and Its Pioneer Families*, p. 16}

TAYLOR, JOHN, see "Daniel Root," q.v.

TAYLOR, MARGARET, see "George Dougherty," q.v.

TAYLOR, RICHARD (Prince George's County), private (substitute) in the Maryland Continental Line by 1781, was discharged on 8 Dec 1781. {Ref: Archives of Maryland Vol. 48, p. 10}

TAYLOR, ROBERT (Charles County), recommended as first lieutenant in the 26th Battalion of Militia of Charles County on 20 Mar 1781. {Ref: Archives of Maryland Vol. 47, p. 136}

TAYLOR, THOMAS (Queen Anne's County), private (substitute) in the Maryland Continental Line by 1781, was discharged on 8 Dec 1781. {Ref: Archives of Maryland Vol. 48, p. 11}

TAYLOR, WILLIAM (Baltimore Privateer), commander of the brigantine *Duke of Leinster*, navigated by 60 men and mounting 16 carriage guns, 2 swivel guns and 20 small arms, was issued Letters of Marque & Reprisal by the Council of Maryland on 8 Aug 1780. {Ref: Archives of Maryland Vol. 43, p. 249}

TAYLOR, WILLIAM (Harford County), private who was enrolled 10 Mar 1776 in Militia Company No. 18 under Capt. John Jolly. {Ref: George W. Archer Collection and Revolutionary War File, Historical Society of Harford County Archives}

TEAGARDEN, ABRAHAM (Western Maryland), private in Capt. Michael Cresap's Company in 1775. {Ref: Howard L. Leckey's *The Tenmile Country and Its Pioneer Families*, p. 16}

TEAMS, PETER (Baltimore County), private who enlisted in Pulaski's Legion in 1778, discharged 15 Nov 1783. {Ref: Maryland Historical Magazine, Vol. 13, No. 3, p. 223}

TEDFORD, JOHN (Baltimore County), private who enlisted in Pulaski's Legion on 12 May 1778 in Baltimore. {Ref: Maryland Historical Magazine, Vol. 13, No. 3, p. 222}

TEMBLIN, JOHN (Frederick County), private (substitute) in the Maryland Continental Line, German Regiment, enrolled in April, 1778 for 3 years or duration of the war. {Ref: Maryland Historical Magazine, Vol. 6, No. 3, p. 257}

TENANT, JAMES (Prince George's County), private (substitute) in the Maryland Continental Line by 1781, was discharged on 8 Dec 1781. {Ref: Archives of Maryland Vol. 48, p. 10}

TERRELL, JOHN (Western Maryland), private in Capt. Michael Cresap's Company in 1775. {Ref: Howard L. Leckey's *The Tenmile Country and Its Pioneer Families*, p. 16}

THOMAS, EDWARD (Western Maryland), private in Capt. Michael Cresap's Company in 1775. {Ref: Howard L. Leckey's *The Tenmile Country and Its Pioneer Families*, p. 16}

THOMAS, ISAAC (Harford County), private who was enrolled 10 Mar 1776 in Militia Company No. 18 under Capt. John Jolly. {Ref: George W. Archer Collection and Revolutionary War File, Historical Society of Harford County Archives}

THOMAS, JAMES (Harford County), ensign on 10 Mar 1776 in Militia Company No. 18 under Capt. John Jolly. {Ref: George W. Archer Collection and Revolutionary War File, Historical Society of Harford County Archives}

THOMAS, JOHN (Western Maryland), private in Capt. Michael Cresap's Company in 1775. {Ref: Howard L. Leckey's *The Tenmile Country and Its Pioneer Families*, p. 16}

THOMAS, JOSEPH (Harford County), private who was enrolled 9 Dec 1775 in Militia Company No. 14 under Capt. William McComas. {Ref: George W. Archer Collection and Revolutionary War File, Historical Society of Harford County Archives}

THOMAS, MARY, see "Benjamin Moore," q.v.

THOMAS, PHILIP (Frederick County), doctor and patriot buried in Mount Olivet Cemetery. {Ref: Information compiled by Dr. Donald Wolf in Maryland Society SAR Newsletter circa 1996}

THOMAS, RICHARD (Montgomery County), patriot who took the Oath of Fidelity and Support to the State of Maryland (affirmed) on 7 Apr 1778. {Ref: Archives of Maryland Vol. 21, p. 13}

THOMAS, SAMUEL (Caroline County), first lieutenant in Col. Richardson's Regiment in 1776 who was recommended for promotion to captain. {Ref: Archives of Maryland Vol. 18, p. 74}

THOMAS, STARLING (Kent County), private (substitute) in the Maryland Continental Line by 1781, was discharged on 8 Dec 1781. {Ref: Archives of Maryland Vol. 48, p. 11}

THOMAS, WILLIAM (Dorchester County Privateer), commander of the schooner *Molly*, navigated by 10 men and mounting 6 carriage guns, 4 swivel guns and 16 small arms, was issued Letters of Marque & Reprisal by the Council of Maryland on 16 Oct 1778; commander of the schooner *Freemason*, navigated by 14 men and mounting 6 swivel guns, was issued Letters of Marque & Reprisal by the Council of Maryland on 19 Jun 1780. {Ref: Archives of Maryland Vol. 21, p. 217 and Vol. 43, p. 199}

THOMAS, WILLIAM, see "John Patrick," q.v.

THOMPSON, ANDREW (Harford County), private who was enrolled 9 Dec 1775 in Militia Company No. 14 under Capt. William McComas. {Ref: George W. Archer Collection and Revolutionary War File, Historical Society of Harford County Archives}

THOMPSON, EDWARD (Harford County, Susquehannah Hundred), private who was enrolled 23 Apr 1776 in Militia Company No. 21 under Capt. George Patterson. {Ref: George W. Archer Collection and Revolutionary War File, Historical Society of Harford County Archives}

THOMPSON, ELIZABETH, see "James Kidd," q.v.

THOMPSON, GEORGE (Maryland Navy), sailor on the State Ship *Defence* in 1777. {Ref: Archives of Maryland Vol. 18, p. 660}

THOMPSON, HANNAH, see "Richard Hope," q.v.

THOMPSON, JAMES (Harford County), private who was enrolled 9 Dec 1775 in Militia Company No. 14 under Capt. William McComas. {Ref: George W. Archer Collection and Revolutionary War File, Historical Society of Harford County Archives}

THOMPSON, JOHN (Baltimore or Frederick County), private in Pulaski's Legion before July, 1782. {Ref: Maryland Historical Magazine, Vol. 13, No. 3, p. 225}

THOMPSON, JOHN (Maryland Navy), seaman or marine on the State Ship *Defence* in 1777. {Ref: Archives of Maryland Vol. 18, p. 660}

THOMPSON, MARY, see "Abraham Mitchell," q.v.

THOMPSON, SAMUEL (Queen Anne's County), first major in the 5th Battalion of Militia, commissioned 8 May 1777; appointed by the Council of Maryland on 27 Jan 1776 as one of three persons in Queen Anne's County to collect all gold and silver coin that can be procured in said county. {Ref: Archives of Maryland Vol. 11, p. 132 and Vol. 16, p. 243}

THOMPSON, WILLIAM (Maryland Privateer), commander of the schooner *Two Sisters*, navigated by 8 men and mounting 4 swivel guns and 6 muskets, was issued Letters of Marque & Reprisal by the Council of Maryland on 13 Mar 1780. {Ref: Archives of Maryland Vol. 43, pp. 109-110}

THOMSON, GEORGE (Baltimore or Frederick County), private who enlisted in Pulaski's Legion on 15 Jun 1779. {Ref: Maryland Historical Magazine, Vol. 13, No. 3, p. 224}

THORNTON, WILLIAM (Anne Arundel County), patriot who took the Oath of Fidelity and Support to the State of Maryland on 9 Apr 1778. {Ref: Archives of Maryland Vol. 21, p. 22}

TIBBITT, JAMES (Maryland Privateer), commander of the sloop *Independence*, was issued Letters of Marque & Reprisal by the Council of Maryland on 30 Sep 1776. {Ref: Archives of Maryland Vol. 12, p. 311}

TIDINGS, CALEB (Anne Arundel County), private (substitute) in the Maryland Continental Line by 1781, was discharged on 8 Dec 1781. {Ref: Archives of Maryland Vol. 48, p. 11}

TILDEN, MARMADUKE (Kent County), patriot who was commissioned one of the three persons in Kent County by the Council of Maryland on 19 Aug 1779 to receive subscriptions for use of the State. {Ref: Archives of Maryland Vol. 21, p. 499}

TILGHMAN, FRISBY, see "William Lamar," q.v.

TILGHMAN, GEORGE, see "David Lynn" and "William Lamar," q.v.

TILGHMAN, RICHARD, OF MATTHEW (Queen Anne's County), first major of the 5th Battalion of Militia, commissioned 8 May 1777. {Ref: Archives of Maryland Vol. 16, p. 243}

TILLEY, ZACHARIAH (Prince George's County), private in the Maryland Continental Line who was drafted to serve until 10 Dec 1781, was discharged on 11 Dec 1781. {Ref: Archives of Maryland Vol. 48, p. 18}

TIPPETT, NOTLEY (Baltimore County), private who enlisted in Pulaski's Legion in July, 1778 or 1779 in Baltimore. {Ref: Maryland Historical Magazine, Vol. 13, No. 3, p. 222}

TISDALE, ---- (Baltimore County?), private in the 7th Maryland Continental Line by 10 May 1780 at which time his wife Catharine Tisdale received 3 days' rations from the Issuing Commissary. {Ref: Archives of Maryland Vol. 43, p. 170}

TODD, EDWARD (Western Maryland), private in Capt. Michael Cresap's Company in 1775. {Ref: Howard L. Leckey's *The Tenmile Country and Its Pioneer Families*, p. 16}

TODD, THOMAS (Western Maryland), private in Capt. Michael Cresap's Company in 1775. {Ref: Howard L. Leckey's *The Tenmile Country and Its Pioneer Families*, p. 16}

TONT, ABRAHAM (Harford County), private who was enrolled 9 Dec 1775 in Militia Company No. 14 under Capt. William McComas. {Ref: George W. Archer Collection and Revolutionary War File, Historical Society of Harford County Archives}

TOOLE, ROBERT (Baltimore County), matross soldier by 7 May 1779 at which time he gave a deposition about his enlistment terms. {Ref: Maryland State Archives Record MdHR 6636-14-83}

TOOLOE, DENNIS (Maryland Navy), marine on the State Ship *Defence* in 1777. {Ref: Archives of Maryland Vol. 18, p. 660}

TOOTELL, JAMES (Anne Arundel County), major in the Severn Battalion of Militia, commissioned 26 Jan 1777 by the Maryland Council of Safety; died by 10 Nov 1809 (date of distribution), leaving children Hellen Tootell, Elizabeth Plater, Ann Tootell, Mary Childs, and Rosanna Tootell; also see "John Davis," q.v. {Ref: Archives of Maryland Vol. 16, p. 77; Anne Arundel County Administration Account JG No. 2, p. 139}

TOOTELL (TOOTLE), RICHARD (Anne Arundel County), patriot and doctor who was *"requested to remove any Soldiers of Infectious Disorders, to be nursed in private Houses"* on 17 Sep 1776 by order of the Council of Maryland; on 17 Dec 1776 the Council of Safety ordered that *"he should have such necessaries out of the Public Store as he may think are wanting for the use of the Hospital."* {Ref: Archives of Maryland Vol. 12, pp. 276, 534}

TOPET, ROBERT (Maryland Navy), marine on the State Ship *Defence* in 1777. {Ref: Archives of Maryland Vol. 18, p. 660}

TOWNSEND, GEORGE (Talbot County), private who was drafted into the Maryland Continental Line, was discharged on 8 Dec 1781. {Ref: Archives of Maryland Vol. 48, p. 10}

TOWNSEND, JOHN (Worcester County), first lieutenant in the county militia, commissioned 21 Jun 1776. {Ref: Archives of Maryland Vol. 11, p. 506}

TOWSON, EZEKIEL (Baltimore County), captain of a guard for the magazine in Baltimore County by 4 Oct 1776 at which time he was engaged by the Maryland Council of Safety to hire 12 men and draw rations for that purpose. {Ref: Archives of Maryland Vol. 12, p. 319}

TRAINER, PATRICK (Frederick County), private (substitute) in the Maryland Continental Line, Williams' Regiment, enrolled in May, 1778 for 3 years or duration of the war. {Ref: Maryland Historical Magazine, Vol. 6, No. 3, p. 261}

TRAINER, SIMON (Maryland Navy), marine on the State Ship *Defence* in 1777. {Ref: Archives of Maryland Vol. 18, p. 660}

TRANTER, THOMAS (Baltimore County), private, aged 21, miller, born in Pennsylvania, enlisted 19 Feb 1776 in Capt. John Fulford's Company of

Matrosses, deserted 28 Feb 1776. {Ref: Maryland Historical Magazine, Vol. 69, No. 1, pp. 95, 97}

TRAVISE, CATHARINE, see "Henry Hoffman," q.v.

TREADWAY, DANIEL (Harford County), private who was enrolled 16 Sep 1775 in Militia Company No. 6 under Capt. Benjamin Rumsey. {Ref: George W. Archer Collection and Revolutionary War File, Historical Society of Harford County Archives}

TREGASHES, JACOB (Maryland Navy), armorer on the State Ship *Defence* in 1777. {Ref: Archives of Maryland Vol. 18, p. 660}

TRIMBLE, ROBERT (Harford County), private who was enrolled 9 Dec 1775 in Militia Company No. 11 under Capt. Thomas Bond. {Ref: Preston's History of Harford County, p. 117, which misspelled the name as "Robert Fremble"}

TRIPPE, LEVIN (Baltimore Privateer), commander of the sloop *Isabella*, mounting 6 carriage guns, 4 swivel guns and 8 small arms, was issued Letters of Marque & Reprisal by the Council of Maryland on 12 Aug 1779; commander of the schooner *Isabella*, navigated by 15 men and mounting 6 carriage guns, 4 swivel guns and 8 muskets, was issued Letters of Marque & Reprisal by the Council of Maryland on 6 Apr 1780. {Ref: Archives of Maryland Vol. 21, p. 491 and Vol. 43, p. 132}

TROT, WILLIAM (Maryland Navy), ordinary sailor on the State Ship *Defence* in 1777. {Ref: Archives of Maryland Vol. 18, p. 660}

TROTTER, LONDON (Western Maryland), private in Capt. Michael Cresap's Company in 1775. {Ref: Howard L. Leckey's *The Tenmile Country and Its Pioneer Families*, p. 16}

TROUP, JOHN (Talbot County), patriot and doctor by 26 Aug 1778 at which time the Council of Maryland recorded, in part, that *"he hath been absent in France for about 7 months last past and hath lately that is to say within 3 Months now last past, returned into this State, appeared before the Council, and before them did take, repeat and Subscribe the Oath of Fidelity and Support to this State Contained in the Act entitled An Act to Punish Certain Crimes and Misdemeanors and to prevent the Growth of Toryism."* He was commissioned one of the three persons in Talbot County by the Council of Maryland on 19 Aug 1779 to receive subscriptions for use of the State. {Ref: Archives of Maryland Vol. 21, pp. 190, 499}

TROUTMAN, MICHAEL (Frederick County), captain in the militia in 1782. {Ref: Archives of Maryland Vol. 48, p. 248}

TROY, JOSEPH (Montgomery County), private (substitute) in the Maryland Continental Line by 1781, was discharged on 8 Dec 1781. {Ref: Archives of Maryland Vol. 48, p. 17}

TRUGARD, WILLIAM (Baltimore County), private who enlisted in Pulaski's Legion on 22 May 1778 in Baltimore, later deserted (no date was given) {Ref: Maryland Historical Magazine, Vol. 13, No. 3, p. 222}

TRUMAN (TRUEMAN), ALEXANDER (Prince George's County), captain in the 2nd and 6th Maryland Continental Lines who received payment for his services in the amount of "1900 Dollars & £3.10s" on 12 Sep 1780. Alexander was active in the military throughout the revolution and became an original member of the Society of the Cincinnati in 1783; he rejoined the U. S. Army in 1790 as a captain, rose to the rank of major, and was killed by Indians while on a peace mission to the Ohio Valley in April, 1792; his daughter Mary Ann Truman later moved to Kentucky, married Byrd Rogers in 1801, and died in Barren County in 1822. {Ref: Archives of Maryland Vol. 45, p. 98; Research by Henry C. Peden, Jr. of Bel Air, Maryland (a direct descendant) in 2001}

TRUMAN (TRUEMAN), JOHN (Anne Arundel County), ensign in the 3rd Maryland Continental Line who received payment for his services in the amount of "1900 Dollars & £3.10s" on 12 Sep 1780. {Ref: Archives of Maryland Vol. 45, p. 98}

TRUMAN (TRUEMAN), THOMAS (Prince George's County), captain (Prince George's County),

TSCHUDY, ELIZABETH, see "William Clemm," q.v.

TUCKER, ISAAC (Anne Arundel County), private by 5 Oct 1776 (made his "+" mark) in Capt. Richard Chew's Militia Company, Weems' Battalion. {Ref: Archives of Maryland Vol. 12, p. 322}

TUCKER, JACOB (Dorchester County), private (substitute) in the Maryland Continental Line by 1781, was discharged on 8 Dec 1781. {Ref: Archives of Maryland Vol. 48, p. 10}

TUCKER, SEABORN (Anne Arundel County), private by 5 Oct 1776 (made his "X" mark) in Capt. Richard Chew's Militia Company, Weems' Battalion. {Ref: Archives of Maryland Vol. 12, p. 322}

TURNBULL, GEORGE (Baltimore County), captain of the State Ship *Defence* in the Maryland Navy in 1777; took the Oath of Fidelity and Allegiance to the State of Maryland on 31 Mar 1778. {Ref: Archives of Maryland Vol. 16, p. 559, and Vol. 18, p. 660 which listed his name as "Turnbull, C. George"}

TURNER, ----, JR. (Harford County), third sergeant, enrolled by 15 Apr 1776 in Militia Company No. 20 under Capt. Robert Glenn. {Ref: George W. Archer Collection and Revolutionary War File, Historical Society of Harford County Archives}

TURNER, ----, SR. (Harford County), second sergeant, enrolled by 15 Apr 1776 in Militia Company No. 20 under Capt. Robert Glenn. {Ref: George W. Archer Collection and Revolutionary War File, Historical Society of Harford County Archives}

TURNER, ABRAHAM (Anne Arundel County), private by 5 Oct 1776 (made his "+" mark) in Capt. Richard Chew's Militia Company, Weems' Battalion. {Ref: Archives of Maryland Vol. 12, p. 323}

TURNER, JOHN (Harford County), private who was enrolled 9 Dec 1775 in Militia Company No. 14 under Capt. William McComas. {Ref: George W. Archer Collection and Revolutionary War File, Historical Society of Harford County Archives}

TURNER, OSBURN (Worcester County), private (substitute) in the Maryland Continental Line by 1781, was discharged on 8 Dec 1781. {Ref: Archives of Maryland Vol. 48, p. 11}

TURNER, ROBERT (Harford County), private who was enrolled by 15 Apr 1776 in Militia Company No. 20 under Capt. Robert Glenn. {Ref: George W. Archer Collection and Revolutionary War File, Historical Society of Harford County Archives}

TURNER, SAMUEL (Harford County), private who was enrolled by 15 Apr 1776 in Militia Company No. 20 under Capt. Robert Glenn. {Ref: George W. Archer Collection and Revolutionary War File, Historical Society of Harford County Archives}

TURNER, THOMAS (Anne Arundel County), private by 5 Oct 1776 (made his "+" mark) in Capt. Richard Chew's Militia Company, Weems' Battalion. {Ref: Archives of Maryland Vol. 12, p. 322}

TURNER, WILLIAM (Anne Arundel County), private by 5 Oct 1776 (made his "+" mark) in Capt. Richard Chew's Militia Company, Weems' Battalion. {Ref: Archives of Maryland Vol. 12, p. 323}

TURNER, ZEPHANIAH (Charles County), patriot who was appointed Auditor General by the Maryland Assembly and qualified before the Governor & Council by taking the several required oaths on 11 Apr 1778. {Ref: Archives of Maryland Vol. 21, p. 29}

TUTWEILER (TUTWILLER), JONATHAN (Washington County), sergeant in the 7th Maryland Continental Line, enlisted 4 Dec 1776 and was discharged 7 Dec 1779; died 19 Jul 1819. {Ref: Archives of Maryland Vol. 18, p. 253; J. Thomas Scharf's *History of Western Maryland*, Vol. II, p. 1056}

TWINER, JOHN (Frederick County), private (substitute) in the Maryland Continental Line, Gunby's Regiment, enrolled in May, 1778 for 3 years or duration of the war. {Ref: Maryland Historical Magazine, Vol. 6, No. 3, p. 259}

TYLER, LITTLETON (Maryland Navy), carpenter on the State Ship *Defence* in 1777. {Ref: Archives of Maryland Vol. 18, p. 660}

UNDERWOOD, SUSAN, see "John Lindsay," q.v.

VALLETTE, ELIE (Annapolis), patriot who was appointed Principal Clerk to the Auditor General and qualified before the Council of Maryland by taking the several required oaths on 6 May 1778. {Ref: Archives of Maryland Vol. 21, p. 68}

VALENTINE, GEORGE (Washington County), private who was enrolled to serve as a substitute in the Maryland Continental Line until 10 Dec 1781, but *"being represented unfit for the service for which he was intended"* was discharged on 30 Oct 1781. {Ref: Archives of Maryland Vol. 45, p. 657}

VALLIANT, ANSON (Caroline County), private who was drafted into the Maryland Continental Line, was discharged on 8 Dec 1781. {Ref: Archives of Maryland Vol. 48, p. 10}

VALLIANT, JOHN (Maryland Privateer), captain of a schooner [not named] in April, 1776; captain of the boat *Polly* which was impressed into service by order of the Council of Maryland on 27 Apr 1780 *"to go to the Head of Elk for the Purpose of Transporting a Detachment of the American Army to the State of Virginia."* {Ref: Archives of Maryland Vol. 11, p. 396 and Vol. 43, p. 155}

VALLIANT, NICHOLAS (Maryland Privateer), captain of the schooner *Sally* which was impressed into service by order of the Council of Maryland on 27 Apr 1780 *"to go to the Head of Elk for the Purpose of Transporting a Detachment of the American Army to the State of Virginia."* {Ref: Archives of Maryland Vol. 43, p. 155}

VAN CAMP, SARAH, see "Josiah Prickett," q.v.

VAN CAMP, LARANCE, see "Josiah Prickett," q.v.

VANSICKLE, GILBERT (Maryland Navy), seaman on the State Ship *Defence* in 1777. {Ref: Archives of Maryland Vol. 18, p. 660}

VAUGHAN, ABRAHAM (Maryland Navy), marine on the State Ship *Defence* in 1777. {Ref: Archives of Maryland Vol. 18, p. 660}

VAUGHAN, CORNELIUS (Frederick County), private (substitute) in the Maryland Continental Line, German Regiment, enrolled in May, 1778 for 3 years or duration of the war. {Ref: Maryland Historical Magazine, Vol. 6, No. 3, p. 260}

VAUN, JOHN (Maryland Navy), marine on the State Ship *Defence* in 1777. {Ref: Archives of Maryland Vol. 18, p. 660}

VERNAY, MARY, see "David Tate," q.v.

VESEY, JOSEPH (Maryland Privateer), commander of the sloop *Adriana*, navigated by 47 men and mounting 9 carriage guns, 6 swivel guns and 36 small arms, was issued Letters of Marque & Reprisal by the Council of Maryland on 8 Oct 1778. {Ref: Archives of Maryland Vol. 21, p. 215}

VEST, GEORGE (Western Maryland), private in Capt. Michael Cresap's Company in 1775. {Ref: Howard L. Leckey's *The Tenmile Country and Its Pioneer Families*, p. 16}

VICKARS, EZEKIEL (Dorchester County), lieutenant colonel of the Lower Battalion of Militia, commissioned 15 Jan 1783. {Ref: Archives of Maryland Vol. 48, p. 344}

VINCENT, AARON (Dorchester County), private (substitute) in the Maryland Continental Line by 1781, was discharged on 8 Dec 1781. {Ref: Archives of Maryland Vol. 48, p. 10}

VINCENT, WILLIAM (Frederick County), private (substitute) in the Maryland Continental Line, German Regiment, enrolled in May, 1778 for 3 years or duration of the war. {Ref: Maryland Historical Magazine, Vol. 6, No. 3, p. 261}

VIRGIN, BRICE (Western Maryland), sergeant in Capt. Michael Cresap's Company in 1775. {Ref: Howard L. Leckey's *The Tenmile Country and Its Pioneer Families*, p. 15}

VIRGIN, JOHN (Western Maryland), private in Capt. Michael Cresap's Company in 1775. {Ref: Howard L. Leckey's *The Tenmile Country and Its Pioneer Families*, p. 16}

VOGAN, JAMES (Harford County), private who was enrolled 9 Dec 1775 in Militia Company No. 14 under Capt. William McComas. {Ref: George W. Archer Collection and Revolutionary War File, Historical Society of Harford County Archives}

VOORHEES, JOHN (Kent County), patriot who was appointed Commissary of Purchases by the Council of Maryland on 8 Jul 1780; a John Voorhees died testate in Kent County by 13 Jan 1792. {Ref: Archives of Maryland Vol. 43, p. 215; Kent County Wills Liber 7, p. 338}

WADE, JOHN (Frederick County), private (substitute) in the Maryland Continental Line, German Regiment, enrolled in May, 1778 for 3 years or duration of the war. {Ref: Maryland Historical Magazine, Vol. 6, No. 3, p. 258}

WADE, JOSEPH (Western Maryland), private in Capt. Michael Cresap's Company in 1775. {Ref: Howard L. Leckey's *The Tenmile Country and Its Pioneer Families*, p. 16}

WADE, ROBERT (Prince George's County), captain who served on a General Court-Martial on 6 Jul 1776. {Ref: Archives of Maryland Vol. 11, p. 553}

WAGGONER, CHRISTOPHER (Frederick County), private who was enrolled to serve as a substitute in the Maryland Continental Line until 10 Dec 1781, but *"being represented unfit for the service for which he was intended"* was discharged on 30 Oct 1781. {Ref: Archives of Maryland Vol. 45, p. 657}

WAINWRIGHT, JOHN (Maryland Privateer), commander of the sloop *Ranger*, navigated by 15 men and mounting 7 carriage guns, 1 swivel gun and 11 small arms, was issued Letters of Marque & Reprisal by the Council of Maryland on 8 Oct 1778. {Ref: Archives of Maryland Vol. 21, p. 215}

WALDRUG, JOHN (Western Maryland), private in Capt. Michael Cresap's Company in 1775. {Ref: Howard L. Leckey's *The Tenmile Country and Its Pioneer Families*, p. 16}

WALER, JOHN (Frederick County), private (substitute) in the Maryland Continental Line, Price's Regiment, enrolled in May, 1778 for 3 years or duration of the war. {Ref: Maryland Historical Magazine, Vol. 6, No. 3, p. 261}

WALKER, JAMES (Harford County), second lieutenant, commissioned -- Feb 1777, Militia Company No. 32. {Ref: George W. Archer Collection and Revolutionary War File, Historical Society of Harford County Archives}

WALKER, JOHN (Harford County), first lieutenant on 9 Dec 1775 in Militia Company No. 14 under Capt. William McComas. {Ref: George W. Archer Collection and Revolutionary War File, Historical Society of Harford County Archives}

WALKER, JOHN (Baltimore County), private, aged 28, labourer, born in England, enlisted 2 Mar 1776 in Capt. John Fulford's Company of Matrosses. {Ref: Maryland Historical Magazine, Vol. 69, No. 1, p. 96}

WALKER, MOSES (Western Maryland), private in Capt. Michael Cresap's Company in 1775. {Ref: Howard L. Leckey's *The Tenmile Country and Its Pioneer Families*, p. 16}

WALKER, SAMUEL (Maryland Navy), master on the State Ship *Defence* in 1777. {Ref: Archives of Maryland Vol. 18, p. 660}

WALKER, THOMAS (Maryland Navy and Annapolis Privateer), lieutenant of marines on the State Ship *Defence* in 1777; commander of the sloop *Dispatch*, mounting no guns, was issued Letters of Marque & Reprisal by the Council of

Maryland on 21 Jun 1779; commander of the schooner *Dispatch*, navigated by 6 men and mounting 4 swivel guns, was issued Letters of Marque & Reprisal by the Council of Maryland on 1 Mar 1780. {Ref: Archives of Maryland Vol. 18, p. 660, Vol. 21, p. 460 and Vol. 43, p. 99}

WALKER, WILLIAM (Baltimore County), private, aged 24, weaver, born in England, enlisted 18 Sep 1776 in Capt. John Fulford's Company of Matrosses. {Ref: Maryland Historical Magazine, Vol. 69, No. 1, p. 96}

WALLACE, BETHULA, see "William Harper," q.v.

WALLACE, JOHN (Queen Anne's County), private (substitute) in the Maryland Continental Line by 1781, was discharged on 8 Dec 1781. {Ref: Archives of Maryland Vol. 48, p. 11}

WALLEY, ZEDEKIAH (Maryland Navy), captain of the barge *Protector*, in the service of this state, commissioned 16 Jun 1781; see "Joseph Handy," q.v. {Ref: Archives of Maryland Vol. 45, p. 476}

WALSH, JOHN (Harford County), private who was enrolled by 15 Apr 1776 in Militia Company No. 20 under Capt. Robert Glenn. {Ref: George W. Archer Collection and Revolutionary War File, Historical Society of Harford County Archives}

WALTER, LEVIN (Maryland Navy), seaman or marine on the State Ship *Defence* in 1777. {Ref: Archives of Maryland Vol. 18, p. 660}

WAND, WEST (Anne Arundel County), private by 5 Oct 1776 in Capt. Richard Chew's Militia Company, Weems' Battalion. {Ref: Archives of Maryland Vol. 12, p. 323}

WARD, CHARLES (Harford County), private who was enrolled 9 Dec 1775 in Militia Company No. 14 under Capt. William McComas. {Ref: George W. Archer Collection and Revolutionary War File, Historical Society of Harford County Archives}

WARD, JAMES, see "James Kidd," q.v.

WARD, JOHN (Cecil County), patriot who was commissioned one of the three persons in Cecil County by the Council of Maryland on 19 Aug 1779 to receive subscriptions for use of the State. {Ref: Archives of Maryland Vol. 21, p. 499}

WARD, JOHN (Queen Anne's County), private (substitute) in the Maryland Continental Line by 1781, was discharged on 8 Dec 1781. {Ref: Archives of Maryland Vol. 48, p. 10}

WARD, JOHN (Harford County), private who was enrolled 9 Dec 1775 in Militia Company No. 14 under Capt. William McComas. {Ref: George W. Archer Collection and Revolutionary War File, Historical Society of Harford County Archives}

WARD, JOHN (Maryland Navy), marine on the State Ship *Defence* in 1777. {Ref: Archives of Maryland Vol. 18, p. 660}

WARD, JOSEPH (Baltimore County), private, aged 23, bricklayer, born in England, enlisted (made his "X" mark) on 20 Jun 1776 in Capt. John Fulford's Company of Matrosses. {Ref: Maryland Historical Magazine, Vol. 69, No. 1, p. 96}

WARD, PHILIP (Washington County), private who was drafted to serve in the Maryland Continental Line until 10 Dec 1781, but *"being represented unfit for*

274

the duty for which he was intended" was discharged on 30 Oct 1781. {Ref: Archives of Maryland Vol. 45, p. 656}

WARD, RACHEL, see "James Kidd," q.v.

WARFIELD, JOSEPH (Montgomery County), lieutenant in the Maryland troops who applied for pension under the Act of June 7, 1832, but the claim was suspended because *"he was not noticed on the rolls of his captain's company and his service as lieutenant was less than six months."* For additional information see Peden's *Revolutionary Patriots of Montgomery County, 1776-1783* (p. 340). {Ref: *Rejected or Suspended Applications for Revolutionary War Pensions* (1850 Report), p. 232}

WARFIELD, JOSHUA (Anne Arundel County), ensign in the Maryland Continental Line who was commissioned on 27 Jul 1780 to serve in the Regiment Extra by order of the Council of Maryland. {Ref: Archives of Maryland Vol. 43, p. 234}

WARFIELD, WALTER (Anne Arundel County), doctor for the 2nd and 6th Maryland Continental Lines who received payment for his services in the amount of "1900 Dollars & £3.10s" on 12 Sep 1780. {Ref: Archives of Maryland Vol. 45, p. 97}

WARFIELD, WILLIAM, see "William Clemm," q.v.

WARREN, GENERAL, see "George Moore," q.v.

WARREN, RICHARD (Harford County), private in the Maryland Continental Line who was *"sent from camp by General Smallwood as unfit for the service"* and was discharged on 22 Jun 1778. {Ref: Archives of Maryland Vol. 21, p. 144}

WARRING (WARING), CLEMENT (Prince George's County Privateer), patriot who was noted by the Council of Maryland on 29 Sep 1778 stating, in part, *"that he hath been absent in parts beyond the Seas for about 14 months last past and hath lately that is to say within 3 months last past, returned into this State, appeared before the Governor & Council, and before them did take, repeat and Subscribe the Oath of Fidelity and Support to this State contained in th Act entitled An Act to punish certain Crimes and Misdemeanors and to prevent the Growth of Toryism."* As commander of the brigantine *Duke of Leinster*, navigated by 14 men and mounting 4 carriage guns, was issued Letters of Marque & Reprisal by the Council of Maryland on 19 Jun 1780. {Ref: Archives of Maryland Vol. 21, p. 212 and Vol. 43, p. 199}

WARRINGTON, JAMES (Charles County), private who was drafted to serve in the Maryland Continental Line until 10 Dec 1781, but *"being represented unfit for the duty for which he was intended"* was discharged on 30 Oct 1781. {Ref: Archives of Maryland Vol. 45, p. 656}

WASHINGTON, GENERAL, see "Jesse Bussey" and "---- Collier" and "George Moore" and "Baruch Williams," q.v.

WATERMAN, PHILIS (Anne Arundel County), patriot who was paid 15 shillings by the Maryland Council of Safety for attending hospital on 5 Oct 1776. {Ref: Archives of Maryland Vol. 12, p. 321}

WATERS, JONATHAN (Maryland Navy), marine on the sloop *Lincoln* who was taken prisoner and confined in New York before 17 Jan 1781 and was subsequently exchanged. {Ref: Archives of Maryland Vol. 45, p. 277}

WATERS, RICHARD (Anne Arundel County), captain in the 1st Maryland Continental Line who received payment for his services in the amount of "1900 Dollars & £3.10s" on 12 Sep 1780. {Ref: Archives of Maryland Vol. 45, p. 97}

WATERS, THOMAS (Dorchester County Privateer), commander of the sloop *Lark*, navigated by 8 men and mounting 4 carriage guns, was issued Letters of Marque & Reprisal by the Council of Maryland on 11 Mar 1780. {Ref: Archives of Maryland Vol. 43, p. 106}

WATERS, WILLIAM (Caroline County), private (substitute) in the Maryland Continental Line, who enlisted to serve until 10 Dec 1781, was discharged on 29 Nov 1781. {Ref: Archives of Maryland Vol. 48, p. 7}

WATHEN, BARTON (Charles County), private who was drafted to serve in the Maryland Continental Line until 10 Dec 1781, but *"being represented unfit for the duty for which he was intended"* was discharged on 30 Oct 1781. {Ref: Archives of Maryland Vol. 45, p. 656}

WATKINS, GASSAWAY (Anne Arundel County), lieutenant in the 7th Maryland Continental Line who received payment for his services in the amount of "1900 Dollars & £3.10s" on 12 Sep 1780. {Ref: Archives of Maryland Vol. 45, p. 98}

WATKINS, JOHN (Baltimore County), soldier in the Maryland troops who was born 5 Mar 1758 near Fork Meeting House about 15 miles from Baltimore; applied for pension on 29 May 1841, aged 83, under the Act of June 7, 1832, but the claim was rejected because he did not serve six months. {Ref: *Rejected or Suspended Applications for Revolutionary War Pensions* (1850 Report), pp. 230, 232; Research by Virgil D. White, citing Federal Pension Application R11191}

WATKINS, SAMUEL (Harford County), private who was enrolled 9 Dec 1775 in Militia Company No. 14 under Capt. William McComas. {Ref: George W. Archer Collection and Revolutionary War File, Historical Society of Harford County Archives}

WATPOLE, JOSEPH (Maryland Navy), sailor on the State Ship *Defence* in 1777. {Ref: Archives of Maryland Vol. 18, p. 660}

WATSON, JAMES (Maryland Navy), patriot who served as *"captain after guard"* on the State Ship *Defence* in 1777. {Ref: Archives of Maryland Vol. 18, p. 660}

WATT, ROBERT (Harford County), private who was enrolled 9 Dec 1775 in Militia Company No. 14 under Capt. William McComas. {Ref: George W. Archer Collection and Revolutionary War File, Historical Society of Harford County Archives}

WATTERS, THOMAS (Harford County), private who was enrolled 9 Dec 1775 in Militia Company No. 14 under Capt. William McComas. {Ref: George W. Archer Collection and Revolutionary War File, Historical Society of Harford County Archives}

WATTS, JOSHUA (Anne Arundel County), patriot who took the Oath of Allegiance and Fidelity in 1778 (see Peden's *Revolutionary Patriots of Maryland, 1775-1783: A Supplement*); stated under oath on 7 Jun 1781 that he was above 50 years of age; apparently rendered service to the State during the war (nature not specified) and on 1 Aug 1781 the Maryland Council *"ordered that the Western Shore Treasurer pay to Joshua Watts three pounds, fifteen shillings of the bills emitted under the Act for the Emission of Bills of Credit not exceeding 200,000 pounds, etc., of the money appropriated for the current campaign due him per account passed by the Deputy Auditor."* He died testate in 1782 (will written in October, 1779), leaving wife Rachel, sons Samuel, Joshua, Nathan, Henry and William, and daughters Betsy, Anne, Mary, Susanna and Rachel. {Ref: Maryland State Archives Records MdHR 6636-30/124 and 6636-33-25/4; Archives of Maryland Vol. 45, p. 532; Anne Arundel County Wills TG1:34, pp. 56-57; Research by Harry Smith of Baltimore, Maryland (a direct descendant) in 2002}

WAUD, WILLIAM (Maryland Privateer), commander of the schooner *Laurens*, navigated by 18 men and mounting 8 carriage guns, was issued Letters of Marque & Reprisal by the Council of Maryland on 9 May 1780. {Ref: Archives of Maryland Vol. 43, pp. 167-168}

WAYLON, DENNIS (Frederick County), private (substitute) in the Maryland Continental Line, Gunby's Regiment, enrolled in May, 1778 for 3 years or duration of the war. {Ref: Maryland Historical Magazine, Vol. 6, No. 3, p. 261}

WAYNE, GENERAL, see "William Lewis" and "George Moore" and "William Richardson," q.v.

WEAN, THOMAS, JR. (Harford County), private who was enrolled 9 Dec 1775 in Militia Company No. 14 under Capt. William McComas. {Ref: George W. Archer Collection and Revolutionary War File, Historical Society of Harford County Archives}

WEARING, THOMAS (Western Maryland), ensign and later lieutenant in Capt. Michael Cresap's Company in 1775. {Ref: Howard L. Leckey's *The Tenmile Country and Its Pioneer Families*, p. 15}

WEATHERBY, JESSE (Maryland Privateer), commander of the schooner *Nelly and Polly*, mounting 6 swivel guns and 8 small arms, was issued Letters of Marque & Reprisal by the Council of Maryland on 19 Dec 1778. {Ref: Archives of Maryland Vol. 21, p. 269}

WEAVER, JACOB (Washington County), private (substitute) in the Maryland Continental Line, who enlisted to serve until 10 Dec 1781, was discharged on 29 Nov 1781. {Ref: Archives of Maryland Vol. 48, p. 7}

WEDDERSTRANDT, CONROD T. (Queen Anne's County), patriot who was appointed Commissary of Purchases by the Council of Maryland on 8 Jul 1780. {Ref: Archives of Maryland Vol. 43, p. 215}

WEDERSTRANDT, JOHN C. (Baltimore Town), patriot and merchant who enrolled in Capt. John Sterrett's Independent Mercantile Company by February, 1777, at which time they were mustered into regular service with the continental army to repress loyalist activities in the Eastern Shore counties of Somerset and Worcester. {Ref: J. Thomas Scharf's *History of Baltimore City and County*, Part I, p. 77}

WEEKS, BENJAMIN (Baltimore Privateer), commander of the brigantine *Cato*, navigated by 40 men and mounting 14 carriage guns, was issued Letters of Marque & Reprisal by the Council of Maryland on 30 Dec 1780. {Ref: Archives of Maryland Vol. 45, p. 257}

WEEKS, MARY, see "Charles Gilbert," q.v.

WEELART, JOHN (Frederick County), private (substitute) in the Maryland Continental Line by 1781, was discharged on 8 Dec 1781. {Ref: Archives of Maryland Vol. 48, p. 11}

WEEMS, DAVID (Frederick County), private who was drafted to serve in the Maryland Continental Line until 10 Dec 1781, but *"being represented unfit for the duty for which he was intended"* was discharged on 30 Oct 1781. {Ref: Archives of Maryland Vol. 45, p. 656}

WEEMS, JOHN (Anne Arundel County), patriot who was appointed by the Council of Maryland on 27 Jan 1776 as one of three persons to collect all the gold and silver coin that can be procured in said county; commissioned on 19 Aug 1779 as one of the three persons in Anne Arundel County to receive subscriptions for use of the State. {Ref: Archives of Maryland Vol. 11, p. 132, and Vol. 21, p. 499}

WEEMS, WILLIAM (Maryland Privateer), commander of the sloop *Little Sam*, mounting 6 carriage guns, 4 swivel guns and 12 small arms, was issued Letters of Marque & Reprisal by the Council of Maryland on 4 Feb 1779; commander of the sloop *Porpoise*, navigated by 16 men and mounting 6 carriage guns, 4 howitz guns and 6 small arms, was issued Letters of Marque & Reprisal by the Council of Maryland on 24 Apr 1780 and again on 1 Jan 1781; commander of the ship *Nantes*, navigated by 30 men and mounting 8 carriage guns, was issued Letters of Marque & Reprisal by the Council of Maryland on 14 Dec 1782. {Ref: Archives of Maryland Vol. 21, p. 292, Vol. 43, p. 150, Vol. 45, pp. 258-259, and Vol. 48, p. 322}

WEIGLE, JOSEPH (Frederick County), private (substitute) in the Maryland Continental Line, German Regiment, enrolled in April, 1778 for 3 years or duration of the war. {Ref: Maryland Historical Magazine, Vol. 6, No. 3, p. 257}

WEIL, APOLLONIA, see "John G. Main," q.v.

WELCH, JAMES (Frederick County), private (substitute) in the Maryland Continental Line, Price's Regiment, enrolled in April, 1778 for 3 years or duration of the war. {Ref: Maryland Historical Magazine, Vol. 6, No. 3, p. 257}

WELLER, DANIEL, see "Frederick Willhide," q.v.

WELLS, CHARLES (Baltimore Privateer), commander of the brigantine *Bantrus*, navigated by 18 men and mounting 6 carriage guns and 6 swivel guns, was issued Letters of Marque & Reprisal by the Council of Maryland on 8 Jun 1778. {Ref: Archives of Maryland Vol. 21, p. 126}

WELLS, JAMES (Baltimore County), private, aged 18, weaver, born in Ireland, enlisted (made his "O" mark) on 21 Feb 1776 in Capt. John Fulford's Company of Matrosses. {Ref: Maryland Historical Magazine, Vol. 69, No. 1, p. 95}

WELLS, WILLIAM (Harford County), private who was enrolled 25 Mar 1776 in Militia Company No. 19 under Capt. William Morgan. {Ref: George W. Archer Collection and Revolutionary War File, Historical Society of Harford County Archives}

WELSH, RICHARD, see "William Armitage," q.v.

WEST, DAVID (Harford County), private who was enrolled 9 Dec 1775 in Militia Company No. 14 under Capt. William McComas. {Ref: George W. Archer Collection and Revolutionary War File, Historical Society of Harford County Archives}

WEST, JONATHAN (Harford County), ensign, commissioned -- Feb 1777, Militia Company No. 31 under Capt. John Ashmead. {Ref: George W. Archer Collection and Revolutionary War File, Historical Society of Harford County Archives}

WEST, JOSEPH (Harford County), private who was enrolled 25 Mar 1776 in Militia Company No. 19 under Capt. William Morgan. {Ref: George W. Archer Collection and Revolutionary War File, Historical Society of Harford County Archives}

WEST, MARGARET, see "John B. Howard," q.v.

WEST, ROBERT (Harford County, Susquehannah Hundred), private who was enrolled 23 Apr 1776 in Militia Company No. 21 under Capt. George Patterson. {Ref: George W. Archer Collection and Revolutionary War File, Historical Society of Harford County Archives}

WEST, STEPHEN (Prince George's County), patriot who was appointed by the Council of Maryland on 27 Jan 1776 as one of three persons in Prince George's County to collect all gold and silver coin that can be procured in said county. {Ref: Archives of Maryland Vol. 11, p. 132}

WEST, THOMAS (Harford County), private who was enrolled 10 Mar 1776 in Militia Company No. 18 under Capt. John Jolly. {Ref: George W. Archer Collection and Revolutionary War File, Historical Society of Harford County Archives}

WEST, WILLIAM, see "Daniel Root," q.v.

WHALIN, LAWRENCE (Frederick County), private (substitute) in the Maryland Continental Line, Gunby's Regiment, enrolled in May, 1778 for 3 years or duration of the war. {Ref: Maryland Historical Magazine, Vol. 6, No. 3, p. 259}

WHALING, JAMES (Baltimore County), private, aged not stated, farmer, born in Maryland, enlisted (made his "X" mark) on 11 Mar 1776 in Capt. John Fulford's Company of Matrosses. {Ref: Maryland Historical Magazine, Vol. 69, No. 1, p. 96}

WHARTON, REVEL (Maryland Navy), seaman or marine on the State Ship *Defence* in 1777. {Ref: Archives of Maryland Vol. 18, p. 660}

WHARTON, THOMAS, see "Benjamin B. Norris," q.v.

WHEELER, BENJAMIN (Maryland Navy), marine on the State Ship *Defence* in 1777. {Ref: Archives of Maryland Vol. 18, p. 660}

WHEELER, HEZEKIAH (Prince George's County), captain who served on a General Court-Martial on 6 Jul 1776; commissioned captain of a Company of Select Militia on 8 Jun 1781; see "William Shircliff," q.v. {Ref: Archives of Maryland Vol. 11, p. 553 and Vol. 45, p. 466}

WHEELER, JOHN (Dorchester County), private (substitute) in the Maryland Continental Line by 1781, was discharged on 8 Dec 1781. {Ref: Archives of Maryland Vol. 48, p. 10}

WHEELER, RICHARD (Frederick County), sergeant who recruited for the Extra Regiment and was ordered to be paid for his services by the Council of Maryland on 17 Aug 1780. {Ref: Archives of Maryland Vol. 43, p. 257}

WHELER, BASILE (Baltimore County), private who enlisted in Pulaski's Legion on 22 Mar 1778 and still in service in November, 1779. {Ref: Maryland Historical Magazine, Vol. 13, No. 3, p. 223}

WHIT, WILLIAM (Frederick County), private (substitute) in the Maryland Continental Line, German Regiment, enrolled in May, 1778 for 3 years or duration of the war. {Ref: Maryland Historical Magazine, Vol. 6, No. 3, p. 259}

WHITAKER, ANN, see "Nathaniel Bayless," q.v.

WHITAKER, JOHN (Harford County), private who was enrolled by 15 Apr 1776 in Militia Company No. 20 under Capt. Robert Glenn. {Ref: George W. Archer Collection and Revolutionary War File, Historical Society of Harford County Archives}

WHITAKER, PLATT, see "Nathaniel Bayless," q.v.

WHITE, ABRAHAM (Frederick County), soldier who allegedly served in the Maryland troops; born in 1745 in York County, Pennsylvania and lived in Frederick County at the time of his enlistment; applied for pension at Baltimore on 18 May 1833, aged 87, under the Act of June 7, 1832, but the claim was rejected *"because he served in the French Army."* {Ref: *Rejected or Suspended Applications for Revolutionary War Pensions* (1850 Report), p. 230; Research by Virgil D. White, citing Federal Pension Application R11400}

WHITE, BENJAMIN (Maryland Navy), seaman on the State Ship *Defence* in 1777. {Ref: Archives of Maryland Vol. 18, p. 660}

WHITE, JOHN (Dorchester County), private (substitute) in the Maryland Continental Line by 1781, was discharged on 8 Dec 1781. {Ref: Archives of Maryland Vol. 48, p. 10}

WHITE, JOSEPH WOOD (Harford County), private who was enrolled 25 Mar 1776 in Militia Company No. 19 under Capt. William Morgan. {Ref: George W. Archer Collection and Revolutionary War File, Historical Society of Harford County Archives}

WHITE, NICHOLAS (Frederick Town), contractor for State Arms in Frederick County in 1781. {Ref: Archives of Maryland Vol. 47, p. 14}

WHITE, PETER (Maryland Navy), seaman on the State Ship *Defence* in 1777. {Ref: Archives of Maryland Vol. 18, p. 660}

WHITE, RICHARD (Harford County, Susquehannah Hundred), private who was enrolled 23 Apr 1776 in Militia Company No. 21 under Capt. George Patterson.

280

{Ref: George W. Archer Collection and Revolutionary War File, Historical Society of Harford County Archives}

WHITE, SIMON (Baltimore Privateer), commander of the schooner *Harliquin*, navigated by 28 men and mounting 6 carriage guns, was issued Letters of Marque & Reprisal by the Council of Maryland on 18 Jul 1782. {Ref: Archives of Maryland Vol. 48, p. 217}

WHITEHOOK, EZEKIEL (Dorchester County), private who was drafted into the Maryland Continental Line, was discharged on 8 Dec 1781. {Ref: Archives of Maryland Vol. 48, p. 10}

WHITING, ISAAC (Frederick County), soldier who allegedly served in the Maryland troops and lived in Prince George's County at the time of his enlistment; applied for pension in Frederick County on 18 Dec 1832, aged 84, under the Act of June 7, 1832, but the claim was suspended because *"he was not on the rolls of the Maryland Continental Line nor was his colonel's (Sands) who was not a continental officer."* In 1852 Benjamin Whiting was his only child and legal heir. {Ref: *Rejected or Suspended Applications for Revolutionary War Pensions* (1850 Report), p. 232; Research by Virgil D. White, citing Federal Pension Application R11461}

WHITLOCK, MICHAEL (Western Maryland), private in Capt. Michael Cresap's Company in 1775. {Ref: Howard L. Leckey's *The Tenmile Country and Its Pioneer Families*, p. 16}

WHITTINGTON, FRANCIS (Anne Arundel County), private by 5 Oct 1776 in Capt. Richard Chew's Militia Company, Weems' Battalion. {Ref: Archives of Maryland Vol. 12, p. 322, which listed his name as "Francis Wettington"}

WHITTINGTON, FRANCIS, JR. (Anne Arundel County), private by 5 Oct 1776 in Capt. Richard Chew's Militia Company, Weems' Battalion. {Ref: Archives of Maryland Vol. 12, p. 322}

WHITTINGTON, WILLIAM (Anne Arundel County), private by 5 Oct 1776 in Capt. Richard Chew's Militia Company, Weems' Battalion. {Ref: Archives of Maryland Vol. 12, p. 322}

WICKARD, ELIZABETH, see "Henry Hoffman," q.v.

WICKERT, MICHAEL (Washington County), private who was enrolled to serve as a substitute in the Maryland Continental Line until 10 Dec 1781, but *"being represented unfit for the service for which he was intended"* was discharged on 30 Oct 1781. {Ref: Archives of Maryland Vol. 45, p. 656}

WICKES, SAMUEL (Queen Anne's County), quartermaster of the 5th Battalion of Militia, commissioned 8 May 1777. {Ref: Archives of Maryland Vol. 16, p. 243}

WIGINS, URIAH (Western Maryland), private in Capt. Michael Cresap's Company in 1775. {Ref: Howard L. Leckey's *The Tenmile Country and Its Pioneer Families*, p. 16}

WILEY, GEORGE (Baltimore Town), patriot and merchant who enrolled in Capt. John Sterrett's Independent Mercantile Company by February, 1777, at which time they were mustered into regular service with the continental army to

repress loyalist activities in the Eastern Shore counties of Somerset and Worcester. {Ref: J. Thomas Scharf's *History of Baltimore City and County*, Part I, p. 77}

WILEY, JAMES, see "Matthew Wiley," q.v.

WILEY, MATTHEW (Harford County), soldier who served in the Pennsylvania Line who lived in Chester County at the time of his enlistment; applied for pension at Bel Air in Harford County on 16 Oct 1832, aged 81, under the Act of June 7, 1832, and stated his general residence was in London Grove Township in Chester County, Pennsylvania; also mentioned James Wiley of York County, a very old and infirm man, but no relationship was given; Matthew's claim was rejected because he did not serve six months. {Ref: *Rejected or Suspended Applications for Revolutionary War Pensions* (1850 Report), p. 230; Research by Virgil D. White, citing Federal Pension Application R11533}

WILGUS, JAMES (Harford County), private who was enrolled by 15 Apr 1776 in Militia Company No. 20 under Capt. Robert Glenn. {Ref: George W. Archer Collection and Revolutionary War File, Historical Society of Harford County Archives}

WILKERSON (WILKINSON), YOUNG (Baltimore County), second lieutenant in the Maryland Artillery, commissioned 25 Feb 1778 and served at Valley Forge; received payment for his services in the amount of "1900 Dollars & £3.10s" on 12 Sep 1780. For additional information see Peden's *Revolutionary Patriots of Baltimore Town and Baltimore County, 1775-1783*, p. 291. {Ref: Archives of Maryland Vol. 45, p. 98}

WILKES, JOSEPH (Baltimore County), matross soldier by 7 May 1779 at which time he gave a deposition about his enlistment terms. {Ref: Maryland State Archives Record MdHR 6636-14-83}

WILKES, THOMAS (Frederick County), private soldier who *"was fined £20 by a Militia Court Martial held at Frederick Town on September 21, 1781 for neglecting to March to George Town"* and it was certified to the Council of Maryland by several named associates on 15 Mar 1783 *"that the said Thomas Wilkes served five Months in Capt. Hilleary's Company of Select Militia in Frederick County and his behaviour during that Time was in every point such as became a true and Faithful soldier and Subject of this State."* The Council therefore ordered that £19 of the £20 fine be remitted to him. {Ref: Archives of Maryland Vol. 48, pp. 381-382}

WILKINSON, JOSEPH (Calvert County), colonel and lieutenant of the county in 1781. {Ref: Archives of Maryland Vol. 45, p. 276}

WILKINSON, ROBERT (Baltimore Town), patriot and merchant who enrolled in Capt. John Sterrett's Independent Mercantile Company by February, 1777, at which time they were mustered into regular service with the continental army to repress loyalist activities in the Eastern Shore counties of Somerset and Worcester. {Ref: J. Thomas Scharf's *History of Baltimore City and County*, Part I, p. 77}

WILLARD, JOHN (Harford County), private (substitute) in the Maryland Continental Line by 1781, was discharged on 10 Dec 1781. {Ref: Archives of Maryland Vol. 48, p. 17}

WILLARD, MARY, see "Daniel Smith," q.v.

WILLEN, CHARLES (Calvert County), private who was drafted to serve in the Maryland Continental Line until 10 Dec 1781, but *"being represented unfit for the duty for which he was intended"* was discharged on 30 Oct 1781. {Ref: Archives of Maryland Vol. 45, p. 656}

WILLHIDE, FREDERICK (Frederick County), sergeant in the Maryland Continental Line who died at the residence of his son-in-law Daniel Weller near Creagerstown on 14 Nov 1838 in his 85th year: *"Major Willhide was born on 2 Nov 1762 and enlisted in the German Regiment for 3 years, during which period he was promoted to Orderly Sergeant and served out his term of enlistment (after which he acted as a volunteer until the close of the war); he was present at the Battles of Brandywine, Germantown, Trenton and Monmouth, and witnessed the closing of the glorious struggle at Yorktown; he afterwards commanded a company of volunteers and was later commissioned a major in the Old Maryland Continental Line, but he never saw any active service after the war; he was accompanied to his grave by the Mechanics-Town Guard."* {Ref: *The Republican Citizen*, 23 Nov 1838}

WILLIAM, ANDREW (Baltimore County), private, aged 27, labourer, born in Amsterdam, enlisted (made his "X" mark) on 12 Mar 1776 in Capt. John Fulford's Company of Matrosses. {Ref: Maryland Historical Magazine, Vol. 69, No. 1, p. 96}

WILLIAMS, ABRAHAM (Harford County), second lieutenant, elected 30 Nov 1776, commissioned 26 Jan 1777, Militia Company No. 30 under Capt. Benjamin Amoss in the 8th Battalion. {Ref: Archives of Maryland Vol. 16, p. 77; George W. Archer Collection and Revolutionary War File, Historical Society of Harford County Archives}

WILLIAMS, BARUCH (Cecil County), lieutenant colonel and patriot who was commissioned one of the three persons in Cecil County by the Council of Maryland on 19 Aug 1779 to receive subscriptions for use of the State and on 8 Jul 1780 he was appointed Commissary of Purchases; on 24 Oct 1782 he was given permission by the Council of Maryland *"to Solicit His Excellency General Washington or the Officers commanding at the Out posts of the American Army for a Flag to go into the City of New York for the purpose of obtaining the Books, Records and other Public Papers belonging to Cecil County which were carried from thence in the year 1777 by the British Army under the command of General Howe on their passage through this State to Philadelphia."* {Ref: Archives of Maryland Vol. 21, p. 499, Vol. 43, p. 215, and Vol. 48, p. 292}

WILLIAMS, BENJAMIN (Baltimore Town), patriot and merchant who enrolled in Capt. John Sterrett's Independent Mercantile Company by February, 1777, at which time they were mustered into regular service with the continental army to repress loyalist activities in the Eastern Shore counties of Somerset and Worcester. {Ref: J. Thomas Scharf's *History of Baltimore City and County*, Part I, p. 77}

WILLIAMS, BENJAMIN (St. Mary's County), captain of the barge *Independence*, commissioned by the Council of Maryland on 16 Jul 1780, who also ordered *"that the Armourer deliver to Capt. Benjamin Williams 45 Muskets complete with Accoutrements, 12 Boarding Pikes and 6 Cutlasses to be delivered over to Richard Barnes, Esq., Lieutenant of St. Mary's County."* {Ref: Archives of Maryland Vol. 43, p. 330}

WILLIAMS, CHARLES (Harford County), private who was enrolled 25 Mar 1776 in Militia Company No. 19 under Capt. William Morgan. {Ref: George W. Archer Collection and Revolutionary War File, Historical Society of Harford County Archives}

WILLIAMS, ELI or ELIE (Frederick and Washington Counties), quartermaster and later colonel, *"an officer who was conspicuous in the revolution like his brother Otho Holland Williams, after which war he took an active interest in the Chesapeake and Ohio Canal and died in Georgetown, D. C. in 1823 in his 73rd year."* {Ref: J. Thomas Scharf's *History of Western Maryland*, Vol. II, p. 1022}

WILLIAMS, ---- [ELISHA?] (Montgomery County?), captain in the 6th Maryland Continental Line who received payment for his services in the amount of "1900 Dollars & £3.10s" on 12 Sep 1780. {Ref: Archives of Maryland Vol. 45, p. 98}

WILLIAMS, FRANCIS (Maryland Navy), cook's mate on the State Ship *Defence* in 1777. {Ref: Archives of Maryland Vol. 18, p. 660}

WILLIAMS, GABRIEL (St. Mary's County), private (substitute) for 9 months in the Maryland Continental Line who was discharged on 18 Jun 1778, *"he having procured James McBride to serve in the Continental Army for the Term of 3 years and having paid him the Sum of $80 in which the State Bounty is included."* {Ref: Archives of Maryland Vol. 21, p. 139}

WILLIAMS, J., JR. (Baltimore Town), patriot and merchant who enrolled in Capt. John Sterrett's Independent Mercantile Company by February, 1777, at which time they were mustered into regular service with the continental army to repress loyalist activities in the Eastern Shore counties of Somerset and Worcester. {Ref: J. Thomas Scharf's *History of Baltimore City and County*, Part I, p. 77}

WILLIAMS, JOHN (Maryland Navy), marine on the State Ship *Defence* in 1777. {Ref: Archives of Maryland Vol. 18, p. 660}

WILLIAMS, JOHN (Western Maryland), private in Capt. Michael Cresap's Company in 1775. {Ref: Howard L. Leckey's *The Tenmile Country and Its Pioneer Families*, p. 16}

WILLIAMS, JOSEPH, see "Richard Williams," q.v.

284

WILLIAMS, MARSHALL (Maryland Navy), seaman on the State Ship *Defence* in 1777. {Ref: Archives of Maryland Vol. 18, p. 660}

WILLIAMS, O. H., JR. (Baltimore Town), patriot and merchant who enrolled in Capt. John Sterrett's Independent Mercantile Company by February, 1777, at which time they were mustered into regular service with the continental army to repress loyalist activities in the Eastern Shore counties of Somerset and Worcester. {Ref: J. Thomas Scharf's *History of Baltimore City and County*, Part I, p. 77}

WILLIAMS, OTHO HOLLAND (Frederick and Washington Counties), colonel in the 6th Maryland Continental Line who received payment for his services in the amount of "1900 Dollars & £3.10s" on 12 Sep 1780; a distinguished officer and founder of Williamsport, General Williams died 15 Jul 1794; also see "Elie Williams," q.v. {Ref: Archives of Maryland Vol. 45, p. 98; J. Thomas Scharf's *History of Western Maryland*, Vol. II, pp. 1022, 1056}

WILLIAMS, RICHARD (Annapolis), son of Joseph Williams who, in his behalf, petitioned the Council of Maryland on 19 May 1778 and they, in turn, informed Robert Smith that *"Joseph Williams has complained to us of your getting his Son, a Boy of 14 Years old, fudled and obtaining his Mark to an Enlistment and that you have since sold him as a Substitute to Mr. Nicholas Gassaway. We are desirous of enquiring into this Matter."* On 20 May 1778 Richard Williams, son of Joseph, a lad of 14 years of age, enlisted as a substitute for Richard Smith and not being an able bodied recruit, was discharged from the service. {Ref: Archives of Maryland Vol. 21, pp. 96-97}

WILLIAMS, SULLIVAN (Southern Maryland?), lieutenant in the 2nd Maryland Continental Line on 10 Apr 1777 and captain on 17 Apr 1777; received payment for his services in the amount of "1900 Dollars & £3.10s" on 12 Sep 1780. {Ref: Archives of Maryland Vol. 18, p. 174, and Vol. 45, p. 97}

WILLIAMS, THOMAS (Queen Anne's County), private in the 5th Maryland Continental Line who had enlisted for 9 months and was discharged on 23 Mar 1779 at which time he received £21.10.0 in clothing. {Ref: Archives of Maryland Vol. 21, p. 326}

WILLIAMS, THOMAS (Charles County), private who was enrolled to serve as a substitute in the 4th Maryland Continental Line until 10 Dec 1781, but *"being represented unfit for the service for which he was intended"* was discharged on 30 Oct 1781. {Ref: Archives of Maryland Vol. 45, p. 657}

WILLIAMS, THOMAS (Worcester County Privateer), commander of the brigantine *Willing Lass*, navigated by 40 men and mounting 16 carriage guns and 22 small arms, was issued Letters of Marque & Reprisal by the Council of Maryland on 3 May 1780. {Ref: Archives of Maryland Vol. 43, p. 162}

WILLIAMSON, DAVID (Western Maryland), private in Capt. Michael Cresap's Company in 1775. {Ref: Howard L. Leckey's *The Tenmile Country and Its Pioneer Families*, p. 16}

WILLIS, JOHN (Dorchester County), private (substitute) in the Maryland Continental Line, who enlisted to serve until 10 Dec 1781, was discharged on 29 Nov 1781. {Ref: Archives of Maryland Vol. 48, p. 7}

WILLOUGHBY, JAMES, see "David Lynn," q.v.

WILLSON, HUGH (Baltimore Privateer), commander of the schooner *Greyhound*, navigated by 20 men and mounting 7 carriage guns, was issued Letters of Marque & Reprisal by the Council of Maryland on 14 Mar 1783. {Ref: Archives of Maryland Vol. 48, p. 381}

WILMER, LAMBERT (Harford County), ensign, commissioned 26 Apr 1776 in Militia Company No. 22 under Capt. Alexander Cowan. {Ref: George W. Archer Collection and Revolutionary War File, Historical Society of Harford County Archives}

WILMOTT, ROBERT (Baltimore County), first lieutenant in the Maryland Artillery, commissioned 24 Nov 1777 and served at Valley Forge; received payment for his services in the amount of "1900 Dollars & £3.10s" on 12 Sep 1780. For additional information see Peden's *Revolutionary Patriots of Baltimore Town and Baltimore County, 1775-1783*, pp. 293-294. {Ref: Archives of Maryland Vol. 45, p. 98}

WILMOTT, WILLIAM (Baltimore County), captain in the 3rd Maryland Continental Line who received payment for his services in the amount of "1900 Dollars & £3.10s" on 12 Sep 1780. {Ref: Archives of Maryland Vol. 45, p. 98}

WILSON, AQUILA (Prince George's County), private in the Maryland Continental Line who was drafted to serve until 10 Dec 1781, was discharged on 29 Nov 1781. {Ref: Archives of Maryland Vol. 48, p. 6}

WILSON, HENRY, JR. (Harford County), captain, commissioned 16 May 1776 in Militia Company No. 28. {Ref: George W. Archer Collection and Revolutionary War File, Historical Society of Harford County Archives}

WILSON, JAMES (Western Maryland), private in Capt. Michael Cresap's Company in 1775. {Ref: Howard L. Leckey's *The Tenmile Country and Its Pioneer Families*, p. 16}

WILSON, JAMES (Harford County), second lieutenant on 10 Mar 1776 in Militia Company No. 18 under Capt. John Jolly. {Ref: George W. Archer Collection and Revolutionary War File, Historical Society of Harford County Archives}

WILSON, JOHN (Harford County), private who was enrolled 10 Mar 1776 in Militia Company No. 18 under Capt. John Jolly. {Ref: George W. Archer Collection and Revolutionary War File, Historical Society of Harford County Archives}

WILSON, JOHN (Maryland Navy), corporal of marines on the State Ship *Defence* in 1777. {Ref: Archives of Maryland Vol. 18, p. 660}

WILSON, JOSEPH (Harford County), ensign, 6th Maryland Regiment of Continental Troops, commissioned 10 Dec 1779. {Ref: Archives of Maryland Vol. 43, p. 34}

WILSON, JOSEPH CRAWFORD (Prince George's County), private (substitute) in the Maryland Continental Line by 1781, was discharged on 8 Dec 1781. {Ref: Archives of Maryland Vol. 48, p. 10}

WILSON, MARY ANN, see "Thomas Adams," q.v.

WILSON, ROBERT (Dorchester County), patriot who took the Oath of Fidelity and Support to the State of Maryland on 1 Apr 1778. {Ref: Archives of Maryland Vol. 21, p. 1}

WILSON, SAMUEL (Somerset County), patriot who was appointed by the Council of Maryland on 27 Jan 1776 as one of three persons in Somerset County to collect all gold and silver coin that can be procured in said county. {Ref: Archives of Maryland Vol. 11, p. 132}

WINCHESTER, J. (Baltimore Town), patriot and merchant who enrolled in Capt. John Sterrett's Independent Mercantile Company by February, 1777, at which time they were mustered into regular service with the continental army to repress loyalist activities in the Eastern Shore counties of Somerset and Worcester. {Ref: J. Thomas Scharf's *History of Baltimore City and County*, Part I, p. 77}

WINDER, LEVIN (Baltimore and Somerset Counties), major in the 1st Maryland Continental Line who received payment for his services in the amount of "1900 Dollars & £3.10s" on 12 Sep 1780. For additional information see Peden's *Revolutionary Patriots of Baltimore Town and Baltimore County, 1775-1783* (p. 296) and *Revolutionary Patriots of Worcester and Somerset Counties, 1775-1783* (p. 340). {Ref: Archives of Maryland Vol. 45, p. 97}

WINDER, WILLIAM (Somerset County), patriot who was commissioned one of the three persons in Somerset County by the Council of Maryland on 19 Aug 1779 to receive subscriptions for use of the State. For additional information see Peden's *Revolutionary Patriots of Worcester and Somerset Counties, 1775-1783* (p. 341). {Ref: Archives of Maryland Vol. 21, p. 499}

WINKFIELDS, JOHN (Western Maryland), private in Capt. Michael Cresap's Company in 1775. {Ref: Howard L. Leckey's *The Tenmile Country and Its Pioneer Families*, p. 16}

WINNING, JOHN (Baltimore Privateer), commander of the sloop *Fly*, navigated by 50 men and mounting 10 carriage guns, 10 swivel guns and 20 muskets, was issued Letters of Marque & Reprisal by the Council of Maryland on 14 Sep 1778. {Ref: Archives of Maryland Vol. 21, p. 202}

WINSET, JOSEPH (St. Mary's County), private (substitute) in the Maryland Continental Line by 1781, was discharged on 8 Dec 1781. {Ref: Archives of Maryland Vol. 48, p. 11}

WINSET, RAPHAEL (St. Mary's County), private in the 2nd Maryland Continental Line by 31 Jan 1780 at which time he was issued clothing *"due him from the Continent."* For additional information see Peden's *Revolutionary Patriots of Calvert and St. Mary's Counties, 1775-1783* (p. 297). {Ref: Archives of Maryland Vol. 43, p. 73}

WISE, THOMAS (St. Mary's County), private (substitute) in the Maryland Continental Line by 1781, was discharged on 8 Dec 1781. {Ref: Archives of Maryland Vol. 48, p. 11}

WISEMAN, WILLIAM (Western Maryland), private in Capt. Michael Cresap's Company in 1775. {Ref: Howard L. Leckey's *The Tenmile Country and Its Pioneer Families*, p. 16}

WISTEL, CATHERINE, see "Robert Purtle," q.v.

WISTEL, WILLIAM, see "Robert Purtle," q.v.

WITMORE, ---- (Frederick County), soldier in the Revolution; his widow Elizabeth Witmore died near Emmittsburg on 4 Jun 1840, aged 95 years, *"having been confined to bed for the last 10 years; she was born in 1745, a member of the Lutheran Church for 75 years, and was the mother of 11 children, 33 grandchildren and 35 great-grandchildren."* {Ref: *Frederick Visiter and Temperance Advocate*, 11 Jun 1840}

WOLFRED, THOMAS (Frederick County), private (substitute) in the Maryland Continental Line, German Regiment, enrolled in May, 1778 for 3 years or duration of the war. {Ref: Maryland Historical Magazine, Vol. 6, No. 3, p. 259}

WOOD, HOPEWELL (Anne Arundel County), private by 5 Oct 1776 (made his "+" mark) in Capt. Richard Chew's Militia Company, Weems' Battalion. {Ref: Archives of Maryland Vol. 12, p. 323}

WOOD, JAMES (Harford County, Susquehannah Hundred), private who was enrolled 23 Apr 1776 in Militia Company No. 21 under Capt. George Patterson. {Ref: George W. Archer Collection and Revolutionary War File, Historical Society of Harford County Archives}

WOOD, JOHN (Anne Arundel County), private by 5 Oct 1776 (made his "X" mark) in Capt. Richard Chew's Militia Company, Weems' Battalion. {Ref: Archives of Maryland Vol. 12, p. 323}

WOOD, JOSHUA (Harford County), private who was enrolled 10 Mar 1776 in Militia Company No. 18 under Capt. John Jolly. {Ref: George W. Archer Collection and Revolutionary War File, Historical Society of Harford County Archives}

WOOD, LT. COL., see "Valentine Moser," q.v.

WOOD, MORGAN (Anne Arundel County), private by 5 Oct 1776 (made his "X" mark) in Capt. Richard Chew's Militia Company, Weems' Battalion. {Ref: Archives of Maryland Vol. 12, p. 323, which listed his name as "Mogan Wood"}

WOOD, THOMAS (Baltimore County), private, aged 35, labourer, born in England, enlisted (made his "X" mark) on 20 Feb 1776 in Capt. John Fulford's Company of Matrosses. {Ref: Maryland Historical Magazine, Vol. 69, No. 1, p. 95}

WOOD, WILLIAM (Anne Arundel County), private by 5 Oct 1776 (made his "+" mark) in Capt. Richard Chew's Militia Company, Weems' Battalion. {Ref: Archives of Maryland Vol. 12, p. 323}

WOODFIELD, JOHN (Anne Arundel County), private in a company of matrosses station in Annapolis on 28 Jan 1780; married Elizabeth Norman, daughter of

William Norman (died by 1791). {Ref: Archives of Maryland Vol. 43, p. 72; Anne Arundel County Administration Account JG No. 1, p. 25}

WOODFIELD, JOHN, see "George Moore," q.v.

WOODS, BENJAMIN (Maryland Navy), mate on the State Ship *Defence* in 1777. {Ref: Archives of Maryland Vol. 18, p. 660}

WOODWARD, JAMES (Kent County), private (substitute) in the Maryland Continental Line by 1781, was discharged on 8 Dec 1781. {Ref: Archives of Maryland Vol. 48, p. 11}

WOOLEN, RICHARD (Harford County), private who was enrolled 16 Sep 1775 in Militia Company No. 6 under Capt. Benjamin Rumsey. {Ref: George W. Archer Collection and Revolutionary War File, Historical Society of Harford County Archives}

WOOLFORD, MARY, see "Thomas Jones," q.v.

WOOLFORD, THOMAS (Dorchester County), lieutenant colonel in the 5th Maryland Continental Line who received payment for his services in the amount of "1900 Dollars & £3.10s" on 12 Sep 1780. {Ref: Archives of Maryland Vol. 45, p. 98}

WOOLFORD, WILLIAM (Dorchester County), lieutenant in the 2nd Maryland Continental Line who received payment for his services in the amount of "1900 Dollars & £3.10s" on 12 Sep 1780. {Ref: Archives of Maryland Vol. 45, p. 97}

WOOLFORD, WILLIAM, see "Thomas Jones," q.v.

WOOLSEY, WILLIAM (Baltimore Privateer), commander of the schooner *Harlequin*, commissioned 6 Jul 1776; commander of the schooner *Centurion*, navigated by 15 men and mounting 6 carriage guns and 13 small arms, was issued Letters of Marque & Reprisal by the Council of Maryland on 18 Mar 1780. {Ref: Archives of Maryland Vol. 11, p. 554 and Vol. 43, p. 115}

WOOTTON, WILLIAM TURNER (Prince George's County), patriot who was appointed by the Council of Maryland on 27 Jan 1776 as one of three persons in Prince George's County to collect all gold and silver coin that can be procured in said county. {Ref: Archives of Maryland Vol. 11, p. 132}

WORIEW, DANIEL (Frederick County), private (substitute) in the Maryland Continental Line, Williams' Regiment, enrolled in May, 1778 for 3 years or duration of the war. {Ref: Maryland Historical Magazine, Vol. 6, No. 3, p. 258}

WORKMAN, WILLIAM (Western Maryland), private in Capt. Michael Cresap's Company in 1775. {Ref: Howard L. Leckey's *The Tenmile Country and Its Pioneer Families*, p. 16}

WORRALL, MARK LINZLY (Baltimore County), private, aged 25, papermaker, born in England, enlisted 8 Mar 1776 in Capt. John Fulford's Company of Matrosses. {Ref: Maryland Historical Magazine, Vol. 69, No. 1, p. 96}

WORTH, JONATHAN (Kent County), first major of the 27th Battalion of Militia, commissioned 8 May 1777; one Jonathan Worth, merchant, died testate in Kent County by 11 Aug 1788. {Ref: Archives of Maryland Vol. 16, p. 243; Kent County Wills Liber 7, p. 207}

WORTHINGTON, ----, see "William Lamar," q.v.

WORTHINGTON, CHARLES, see "Edward Markland," q.v.

WORTHINGTON, MARGARET, see "William Lamar," q.v.

WORTHINGTON, NICHOLAS (Anne Arundel County), colonel of the Severn Battalion of Militia, commissioned 26 Jan 1777 by the Maryland Council of Safety. {Ref: Archives of Maryland Vol. 16, p. 77}

WRIGHT, BENJAMIN (Queen Anne's County), private (substitute) in the Maryland Continental Line by 1781, was discharged on 8 Dec 1781. {Ref: Archives of Maryland Vol. 48, p. 11}

WRIGHT, CORNELIA, see "Jacob Norris," q.v.

WRIGHT, JAMES (Charles County), private who was drafted into the Maryland Continental Line, was discharged on 8 Dec 1781. {Ref: Archives of Maryland Vol. 48, p. 10}

WRIGHT, JOHN (Maryland Navy), seaman on the State Ship *Defence* in 1777. {Ref: Archives of Maryland Vol. 18, p. 660}

WRIGHT, JOHN (Maryland Navy), quartermaster on the State Ship *Defence* in 1777. {Ref: Archives of Maryland Vol. 18, p. 661}

WRIGHT, SILAS, JR., see "Henry Hill," q.v.

WRIGHT, THOMAS (Washington County), private who was enrolled to serve as a substitute in the Maryland Continental Line until 10 Dec 1781, but *"being represented unfit for the service for which he was intended"* was discharged on 30 Oct 1781. {Ref: Archives of Maryland Vol. 45, p. 656}

WRIGHT, TURBUTT (Queen Anne's County), patriot who was appointed by the Council of Maryland on 27 Jan 1776 as one of three persons in Queen Anne's County to collect all gold and silver coin that can be procured in said county. {Ref: Archives of Maryland Vol. 11, p. 132}

WROTH, MARTHA, see "William B. Rasin," q.v.

WRYAN, PATRICK (Frederick County), private (substitute) in the Maryland Continental Line, enrolled in April, 1778 for 3 years or duration of the war. {Ref: Maryland Historical Magazine, Vol. 6, No. 3, p. 256}

YARDSLEY, WILLIAM (Maryland Privateer), commander of the schooner *Johnson*, navigated by 8 men and mounting 5 swivel guns and 6 muskets, was issued Letters of Marque & Reprisal by the Council of Maryland on 28 May 1778. {Ref: Archives of Maryland Vol. 21, p. 113}

YATES, RICHARD (Maryland Navy), boatswain's mate on the State Ship *Defence* in 1777. {Ref: Archives of Maryland Vol. 18, p. 661}

YATES, VACHEL (Maryland Navy), sergeant of marines on the State Ship *Defence* in 1777; lieutenant of marines from 15 Feb to 15 Oct 1777; captain of marines from 15 Oct to 15 Dec 1777. {Ref: Archives of Maryland Vol. 18, p. 661}

YEARLY, NATHAN, see "Jonathan Ady," q.v.

YEATES, BENJAMIN (Frederick County), private (substitute) in the Maryland Continental Line by 1781, was discharged on 8 Dec 1781. {Ref: Archives of Maryland Vol. 48, p. 11}

YEATES, THOMAS (Baltimore County), private (substitute) in the Maryland Continental Line by 1781, was discharged on 8 Dec 1781. {Ref: Archives of Maryland Vol. 48, p. 11}

YEATES, WILLIAM (Washington County), patriot who was commissioned one of the three persons in Washington County by the Council of Maryland on 19 Aug 1779 to receive subscriptions for use of the State. {Ref: Archives of Maryland Vol. 21, p. 499}

YELLOT (YELLET), JEREMIAH (Baltimore Privateer), commander of the schooner *Felicity*, mounting 6 carriage guns, 6 swivel guns and 12 small arms, was issued Letters of Marque & Reprisal by the Council of Maryland on 19 Jul 1779; commander of the schooner *Antilope*, navigated by 40 men and mounting 14 carriage guns, was issued Letters of Marque & Reprisal by the Council of Maryland on 17 Aug 1780. {Ref: Archives of Maryland Vol. 21, p. 477 and Vol. 43, p. 257}

YORKE, REBECCA, see "Jonathan Ady," q.v.

YOST, JOHN (Frederick or Montgomery County), contractor for State Arms in 1781. {Ref: Archives of Maryland Vol. 47, p. 14}

YOUNG, BENJAMIN (Anne Arundel County), private in the Maryland Continental Line who enlisted in Anne Arundel County and applied for pension in Baltimore County on 9 Apr 1819, aged 65. {Ref: Research by Virgil D. White, citing Federal Pension Application S35164}

YOUNG, CASPER, see "Henry Young," q.v.

YOUNG, CONRAD, see "Henry Young," q.v.

YOUNG, ELIZABETH, see "Henry Young," q.v.

YOUNG, HENRY (Frederick County), private who was enrolled to serve as a substitute in the 7th Maryland Continental Line until 10 Dec 1781, but *"being represented unfit for the service for which he was intended"* was discharged on 30 Oct 1781; married Mary ---- prior to 1776 and died circa 1793 (widow Mary Young married Vincent Sanders in May, 1818 and he died in July, 1840; she died 17 Feb 1843); the known children of Henry and Mary Young were: George Young; Casper Young; Jacob Young; Conrad Young; Mary Young (married a Hoffman and applied for pension in Frederick County on 27 Jul 1855, aged 72); Nancy Young; and, Elizabeth Young. {Ref: Archives of Maryland Vol. 45, p. 657; Research by Virgil D. White, citing Federal Pension Application R9182}

YOUNG, JACOB, see "Henry Young," q.v.

YOUNG, JACOB W. (Caroline County), private who lived in Caroline County at the time of his enlistment in the Maryland Continental Line, but was born in Queen Anne's County on 21 Nov 1762; also served as a privateer; applied for pension in Maury County, Tennessee on 12 Dec 1832. {Ref: Research by Virgil D. White, citing Federal Pension Application S3954}

YOUNG, JOHN, see "Jesse Dungan," q.v.

YOUNG, JOSEPH (Baltimore Town), patriot and merchant who enrolled in Capt. John Sterrett's Independent Mercantile Company by February, 1777, at which time they were mustered into regular service with the continental army to repress loyalist activities in the Eastern Shore counties of Somerset and Worcester. {Ref: J. Thomas Scharf's *History of Baltimore City and County*, Part I, p. 77}

YOUNG, MARY, see "Henry Young," q.v.

YOUNG, MICHAEL (Baltimore County), private, aged 22, labourer, born in Redding Town, enlisted (made his "M" mark) on 13 Feb 1776 in Capt. John Fulford's Company of Matrosses. {Ref: Maryland Historical Magazine, Vol. 69, No. 1, p. 94}

YOUNG, NANCY, see "Henry Young," q.v.

YOUNG, ROBERT (Anne Arundel County), private by 5 Oct 1776 in Capt. Richard Chew's Militia Company, Weems' Battalion. {Ref: Archives of Maryland Vol. 12, p. 323}

YOUNG, WILLIAM (Montgomery County), private (substitute) in the Maryland Continental Line by 1781, was discharged on 8 Dec 1781. {Ref: Archives of Maryland Vol. 48, p. 11}

YOUNGER, TELLER (Washington County), private who was drafted to serve in the Maryland Continental Line until 10 Dec 1781, but *"being represented unfit for the duty for which he was intended"* was discharged on 30 Oct 1781. {Ref: Archives of Maryland Vol. 45, p. 656}

ZIMMERMAN, GEORGE, SR. (Baltimore County), patriot who took the Oath of Fidelity and Allegiance in 1778; born in July, 1730, married Catherine ---- circa 1767, and died 20 Jul 1817. [*Ed. Note:* The family information first published in Peden's *Revolutionary Patriots of Baltimore Town and Baltimore County, 1775-1783* should be corrected to read as follows]. The children of George and Catherine Zimmerman were: John Zimmerman (married Mary Hissey on 15 Jun 1798); George Zimmerman, Jr.; Elizabeth Zimmerman (married a Peddicoard); Magdalen Zimmerman (married a Stinchcomb); Mary Zimmerman (married a Lee); Catherine Zimmerman (married an Owings); and, Sarah Zimmerman (married an Emmart). {Ref: Research by Kenneth E. Zimmerman of Woodstock, Maryland (a direct descendant) in 2001, citing Baltimore County Land Records dated 16 Oct 1813 and 4 Nov 1813, and Maryland State Archives Record MdHR 4647-13, Box 3}

ZINK, JOHN (Baltimore County), private, aged 25, born in England, enlisted (made his "Z" mark) on 20 Feb 1776 in Capt. John Fulford's Company of Matrosses. {Ref: Maryland Historical Magazine, Vol. 69, No. 1, p. 95}